In the Name of Allah,
The Merciful, The Most Beneficent

A JOURNEY THROUGH THE QUR'AN

Themes and Messages of the Holy Qur'an

Muhammad al-Ghazali

Abridged by Abdalhaqq Bewley

Dar Al-Taqwa

© Dar Al Taqwa Ltd. 1998

ISBN 1-870582-90-X

Translation: Aisha Bewley

Editors: Abdalhaqq Bewley and Muhammad Isa Waley

Production: Bookwork, Norwich

Published by:
    Dar Al Taqwa Ltd.
    7A Melcombe Street
    Baker Street
    London NW1 6AE

Printed by Redwood Books Limited

Table of Contents

Preface

This book represents an entirely new way of approaching the Noble Qur'an although it does incorporate a number of ideas from already existing *tafsirs*. It has arisen from my desire to have a greater understanding of the Qur'an. In spite of my feeling of inadequacy in the face of the incomparable majesty of the Qur'an, I said to myself, "I will explore a previously untried method in the hope of opening up a new avenue to understanding the Qur'an," while acknowledging, of course, that the wonders of the Qur'an are infinite and that it is impossible to plumb its depths.

What I have done is attempt to produce a kind of *tafsir* which deals with each *sura* of the Mighty Book according to its general subject matter, rather than use the *ayat* by *ayat* approach of normal *tafsirs*. I have tried to give a picture of the whole *sura* from beginning to end, recognising the hidden connections which bind it together, showing how its beginning leads to its end and how its end is a confirmation of its beginning. My concern has been the unity of the subject matter of each *sura*, even if many different themes are involved, taking as my model Shaykh Muhammad 'Abdallah Darraz who used this method when dealing with *Surat al-Baqara*, the longest of the *suras* of the Noble Qur'an, and showed it to be one variegated, multi-layered whole in his book, *an-Naba' al-'Azim*, which was, I believe the first *tafsir* to treat the Qur'an in this way. The scholars of the Qur'an are merely receptors for whatever understanding what Allah has given them of it, so all credit belongs absolutely to Him who conferred it on them, may His Name be exalted!

I have become aware through my own experience that there is a real need among the Muslims for a *tafsir* of this kind. Although I have been familiar with the Qur'an since my early childhood and

1

memorised it by the age of ten, and still recite it now at more than eighty years of age, it became clear to me that I was in fact grasping very little of its significance beyond the immediate meaning of the actual *ayat* I was reciting, which led me in turn to the realisation that I was certainly not reflecting on the Qur'an in the way that we have been commanded to by Him who sent it down for us. It occurred to me that I should delve into the depths of each *ayat* with a view to ascertaining its connection to what is before and after it and acquainting myself with the entire *sura* as a cohesive and coherent whole.

Having started on this task I soon felt that I was not up to it and almost stopped! But then I said to myself, "It is better to make an real attempt at this than just to fall at the first hurdle," so I continued, seeking Allah's help and relying on Him, and set to work writing this, hoping that my time would not come until I had finished it, knowing that the future is in the hand of Allah Alone.

I repeat that I am inadequate to the task I have undertaken and that the river bed from which my knowledge flows is a very shallow one. However, I hope that it will encourage others to go further and help them to reach the highest peaks in the service of the Qur'an and to uncover many more of its splendours and marvels.

One word of warning: this kind of holistic *tafsir* will never supplant the classical *tafsirs* and can only be viewed as a kind of extension of them and an effort to supplement them. However, there is no doubt in my mind that Qur'anic study needs this added dimension. What is certain is that the Noble Qur'an is the constitution of Islam and its lasting miracle and a continual source of inspiration for all Muslims for all time. We will need to refer to it ceaselessly until the end of time.

Praise belongs to Allah who revealed the Book to His slave and made it the goal of those with intelligence and preserved it from error.

Muhammad al-Ghazali

Sura 1

Al-Fatiha: The Opening

In the Name of Allah, the best of all names.

In the Name of Allah with which nothing in the heaven or the earth can come to any harm.

Despite being one of the shorter *suras* of the Qur'an, the *Sura* of Praise is nevertheless the Mother of the Book and its greatest *sura*. It comprises a brief summary of the basic beliefs of Islam, a binding contract between mankind and their Lord which establishes our function in existence, and a supplication to Allah to guide us on the Straight Path, give us success in following it, and keep us from misguidance.

It starts with the words: *"Praise belongs to Allah, Lord of all the worlds."* Praise (*al-hamd*) is a word which has three meanings. It signifies firstly that pure praise of Allah which proclaims the glories of the Highest Essence, declaring the Majesty, Beauty and Perfection of Allah. It also embraces praise for the Giver of gifts and blessings for His graciousness and generosity to us. And finally it expresses thankfulness for all the good which comes and all the favours we receive. We start the day, for instance, by saying, "Praise belongs to Allah who has brought us to life after we were dead and to Him is the gathering," and in doing so we glorify Him, praise Him and thank Him.

"Lord of all the worlds" means that He is the Master of every single dimension of existence, the Celestial and terrestrial, this world and the Next World, animal, vegetable and mineral, angelic and human, everything seen and Unseen. A 'world' (*'alam*) is something that is other than Allah; and everything other than Allah is absolutely subject to Him and in need of Him. Indeed, everything other than Allah is His slave and the outcome of His bless-

ing: *"To Allah belongs all praise, Lord of the heavens and Lord of the earth, the Lord of all the worlds. All glory in the heavens and earth belongs to Him. He is the Almighty, the All-Wise."* (45:36-37)

"All Merciful, Most Merciful." We live in Allah's Mercy. His Mercy and Knowledge encompass everything in existence. Were it not that Allah is Forgiving and Merciful, our acts of disobedience would destroy us and our denial of Him and our excesses would cause our immediate devastation.

"King of the Day of Repayment (deen)." What is meant by *"deen"* here is repayment. It is the first stage of the Next World. The Next Life is simply requital for this present life. The materialistic culture which now dominates the world does not take this implacable reality into account. Indeed, it frequently mocks the concept of accountability in the Next World and deliberately neglects it where education, legislation, and government are concerned.

"You alone we worship. You alone we ask for help." We worship You alone, O Allah. We seek Your help and not the help of anyone else. Everything other than You is in absolute need of You. We have the famous supplication of the Prophet, may Allah bless him and grant him peace: "O Allah, help me to remember You and thank You and worship You in the best way." And also his words: "When you ask, ask Allah. When you seek help, seek Allah's help."

"Guide us on the Straight Path, the path of those You have blessed." A straight line is the shortest path between two points. That is why there is only one Straight Path and why all who go straight are guided to Allah. *"My Lord is on a straight path."* (11:56) There is only one *deen* of Allah and all the different Prophets brought it in their own times for their own communities. Its basis is that there is only one God and that all the inhabitants of heaven and earth are in need of Him. Perhaps this may prove a point of disagreement with the followers of some other contemporary religions, but the Muslims are certain that everything other than Allah is a slave to Him, subject to His judgement, subject to His command in this world and the Next.

It is impossible for any creature to transcend this reality. All who cling to it are saved and all who deviate from it are destroyed. Those who truly obey Allah and His Messengers will be among the blessed: *"All who obey Allah and the Messenger, they are with the people Allah has blessed: the Prophets, the men of truth, the martyrs, the righteous. And such people are the best of company!"* (4:69) But those who attribute partners to Allah or refuse to obey His commands will be subject either to misguidance or to wrath without hope of deliverance, *"… not of those with anger upon them, nor of the misguided."* It is up to each individual to be sincere in his aspiration and in his search for the truth and, if he is guided to the truth, to act by it and be humble to his Lord and compassionate to His creatures.

Allah has made it obligatory to recite this *sura* in every prayer so that it is a continually repeated and accepted means of communion between mankind and their Lord. It contains great truths and is at the same time the earnest entreaty of a slave seeking the pleasure of his Lord.

Allah said on the tongue of His Prophet, may Allah bless him and grant him peace, in a *hadith qudsi*, "I have divided the prayer in half between Me and My slave, and My slave will have what he asks for. When he says, *'Praise belongs to Allah, Lord of all the worlds,'* Allah says, 'My slave has praised Me!' When he says, *'All-Merciful, Most Merciful,'* Allah says, 'My slave has lauded Me!' When he says, *'Master of the Day of Repayment,'* Allah says, 'My slave has glorified Me,' or 'My slave has entrusted himself to Me!' When he says, *'You alone we worship. You alone we ask for help,'* Allah says, 'This is between Me and My slave, and My slave will have what he asks for.' When he says, *'Guide us on the Straight Path, the path of those You have blessed, not of those with anger upon them, nor of the misguided,'* Allah says, 'This is for My slave and My slave will have what he asks for.'"

We repeat this *sura* in the same way that we wash ourselves repeatedly, because there never ceases to be cause for so to do so. It is not enough to wash the human body once or twice in a lifetime to keep it clean it: the washing must be repeated continually. It is the same with the repetition of the *Fatiha*. Human nature will not be perfected by one or two prayers. It is necessary for us to stand in the presence of our Lord time and time again because the heedlessness of the self and the whisperings of Shaytan never cease. So the prayer must be repeated continually and our entreaty never cease: *"The prayer is prescribed for the believers at set times."* (4:103)

So to sum up, the *Fatiha* embodies in the most complete way the nature of the connection between mankind and their Lord: acknowledgement of Him; praise of Him; preparation to meet Him; the contract to worship Him; and then the supplication that He may make us pleasing to Him.

Sura 2
Al-Baqara: The Cow

After the *Hijra*, the main thrust of the Muslims was to establish the first Islamic polity in Madina. The Muslims had succeeded as individuals in the face of the trials of idolatry and had proved sincere in their *deen*. Now they had found a place where they could gather as a community and where they could establish governance. However they were soon faced with a new kind of enmity, that of the Jews who thought that they had a monopoly on religion and frowned on their new rivals. They soon began to oppose the Muslims and plotted secretly and openly against them.

The Jewish tribes who lived in the fertile areas of the Hijaz arrived there after fleeing, to save their faith, from the power of the Byzantines and took up residence among the illiterate Arabs, thinking themselves superior to them. They did not try to combat idolatry or call the local people to the worship of Allah and never presented their Divine teachings to those around them. They remained aloof and relied on their heritage, considering that faith in God was their unique privilege and should not be shared with anyone. So when Islam appeared with the same teaching they opposed it and tried to make things difficult for it.

The Final Prophet, may Allah bless him and grant him peace, made every effort to placate them and co-operate with them for the common good but nonetheless their malice prevailed and their mischief became more and more harmful. So in the place to which they had emigrated the Muslims were having to build up their community with one hand and combat increasing hostility with the other. They were setting up their society on the firm foundations of the Revelation and at the same time having to defend it against enemies who could not conceal their ill will. It was in this environment and atmosphere that Allah revealed *Surat al-Baqara*, the longest *sura* of the Noble Qur'an and the most laden with varied instructions.

From the very beginning it hints at the spuriousness of what was left of the Jewish tradition: *"That is the Book with no doubt. In it is guidance for the godfearing."* (2:2) It is as if all previous Books are open to doubt; as if there is error in them which will not produce fear of Allah or purify the behaviour of their adherents. Fear of Allah is in fact the keynote of *Surat al-Baqara.* Many of the characteristics of the godfearing are enumerated in *Surat al-Baqara* and the term *taqwa* (active fear of Allah) is repeated during the *sura* about thirty times, which is not the case in any other *sura. Taqwa* is that universal quality which is the aspiration of every nation who receive Divine guidance: *"Everything in the heavens and everything in the earth belongs to Allah. We have instructed those given the Book before you, and you yourselves, to fear Allah."* (4:131)

Surat al-Baqara is distinguished by including each of the five pillars of Islam within its scope: *"O Mankind! Worship your Lord, who created you and those before you"* (1:21); *"Guard the prayers well - especially the middle prayer. Stand in obedience to Allah"* (2:238); *"O you who believe! Give away some of what We have provided for you before a day comes on which there is no trading, no close friendship and no intercession"* (2:254); *"O you who believe! Fasting is prescribed for you, as it was prescribed for those before you"* (2:183); and *"Carry out the Hajj and 'Umra for Allah."* (2:196)

The *sura* remained open so that Allah could add to it whatever supplementary revelations connected to its main themes He wished to include in it. It is known that the last *ayat* of the entire Qur'an to be revealed was His words: *"Fear a Day on which you will be returned to Allah. Then every self will be paid in full for what it earned. They will not be wronged."* (2:281) The Prophet, may Allah bless him and grant him peace, was commanded to add this to the *ayats* about usury at the end of *Surat al-Baqara.*

Looking at the first pages of the *sura,* we find that it describes the godfearing in three *ayats,* the unbelievers in two *ayats* and then takes thirteen *ayats* to describe the Hypocrites! That reflects the extent of their evil and the magnitude of the danger they represent for the entire community. Then, after a general invitation to believe in Allah and the Last Day and a brief mention of the inimitability of the Noble Qur'an, the truthfulnesness of the one who brings it and the irreparable loss of all who oppose it, the discussion about the categories of people in respect of the Message continues, making their position clear. They are either believers or unbelievers, fulfillers or breakers of their contract with Allah. But is it fitting repayment for the great blessing which has been conferred upon us, that of existence itself and continual sustenance, that its Giver should be rejected with such blatant ingratitude? *"How can you reject Allah when you were dead and then He gave you life; then will cause you to die and bring you back to life; then to Him you will be returned?"* (2:28)

Following on from this it is only natural to mention the beginning of creation, the commissioning of man and the endless struggle between Adam and his descendants and Iblis and his progeny. This struggle took on an historical form in the bitter enmity shown by the tribe of Israel to the Prophets who were sent to them. They chose to enlist in the armies of Iblis in his ceaseless battle against the Truth. *Surat al-Baqara,* being the first *sura* to be revealed in Madina, was therefore bound to confront the tribe of Israel, refuting their opinion regarding the Final Message and unveiling their unsavoury tactics, both past and present. This theme is introduced when the Almighty says: *"O tribe of Israel! Remember the blessing I conferred on you. Honour My contract and I will honour your contract. Dread Me alone. Believe in what I have sent down, confirming what you already have. Do not be the first to reject it."* (2:40-41)

The Qur'an's affirmation of the Jews is a general one, showing that the People of the Book are not the same as the idolaters in respect of disbelief in Allah and denial of the Revelation sent to the Messengers. The Qur'an confirms them in their professed belief in Allah, in their confirmation of Revelation, in their acceptance of accountability and reckoning for their actions, but it does not confirm them with regard to the many deviations they later

introduced. It does not confirm their ancient account stating that
Allah descended to the earth and visited His Prophet Ibrahim and
ate with him! It does not confirm their assertion that Jacob struggled with Allah all night and did not release Him until He gave
him the name of Israel! The confirmation of what the tribe of
Israel have is general, not particular, and a summary of what is
true in it is mentioned so that the reckoning they receive in the
light of it will be fair. *Surat al-Baqara* recalls more than sixteen
events which occurred to the Jews during their long history, events
which are also recorded in the Torah, but, in spite of that, they did
not take the opportunity to reflect on what had happened to them
or thank Allah for His blessings to them.

This enumeration begins with the words of the Almighty:
*"When We rescued you from the people of Pharaoh. They were
inflicting an evil punishment on you."* (2:49) Did they show thanks
for their rescue when Allah punished their enemies and drowned
them in front of their eyes? Were they aware of the justice
involved in this retaliation and did they praise their Lord for the
destruction of injustice? The Qur'anic account continues through
many pages and reminds the Jews of Allah's great blessings to
them and their past ingratitude to Allah and asks them whether
they are going to continue in their hostility to the Truth by rejecting the Prophet of the Qur'an even more violently than the idolaters did. The importance of this discussion of the history of the
tribe of Israel in *Surat al-Baqara* and the attitude of the Jews to
their own Prophets and to the coming of Islam is all too plain in
the context of the world today.

To counter them the Noble Qur'an goes on from here to discuss
and demonstrate the truly universal character of the *deen* of Allah.
In the face of the narrow religious sectarianism of the previous
religions, Islam gives to all mankind the possibility of true religious unity based on the natural form of man and his spiritual and
social needs. The Jews and Christians both believe that they have a
monopoly on the Truth and that salvation will be obtained by no
one but them. *"They say, 'No one will enter the Garden except a
Jew or a Christian.' Such is their vain hope. Say, 'Produce your
evidence if you are telling the truth.'"* (2:111) What about all the

other people who recognise Allah and submit to Him and are sincere in their intentions and do righteous deeds? Why should their efforts be wasted? *"Not so! Anyone who submits himself completely to Allah and is a good-doer will find his wage with his Lord. They will feel no fear; they will know no sorrow."* (2:112)

The Qur'an therefore advises the People of the Book to believe in Allah and all His Messengers and to rid themselves of their presumption which makes every group pride itself on sole possession of the truth: *"They say, 'Be Jews or Christians and you will be guided.' Say: 'Rather take the religion of Ibrahim, a man of pure natural belief. He was not an idolater.'"* (2:135) Then the Qur'an tells them to expand their faith to embrace every Prophet whom Allah sent to guide mankind. It is not permitted to exclude any of them: *"Say: 'We believe in Allah and what has been sent down to us and what was sent down to Ibrahim and Isma'il and Ishaq and Ya'qub and the Tribes, and what Musa and 'Isa were given, and what all the Prophets were given by their Lord. We do not differentiate between any of them. We are Muslims who have submitted to Him.'"* (2:136)

These are the bases of religious unity which *Surat al-Baqara* sets out and offers to the Jews and Christians in the name of Islam so that they may enter it and become brothers with the Muslims, having already made it clear that what is offered is not something new but, in fact, the same *deen* as was brought by all the earlier Prophets. The Jews boast of the fact that they are the descendants of Ya'qub who later took the name Israel - the name also chosen by them for their state today! But who was Ya'qub? Ya'qub was a man devoted to Allah with complete recognition of Him and who submitted to His Decree. He called on his children to believe in Him and asked them to make a covenant before his death that they would not neglect any aspect of this *deen*: *"Or were you present when death came to Ya'qub and he said to his sons, 'What will you worship after me?' They said, 'We will worship your God, the God of your fathers, Ibrahim and Isma'il and Ishaq: One God. We are Muslims submitting to Him.'"* (2:133)

Islam is in fact the sole link between human beings and their Creator, between mankind and their Lord. Is it not the right of Him who brought things into being that beings should bow to Him in humble worship? Muhammad, may Allah bless him and grant him peace, took things right back to their root and offered the guidance of a way to Allah and nothing else: *"If they believe in the same thing you believe in, they are guided. But if they turn away, they place themselves in hostile opposition. Allah will be enough for you against them. And He is the All-Hearing, the All-Knowing."* (2:137)

The explanation of the universality of Islam given in this *sura* clarifies something which has proved a source of confusion for some people. How can it be said that all the Messengers were Muslims when it is known that Islam is what Muhammad brought to the world? The confirmed truth is that the *deen* has been one since the beginning of time: belief in Allah accompanied by righteous action. This is the meaning of Islam.

Recognition of Allah alone is not sufficient. As well as having recognition, we must also say to our Lord, *"We hear and obey. Forgive us, O our Lord! To Yo is the final journey's end."* (2:285) Iblis's recognition that Allah was One and had created everything did not help him at all. Recognition must be accompanied by submission to Allah's commands and striving to please Him. Failure to do this will result in being banished from Allah's mercy. The Messengers all came to proclaim both their recognition of Allah and also their obedience to Allah in all that He obliges His slaves to do. This is Islam. It is what Nuh and Ibrahim did. It is also what Musa, 'Isa and Muhammad did. We will not present here all the *ayats* in which their Islam is announced because that would take up too much time, but it is clear that all of them called people to Islam, even if the details of their legal precepts differed at different times.

When someone comes into the world he is given a name and that name does not change as he grows older even though the scope of his actions becomes wider and more varied. It is not logical to think that godliness in this age will necessarily take on exactly the same form as it did in the time of Nuh; and yet its central point remains the same even though its circumference may have expanded with the expansion of human development.

Muhammad, may Allah bless him and grant him peace, appeared after Musa and 'Isa, peace be upon them, had endured terrible trials with their people. Is it surprising, then, that the Final *Deen* should correct some deviations which had occurred, should straighten paths which had become crooked, should eradicate innovations which had arisen, and should set out in a new Book the details of truths which had been forgotten?

The mission of Muhammad was urgently needed to correct the errors of humanity and to call the attention of the People of the Book to the calamities they had caused mankind. The Christians had to be reminded of the unity of Allah and shown that 'Isa was a servant of Allah like other creatures, and informed anew that he and his Disciples called people to true Islam. The Jews had to be admonished for their arrogance, their claim of exclusive right to Revelation had to be wrenched from their talons, and they had to be told that Allah does not have a special relationship with any particular race or group.

The truly righteous among the followers of Musa and 'Isa are connected to the followers of Muhammad: *"Those who believe, those who are Jews, and the Christians and Sabaeans, all who believe in Allah and the Last Day and act rightly, will find their wage with their Lord. They will feel no fear; they will know no sorrow."* (2:62) However, as for the remnants of the People of the Book alive now, they do not know what the Book is or what belief is; they pursue the appetites of this world in a race with the idolaters and have no acceptable claim to true faith. They have obstinately clung to their original deviations and have added to them implacable hostility towards those who truly affirm Allah's unity, destroying their mosques and shattering their societies. *"Who could do greater wrong than someone who bars access to the mosques of Allah, preventing His Name from being remembered in them, and goes about destroying them? Such people will never be able to enter them – except in fear. They will have disgrace in this world and in the Next World they will have a terrible punishment."* (2:114)

This *sura,* which was revealed immediately after the *hijra* and coincided with the laying of the foundations of Islamic society, decided the basis on which relations between the followers of different religions were to be established while at the same time calling for the unity of the *deen* by returning to the core teaching of all of the previous Prophets and Messengers.

The first reaction of the Jews to Islam was one of rejection and hatred. They thought that the *deen* was their monopoly and should not be extended to any other people. After the *hijra* had been made and the reality of Islam was on their doorstep, they decided to plot to devise ways of fighting it and of deluding its followers.

The Prophet, may Allah bless him and grant him peace, drew up a document in which the relations between the Muslims and all the other inhabitants of Madina were set out on the basis of alliance and mutual support. The Jews accepted this document grudgingly but continued to mock the new *deen*, conspire against it and attack it. The Qur'an therefore continued to rebuke the Jews for their attitude and censure them for the faults they had demonstrated throughout their long history, but that had no effect at all in stopping their deception or softening their hearts! Their own opinion is that they alone are the people of Revelation and that Allah will not allow any Prophet except among them.

The Noble Qur'an refutes all their claims. If they believe in what they have, then why do they deny what confirms it? *"When they are told, 'Believe in what Allah has revealed,' They say, 'We believe in what was revealed to us,' and they reject anything beyond that, even though it is the truth, confirming what they have. Say, 'Why then, if you are believers, did you previously kill the Prophets of Allah?'"* (2:91) The Qur'an shows that their pretension to faith is a lie because otherwise they would not have slain the Prophets and broken their covenant and committed acts of disobedience. Their record is an eloquent denial of their claim: *"What an evil thing it is that your belief has directed you to do if you are believers!"* (2:93)

The Jews concentrated on the form rather than the content of the *deen*, and latched onto on superficialities while forgetting the core. Therefore the Muslims are cautioned against making the same mistake, and directed to hold to the basic truth and the pillars which uphold it: *"It is not piety to turn your faces to the East or to* the West. *Rather, those with true piety are those who believe in Allah and the Last Day."* (2:177) This pivotal *ayat* continues by outlining the basic pillars of the *deen* which explain the reality of piety and constitute the bases of *taqwa*.

✳✳✳✳✳

This *sura* then concentrates on the building of the new society, detailing the five pillars of Islam and moving on to discuss the nature of the Muslim family, the central element of Muslim society, outlining many precepts to assist its sound development and firm establishment. It does not forget, while proceeding with this aim, to indicate, by way of warning, what had happened to the Jews. It mentions how many times the Signs of Allah were repeated to them but how they nevertheless treated them with disdain with the result that the Word of the Lord was realised against them: *"Ask the tribe of Israel how many clear signs We gave to them. If anyone alters Allah's blessing after it has come to him, Allah is Fierce in Retribution."* (2:211)

This *sura* mentions how the protection of society as a whole is accomplished through *jihad* while the protection of society in its constituent parts is achieved through safeguarding the family unit by the clear application of legal judgements. However, we Muslims have now abandoned both of these vital matters. We will defer discussing the Muslim family until later, but take this opportunity to deal briefly with the matter of fighting and show how the Noble Qur'an explains it in a way that precludes any imputation of naked aggression.

Muslims do not like wars, with their inevitable consequences of destruction and loss, any more than anyone else. Like everyone else we prefer well-being and stability. Peace is eminently desirable so long as people's rights are protected and their faith respected. However, when peace can only be secured at the cost of the surrender of basic rights and the acceptance of domination by unbelief, then it is not an option in spite of people's basic reluctance to fight: *"Fighting is prescribed for you even though it is hateful to you. It may be that you hate a thing when it is good for*

*you and it may be that you love a thing when it is bad for you.
Allah knows and you do not know."* (2:216)

This whole matter is made clear in the discussion in the Qur'an
about the violation of the Sacred Month which begins: *"They will
ask you about the Sacred Month and fighting in it. Say: 'Fighting
in it is a serious thing,'"* meaning that it is not strictly permitted.
What is the position, however, when there is blatant aggression
and people are expelled from their homes and the right to worship
is taken from them? The Qur'an makes it clear that it is obligatory
to repel aggression and protect people's rights under any circumstances: *"But barring access to the Way of Allah and rejecting
Him and barring access to the Sacred Mosque and expelling its
people from it are far more serious in Allah's sight,"* because
"Idolatry is worse than killing." (2:217) Fighting is necessary in
defence of sacred things and faith. If we are faced with people who
are determined to make us abandon what we have and enter into
their religion we have no choice but to fight and we will be held
accountable for it if we do not.

It is in this light that we understand the meaning of the words
of the Almighty in *Surat al-Baqara*: *"Fight in the Way of Allah
against those who fight you, but do not go beyond the limits. Allah
does not love those who go beyond the limits."* (2:190) This is an
order which will remain in force till the Last Day. There is nothing
in the Noble Qur'an from the first page to the last which does not
accord with this judgement. It is necessary at this point to state
clearly that the fighting referred to in the Noble Qur'an is condi-
tional on its being for the sake of Allah and not for any other reason. Fighting for the sake of personal glory or private benefit or
aggressive nationalism, for instance, has no Qur'anic mandate
whatsoever.

The fighting which has dominated the world in recent times,
fighting for national or tribal domination or to gain the wealth of
weaker nations by colonising their lands, is certainly not fighting
for the sake of Allah. It is fighting for the sake of Shaytan.
Fighting for the sake of Allah means fighting so that the worship
of Allah may be established and maintained and the worship of
Shaytan overthrown. This kind of fighting has been incumbent on

the righteous since the beginning of time in order that the houses of Allah shall remain inhabited by people who worship Him: *"If it were not for Allah's driving some people back by means of others, the earth would have been corrupted. But Allah has overflowing favour for all the worlds."* (2:251) Indeed, the continued survival of the Truth is dependent on the courage of its adherents and their determination to raise its banner and ensure its future existence.

✳✳✳✳✳

Surat al-Baqara contains many injunctions concerning the family but although the *sura* comes at the beginning of the Noble Qur'an, it must be remembered that two-thirds of the Noble Qur'an had already been revealed before it came. So before we examine these injunctions it is necessary for us to look at the preliminary injunctions which underlie them if we want to understand them properly.

One of them is the basic equality between male and female. Confirmation of this comes in *Surat an-Nahl*: *"Anyone who acts rightly, whether male or female, being a believer, We will give them a good life and We will recompense them according to the best of what they did."* (16:97) We also find this judgement confirmed by the believer of the house of Pharaoh who says while advising the unbelievers of his time: *"Anyone who does an evil act will only be repaid the same as it. But anyone who acts rightly, whether male or female, being a believer, will enter the Garden, provided for in it without any reckoning."* (40:40)

The subject of the status of women is also referred to in *Surat ar-Rum* when it is discussing the signs of Allah: *"Among His signs is that He created for you spouses from yourselves so that you might find repose with them. And He has placed between you affection and mercy."* (30:21) And again in *Surat an-Nahl* when Allah is recounting the blessings He has bestowed on His slaves: *"Allah has given you wives from among yourselves, and given you children and grandchildren from your wives."* (16:72)

Thus it can be seen that the status of woman and the importance of the family had already been discussed in the Qur'an and so it is not strange that *Surat al-Baqara*, coming as it did at the time when Muslim society and the life of the family within it were finding their concrete expression in Madina, should contain specific guidance as to what to do if disputes occur, or refer to situations concerning which people must learn the judgement of Allah. It is quite logical that is should refer, for instance, to the different kinds of divorce, and to birth, suckling, and other matters concerning family life.

We find that the laws governing family life are based on the restraints of morality, faith and fear of Allah. Look at the basic *ayat* of divorce: *"When you divorce women and they reach the end of their waiting-period, then either retain them with correctness and courtesy, or release them with correctness and courtesy. Do not retain them by force, thus going beyond the limits. Anyone who does that has wronged himself. Do not make a mockery of Allah's Signs. Remember Allah's blessing to you and the Book and Wisdom He has sent down to you to admonish you. Fear Allah and know that Allah has knowledge of everything."* (2:231) What more could be done to uphold consideration and courtesy and allow for present and future contingencies?

Women have been oppressed and mistreated in many societies but it is strange that such injustice is imputed to Islam when it in fact lays great emphasis on justice for women. Allah Almighty says: *"Women possess rights similar to those held over them to be honoured with fairness; but men have a degree above them."* (2:228) The *ayat* is clear about mutual rights and obligations and affirms man's degree of leadership within the context of this mutual obligation.

Unfortunately this does not mean that there are not many places where this clear injunction is ignored by Muslims, where a woman has duties but no rights and where she is treated with harshness and cruelty; but this abuse cannot be ascribed to Islam itself. There are many Western organisations of both a religious and secular nature who take advantage of this to seduce Muslim women from their *deen*, and indeed many have fallen into their snare, but this is only possible where the basic tenets of Islam are ignored. The solution to this problem is good education and clinging to fear of

Allah and stopping at the limits of Allah. One difficulty is that some of those who speak about the *deen* are themselves ignorant and mediocre. For example some scholars limit a woman's right to *khul'*[1] divorce, saying that the *qadi* can only grant a divorce in the case of injury. But the truth is that if a woman finds that she cannot stand her husband for reasons which she either reveals or conceals and offers to return to him the dowry she received, the *qadi* has the right to grant her a divorce even if her husband does not agree.

When a woman gives birth, the benefits and expenses are shared between the couple: *"No self is charged save with what it can bear. No mother should be put under pressure in respect of her child nor any father in respect of his child,"* and they have to consult one another about the time of weaning: *"If the couple both wish weaning to take place after mutual agreement and consultation, there is nothing blameworthy for them in that."* (2:233)

All Muslims must consult their Book and the *Sunna* of their Prophet in learning the rules which govern family life, for it is only by truly understanding them and submitting to them that correct balance will be returned to human society and the social message of Islam which is so needed in the world today can be transmitted.

❋❋❋❋❋

After the *Hijra* the Muslims continued to receive the guidance of the Noble Qur'an as they had during the previous thirteen years but in a different kind of environment. The historical discussion about the Jews set the scene making clear their involvement in an ongoing struggle which would touch both present and future. The prayers had first been established on an individual basis. Now the *adhan* was given from the mosque to tell the Muslims to attend the prayer together, and the communal prayer became one of the hallmarks of Islam. Only hypocrites or people with valid excuses would fail to attend the prayer. The characteristics of the new society now began to emerge, individual virtue being augmented by shared loyalty to a prescribed *deen* which put its stamp on every

---

1. A form of divorce initiated by the wife.

aspect of people's lives. The unlawful was all but eliminated in both the public and private domains, based on the commanding of the right and the forbidding of the wrong. Military expeditions began to ensure the protection of faith in its new homeland and to check those who initiated aggression. The Revelation continued hand in hand with this process, underpinning it and moulding it.

From the very beginning the cornerstone of the whole edifice of Islam had been *tawhid,* that teaching about Divine Unity which had permeated the Revelation from its inception. The Makkan *suras* were full of *ayats* affirming Allah's Oneness and refuting idolatry in all its forms. This is continued and expanded in the Madinan period with more clarification, details and evidence as can be seen in the words of the Almighty: *"Your God is One God. There is no god but Him, the All-Merciful, the Most Merciful"* (2:163), which are immediately followed by evidence of Allah's unity derived from the earth and the sky: *"In the creation of the heavens and the earth, and the alternation of the night and day, and the ships which sail on the sea to people's benefit, and the water which Allah sends down from the sky, by which He brings the dead earth back to life and spreads about in it beasts of every kind, and the varying direction of the winds, and the clouds held subservient between heaven and earth, there are signs for people who use their understanding."* (2:164)

The *ayats* which follow this go further by explaining how knowledge of unity leads to a feeling of love which is then incorporated in behaviour. So the believer loves his Lord with a love stronger than he has for anything else and the fruits of this overpowering love appear in what he does. Allah the All-Glorious is worthy of this love because all glory and might belong to Him alone. Here we find the greatest of the *ayats* of the Noble Qur'an - the Throne Verse: *"Allah. There is no god but Him, the Living, the Self-Sustaining. He is not subject to drowsiness or sleep. Everything in the heavens and the earth belongs to Him ..."* (2:255) This uncompromising affirmation of Allah's oneness irresistibly annuls any attempt to associate anyone or anything else with His Sovereignty and Power. So we see in *Surat al-Baqara,* the first Madinan Revelation, a new kind of Qur'anic exposition of the most important aspects of belief, although of course there was no change in the fundamental principles.

The Companions of Muhammad succeeded in responding to what was sent down to them in this *sura* and what followed it. The Qur'an was sent down and they acted. It commanded and they obeyed. It prescribed for the individual and society and state, and they implemented. With its new men and new order Madina became the unique capital of the Message, the 'Middlemost Nation' which was *"the best nation ever to be manifested to mankind."* (3:110) Allah informed His Messenger by revelation and the Muslims learned from their Messenger what was of benefit to them and all mankind: *"In this way We have made you a middlemost nation, so that you could be witnesses against mankind and the Messenger could be a witness against you."* (2:143)

Allah Almighty makes it clear in the last two *ayats* of *Surat al-Baqara* that the Prophet and those with him have been true to Allah and therefore Allah is also true to them. They carried out the decrees He sent down to them in this *sura* and what followed it and were constant in it and did all they could to implement them in the best manner. They were far better in this respect than the previous people to whom Revelation had come, who said: *"We hear and disobey."* (2:92)

The Arabs were a basically illiterate people who had no recognised culture as far as the other world civilisations were concerned. Then the Qur'an was sent down among them and began to purify their behaviour and elevate them and they continued to climb the ascending steps of Divine guidance until they had risen above all other nations and become stronger and nobler than every other people in respect of both individual purity of character and the establishment of social justice.

The civilisation which they created was not based on racial pride or material aspiration or earthly goals but on the sincere acknowledgement of Allah's sovereignty and making this world the threshold of the Next World. That is why Allah Almighty says at the end of this *sura*: *"The Messenger believes in what has been sent down to him from his Lord, and so do the believers. Each one believes in Allah and His angels and His Books and His Messen-*

gers. We do not differentiate between any of His Messengers. They say, 'We hear and obey. Forgive us, O our Lord! To You is the final journey's end.'" (2:285)

The people of Islam have no race to be fanatic about, no homeland with which they identify themselves. Their fealty is to Allah, the Lord of the heavens and the earth, the Creator of all mankind. The only way one person can be better than another is by *taqwa* and no people is better than another except by their adherence to the *deen*.

Madina witnessed the first formation of the Islamic community and this occurred through their recognition of the Revelation connecting them to Allah and therefore directly to His guidance. Thus there were the Muslim household, the Muslim market, and the general expression of Islam in every area of life, whether legal, educational, commercial and agricultural, or intimately personal. Everything proceeded in accordance with the Revelation sent down in the Book and under the guiding leadership of him whose task was the complete implementation of Allah's final Message, may Allah bless him and grant him peace.

Sura 3

Ali 'Imran: The Family of 'Imran

The reader of *Surat Ali 'Imran* can quickly ascertain that this noble *sura* deals with two major themes: a discussion with the People of the Book who disputed with Islam inside Madina and an analysis of the setback of Uhud which inflicted a deep wound on the Muslims and brought grief to dozens of families. Both are first discussed on their own, the former at the beginning of the *sura* and the latter in the middle, and then discussion and commentary on both issues are combined at the end of the *sura*, implying that the implementation of the Message involves firm understanding of both of these important matters. The Muslims are made aware of the necessity of a common need to confront the deceit of the Jews inside Madina and the aggression of the idolaters from outside it.

Islam should be presented to all parties without either aggression or tyranny. Those who accept it become brothers in the faith, those who turn away are left alone, but those who commit aggression must be confronted. This position is made clear in the words of Allah in this *sura*: *"If they argue with you, say: 'I have submitted completely to Allah, and so have all who follow me.' Say to those given the Book and those who have no Book: 'Have you become Muslim?' If they become Muslim, they are guided. If they turn away, you are only responsible for conveying the Message. Allah sees His slaves."* (3:20)

The *sura* begins by clarifying that Islam is guidance for all people. The Qur'an is simply a confirmation of what was revealed before it. The purpose of all Divine Revelation is to discriminate between truth and falsehood. Musa, 'Isa and Muhammad all say basically the same thing and the term "Islam" embraces all true *deens* in their different times and places. Allah calls the Torah,

Gospel and Qur'an equally *Signs of Allah"*. This expression, *"Signs of Allah"*, is repeated ten times in this *sura*: the first time when Allah says, *"Those who reject the Signs of Allah will have a terrible punishment. Allah is Almighty, Exactor of Revenge,"* (3:4) and the last when He says, *"But among the people of the Book there are some who believe in Allah and what has been sent down to you and what was sent down to them, and who are humble before Allah. They do not sell Allah's Signs for a paltry price."* (3:199)

There is no contradiction between the fundamentals of faith revealed to Muhammad and those revealed to his two previous brother Prophets, Musa and 'Isa. Any disparity which has come to exist is only due to human lies. Faith, as the Qur'an makes clear, constitutes belief in what was revealed for us and what was revealed before us, and those who differ must return to their original right guidance.

The People of the Book fall into two categories: the Jews and the Christians. There was no heated debate between the Muslims and the Christians in Madina but there was heated dispute between the Muslims and the Jews, both those who were living in Madina itself and those living in northern Hijaz, all of whom created barriers against Islam, denied Allah and His Messenger, attacked the Revelation and rallied the idolaters against it in various places.

This incessant hostility was due to the fact that they had amassed much property and goods and possessed wealth and fortresses which were threatened by the coming of Islam. That is the reason for the reiterated denigration of their supposed strength in this noble *sura*: *"As for those who reject, their wealth and children will not avail them against Allah in any way. They are the fuel of the Fire."* (3:10) *"As for those who reject the Signs of Allah and kill the Prophets without any right and kill those who command justice, give them good news of a painful punishment."* (3:21) *"Do not be deceived by the fact that the people who reject move freely about the earth. A brief enjoyment; then their refuge is Jahannam. What an evil resting-place!"* (3:196) The truth is that arrogant wealth and forgetfulness of Allah do not constitute strength but simply mislead both individuals and societies.

When they first settled in the Hijaz, the cultural and economic level of the Jews was far above that of the Arabs of the peninsula but they did not make use of this attainment for the betterment of the ignorant idolatrous society which surrounded them. When the Final Prophet was sent to undertake this task they were misguided into contending with him and rejecting him, with the result that their force was shattered and all their hopes destroyed. They had been the favoured recipients of Divine Revelation for many generations and it had remained among them for so long that they claimed sole right to it, saying that it was impossible for it to go to anyone else. The truth is, however, that if someone ceases to be worthy of a certain privilege it will be removed from them, and by this time in their history the Jews had become completely unworthy of the Revelation they had received. Their hearts were like stones, their character base, their egoism overweening, and their first and last concern was to have their fill of this world and to devote themselves to it and to be insolent towards Allah, rejecting His commands and judgements.

It was now necessary, therefore, for the Revelation to move to another people who would respect it and implement it properly. This is the key to the words of the Almighty: *"Say, 'O Allah! Owner of the Kingdom! You give the kingdom to those You will and You take the kingdom from those You will. You exalt those You will and You abase those You will. All good is in Your hands. You have power over everything.'"* (2:26) This *ayat* is preceded by other *ayats* which lead up to it, such as the words of the Almighty directly before this *ayat*: *"Do you not see those who have been given a portion of the Book being called upon to let Allah's Book judge between them? But then a group of them turn away in aversion. That is because they say: 'The Fire will only touch us for a number of days.'"* (2:23-24) They felt safe from punishment and lifted the banner of rebellion. They decided to revoke unilaterally the Divine Law and its judgements.

The Divine response was to confirm universal justice between all categories of men and that racial and religious pretensions bear no weight in the scale of things: *"But how will it be when We gather them together for a Day about which there is no doubt?*

Every self will be paid in full for what it earned. They will not be wronged." (3:25) The spurious claims of individuals will prove worthless on the Day of Judgement. The naked human self will receive repayment for what it did and people will be gathered naked as they were created in the first place. The only clothing they will have is the garments of *taqwa* – if they were people who possessed it!

Even though the words rebuke the Jews, they also contain a hidden message for all people. Allah would not punish the tribe of Israel for their corruption and then leave the Muslims unpunished if they did the same thing. Similar actions will incur a similar punishment. The Jews did not think that they had been honoured by being given the Torah; they thought that the Torah had been honoured by being given to them and that they were far too precious to be destroyed. In the same way you now see Arabs who refuse to view Islam as the only source of their glory and who talk of their Arabness. Do you think that their end will be any better than that of the tribe of Israel who were turned into apes and pigs? The habitual practice of Allah does not change. All people are the same in His sight.

The discussion devoted to the People of the Book goes on for about ten pages, sometimes directed to the Jews, sometimes to the Christians, and sometimes to both. The origin of the Jews' hatred of the Arabs was that prophethood had been taken from them and given to Muhammad for the reasons we have already seen. When they saw the Revelation descending among the Arabs, they went mad and started to vent their hatred on everything. Divine Words were addressed to them to rebuke them: *"O People of the Book! Why do you reject Allah's Signs when you yourselves are there as witnesses? O People of the Book! Why do you mix up truth with falsehood and knowingly conceal the truth?"* (3:70-71)

It is clear from this rebuke that the Jews recognised with certainty that Muhammad was a true Prophet and that he spoke in the Name of Allah and that they were aware that Allah would punish them for their rebellion; but instead of putting things right with Allah, they continued to dispute and challenge the truth, denying the final prophethood, attacking it with both words and weapons, and orchestrating plots with the idolaters in order to divert them from sound belief.

Allah upbraids the Jews for the malicious position they adopted in several places: *"How is it possible for Allah to guide a people who have rejected after having had belief? They bore witness that the Messenger was true and that the clear Signs had come to them."* (3:86) And again: *"Say, 'People of the Book! Why do you reject Allah's Signs when Allah is witness of everything you do?' Say, 'People of the Book! Why do you obstruct those who believe from the Way of Allah, desiring to make it crooked when you yourselves are witnesses to it? Allah is not unmindful of what you do.'"* (3:98-99)

Jewish deviousness devised a cunning trick to turn people away from Islam and bar them from the Way of Allah. They said: "People suspect us of being fanatical about our own religion and think that we hate Islam on that account; why don't we pretend to embrace Islam, so that people think that we are liberal-minded and have left our religion for another? Then when we find the change is not beneficial we will change back again; but then it will appear to be because of something in Islam, not something in us!" *"A group of the People of the Book say, 'At the beginning of the day believe in what was sent down to those who believe and then at the end of the day reject it, so that perhaps they will revert."* (3:72)

They continued to show persistent aversion to the new Revelation and the transference of the Message away from themselves. They said: *"Do not believe anyone but those who follow your own deen."* (3:73) "Do not admit the possibility of anyone being given the like of what you were given. It is not possible for anyone but a Jew to receive Revelation." They hated what Allah had done and were enraged that He had preferred the Arabs to them and singled them out for the new Revelation. They wanted Him to change His decree and return Revelation to them but Allah's response was definitive: *"All favour is in Allah's hand and He gives it to anyone He wills. Allah is Boundless, All-Knowing. He singles out for His mercy anyone He wills. Allah possesses vast overflowing favour."* (3:73-74)

The vices of pride, hard-heartedness and self-delusion all meet together in the tribe of Israel. They are vices which are concealed by cowardice when their possessor is weak, and turn into hidden malice. But wealth and dominance lead to their open manifestation in overt enmity. Such has been the history of the Jews in this age, firstly in their ghettos in the capitals of the east and west when they concealed their evil opinion of all other people in supposed superiority and mockery. and now they have gained power in their arrogant hostility towards all who stand in their way. This *sura* gives their own justification for the position they take: *"That is because they say, 'We are under no obligation where the Gentiles are concerned.' They tell a lie against Allah and they know it."* (3:75)

The word translated as 'Gentiles' is a plural derived from the root *umm* which might mean 'illiterate', referring to the Arabs since illiteracy was widespread among them, or might mean 'nations', referring to all other people. The latter meaning is most likely given the character of the Jews and the claims which they put forward in their versions of the Torah and Talmud. It is this which made all the nations of Europe disown them and inflict punishment on them. Hitler was the latest in that succession of violent rulers and he will not be the last.

The noble Qur'an explains that the connection between mankind and their Lord is based not on false claims but on noble character, fidelity and fear of God: *"If people honour their contracts and are godfearing, Allah loves all godfearing people."* (3:76)

It might be asked, given that the first half of *Sura Ali 'Imran* is devoted to the People of the Book and their relationship to Islam, why mention is made in it of forbidden and permitted foods and the *Hajj*. The reason for the former is that when Islam was offered to the Jews they asked how they could follow a religion which allowed foods forbidden to them and which they avoided at all costs. They were told that the prohibition imposed on them was temporary and self-imposed. All foods had been lawful for them but when they deviated and transgressed, certain things were forbidden them as a punishment from Allah. *"All food was lawful for the tribe of Israel except what Israel made unlawful for himself before the Torah was sent down."* (3:93) It is known that the Message of 'Isa lifted some of the burdens of the Jews, a fact confirmed by the words of the Almighty on the tongue of the Messiah: *"I come confirming the Torah that is already there, and to make lawful for you some of what was forbidden to you."* (3:50) When the Noble Qur'an was revealed, the prohibited categories reverted to their original minimal prescription: carrion, pig meat, spilled blood, and what is consecrated to other than Allah. Everything else is permitted.

The mention of the *Hajj* must be understood in the context of the new *qibla* because it must be remembered that when the Muslims first went to Madina they faced Jerusalem to pray. The Sacred House in Makka was the first and last *qibla* for all people: *"The first House established for mankind was the one at Bakka, a place of blessing, and a guidance for all beings."* (3:96) Then Jerusalem became the *qibla* because of temporary circumstances and when these circumstances changed, the waters returned to their course and honour reverted to the House which had originally been founded as a stronghold of *tawhid* in ancient times. It is therefore the symbol for the unchanging nature of the universal principles which have underpinned Allah's *deen* throughout human history.

Overlooking the transient differences between the various *Shari'as* it is clear that the fundamental guidance for all human communities in different eras has been immutable. In reference to this we find at the beginning of *Surat Ali 'Imran* an exposition of the mainsprings of basic human nature: *"The love of worldly appetites is made to seem fair to mankind: of women and children, and heaped-up mounds of gold and silver, and horses with fine markings, and livestock, and fertile farmland. All that is merely the enjoyment of the life of this world. But the best homecoming is to the Presence of Allah."* (3:14)

Some of these instincts are necessary. Were it not for the sexual instinct, for instance, life on earth would cease to exist, and the same applies in varying degrees to the other instincts. What is important is that the correct balance is not exceeded. Otherwise you will go astray from the straight path. Islam permits what is beneficial and makes unlawful what is harmful. The lawful and unlawful are based on belief and right action and their starting point is *taqwa,* the dynamic of human connection with Allah and the Last Day.

This is the basis of all morality and applies equally to all human beings no matter what their beliefs. Human individuals and societies will inevitably receive endless trouble from their lower appetites unless they confine them within those Divine limits which define their correct balance, and they will never do this unless they understand and act on the words of Allah Almighty which follow the preceding *ayat: "Say: 'Shall I tell you of something better than that?' Those who are godfearing will find Gardens with their Lord, with rivers flowing under them, remaining in them timelessly, forever, and purified wives, and the Pleasure of Allah. Allah sees His slaves: those who say, 'Our Lord, we believe, so forgive us our wrong actions and safeguard us from the punishment of the Fire.' The steadfast and the truthful and the obedient and the givers and those who seek forgiveness before dawn."* (3:15-17) So this is a reminder for the People of the Book that the key to salvation is firstly recognition of the Unity of Allah and then confining human nature within the bounds of natural purity, avoiding excess and negligence.

❋❋❋❋❋

Now we come to that part of the *sura* addressed specifically to the Christians, the core of which is the correction of their absolutely baseless and fallacious claim of divinity for 'Isa son of Maryam. One reason for this error was the miraculous nature of 'Isa's birth since it is absolutely clear that no human being was involved with Maryam when she gave birth to her son, a fact which led some people to say, "'Isa is the son of God." This is gross ignorance of the Divine Nature and the Holiness which it possesses. The birth of 'Isa was of course a miracle, a case of the direct manifestation of Divine will with no intermediary of any kind, one of the numerous miracles which Allah makes happen among mankind to teach people that He controls the law of causality and is not controlled by it. That is why the story of Maryam and her son is related here together with the story of Zakariyya and his wife, who also gave birth in a miraculous way.

The mother of Maryam, expecting a boy, had pledged what was in her womb to be a servant of the Temple to protect its practices and to establish the worship of Allah in it: *"When the wife of 'Imran said, '"My Lord, I have pledged what is in my womb to You, devoting it to Your service. Please accept my prayer. You are the All-Hearing, the All-Knowing.'"* (3:35) But the child turned out to be a girl! What could a girl do to realise her mother's hopes and carry out duties which were a male prerogative? She did not know that her daughter would give birth to a man of supreme importance in this world and the Next. Maryam's mother's words upon giving birth are recorded in the *sura: "'O my Lord! I have given birth to a girl' – and Allah knew very well what she had given birth to, male is not like female – 'and I have named her Maryam and placed her and her children in Your safekeeping from the Accursed Shaytan.' Her Lord accepted her with approval and made her grow in health and beauty."* (3:36-37)

Zakariyya became Maryam's guardian. He was a very old man whose bones had become weak and whose wife was barren and had not borne any children. He was unhappy because there was no one to inherit the leadership of the tribe of Israel from him and he had a bad opinion of the Jews and feared what might happen after his death. However, he was happy to take on the guardianship of Maryam and soon became aware of the great blessing she brought to his house. Provision from the Unseen was sent to this unusual girl who had been placed in his care. *"He said, 'Maryam, how did you get this?' She said, 'It is from Allah. Allah provides for anyone He wills without any reckoning.'"* (3:37)

The deep understanding of Allah's Power implicit in her answer profoundly impressed Zakariyya and inspired him to called on his Lord in his own need, realising that his own old age and his wife's barrenness did not constitute any kind of barrier for Allah: *"There and then Zakariyya called on his Lord and said, 'O Lord, grant me, from Your favour, an upright descendant. You are the Hearer of Prayer.' The angels called out to him while he was standing in prayer in the Upper Room: 'Allah gives you the good news of Yahya, who will come to confirm a Word from Allah.'"* (3:38-39)

Vigour returned to the barren couple: the old man regained his potency and made his wife pregnant and the barren woman gave birth when she had never been able to before. When Allah wills something, causes obey His command and He creates whatever He wills and does whatever He pleases. Maryam grew up in this devout environment which was so full of blessings and thrived accordingly. The atmosphere of spiritual purity in which she lived prepared her for the angelic visitation which occurred after she reached maturity: *"When the angels said, 'Maryam, your Lord gives you the good news of a Word from Him. His name is the Messiah, 'Isa, son of Maryam, of high esteem in this world and the Next World, one of those brought near. He will speak to people in the cradle, and also when fully grown, and will be one of the righteous.' She said, 'My Lord! How can I possibly have a son when no man has ever touched me?' He said, 'It will be so. Allah creates anything He wills. When He decides on something, He just says to it, 'Be!' and it is."* (3:45-47)

This was clearly a severe ordeal for Maryam but the Decree of Allah was fulfilled and 'Isa son of Maryam was born in this unprecedented way. He was sent as a Messenger to the tribe of Israel in order to straighten their crookedness, shatter their delusions and oblige them to worship humbly and to be gentle towards Allah and other people. The tribe of Israel denied the miracle which had occurred in their midst and refused to acknowledge 'Isa's message. Their disbelief was made worse by their monstrous assertion that 'Isa's birth was not a Divine miracle but a human crime which had been committed by Maryam. Thus they combined disbelief and slander.

'Isa sought the help of good, truthful people and the Disciples supported him and gathered around him, saying: *"Our Lord, we believe in what You have sent down and have followed the Messenger, so write us down among the witnesses."* (3:53) The Jews continued their efforts, trying to delude 'Isa and his followers, but in spite of this 'Isa conveyed his Message and performed his Mission and Allah took him back to Himself, delivering him from the plots of the Jews and placing him in the highest part of Paradise, from where he will return near the end of time to join the Muslims in the affirmation of the oneness of Allah and support their ranks in their fight against the enemies of Allah. The vital point to grasp from all of this is that 'Isa is the slave of Allah and His Messenger. He is not a god nor is he the son of God.

Surat Ali 'Imran gives us an account of the clerical delegation which came to Madina to argue with the Messenger about his belief in Divine Unity. They said to him about 'Isa, "If he was a mortal, then who was his father? God was his father and he was only a mortal in form alone." The Messenger, may Allah bless him and grant him peace, argued that the absence of a human father did not mean that he had to be the son of God. If that had been the case, then Adam would have been more entitled to divinity since he had neither father nor mother. *"The likeness of 'Isa in Allah's sight is the same as that of Adam. He created him from earth and then He said to him, 'Be!' and there he was. It is the truth from your Lord. So do not be among the doubters."* (2:59-60)

However, the priests persisted in their opinion, and opposed him vigorously. So Allah revealed a way to resolve the impasse: *"If anyone argues with you about him after the knowledge that has come to you, say, 'Come then! Let us summon our sons and your sons, our women and your women, ourselves and yourselves. Then let us make earnest supplication and call down the curse of Allah upon the liars.' This is the true account. There is no god other than Allah. Allah. He is the Almighty, the All-Wise."* (3:61-62) The Christian delegation refused to take advantage of this possibility and both of the parties remain until today with people following their own *deen*. It appears that it is 'Isa alone who will resolve the situation when he descends at the end of time. He will make it clear to his worshippers that they were mistaken and that there is only one Lord: Allah, the One, the All-Conquering.

This discussion about the People of the Book now gives place to the considerable amount of Revelation received concerning the many ramifications of the Battle of Uhud, a battle in which the Muslims suffered a painful setback and sustained heavy losses. The battle was fought against the idolaters who had outdone the People of the Book in their opposition to Islam and expelled its followers from Makka. The enemies of the Muslims have rarely come from only one direction, and throughout the course of their history down to the present day the Muslims have always found themselves fighting on several fronts at the same time!

The discussion begins when the Almighty says to His Prophet, *"When you left your family early in the day to settle the believers in their battle stations. Allah is All-Hearing, All-Knowing."* (2:121) The thread of the narrative is apparently broken after a few *ayats* by an interpolation reinforcing the prohibition against usury and urging spending in both ease and hardship and hastening to repentance after yielding to wrong action, after which the Revelation reverts to discussing in detail the results of the Battle of Uhud. Nothing about Allah's Words is in any way haphazard and it is clear that the goal of this interpolation is to reinforce the inner front-line and purify it from every deviation until it is worthy of victory. *Jihad* is not about the victory of individuals but about the victory of Allah's *deen* as a whole. It is particularly important for us in this time to note the fact that Allah chose this juncture to remind us of His prohibition of usury. It is as if He were pointing out to us the direction in which our hidden enemy lies; and there is no doubt that usury has played a pivotal role in the downfall of the Muslims in our time.

It is also clear that there must be no personal element involved when fighting *Jihad*. Allah says to His Prophet: *"You have no part in the affair. Either He will turn to them or He will punish them, for they are the wrongdoers."* (3:128) No one knows whether the opponent of yesterday or today will put himself right with Allah and enter His *deen*. Love and hate must be for the sake of Allah alone. There is no room whatsoever for personal vendettas or enmities.

There is a clear wisdom in the setback of Uhud. The victory of Badr opened up an avenue for adventurers and those seeking worldly benefit to join the new *deen*, when it became apparent that the future belonged to it. Did not the leader of the Hypocrites, 'Abdullah ibn Ubayy, say after the sudden victory in Badr: "This business has taken a turn for the good" and encourage his followers to throw in their lot with the Muslims? That is why Allah Almighty says: *"Allah would never abandon the believers in the state in which you find yourselves – only until He sifts out the bad from the good. And Allah does not give you access to the Unseen."* (3:179) Therefore a setback was needed to sort out friend from foe and to sift out those who merely sought material gain and reputation from the people of true sincerity who would support their Prophet through good and bad times and stand by their commitment to their Lord no matter what turn events took.

The Muslims in Madina were divided into two groups: one was devoted to the Truth no matter what happened but the other had a hidden agenda: *"whereas another group filled themselves with anxious thoughts."* (3:154) Their striving was in reality only for their own ends and they found themselves *"thinking other than the truth about Allah – thoughts belonging to the Age of Ignorance – saying, 'Do we have any say in the affair at all?'"* (3:154) They were angry because their suggestions had not been taken and because they were not advanced and esteemed. Belief is not helped by the likes of such people.

The setback of Uhud did not arise from poor planning, as some people say, but from negligence in carrying out orders. If every soldier had played his prescribed part it would not have occurred, but some forgot their duty owing to their impulsive greed at the sight of the piles of booty which became available when the Muslims gained the upper hand in the first part of the battle: *"Allah fulfilled His promise to you when you were slaughtering them by His permission. But then you faltered and disputed the command, and disobeyed after He showed you what you love. Some of you are people who want this world and some of you are people who want the Next World. Then He turned you from them in order to test you; but He has pardoned you - Allah possesses over-flowing favour for the believers."* (3:152)

The Muslims were severely shocked by this serious setback and were taken aback by its evil effects. They did not understand how such a thing was possible. The explanation was not long in coming: *"Why is it that when a calamity happens to you, when you have already inflicted twice as much, you ask, 'How could this possibly happen?'? Say: 'It has come from yourselves.' Allah has power over everything."* (3:165) Allah was telling the Muslims that their defeat at Uhud was only half that suffered by the idolaters at Badr and that fact alone should be enough for them, despite what had occurred. Moreover, they alone were responsible for what had happened to them. Had they observed the obedience mandatory for every soldier, and the devotion asked of every believer, victory would have been theirs.

However Allah is not interested in apportioning blame and desires the Muslims to gain as much benefit as possible from what happened, and so He consoles and encourages the believers: *"Whole societies have passed away before your time, so travel the earth and see the end result of the deniers. This is a clear explanation for all mankind, and guidance and admonition for the god-fearing. Do not give up and do not be down-hearted. You shall be uppermost if you are believers."* (3:137-139) Unbelief has no future. Allah has reported to His slaves the histories of previous nations. They all were destroyed because they clung to unbelief and persisted in it. The victory of Quraysh was only a brief and transient interlude which was definitely to be overturned because the future belonged to faith alone. However, victory for the Muslims would require two things: sincere intention and efficient execution. Both are necessary. The Muslims of our time particularly need to recognise the second ingredient and confirm it.

Some imagine that righteousness alone will achieve the desired result, as if the angels will descend to compensate for the believers' lack of preparation for battle or their ill-prepared rush into it. This is extremely unlikely. Expend all the faith, action, sincerity and skill you can muster and then expect good, even if your forces are small. In that case you have done everything you can and Allah will not disappoint you. The worst kind of fight is when a man is defeated not by his opponents' strength but by his own lack of fitness and preparation. The battles of the Muslims throughout the course of history show us that their defeats did not come from the zeal of the enemy against them but from their own disagreements and broken ranks, so that their disasters were almost always of their own making. When they repaired the damage, things turned in their favour.

This is what the *sura* insists on here: *"Do not give up and do not be down-hearted. You are uppermost if you are believers. If a wound has been inflicted on you, a similar wound has already been inflicted on them. We send such days to people in turns, so that Allah may know those who believe and can gather martyrs from among you. Allah does not love wrongdoers."* (3:139-140) The story of this life is one of constant struggle between differing opinions and codes of conduct: *"But they persist in their differences, except for those your Lord has mercy on. That is the reason He created them."* (11:118-119) So evil is a test of good and ugliness is a test of beauty and censure is a test of honour. *"But We have made some of you a trial for others. Will you be steadfast? Your Lord is All-Seeing."* (25:20)

If Allah wanted He could defeat unbelief and punish its supporters by Himself – but then there would be nothing left for the people of truth to do. The struggle between believers and unbelievers is part of Allah's plan: *"That is how it is. If Allah willed, He would avenge Himself on them. However it is so in order that He may test some of you by means of others."* (47:4) This has always been the way with the Prophets and their followers throughout history. No place of worship was ever established without struggle and sacrifice on the part of the believers. *"If Allah had not driven some people back by means of others, monasteries, churches, synagogues and mosques, where Allah's Name is mentioned much, would have been pulled down and destroyed. Allah will certainly help those who help Him."* (22:40)

Allah reminds the followers of Muhammad of this fact when consoling them for their losses at Uhud, when He says: *"How many a Prophet has fought, and many thousands with him, who did not give up in the face of what assailed them in the way of Allah, nor did they weaken, nor did they yield. Allah loves the steadfast. All they said was, 'Our Lord, forgive us our wrong actions and our extravagant excesses in our lives; and make our feet firm and help us against the people who reject.'"* (3:146-147)

The *sura* continues to apply a salve to the wound of defeat and to encourage firm resolve. It restores the cohesion and trust of the believers. And we must not forget the role that the Battle of Uhud played in uncovering precious gems. There were men who kicked aside this world and went to Allah undistracted by anything. There were men who remained firm in hopeless positions where they were steadfast to their last breath. There were women who went to the battlefield with courage and sacrifice: while weak men hung back, those believing women flew to the fray. The battle etched reminders in the hearts of the believers so that it would never be forgotten and Uhud continued to be remembered by of our Messenger, may Allah bless him and grant him peace, to the very end of his life. He would pray over its martyrs, saying, "Uhud is a mountain which loves us and which we love."

Martyrdom is a high station for which Allah chooses whomever He pleases of His slaves. He says in this *sura*, *"So that He can gather martyrs from among you."* (3:140) Martyrdom is one of the highest human possibilities to be met with on the way to the victory of Allah and His Messenger. The concern of those believers chosen for this rank is to exalt the Word of Allah and spend their time in supporting Islam and protecting it and repelling its enemies. Those killed at Uhud were unique examples of those qualities.

Consider the life of Mus'ab ibn 'Umayr, one of the wealthiest young men of Makka, who embraced Islam and lost all his wealth, dying a poor man. After being used to silken clothes he had to wear coarse wool. He emigrated to Madina before the rest of the Muhajirun, charged by the Messenger of Allah with spreading Islam, and there was no house of importance in Madina which he did not enter. He was one of those killed at Uhud, an exile from his birthplace, wearing a garment which was not even long enough to shroud his whole body so that his feet had to be covered with herbs.

Consider the life of 'Abdullah ibn Haram. He was a father with six daughters and one son - Jabir ibn 'Abdullah. He told his son: "The six girls should not be left without a man. I am not happy to let the Messenger go out to fight while I remain at home! You stay with them. I am going to fight." He went and was martyred in the battle.

Allah Almighty says about the martyrs: *"Do not suppose that those killed in the way of Allah are dead."* Then He describes them with five qualities: *"No indeed! They are alive, well provided for in the very presence of their Lord, delighting in the overflowing favour Allah has bestowed on them, rejoicing over those left behind who have not yet joined them, feeling no fear and knowing no sorrow."* (3:169-170)

The position of the Muslims was exposed and very compromised when the archers disobeyed their orders and abandoned their position. That is why seventy Muslims were killed as heroes in a spirited defence during which it was even rumoured that the Messenger himself had been killed. Quraysh found themselves up against a hard wall that would not give and, realising they could not achieve more than they already had, gathered their men together and returned to Makka.

It is useful to mention what the Muslims did after their temporary defeat. They regrouped and, braving their wounds, set out towards Makka in pursuit of the army of the unbelievers which was travelling slowly, debating whether or not to return and complete what it had begun. But when they became aware of the Muslims advancing in pursuit, they gave up any hopes they had of finishing off the Muslims and hurried back to Makka. The Muslims returned, as the Revelation describes: *"Those who responded to Allah and the Messenger after the wound had been inflicted on them; those among them who did good and were godfearing will have an enormous wage."* (3:172)

At this point the commentary on the Battle of Uhud stops for a time and the *sura* again discusses the Jews. From this point the *sura* deals with both issues simultaneously, going to and fro between one and the other. Sometimes it talks of the Jews and sometimes of the idolaters, which is not surprising since the *jihad* of the Message is against both groups, as the Almighty says: *"You will be tested in your wealth and in your selves and you will hear many harmful words from those given the Book before you and from those who worship idols. But if you are steadfast and god-fearing, that shows true resolve."* (3:186)

In their disbelief the Jews descended to such a low level that even the most forbearing person would have become exasperated. The Qur'an encourages the believers to spend in the way of Allah, to defend the truth, and to help the poor and destitute: *"Who is there who will make Allah a generous loan so that He may multiply it for him many times? Allah both constricts and expands. And you will be returned to Him."* (2:245) But the response of the Jews to this was to say, "Allah is poor so that He has to borrow from His slaves!" They said, "He forbids usury and then employs it Himself!" *"Allah has heard the words of those who said: 'Allah is poor and we are rich.' We will write down what they said and their killing of the Prophets without any right and We will say: 'Taste the punishment of the Burning.'"* (2:181)

These are people with no faith or fear of Allah in their hearts, people of notorious meanness. They meet faith with disdain, rancour and resentment. The Jews think that they are Allah's chosen people. But does election consist in teaching people and being good to them or does it consist in feeling superior to them and then exploiting and ruining them? Jewish history has not been one of generous giving but one of arrogance and misappropriation.

This *sura* contains a succinct analysis of the behaviour of the Jews: *"When Allah made a covenant with those given the Book: 'You must make it clear to people and not conceal it.' But they cast it in disdain behind their backs and sell it for a paltry price. How evil is the sale that they make! Do not suppose that those who exult in what they have done and love to be praised for what they have not done, do not suppose them to have won safety from the punishment. They will have a painful punishment."* (3:187-188)

Surat Ali 'Imran comes to a climax with a glorious passage addressed at the deepest level to all human beings, cutting through all differences of race and religion by reminding them of their common purpose and destiny. Sincere unprejudiced reflection on the universe is bound to lead us to acknowledgement of the existence of Allah and to glorifying His praise and affirming His might and power. The objective use of the intellect will reveal the insignificance of man-made religious disagreements and the overwhelming importance of understanding the true nature of existence. Let us reflect on what will happen to us after this life. Then it will be clear that we must not forget our Lord and leave the Straight Path He has shown us. We have no choice but to turn to Him and seek His shelter.

This is the context within which the coming of Islam should be viewed. A man has appeared announcing to the people of the earth that they should return to right guidance and believe in their Lord. How can he be denied? Does he not deserve every consideration? *"Our Lord, we have heard a caller calling to belief: 'Believe in your Lord!' and we have believed. Our Lord, forgive us our wrong actions and erase our bad actions from us and take us back with the people of true piety."* (3:193) Allah answers this by telling us that He will not *"let the deeds of any doer among you go to waste,"* man or jinn, black or white, and He is not concerned with race or lineage. What is important is righteous action. Why should people not believe in a man who does nothing but call them to righteousness, humility towards Allah, and preparation for the inevitable meeting with Him?

And yet the blindness of the idolaters and the obstinate prejudice of the People of the Book made them band together against him and fight him and forced his followers to emigrate from their homeland and endure all sorts of injury for the sake of their belief, so their repayment will be as Allah describes: *"Their Lord responds to them: 'I will not let the deeds of any doer among you go to waste, whether male or female – the one is as the other. Those who emigrated and were driven from their homes and suffered harm in My way, and fought and were killed, I will erase their bad actions from them and I will admit them into Gardens with rivers flowing under them.'"* (3:195) The unbelievers have raised their banner and sought the help of their armies but their success will only be short-lived: *"Do not be deceived by the fact that the people who reject move freely about the earth. A brief enjoyment; then their refuge is Jahannam. What an evil resting-place!"* (3:196-197) The idolaters were victorious for a day at Uhud, causing a slight check in the onward flow of the Truth which then resumed its course, unstoppable. *"And the best end result is gained by fear of Allah!"* (20:132)

Surat Ali 'Imran then concludes with two *ayats*, the first of which generously opens a door to the people of the Book: *"But among the people of the Book there are some who believe in Allah and what has been sent down to you and what was sent down to them, and who are humble before Allah. They do not sell Allah's signs for a paltry price. Such people will have their wage with their Lord."* (3:199) The *ayat* directs the People of the Book, Jew or Christian, until the end of time, to listen to the Final Prophet and believe in what he has brought.

The final *ayat, "O you who believe! Be steadfast. Excel the enemy in steadfastness. Be firm on the battlefield and fear Allah so that perhaps you will be successful,"* (3:200) is the summation of all the lessons to be learned from Uhud. Allah tells the Muslims that they must not allow anything to divert them from their task of establishing His *deen*. The virtue of steadfastness is triply emphasised to impress on the Muslims that upholding the Truth with which Allah has honoured them is no easy task and that they must never let up in their struggle against the forces of unbelief. Unfortunately, of course, the Muslims have not heeded this and have allowed themselves to be almost totally dominated by the forces of unbelief. This is, therefore, also a call to us, the Muslims of this time. Are we responding?

Sura 4
An-Nisa': Women

Surat an-Nisa' is almost entirely devoted to the social issues which were facing the burgeoning Muslim polity in Madina. The first third deals with the family and its issues, the family being society in miniature. The remaining two-thirds discuss the community and its affairs, the community being society as a whole. The entire *sura* deals with social relationships and the necessity of getting them right.

This theme is addressed right from the very first words of the *sura*: *"O Mankind! Fear your Lord who created you from a single self and created its mate from it and then disseminated many men and women from the two of them. Fear Allah in whose Name you make demands on one another and also fear Him in respect of your families. Allah watches over you continually."* (4:1) All of mankind, even if they seem to be strangers, are in reality related to one another. All of us originated from a single couple. Every human being must remember this relationship and maintain ties with both immediate and distant kin. Indeed, maintaining ties of kinship is one of the hallmarks of Islam. Although the usual position is that family only means the direct relationship of parents and children, the net of human co-operation must be spread wider and there must be mutual help between different tribes and races.

The *ayat* makes it clear that the basis of this relationship has to be fear of Allah, the All-Powerful Creator, and awareness of His all-encompassing control, although the *sura* mitigates this by a number of *ayats* showing that Allah is aware of our frailty as human beings and always ready to forgive our shortcomings: *"If you avoid the serious wrong actions you have been forbidden to do, We will erase your bad actions for you"* (4:31); *"Anyone who does evil or wrongs himself and then asks Allah's forgiveness will find Allah All-Forgiving, Most Merciful"* (4:110); *"Allah does not forgive partners being attributed to Him but He forgives anything besides that to anyone He wills"* (4:48); *"Allah only accepts the repentance of people who do evil in ignorance and then very soon repent of doing it"* (4:17); and *"Allah desires to make things clear to you and to guide you to the practices of those who came before you and to turn towards you. Allah is All-Knowing, All-Wise. Allah desires to turn towards you, but those who pursue their base appetites desire to make you deviate completely. Allah desires to make things lighter for you. Man was created weak."* (4:26-28)

Allah does not want to burden His slaves with acts of worship which will be too much for them. Their exertions are to be bearable and fruitful ones, such as those of learners in search of knowledge and educated people in their search to achieve perfection. Fear of the All-Watchful and All-Powerful and hope in the All-Merciful and All-Forgiving gives life to the believers and prepares them for the inevitable meeting with their Lord whether that comes sooner or later.

The section dealing with family matters begins with words about the rights of orphans because, as we saw at the end of the previous *sura*, the Muslims are a nation who are in continual *jihad* against the enemies of Islam and so it is not surprising that there are numerous people killed and therefore many orphans. This matter has received added urgency in our own time when orphans have become a target for missionary groups and faith thieves, so that now it is more necessary than ever for the Muslims to take care of their orphans and protect their rights.

Within the framework of this discussion about orphans, marriage is mentioned and sanctioned, both monogamous and polygamous. In this respect Islam in no way deviates from the customs of previous religions. There was no religion which ever forbade polygamy by a command from Allah. When you look at the reality of people in our time, you see that the Europeans and Americans are the worst of people in relation to women and that polygamy is in fact rife among them, except that it is polygamy of an illicit kind with no protection of any kind for the women involved. Any man who wants can, and frequently does, have relations with an unlimited number of women. The Islamic permission for polygamy has a strictly defined scope. For instance unmarried men are instructed to fast if they cannot afford marriage, so it is scarcely likely that a man who already has one wife would be permitted to take another he cannot provide for. And even if he can provide for more, he still has to be able to be fair between them. A woman cannot be forced to marry and therefore it is open to any woman to refuse to enter a polygamous marriage. Furthermore, any woman who fears that her husband might take another wife can stipulate in her own marriage contract that she will not have a co-wife. As Ahmad ibn Hanbal made clear, the husband has to abide by this condition and fulfil the contract. Otherwise the woman is divorced.

The *sura* then mentions the judgements of inheritance. A wife automatically receives a given share of her husband's estate, even if before his death she had not received anything at all. It is recommended to give something from every estate to the poor and weak. People are also allowed to leave up to a third of their property in any way they wish. In general terms the portion of a woman is half that of a man. That is because a man has to shoulder more responsibilities than a woman. He has to pay a dowry and is obliged to support his household. Ample provision is to be made for the care of women either by their families or the Public Treasury so that women will not be exposed to that degradation which is so often their lot in the West despite its continual boast about being the defender of women!

This is not to defend those Muslims lacking in heart and intellect who despise women and demean their wives, sisters and daughters, practically imprisoning them, keeping them in ignorance and behaving arrogantly towards them. There is a *hadith* from 'A'isha, in which the Messenger of Allah, may Allah bless him and grant him peace, said, "The believer with the most complete faith is the one who is the best in character and kindest to his family." Ibn 'Abbas said that the Messenger of Allah said, "The best of you is the best of you to his family and I am the best of you to his family." It is regrettable that a number of 'religious' people think that *taqwa* means being harsh to women, treating them badly and lowering their status. This incorrect understanding has caused women throughout the world to dislike Islam and fear its control over society.

Before the advent of Islam a woman had no rights whatsoever and when her husband died, his closest relative came and took possession of her as if she were part of his goods. That was also the case in Jewish law: when a woman's husband died, his closest relative was obliged to marry her and have children by her which were ascribed to the dead man. (Deuteronomy 25) Allah put an end to this practice: *"O you who believe! It is not lawful for you to inherit women by force,"* and then He says, *"And do not prevent them from remarrying in order to make off with part of what you have given them – unless they have committed an act of flagrant disobedience."* (4:19)

Men are commanded to behave honourably towards their wives even in situations when there is no harmony between the couple: *"Live together with them correctly and courteously. If you dislike them, it may well be that you dislike something when Allah has placed a great deal of good in it."* (4:19) If a man does want a divorce, he is not permitted to bargain with his wife in order to reduce the dowry she received from him, however large it was. It became her personal property on her marriage: *"If you desire to exchange one wife for another one, and you have given one of them a large amount, do not take any of it. Would you take it by means of slander and downright crime? How could you take it when you have been intimate with each other and they have made a binding contract with you?"* (4:20-21)

Before advocating the need for forbearance within marriage, two pernicious social evils connected with this issue are mentioned: fornication and homosexuality. Combating these two crimes is defending the integrity of the family and protecting its purity, and so mentioning such matters at this point is entirely consistent with the subject under discussion. Regarding the first, the Almighty says: *"If any of your women commit fornication, four of you must appear as witnesses against them. And if they do bear witness, detain them in their homes until death comes to them or Allah ordains some other way for them."* (4:15) About homosexuality, the Almighty says: *"If two among you do it, castigate both of them."* (4:16)

One aspect of the West's forgetfulness of Allah and the encounter with Him and its consequent abandonment of Allah's *deen* and its teachings is that it makes light of these crimes with the inevitable consequence of the rampant spread of AIDS and other sexually transmitted diseases. The truth is that western civilisation is rotten through and through and only continues because of the absence of its rightful heirs, namely the Muslims, who have themselves forgotten their *deen* and failed to take on their divinely appointed task of re-establishing Allah's guidance for the whole of mankind.

In order for the family successfully to fulfil its appointed social role, people's natures must be disciplined and their innate selfishness suppressed. Both parties to a marriage must train themselves to be virtuous and to co-operate positively with their partner. Lack of co-operation, particularly sexually, can be very destructive and, in this case, Islam permits the punishment of a recalcitrant woman, starting with admonishment and progressing first to separation and finally to beating, although it is a condition that the beating is not hard and the husband avoids striking his wife's face. In fact there is no justification in the *Sunna* for the last punishment except when a woman refuses to have sexual relations with her husband or allows a stranger in the house without his permission, both of which can lead to very serious repercussions.

After these specifically familial instructions the *sura* opens out to address society as a whole: *"Worship Allah and do not attribute partners to Him. Be good to your parents and relatives and to orphans and the very poor."* (4:36) This directive embraces all society, although the family is indicated first. It also introduces the whole matter of expenditure, saying that it should involve neither stinginess nor extravagance. The Qur'an then mentions people who embody the vices of miserliness and prodigal extravagance. One group are miserly at times, commanding others to be stingy as well, and are profligate at other times for the sake of showing off and reputation. It is better to spend money according to the will of the One who provides it and that is the desired course of action:

"What harm would it have done them to believe in Allah and the Last Day and give of what Allah has provided for them? Allah knows them." (4:39)

After a little further discussion concerning the present and future Muslim community, the *sura* then changes tack to speak of the situations of the various groups which made up society at the time the Qur'an was being revealed. The strange thing is that these groups are the same ones which still exist today.

The Muslims were very eager at first to make friends with the Jews, acknowledging that they had the prior Revelation, and expected them to take their side when there was a fight between them and the idolaters. However the Jews had other ideas, not being concerned with treaties or their neighbours, and tried to do as much damage to Islam as they could. In wonder and disapproval at what they did, Allah says to His Prophet: *"Do you not see those who were given a portion of the Book paying a high price for error and wanting you to be misguided from the way? Allah knows best who your enemies are."* (4:44-45) The statement that they possess only a portion of the Book shows that they had lost much of the Revelation which had been sent to them. The truth is that the loss of their Book was due to a succession of inadequate custodians who had allowed part of it to become lost and the rest to be altered almost beyond recognition. And even then they did not act according to the part they still had. Today, for instance, the Jews are behind the spread of usury and fornication throughout the entire world in spite of the fact that both are specifically forbidden to them.

False religiosity can be more harmful than an empty and negligent heart. That is why it is said that the corrupt go more swiftly to the Fire than the idolaters. The corruption in the hearts of the Jews is what made them prefer misguidance to guidance and gave them their attraction to sin and their strange desire to see the Muslims forget the Qur'an and revert to idolatry.

Allah promises the Muslims that He will support them in their obligatory fight to establish His *deen* and that He will be their Protector and Helper. *"Allah is enough as a Protector. Allah is enough as a Helper."* (4:45) But this protection and help is not for those who hang back, and is likely to be denied to those who neglect to defend themselves and are negligent in making plans and fortifying their positions.

Then the Noble Qur'an explains what the Jews did to their *deen* so that the Muslims may be careful not to do the same. Allah says: *"Some of the Jews distort the true meaning of words ..."* (4:46) This distortion takes various forms. The first involves changing the literal meaning of words because of dislike for what they imply. For instance, they received the good news of an expected Messenger but made the words mean something else which they wanted to hear so that they would not have to affirm Muhammad or bear witness to the truth of his Message.

Another kind of distortion involves deliberately adding extraneous material to the revealed text which has nothing to do with Revelation. The Indian shaykh, M. E. Kairanvi, may Allah have mercy on him, included in his Book, *Izhar al-Haqq*, a hundred instances of this deliberate distortion of the Holy Bible: *"They say, 'It is from Allah,' but it is not from Allah. They tell a lie against Allah and they know it."* (3:78) *Izhar al-Haqq* is the most complete book available on this subject.

Another aspect of the distortion of language on the part of the Jews and their bad-mannered insolence is exemplified by their words to the Messenger: *"'We hear and disobey,' and 'Listen without listening,' and* 'Ra'ina[1] (from flippancy)!' *twisting them with their tongues, disparaging the* deen.*"* (4:46)

Allah threatens the Jews that if they continue in their obduracy, He will strike them down. He says: *"O you who have been given the Book! Believe in what We have sent down confirming what you already have, before We obliterate your faces, turning them inside out, or We curse you as We cursed the Companions of the Sabbath. Allah's command is carried out."* (4:47) However, the Jews persisted in their obduracy and so Allah obliterated all trace of them in the Hijaz.

Allah goes on to explain precisely why they have brought down Allah's curse on themselves. Allah Almighty says: *"Allah does not*

---

1. An ambiguous play on words which changed the meaning from 'look at us' to 'our little shepherd'.

forgive partners being attributed to Him but He forgives anything besides that to anyone He wills." (4:48) There is more than one way of attributing partners to Allah: the first, and most obvious, is to believe in a multiplicity of actual deities. Another, which is more pernicious because it is not so blatant, is to resort to and rely on other than Allah in legislation. The Jews were not guilty of the first type but of the second, which involves altering the laws of Allah. Both types of attributing partners are unforgiveable crimes because they involve a deep corruption of the human soul.

The depths of Jewish malice reached such a point that when the Jewish leaders were asked which of the two groups were more entitled to victory and closer to the truth, their reply was that idolatry was better than Islam and defending ignorant idolaters better than supporting the Companions of Muhammad! Religion in the case of the tribe of Israel does not mean justice and generosity and humility. It is simply a means of inflaming people with racial pride and satisfying their egotism and indulging self-delusion.

They disliked the Arabs and still do because they are the nation whom Allah chose to bear the responsibility of the Revelation after the Israelites exploited it and refused to live by it. The sons of Ya'qub are only one part of the family of Ibrahim. Why should they monopolise the blessing of Allah to Ibrahim and his family so that the sons of Isma'il have no portion of it? Why should they take revenge on their cousins for the bounty of Allah they have received and support idolaters against them? *"Those are the people Allah has cursed. And if Allah curses someone you will never find any helper for him. Or do they indeed really own a portion of the Kingdom? In that case they do not give to people the tiniest speck."* (4:52-53)

This *ayat* emphasises the notorious miserliness of the Jews. Even if they were to possess all the treasures of Allah, they still would not release a single one of them as a gift for a needy person. They envy the Arabs for the blessing they have been granted. *"Or do they in fact envy people for the overflowing favour Allah has given them? We gave the family of Ibrahim the Book and the Wisdom, and We gave them an immense dominion."* (4:54)

The Jews, because of their fury at the transfer of Revelation away from them to the Arabs, have continued in their denial of Muhammad and opposition to his people and have characteristically never forgotten their expulsion from Hijaz. After fourteen centuries they returned to Palestine, seeking to regain their past glory, taking advantage of the opportunity offered them by the Muslims who had neglected the legacy of Islam and were overcome by distraction and self-indulgence. People who were present when they entered Jerusalem heard them shouting: "O revenge for Khaybar! Muhammad died and left nothing but daughters!"

After this passage about the Jews, the *sura* begins to talk about another group which had great importance for Islam and the Muslims: the hypocrites who make an open display of faith while in fact concealing disbelief until eventually their actions betray them and their secrets are disclosed. The discussion about them begins with the words of the Almighty: *"Do you not see those who claim that they believe in what has been sent down to you and what was sent down before you, still desiring to turn to false gods for judgement in spite of being commanded to reject them? Shaytan wants to misguide them far away."* (4:60) The use of the word 'claim' indicates the falseness of their declaration and the 'false gods' referred to are any source of judgement other than Allah – whether human or jinn or inanimate!

Faith implies rejection of all false gods. The Almighty says: *"Allah is the Protector of those who believe, drawing them out of darkness into the light. Those who reject – their protectors are the false gods who drive them out of the light into darkness."* (2:257) He says in this *sura*: *"Those who believe fight in the Way of Allah and those who reject fight for the cause of false gods."* (4:76) A 'false god' is anything that distances one from Allah and bars from His way and disputes His *Shari'a*. The hypocrites hear the advice of the believers to follow Allah and His Messenger but continue blindly on their way. Every step they take is governed by obduracy and misguidance and after they have gone some distance down their evil path, the voice of good counsel almost fails to reach them: *"Those are called out to from a distant place."* (41:44)

A hypocrite may be physically close to you but will be far from you in his heart, which is made heedless by his passions, and so he does not heed or follow what is said to him: *"When they are told, 'Come to what Allah has sent down and to the Messenger,' you see the hypocrites turning away from you completely."* (4:61) And in another *sura* we find: *"When it is said to them, 'Come on, and the Messenger of Allah will ask forgiveness for you,' they avert their heads and you see them turn away with haughty arrogance."* (63:5) The clear-cut unbeliever or hypocrite has a point of view which he clings to and argues for and will not abandon for the truth even after it is made clear to him. But the evil results of such a course of action are bound to manifest themselves sooner or later and when that happens those people will come trying to excuse themselves: *"How will it be when a calamity strikes them because of what they have done, and then they come to you swearing by Allah, 'We desired nothing but goodness and reconciliation'?"* (4:62)

In our time the proponents of man-made laws defend them and suppose that they have some solid foundation, and then when strife dominates the land and crimes increase, they reflect and retreat and offer excuses: *"Such people, Allah knows what is in their hearts. So turn away from them and warn them and speak to them with deeply penetrating words about themselves."* (4:63)

There are two situations in which hypocrisy is always exposed and its ugly face appears. The first is when a hypocrite is asked to judge by what Allah has sent down and the other is when he is asked to defend the Truth and fight in the Way of Allah. Hypocrites also generally feel distaste for acts of obedience to Allah such as prayer and charity but they usually manage to conceal this. When they are faced with submitting to Allah's judgement or *jihad* for His Cause, however, their inward sickness is exposed and they are disgraced.

The Messengers come from Allah with a complete programme for a rightly-guided life and, starting with belief and obedience, the followers of the Messenger implement Allah's guidance and go straight on the Path. There is only this course before them. That is why the Almighty says: *"No, by your Lord, they are not believers until they make you the judge in the disputes that break out between them, and then find no resistance within themselves against what you decide, and submit themselves completely."* (4:65) There is nothing in the teachings of the *deen* to constrict people, but the feeble and those with weak resolve find *jihad* and certain other acts of obedience burdensome when in fact the easiest course is to strive and be true.

Surat an-Nisa' continues to spell out the characteristics of the Hypocrites and identifies a secondary group which always exists alongside them: believers of weak faith whose hearts are sick and require wise and lengthy treatment. There is a natural connection between the sick and the dead, between absence of faith and defective belief which will disappear if not treated properly.

This ailing faith takes various forms. The evidence of one form is clear in Allah's words: *"Among you are people who hang back, and if you encounter a setback, they say, 'Allah has blessed me in that I was not there with them.' But if you encounter favour from Allah, they say, as if there were no bond between you and them, 'Oh, If only I had been with them so that I too might have won a great victory!'"* (4:72-73) This is a man moved by his own desires, whose hopes are all connected to his personal interests, not to the advancement and future of the *deen*. His heart is ambivalent, wavering between sincerity and self-interest. Similar to him is another man who prays and fasts and does everything he should until the command to fight *jihad* reaches him, when he becomes alarmed and unsettled and seeks a deferral: *"Do you not see those who were told: 'Restrain yourselves from fighting and establish the prayer and pay* zakat'*? Then when fighting is prescribed for them, a group of them fear people as they should fear Allah, or even more than that."* (4:77)

Those who vacillate between hypocrisy and weak faith are marked by many different characteristics, some of which are enumerated in *Surat an-Nisa'*. The Almighty says: *"If a good thing happens to them, they say, 'This is from Allah.' If a bad thing happens to them, they say, 'This has come from you.' Say: 'Everything*

53

is from Allah.'" (4:78) The truth is that Allah is the One who harms and benefits, abases and exalts. He is the Creator and Impeller of everything. A human being has no power to create or originate but we do have volition and a certain capacity to act within a defined area of the vastness of Allah's creation of which we know so little. This is the meaning of the words: *"Say: 'Everything is from Allah.'"* (4:78)

Then comes another *ayat* which makes it clear that most of the evils which befall people are due to the bad actions which they commit and which then come back on them. This is the meaning of: *"Anything good that happens to you comes from Allah. Anything bad that happens to you comes from yourself."* (4:79) And in the case of the believer even the bad things that happen are on the whole a mercy because they are the means by which Allah raises people's rank. If high standing in the sight of Allah has been previously decreed for a person and he does not reach it by good action, he will be visited with affliction and raised to it by his steadfastness and submission.

Another characteristic of sick hearts is the tendency to think they know best when they are in fact ignorant: *"When news of any matter reaches them they publicise it, whether it is of a reassuring or disquieting nature. If they had only referred it to the Messenger and those in command among them, those among them able to discern the truth about it would have known of it."* (4:83) It is unfortunate that people occupy themselves with major affairs of state and proffer opinions about matters of which they know virtually nothing at all. I have seen people with no real knowledge of *fiqh* discussing it as if they were experts capable of delivering legal judgements, and people with no idea at all of politics rattling on about matters of war and peace as if they knew all the answers to the world's problems. How many people there are who desire to put the world to rights when they are unable to even put their own houses in order!

O bow-shaper who cannot do it well, do not damage the bow.
Give the bow to the one who knows best how to shape it!

Allah commanded His Prophet to pay no attention to the irresolute cowards and the sick of heart and to put all his strength into fighting the enemy until their cohesion was broken and they had been rendered powerless: *"So fight in the Way of Allah. You have only to answer for yourself only. And spur on the believers. It may well be that Allah will curb the force of those who reject ..."* (4:84) The hope of the army of Allah is in Allah alone and the *ayat* ends by indicating that even if the forces of the unbelievers are strong and their capacity to cause injury far-reaching, Allah is greater: *"Allah has greater force and greater power to punish."* (4:84)

There is an interesting interpolation at this point about greeting: *"When you are greeted with a greeting, then greet with one better than it or at least return it."* (4:86) It is important that courtesy and respect should be maintained under all circumstances. The Muslims used to greet everyone and return the greeting to anyone who greeted them until the Jews distorted the greeting, changing it to "Poison be upon you." (with *sâm* instead of *salâm*). So the believers were commanded to answer, "And upon you too," turning it back against them.

Then the Noble Qur'an returns to the subject of Hypocrites and the position to be taken towards them, meaning in this instance not the Hypocrites of Madina who made an outward show of Islam while in fact concealing disbelief, such as 'Abdullah ibn Ubayy and his adherents, but the distant tribes or, in modern parlance, foreign nations, who had made a show of friendship and support for Islam while conspiring against it in secret. Some of the believers were deceived by their apparent support until the Revelation disclosed the true state of affairs and the Almighty said: *"Why is it that you have become two parties regarding the Hypocrites, when Allah has returned them to unbelief for what they did? Do you desire to guide people Allah has misguided? If Allah misguides someone, you will never find a way for him."* (4:88)

Then the *ayat* lists the characteristics of such people, saying that in reality they desire adversity for you and hope that you will revert to being unbelievers and that they are waiting for reverses to befall you: *"Do not take any of them as friends until they have emigrated in the Way of Allah. But if they run away then seize them and kill them wherever you find them. Do not take any of them either as a friend or as a helper."* (4:89) Some people really are neutral, neither with you nor against you, and they should be left alone: *"If they keep away from you and do not fight you and submit to you, Allah has not given you any way against such people."* (4:90) But the opportunists who want to play both sides must be dealt with harshly: *"You will find others who desire to be safe from you and safe from their own people. Each time they are returned to unbelief they are overwhelmed by it. If they do not keep away from you or submit to you or refrain from fighting, then seize them and kill them wherever you find them. Over such people We have given you clear authority."* (4:91)

Then the *sura* talks about the legal judgements for accidental and deliberate homicide. It seems that the cause of this was an incident which occurred during the fighting, in which a man who proclaimed himself a Muslim was killed by Usama ibn Zayd because it was thought that he only did it to save his life. When the Messenger heard about what had happened he rebuked Usama for what he had done, saying to him: "How could you do that when he had said 'There is no god but Allah'?" Usama said, "He only said it out of fear of our weapons." The Messenger replied to him, "Did you split open his heart so that you could tell whether or not he said it out of fear?" Usama said, "The Messenger of Allah continued to rebuke me until I wished that I had not become Muslim until that day."

The *sura* continues: *"O you who believe! When you go out to fight in the Way of Allah verify things carefully. Do not say, 'You are not a believer,' to someone who gives you the Muslim greeting, simply out of desire for the goods of this world. With Allah there is booty in abundance. That is the way you were before but Allah has been very kind to you. So verify things carefully. Allah is aware of what you do."* (4:94) Of course if the man was a believer he should not have remained among the unbelievers, and the Qur'an goes on to make it clear that there is no excuse for staying in a place where you are unable to express your faith: *"Those whom the angels take while they are wronging themselves, ask them,*

56

'What were your circumstances?' They say, 'We were oppressed in the earth.' The angels say, 'Was Allah's earth not wide enough for you to have emigrated elsewhere in it?' For those people their refuge is Jahannam. What an evil destination! Except for those men, women and children who really are oppressed ...' (4:97-98) It is not acceptable for Muslims to accept domination by unbelievers, especially when Allah has promised a most agreeable future and abundant good in this world and the Next to those who emigrate for His sake.

This leads to the instruction allowing the prescribed prayers to be shortened on journeys: *"When you are travelling in the land, there is nothing blameworthy for you in shortening the prayer if you fear that those who reject might harass you."* (4:101) Next we are instructed how to pray in a situation of imminent danger with what is known as the Fear prayer: *"When you are with them and are leading them in the prayer, a group of them should stand with you, keeping hold of their weapons. When they prostrate, the others should be behind you. Then the other group who have not prayed should come and pray with you. They too should be careful and keep hold of their weapons..."* (4:102)

❋❋❋❋❋

Sura an-Nisa' now returns to the theme of people with weak faith and sick hearts, focusing for ten *ayats* on an incident in which a Jew was wrongfully accused of theft by a group of deceitful Muslims which almost caused an injustice to be done: *"Were it not for Allah's favour to you and His mercy, a group of them would have almost managed to mislead you. But they mislead no one but themselves and do not harm you in any way. Allah has sent down the Book and Wisdom to you and taught you what you did not know before."* (4:113) In dealing with the case, Allah calls attention to the personal responsibility of someone who tries to wrongfully attribute blame to someone else to save himself: *"Whoever commits an error or an evil action, and then attributes it to someone who is innocent, has loaded himself with slander and clear wrongdoing."* (4:112) But recognising that people are fallible,

Allah declares: "*Anyone who does evil or wrongs himself and then asks Allah's forgiveness will find Allah All-Forgiving, Most Merciful.*" (4:110)

The whole passage shows how vital it is for the truth to prevail and the false to be proved false, and for justice to be done under all circumstances.

After this the Revelation turns to yet another group of people who were still living in Madina: the residual pagans. They were Arabs who had still not given up worshipping idols. Allah says in conclusion: "*Allah does not forgive partners being attributed to Him but He forgives anything besides that to anyone He wills. Anyone who attributes partners to Allah is misguided, far off the path.*" (4:116) This re-emphasises the core teaching of Islam, insistence on the absolute unity of Allah. A Muslim is meticulous about submitting himself to Allah alone, accepting Him alone as Lawgiver and sees Him alone as the Author of everything, fearing none Him and seeking the help of none but Him. Idolaters are people who live in a dream world, chasing a mirage, letting their lives go to waste. They are the dupes of Shaytan: "*He makes promises to them and fills them with false hopes. But what Shaytan promises them is nothing but delusion.*" (4:120) The pride people take in their different religions and systems is of no benefit to them at all. This also applies to Muslims who view Islam in the same way. The only important thing is correct belief, sincere action and right conduct. Allah Almighty makes this absolutely clear when He says: "*It will not come about by wishful thinking on your part, nor by the wishful thinking of the People of the Book. Anyone who does evil will be repaid for it. He will find no protector or helper besides Allah.*" (4:123)

The *sura* then returns to its original theme - family relations - concentrating on what to do when difficulties crop up within marriage, advocating reconciliation whenever feasible but allowing for the possibility of complete marital breakdown: "*If a couple do separate, Allah will enrich each of them from His boundless wealth. Allah is Boundless, All-Wise.*" (4:130) Allah also stresses that when this happens they should not be overwhelmed by fear of financial difficulties. There are three *ayats* which stress that Allah is the Provider and is in control of everything in the heavens and the earth, including our provision.

The emphasis on the family is balanced by stressing the need for justice and equity even in the face of family interests: *"O you who believe! Be upholders of justice, bearing witness for Allah alone, even against yourselves or your parents and relatives ..."* (4:135) Establishing justice is something which the missions of all the Prophets have in common. *"We sent Our Messengers with the clear signs and sent down with them the Book and the Balance so that people might establish justice."* (57:25)

❋❋❋❋❋

Sura an-Nisa' has dealt with various hostile social groups which the Muslims face in their struggle to implement the Allah's *deen* and now it returns to perhaps the most dangerous of all of them – the Hypocrites. It has already uncovered them and warned against them and now returns to them to make an example of them and caution the Muslims against being involved with them in any way.

A true believer respects the Words of his Lord and always treats them with reverence and respect. He automatically leaves any gathering in which they are maligned and insolence is expressed towards them, and abandons and rejects the people concerned. But people whose faith is not strong are sometimes tempted to remain in a place where the Revelation is being denigrated and its judgements criticised. Allah addresses them here: *"Give the good news to the Hypocrites that they will have a painful punishment. Those who take as protectors the people who reject rather than the believers, do they hope to find power and strength with them? All power and strength belong entirely to Allah. He has sent down to you in the Book that when you hear Allah's Signs being rejected and mocked at by people you must not sit with them until they start to talk of other things; if you did so you would be the same as them."* (4:138-140) The plots of the Hypocrites harassed the Muslims throughout the time of the Prophet and indeed have continued to do so ever since; so it is not surprising that they are dealt with comprehensively here and elsewhere in the Revelation.

The *sura* then returns to a further discussion of those other implacable enemies of Islam, the Jews, showing how their present attitude of rejection is the fruit of their past rebelliousness and evil actions. Otherwise they would have been able to see that the new Revelation was nothing but the fulfilment of their own tradition: *"Those who reject Allah and His Messengers and desire to differentiate between Allah and His Messengers, saying, 'We believe in some and reject some,' wanting to take a pathway in between, such people are the true rejectors, and We have prepared a humiliating punishment for the rejectors. Those who believe in Allah and His Messengers and do not differentiate between any of them, We will pay them their wages. Allah is Ever-Forgiving, Most Merciful."* (4:150-152) *"We have revealed to you as We revealed to Nuh and the Prophets who came after him. And We revealed to Ibrahim and Isma'il and Ishaq and Ya'qub and the Tribes, and 'Isa and Ayyub and Yunus and Harun and Sulayman. And We gave Da'ud the* Zabur.*"* (4:163)

An unbiased look at the Qur'an will confirm that it is unparalleled among the Revelations of all the Prophets, just as an unbiased look at the life of Muhammad, may Allah bless him and grant him peace, will indicate that he is paramount in remembrance, thankfulness, steadfastness and trust in Allah: *"Allah bears witness to what He has sent down to you. He has sent it down with His knowledge. The angels bear witness as well. And Allah is enough as a witness."* (4:165) However, of all mankind the Jews are the people with the most churlish nature and the hardest hearts. The Almighty says: "Because *of the fact that they broke their covenant, and rejected Allah's Signs, and killed the Prophets without any right and said, 'Our hearts have lids on them,' Allah has stamped them with unbelief. So they do not believe except for a very few. And for their unbelief, and for their utterance of a monstrous slander against Maryam…"* (4:155-156)

This listing of the past iniquities of the Jews also gives Allah the opportunity to state the truth about what happened and did not happen to 'Isa, peace be upon him: *"They did not kill him and they did not crucify him, but it was made to seem so to them. Those who argue about him are in doubt about it. They have no real knowledge of it, merely conjecture. They certainly did not kill him. Allah raised him up to Himself."* (4:157-158) The rightly guided among the People of the Book accept the new Revelation without reservation: *"But those of them who are firmly rooted in knowledge, and the believers, believe in what has been sent down to you and what was sent down before you, those who perform the prayer and pay* zakat, *and believe in Allah and the Last Day – We will pay these people an enormous wage."* (4:162) But the vast majority of Christians believe that this unthinkable atrocity really took place and even they have invented a whole religious doctrine based on it which in turn led to all the other heresies which they hold to be true.

Then Allah mercifully holds out the rope of true guidance to them: *"O People of the Book! Do not go to excess in your* deen. *Say nothing but the truth about Allah. The Messiah, 'Isa son of Maryam, was only the Messenger of Allah and His Word, which He cast into Maryam, and a Spirit from Him. So believe in Allah and His Messengers. Do not say, 'Three.' It is better that you stop. Allah is only One God. Glory be to Him! That He should have a child! Everything in the heavens and everything in the earth belongs to Him. Allah is enough as a Guardian. The Messiah would never disdain to be a slave to Allah nor would the angels brought near. If any do disdain to worship Him and grow arrogant, He will in any case gather them all to Him."* (4:171-172)

Surat an-Nisa' ends by returning to its original theme with an *ayat* which explains the inheritance of people who die without any direct heirs, concluding as it began with the family and its protection and thus unifying the subject matter of the whole *sura*. So the entire *sura* is a general treatment of all society, from its smallest unit, the family, to all the other groups which make it up, including women, from whom the *sura* takes its name. "The family is the small society and society is the large family." It is quite clear that far from being made up of disconnected parts the *sura* is a unified whole. The guidance of Allah embraces all society because He has knowledge of everything. *"Allah makes things clear to you so that you may not go astray. Allah has knowledge of everything."* (4:176)

Sura 4

Al-Ma'ida: The Table

Surat al-Ma'ida is also sometimes called the *Sura of Contracts* and this latter designation denotes its main theme. The first name derives from the incident referred to in the *sura* when the Disciples ask 'Isa to send down to them a table from heaven, which takes up only four *ayats*, but the majority of the *sura* in fact deals with contracts of various kinds. When the *sura* is examined closely it will seen that there are many passages in which people are addressed directly by Allah. There are sixteen instances when the believers are addressed:

1. *"O you who believe! Fulfil your contracts!"* (5:1)
2. *"O you who believe! Do not profane the sacred rites of Allah."* (5:2)
3. *"O you who believe! When you get up intending to do the prayer, wash your faces and your hands."* (5:6)
4. *"O you who believe! Show integrity for the sake of Allah, bearing witness with justice."* (5:8)
5. *"O you who believe! Remember Allah's blessing to you."* (5:11)
6. *"O you who believe! Fear Allah, and seek the means to draw near to Him."* (5:35)
7. *"O you who believe! Do not take the Jews and Christians as friends."* (5:51)
8. *"O you who believe! If any of you renounce their* deen, *Allah will bring forward a people whom He loves and who love Him."* (5:54)

9. *"O you who believe! Do not take any of those given the Book before you, or the rejectors, as your friends."* (5:57)

10. *O you who believe! Do not make unlawful the good things Allah has made lawful for you."* (5:87)

11. *"O you who believe! Wine, gambling, stone altars and divining arrows are disgusting things of Shaytan's handiwork."* (5:90)

12. *"O you who believe! Allah will test you with some game animals."* (5:94)

13. *"O you who believe! Do not kill game while you are in* ihram. *"* (5:95)

14. *"O you who believe! Do not ask about matters which, if they were made known to you, would make things difficult for you."* (5:101)

15. *"O you who believe! You are responsible for yourselves."* (5:105)

16. *"O you who believe! When one of you is near to death and makes a will…"* (5:106)

The Messenger himself is addressed directly twice:

1. *"O Messenger! Do not be grieved by those who rush into rejection."* (5:41)

2. *"O Messenger! Transmit what has been sent down to you from your Lord."* (5:67)

The People of the Book are addressed five times:

1. *"O People of the Book! Our Messenger has come to you, making clear to you…"* (5:15)

2. *"O People of the Book! Our Messenger has come to you, making things clear to you, after a period with no Messengers."* (5:19)

3. *"Say: 'O People of the Book! Do you resent us for any other reason than that we believe in Allah?'"* (5:59)

4. *"Say: 'O People of the Book! Do not go to extremes in your* deen.'"* (5:77)

5. *"Say: 'O People of the Book! You have no ground to stand on until you implement the Torah and the* Injil *and what was sent down to you from your Lord.'"* (5:68)

These pronouncements are followed by information, insights, teachings and directives which the group addressed needs in order to implement the command of Allah and go straight on His Path. These are in fact contracts which should be fulfilled. *Jihad* is a contract between Allah and His servants. *"Allah has bought from the believers their selves and their wealth so that they may have the Garden."* (9:111) The believers are instructed to do *wudu'* before prayer, and the prayer itself is the first stipulation of the covenant Allah made with the Tribe of Israel.

After a number of such ordinances which Allah prescribes for the formation of Islamic society, the Almighty says: *"Remember Allah's blessing to you and the covenant He made with you when you said, 'We hear and obey.' Fear Allah: Allah knows what the breasts contain."* (5:7) Firm undertakings require rigorous observance and fitting action. Honouring the Command of Allah is one of the signs of belief. This *sura* makes it clear that Allah has a contract with the Muslims that they shall believe in Him alone and act for Him alone and call other people to His *deen* and be a model from which people can learn the good of this world and the Next.

The Muslims were not the first people to make this contract. Allah also made an agreement with the people before them that they would follow His guidance and live as He commanded: *"Allah made a covenant with the Tribe of Israel and We raised up twelve leaders from them. Allah said, 'I am with you. If you establish the prayer and pay the* zakat, *and believe in My Messengers and respect and support them, and lend a generous loan to Allah, I will erase your wrong actions from you and admit you into Gardens with rivers flowing under them. Any of you who reject after that, have gone astray from the right way.'"* (5:12) But the Tribe of Israel did not fulfil the terms of this contract. Instead they broke it and that brought Allah's curse down upon them and made their hearts hard.

A hard heart is of all things the furthest from Allah. Being hard-hearted is a curse from Allah from which we seek refuge with Him and the Jews are famous for being the most hard-hearted of all people. Their behaviour throughout the ages in the various communities in which they have lived has provided ample evidence of this. We must always be on our guard where they are concerned and beware of the danger of becoming like them. Even their sometimes scrupulous religiosity has no good in it. Allah says of them: *"You will never cease to come upon some act of treachery on their part."* (5:13)

Just as Allah made a contract with the Jews, He also made one with the Christians. The words revealed about that give pause for reflection because it shows the extent of the split between 'Isa and the Disciples who possessed the true *deen,* and the Christians of later times: *"We also made a covenant with those who say, 'We are Christians,' and they too forgot a good part of what they were reminded of. So We stirred up enmity and hatred between them until the Day of Rising when Allah will inform them about what they accomplished."* (5:14)

The bloody history of the Christians has been a constant demonstration of the truth of these words and the blood continues to flow. How many religious wars have filled the fields of Europe with Christian blood? This undying hatred can still be seen expressed daily on the streets of Northern Ireland and no amount of secularist propaganda has been able to expunge it from people's hearts. Any truce is only transitory and the conflict will always resurface when the conditions for it appear. It is only Islam which can resolve it, through its true belief in the Divine Unity: *"Our Messenger has come to you, making clear to you a great deal of the Book that you were hiding, and passing over a great deal. A Light has come to you from Allah, and a Clear Book by which Allah guides to the ways of Peace anyone who follows what pleases Him. He will bring them out of the darkness into the light by His permission, and guide them to a Straight Path."* (5:15-16) Nations divided by falsehood will only be united by the Truth!

The basis of the human contract with Allah is belief in the Divine Unity and although the Christians claim to believe in One

God their position in relation to 'Isa is shrouded in thick fog. If they worship Allah alone what place can 'Isa hold in this worship? If God is truly one then 'Isa must be His servant. The truth is that the Christians have no historical evidence for their claims about 'Isa son of Maryam, and their position is in fact based entirely on conjecture as we saw in *Surat an-Nisa'* where Allah says: *"They have no real knowledge of it, merely conjecture. They certainly did not kill him."* (4:157) Allah Himself is our sole guaranteed source of Truth. That is the reason for Allah's anger when He says in this *sura*: *"Those who say, 'Allah is the Messiah, son of Maryam,' have definitely disbelieved. Say: 'Who possesses any power at all over Allah if He desires to destroy the Messiah, son of Maryam, and his mother, and everyone else on the earth?' The sovereignty of the heavens and the earth and everything in between them belong to Allah."* (5:17)

Although the Jews deny the Trinity, they describe Allah as having base qualities. The things they say about Him show presumption and contempt towards Him. Their hearts contain neither humility nor sincerity. In spite of that, they claim that they are the Chosen People and that Allah created the world for their sake and for their service. Both groups of the People of the Book claim that they have a special relationship with Allah and a unique position with Him but that is merely wishful thinking on their part.

> All claim a connection to Layla –
> but Layla does not support that claim!

True belief and righteous action are the only solid grounds for expecting Divine approval and it is only through them that either individuals or nations advance. The Muslims are only honoured according to their sincerity towards Allah, their obedience to Him and their courage in helping Him against His enemies. Mere verbal allegiance to Muhammad, peace and blessings be upon him, who is certainly the Best of Creation, is of no use at all without action to back it up. *Surat al-Ma'ida* gives us two clear illustrations of the insufficiency of verbal agreements which are not fulfilled by being acted upon. *"When Musa said to his people, 'O my people!*

Remember Allah's blessing upon you when He appointed Prophets among you and appointed kings for you, and gave you what He had not given to anyone else in all the worlds! O my people! Enter the Holy Land which Allah has ordained for you. Do not turn back in your tracks and so be transformed into losers.'" (5:20-21)

The first is the story of the Tribe of Israel when they were told that their entrance into the Promised Land was dependant upon their fighting the tyrants who were in possession of it. Musa roused them and reminded them of Allah's blessings to them and exhorted them to take the action necessary for them to achieve the promised result but they refused to obey Allah's command.

They refused to obey Allah's commands and their presumption went so far that they said to Musa: *"So you and your Lord go and fight. We will stay sitting here."* (5:24) Because of this Allah made them wander in the desert for forty years, unable to get out until most of them had died. This incident makes it very clear that firm action is an essential part of the contract between Allah and His human slaves.

The second is the story of the two sons of Adam, one of whom killed the other. One of them was stupid and worthless and avenged himself on his brother who was better than him, thinking that he would somehow acquire new strength by getting rid of him. This is of course an impossibility. You cannot improve yourself by destroying someone else. You will remain as you are. Righteousness is a positive effort to strengthen and purify the self, not aggression: *"Allah only accepts from the godfearing."* (5:32)

Allah Almighty considers murder a crime against all humanity and not just against a single individual: *"If someone kills another person – unless in retaliation for someone else or for causing corruption in the earth – it is as if he had murdered all mankind. And if anyone gives life to another person, it is as if he had given life to all mankind."* (5:32)

The Noble Qur'an uses the lessons of the past to teach the Muslims and prescribes for them precepts which will enable them to avoid the pitfalls of earlier nations. Therefore following this story, Allah gives us the judgement against those who commit corruption in the earth by attacking people's lives and property, prescribing the punishments for highway robbery and theft, making it clear that it is lack of fear of Allah which makes such crimes possible. The son of Adam came to grief because his heart was devoid of fear of Allah and believers must avoid the same fate: *"O you who believe! Fear Allah, and seek the means to draw near to Him, and do* jihad *in His way, so that perhaps you will be successful."* (5:35) Belief and right action together will overcome all obstacles and deem all sacrifices insignificant. This is the *jihad* which leads to success.

Divine Revelation is the unique source of the laws governing acts of worship, inheritance, *hudud* punishments and retaliation. There is no place for opinion or analogy regarding any of these things. This was the same for the people of all true religions but sometimes they abandoned Divine Law because their whims and desires overpowered them and eroded their obedience to it.

Crimes against life, property and reputation have serious social consequences which is why Allah Almighty takes charge of the judgements concerning them and does not leave them to human discretion, because that inevitably leads to laxity in application and attempting to come up with substitutes which can never serve the purpose. When human beings make laws they put themselves in the place of the criminal and tend on that account to lighten the punishment; and if they do not do that they think of their sons and relatives and show mercy to the criminals.

Sometimes social pressures result in the weak being punished and the influential being pardoned. That was a common failing among the people of the earlier Revelations. The Messenger of Allah, may Allah bless him and grant him peace, said, "Those before you were destroyed because when one of their nobles stole they left him alone but when one of their common people stole they carried out the punishment on him. By Allah, if Fatima the daughter of Muhammad were to steal, I would cut off her hand!" In the case of the People of the Book, the penalty of amputation for theft has been abandoned and forgotten, and replaced with custodial sentences for various terms. That has led to a catastrophic increase in crimes of theft of all kinds. The end result of this process is the jettisoning of all the *hudud*!

Examination of societies where this has happened shows that the consequences of such negligence are material and spiritual losses on a huge scale. This is an eloquent testimonial to the words of the Messenger of Allah, may Allah bless him and grant him peace: "A *hadd* established on the earth is better for the people of the earth than thirty days of rain," and, "Establish the *hudud* of Allah on the near and far and for Allah's sake do not let yourselves be stopped by the criticism of any critic."

Throughout their long history the Muslims established the *hudud* and protected the lives, property and reputation of all those under their jurisdiction. They did not abandon the Divine judgements until the Mongols attacked them and Divine law was replaced by teachings invented by their tyrants in a book called the *Yasaq*. This disaster was repeated when the Europeans invaded the Muslim world and put man-made laws in place of the Divine legislation so that widespread corruption spread throughout the entire world. In their laws the Europeans permit fornication as long it is by mutual consent and the most highly evolved nations even permit sodomy! They have discredited the laws of *hudud* and retaliation and no one can speak about them without exposing himself to ridicule, censure and even chastisement.

In doing this the Europeans are simply following their forebears. When the Messenger emigrated to Madina the Jews brought him a couple who had fornicated and asked him to look into their case. The Messenger asked them what penalty there was for the crime in their Scripture; they replied that it was flogging and blackening the faces of the perpetrators. The Messenger, may Allah bless him and grant him peace, said to them, "That is not true. The punishment among you is stoning to death." They continued to contradict him until the Torah was produced, and the punishment elicited from it was indeed the stoning which they wanted to abolish. Allah revealed about this: *"O Messenger! Do not be grieved by those who rush into unbelief from among those who say with their mouths, 'We believe,' when their hearts do not believe; nor by those Jews who listen to lies, listening to other people who have not come to you, distorting words from their proper meanings, saying, 'If you are given this, then take it. If you are not given it, then beware!'"* (5:41)

This *ayat* equates the hypocrites and the Jews. Both groups have empty hearts and are hostile to Divine law. It is clear that stoning is an authentic component of what remains of the Torah and that the Jews wanted to abolish it. The Messenger of Allah refused to be lenient about this matter even in the face of strong opposition: *"If Allah desires trouble for someone, you possess no power to help him against Allah in any way. Those are the people whose hearts Allah does not want to purify. There will be disgrace for them in this world and in the Next World they will have a terrible punishment."* (5:41)

As People of the Book the Jews within the Muslim polity are an independent entity and the treaties which were concluded with them at the beginning of the *hijra* did not violate this independence. The Messenger's intervention in this instance was made because he had been applied to by the Jews and was therefore obliged to deliver the correct sentence: *"If they come to you, you may either judge between them or turn away from them. If you turn away from them, they will not harm you in any way. But if you do judge, judge between them justly."* (5:42)

The position regarding stoning in the Book of Deuteronomy is as follows: If someone marries a virgin and then finds that she is not a virgin, she should be stoned at the door of her father's house. If a man is found lying with a married woman, the husband should kill both of them. (Deut. 22:21-22) The same book says: "If a damsel that is a virgin be betrothed unto an husband, and a man find her in the city, and lie with her; then ye shall bring them both out unto the gate of that city, and ye shall stone them with stones that they die; the damsel, because she cried not, being in the city; and the man, because he hath humbled his neighbour's wife: so thou shalt put away evil from among you." (Deut. 22:23-24)

Then the Noble Qur'an gives a brief history of the position of the People of the Book in relation to the laws of blood and honour. It is clear that they were revealed in the Torah and so were binding on the Jews, and that they were then corroborated by the Gospel so that the Christians should also implement them. Abandoning them because of unbelief or injustice or immorality goes beyond the bounds of injustice into the realm of actual disbelief. *"Those who do not judge by what Allah has sent down, they are unbelievers."* (5:46)

However, the truth is that the Torah was binding on its followers only until the Gospel came to put right deviations which had occurred, whereupon judgement was transferred to it. When the Qur'an came both Jews and Christians should have turned to the new Revelation and relied on that, especially in view of the fact that it corrected all previous errors, establishing definitively the truth: *"And We have sent down the Book to you with truth, confirming what came and conserving preceding Books. So judge between them by what Allah has sent down and do not follow their whims and desires, deviating from the Truth that has come to you. To each of you We have assigned a law and a clear practice."* (5:48)

There are two messages contained in this *ayat*. The first is that the *deen* was perfected in all respects in the Message of Muhammad and the second is that the Message of Muhammad will last until the end of time. It is in absolute harmony with human nature and this is clear in all its teachings. The legacy of the two previous Peoples of the Book is like a medicine whose potency is limited to a specific term after which it is no longer effective and indeed if employed can aggravate the illness. Jewish law is based on severity because it is dealing with people accustomed to slavehood and abasement. Christianity did not abrogate this law but wished to alleviate its harshness by introducing an element of compassion. The laws of Islam combine all the necessary elements and unite spirit and body, heart and intellect, this world and the Next World. Islam ennobles and elevates people and establishes their relationship with Allah and with other people on firm and wise foundations.

The Jews and Christians, then, are people who reject the truth, as is shown in our time by the fact that they prefer secularist legal systems to Divinely-revealed law, and so Allah warns the Muslims against them: *"O you who believe! Do not take the Jews and Christians as friends."* (5:49) And also against those who follow them: *"Yet you see those with sickness in their hearts rushing towards them, saying, 'We fear the wheel of fortune may turn against us.' But it may well be that Allah will grant victory or something else from His presence. Then they will be bitterly regretful about what they kept secret inside themselves."* (5:52) All such people desire to demean Islam: *"O you who believe! Do not take any of those given the Book before you, or the rejectors, as your friends, those who make a mockery and a game out of your deen. Fear Allah if you are believers. When you call to the prayer, they make a mockery and a game of it. That is because they are a people who have no understanding."* (5:57-58)

They cannot stand to hear the truth because they have abandoned Allah's contract with them and know in their heart of hearts that the Muslims are right: *"Say: 'O People of the Book! Do you resent us for any other reason than that we believe in Allah and what was sent down to us, and what was sent down before, and that most of you are people who are wantonly deviant?'"* (5:59) Friendship and allegiance can only be based on active acceptance of the truth: *"Your friend is only Allah and His Messenger and those who believe: those who establish the prayer and pay the* zakat, *and bow down. As for those who make Allah their Friend, and His Messenger and those who believe, it is the Party of Allah who are the victors!"* (5:55-56)

One of the tokens of Islam is love for the sake of Allah and hatred for the sake of Allah but this implies a love with no selfishness and a hatred with no injustice. One of the characteristics of the true *deen* is that it overlooks momentary error but is severe against shameless deviation. The Prophet, may Allah bless him and grant him peace, chose the merciful course as long as it was open to him to do so but once a crime was definitively established he was implacable in carrying out the prescribed punishment.

All Prophetic teaching is geared towards preventing crime from becoming habitual but the People of the Book, now and in the past, are characterised by a strange indifference towards acts of disobedience to Allah, to the point that western civilisation is filled with all sorts of corruption accompanied by silence and impotence on the part of the priests who witness it. They hate Islam and make peace with apostasy. They hold public prayers for AIDS sufferers but largely ignore the innocent victims of Zionism.

The *sura* goes on examining this inconsistency on the part of the People of the Book, annulling their claim to right guidance: *"You see many of them plunging into wrongdoing and hostility and acquiring unlawful wealth. What an evil thing it is they do! Why do the scholars and rabbis not prohibit them from speaking falsehood and from acquiring unlawful wealth? What an evil thing it is they fabricate!"* (5:62-63) It makes it clear that their abandonment of their own contract with their Lord has removed any claims they might have had: *"Say: 'O People of the Book! You have no ground to stand on until you implement the Torah and the* Injil *and what was sent down to you from your Lord.' What has been sent down to you from your Lord increases the insolence and rejection of many of them, so do not waste grief on the people of the unbelievers."* (5:68)

Had they kept to their contract their situation would have been very different: *"If only the People of the Book had believed and been godfearing, We would have erased their evil deeds from them and admitted them into Gardens of Delight. If only they had implemented the Torah and the* Injil *and what was sent down to them from their Lord, they would have been provided for from above their heads and beneath their feet."* (5:65-66)

This, of course, does not only apply to the Jews and Christians. The scholars of Islam bear the same responsibility with respect to the Muslims as did their predecessors among the People of the Book, and it is clear from the political and legal systems in all the Muslim lands that they have gone the same way as those before them. One needs to look no further than this to understand the present plight of the Muslim nation and its subservience and humiliation at the hands of the enemies of Allah and His Messenger.

As we have already seen, the basis of the Divine Contract is correct belief in Allah and His Messengers and this is why the *sura* returns once more to this essential matter. The Jewish error is to deny and denigrate their Messengers: *"We made a covenant with the Tribe of Israel and We sent Messengers to them. Each time a Messenger came to them with something their lower selves* did not desire, they denied some and they murdered others." (5:70)

The Christians on the other hand elevate their Messengers, the Archangel Jibril and 'Isa son of Maryam into divinities: *"Those who say 'Allah is the third of three' are unbelievers. There is no god but the one God. If they do not stop saying what they say, a painful punishment will afflict those among them who reject."* (5:73) And: *"Say: 'O People of the Book! Do not go to extremes in your* deen, *asserting other than the truth, and do not follow the whims and desires of a people who were misguided before, and have misguided many others, and are misguided from the right way.'"* (5:77) It is clear that this situation will remain until the Final Hour comes, when Allah will send down His servant 'Isa to resolve it by announcing that he is Allah's slave and to fight those who attribute equals to Allah.

Nevertheless, in spite of all this, there is a difference between the Jews and Christians: "You *will find the people most implacably hostile to those who believe to be the Jews and those who worship idols. You will find those warmest in affection to those who believe to be those who say, 'We are Christians.' That is because some of them are priests and monks and because they are not arrogant. When they listen to what has been sent down to the Messenger, you see their eyes overflowing with tears because of what they recognise of the truth. They say, 'Our Lord, we believe! So write us down among the witnesses.'"* (5:82-83) History shows us what happened at the time of the mission. The idolaters of Makka and the Jews of Madina were the most vehemently hostile to Islam while the Muslims found goodness in the Christians of Abyssinia.

True Christians find themselves accepting Islam when it is presented to them: *"It is the truth from our Lord. We were already Muslims before it came."* (28:53) And indeed after the break-up of Byzantine power, almost all of Asia Minor and North Africa, which was all Christian before, became Muslim. The trouble between Islam and Christianity was in fact with that part of Christianity which was in reality identified with and the inheritor of the old Roman empire. This erupted in the Crusades and has been a continual source of hostility ever since.

After this presentation of the truth of the relationship between Islam and the People of the Book, there follows a whole series of *ayats* elaborating the legal foundations of Islamic society: laying down the penalty for breaking oaths, forbidding gambling and intoxicants, forbidding hunting while in *ihram*, permitting all seafood, making clear what is really sacred and what is merely ignorant superstition, and how to make a will while travelling. All these elements are further reasons why the *sura* is called the *Sura of Contracts* since all of them form part of the basic contractual relationship between each person and their Lord.

Taking the Christians as the example, the *sura* concludes by reminding us of the nature of the contract we have with our Lord and that its fulfilment lies beyond this world, on the Last Day. If we hold to it sincerely we will receive the promised reward. If we break it, it will be on our own heads: *"This is the Day when the truthfulness of the truthful will benefit them. They will have Gardens with rivers flowing under them, remaining in them time-lessly, forever without end. Allah is pleased with them and they are pleased with Him. That is the Great Triumph. The kingdom of the heavens and the earth and everything in them belongs to Allah. He has power over everything."* (5:119-120)

Sura 6
Al-An'am: Livestock

Surat al-An'am is the first Makkan *sura* of the seven long ones at the beginning of the Noble Qur'an. The first people to be addressed by the Qur'an were the Arab pagans of Makka who were heedless of Allah and denied His Oneness. They were people who were fiercely devoted to their idols, stuck in their ancestral traditions, and they vehemently resisted every call to emancipation from this darkness.

One technique Allah uses in His Noble Book to open the eyes of the unbelievers to the realities of existence is that of argument backed up by evidence, and *Surat al-An'am* is a supreme example of this. It is full of words about Allah Almighty which reveal His immensity and call people's attention to His Signs in themselves and in the universe. It stimulates the awe and repentance hidden deep in the human heart, the remnants of that natural disposition which the darkness of ignorance has covered up. *Surat al-An'am* is a dazzling succession of irrefutable arguments, statements and demonstrations by which Allah makes His own existence known beyond doubt and shows the absolute futility of worshipping anything besides Him.

The first *ayat* sets the tone: *"Praise belongs to Allah who created the heavens and the earth and appointed darkness and light."* (6:1) Allah is the Creator of the universe and all the differentiation in it, yet human beings still equate with Him other things which are in reality totally impotent. But the human life-span in this world is very short, and even the existence of the universe is finite, whereas the existence of Allah is infinite and eternal and everything is recorded by Him: *"He is Allah in the heavens and in the*

77

earth. He knows what you keep secret and what you make public and He knows what you earn." (6:3)

The *sura* often speaks of Allah using the third person pronoun: *"It is He who has appointed the stars for you so you may be guided by them in the darkness of the land and sea"* (6:97); and *"It is He who first produced you from a single self, then from a resting-place and a repository."* (6:98) The truth is that the third person pronoun here makes the listener or reader present, as if Allah were addressing him directly. Do not suppose that this was for the Makkan idolaters alone. No, people of all other religions can gain from this immediacy a living recognition which is not available to them in their own traditions and which may have the greatest of effects on their hearts. No other Revealed Book speaks about Allah with such directness, and this brings about a vivid awareness of Allah's presence which in turn completely dispossesses people of the blind traditions with which they are familiar and cuts through the heedlessness which is prevalent among them.

In addition to this use of the third person, there are many instances in this *sura* when Allah tells his Prophet while he is arguing with the idolaters to: "Say this and that to them." Sometimes this is done twice in the same *ayat*: *"Say: 'To whom does everything in the heavens and earth belong?' Say: 'To Allah. He has made mercy incumbent on Himself. He will gather you to the Day of Rising about which there is no doubt.'"* (6:12) And on one occasion four times: *"Say: 'What thing is greatest as a witness?' Say: 'Allah. He is Witness between me and you. This Qur'an has been revealed to me so that I may warn you by it, and anyone else it reaches. Do you then bear witness that there are other gods together with Allah?' Say: 'I do not bear witness.' Say: 'He is only One God, and I am free of any partner you attribute to Him.'"* (6:19) Doing this also brings the presence of Allah right into the dialogue between the Prophet and his auditors. This device is used altogether forty-four times in *Surat al-An'am*.

It is clear that *Surat al-An'am* was sent down at the peak of the furious battle which was waged in Makka between the Truth and falsehood and according to most scholars it was revealed, in spite of its length, all at one time. Some maintain that the references in it to the People of the Book show that some of its *ayats* were revealed in Madina. This is an error resembling that of the people who think that the obligation of *zakat* was imposed in Madina. The truth is that *zakat* was first imposed in Makka but the details of the amount to be given were specified in Madina. So the *sura* was sent down at one time accompanied by tens of thousands of angels and the Messenger knew it all by heart the moment it arrived. His mind was quicker than lighting and his memory more exact than the tape recordings made today. The moment it came he summoned memorisers and scribes and dictated to them what had come from Allah.

One of the first things the *sura* deals with is the inevitable end of the wrongdoers, however long they live. Their denial of the Prophets takes place in successive stages which begin with aversion, continue with denial, lapse into continuous mockery and end up with outright hostility and aggression. It is Allah's will that this process should be allowed to run its course as a test for both believers and unbelievers. This is the nature of the life of this world. However, the outcome for the unbelievers is inevitable destruction: *"Have they not seen how many generations We destroyed before them which We had established on the earth far more firmly than We have established you? We sent heaven down on them in abundant rainfall and made rivers flow under them. But We destroyed them for their wrong actions and raised up further generations after them."* (6:6)

And this does not only apply to pure disbelief but is a universal law which applies to both unbelievers and also to other nations which mix truth with falsehood, and their own whims and desires with true guidance: in other words, to people who received guidance and then turned their backs on it: *"We sent Messengers to nations before you, and seized them with poverty and illness so that perhaps they might humble themselves. If only they had humbled themselves when Our violent force came upon them! But their hearts were hard and Shaytan made what they were doing seem good to them. When they forgot what they had been reminded of, We opened up for them the doors to everything until, when they were exulting in what they had been given, We suddenly seized them and at once they were in despair. So the last remnant of the people who did wrong was rooted out. Praise belongs to Allah, the Lord of all the worlds!"* (6:42-45)

The Muslims are not exempt from this and it is clear from history that the same implacable process has befallen the Islamic nation several times since the coming of the final Revelation, sometimes from outside and sometimes actually from within the community: *"Say: 'He possesses the power to send you punishment from above your heads or from underneath your feet, or to mix you up into sects and make you taste each other's violence.' See how We diversify the Signs so that perhaps they may understand. Your people deny it and yet it is the Truth. Say: 'I am not here as your guardian. Every piece of information has its time, and you will certainly come to know."* (6:65-67)

✻✻✻✻✻

If you give a man advice, telling him to honour and rely on his intellect, and he responds by asking you for a miracle to prove the soundness of your good counsel, what can you do? You call him to reason and he responds with irrationality!

The truth is that miracles are in any case useless without the application of intellect and the misfortune of all idolaters, ancient and modern, is that they are held back by their intellectual inadequacy. Such people are blinded by irrational prejudices to such an extent that the truly miraculous would in any case be subsumed within the narrow confines of their own world view: *"Even if We were to send down to you a Book on parchment pages and they were actually to touch it with their own hands, those who reject would still say, 'This is nothing but downright magic.'"* (6:7) And later in the *sura* this tendency is reconfirmed: *"They have sworn by Allah with their most earnest oaths that if a Sign comes to them, they will believe in it. Say: 'The Signs are in Allah's hands alone.' What will make you realise that even when a Sign does come, they still will not believe? We will overturn their hearts and sight, just as when they did not believe in it at first, and We will abandon them to wander blindly in their overweening insolence."* (6:109-110)

The idolaters of Makka claimed that if the Messenger had been accompanied by an angel they would have believed in him but this is, of course, pure ignorance on their part, a complete misunderstanding of the nature of existence: *"They say, 'Why has an angel not been sent down to him?' If We were to send down an angel, that would be the end of the affair and they would not be reprieved. And if We had made him an angel We would still have made him a man, and further confused for them the very thing they are confused about."* (6:8-9)

True to form the Arab idolaters, like their predecessors of earlier times, resisted Islam and denied its Messenger and mocked him, refusing to budge from their position; but Allah advised His Prophet to be patient and to continue with his task of calling to the truth, trying to stimulate their torpid intellects and hearts. The Prophet, peace and blessings be upon him, was grieved by their obduracy and it affected him. A noble man is inevitably pained by denial and mockery from people for whom he desires nothing but good. So Allah consoles him, reminding him that this is simply part of the nature of things, that the task of the Prophet and his followers is to be steadfast in delivering the Message – guidance is in the hands of Allah alone: *"We know that what they say distresses you. It is not that they are calling you a liar. The wrongdoers are simply refuting Allah's Signs. Messengers before you were also denied but they were steadfast in the face of the denial and injury they suffered until Our help arrived. There is no changing the Words of Allah. News of the Messengers has come to you."* (6: 33-34)

Having made this clear Allah proceeds, through His Messenger, to bombard the unbelievers with a barrage of eloquent arguments to storm and breach their defensive walls of obstinate denial. In the end, however, *"Only those who can hear respond. As for the dead, Allah will raise them up, then to Him they will be returned."* (6:36) and *"Those who deny Our Signs are deaf and dumb in utter darkness. Allah misguides whom He wills, and puts whom He wills on a Straight Path."* (6:40)

So following this the Prophet is reminded by the Revelation who his true followers are: *"Do not chase away those who call on their Lord morning and evening, seeking His Pleasure."* (6:52) and He is instructed to convey the good news to those who believe that Allah is with them with His forgiveness and pleasure: *"When those who believe in Our Signs come to you, say, 'Peace be upon you! Allah has made mercy incumbent on Himself. If anyone among you does evil out of ignorance and then afterwards repents and puts things right, He is Ever-Forgiving, Most Merciful.'"* (6:54)

Next, the Messenger is ordered to restate to the unbelievers the uncompromising basic position of Islam: *"Say: 'I am forbidden to worship those you call upon besides Allah.' Say: 'I do not follow your whims and desires. If I did so I would be misguided and not among the guided.' Say: 'I stand on a clear Sign from my Lord and yet you have denied it. I do not have in my possession what you are in such haste to bring about. Jurisdiction over it belongs to none but Allah. He states the Truth. And He is the best of Deciders.'"* (6:56-57)

The next *ayat*, *"Say: 'If I did have in my possession what you are in such haste to bring about, the affair between me and you would have been settled. Allah knows best the wrongdoers'"* (6:58), links the preceding section of the *sura* with a glorious passage in which Allah affirms His absolute Power over, and Awareness of, everything and every individual in existence. It begins with His Words: *"The keys of the Unseen are in His possession. No one knows them except for Him. He knows everything in the land and sea. Not a leaf falls without His knowing it. There is no seed in the darkness of the earth, and nothing wet or dry, but it is in a Clear Book."* (6:59) and ending with the warning: *"Your people deny it and yet it is the Truth. Say: 'I am not here as your guardian. Every piece of information has its time, and you will certainly come to know.'"*

It must not be forgotten that the great miracle granted to the Prophet Muhammad, may Allah bless him and grant him peace, was the Qur'an itself and no miracle the Prophet might have performed could possibly have provided more evidence of Allah than *Surat al-An'am*. These *ayats* convey to us the closeness of the presence of Allah and His minute awareness of every atom in existence: *"He knows everything in the land and sea. Not a leaf falls without His knowing it. There is no seed in the darkness of the earth, and nothing wet or dry, but it is in a Clear Book."* (6:59) And not only that, but every aspect of the lives of every one of the billions of human beings on the earth, and not only they but all those who have existed and all those who will, are the subject of His direct and continual concern: *"It is He who takes you back to Himself at night, while knowing the things you perpetrate by day, and then wakes you up again, so that a specified term may be completed. Then you will return to Him, and then He will inform you about the things you did."* (6:60) Again, *"Say: 'Who rescues you from the darkness of the land and sea? You call on Him humbly and secretly: "If you rescue us from this, we will truly be among the thankful."'" Say: 'Allah rescues you from it, and from every distress. Then you attribute partners to Him.'"* (6:63-64) It is an irony that the Makkans, who were demanding a miracle from the Prophet, were unable to appreciate what was right in front of them.

Because of that the believers should avoid them and people like them who disparage the great gift they have been given: *"When you see people involved in mockery of Our Signs, turn from them until they are involved in other talk. And if Shaytan should ever cause you to forget, once you remember, do not remain sitting with the people of the wrongdoers."* (6:68) and again: *"Abandon those who have made their* deen *into game-playing and diversion and whom the life of this world has deluded."* (6:70)

This leads into a discussion about the senselessness of what such people offer as an alternative to the true guidance available to them: *"Say: 'Are we to call on something other than Allah which can neither benefit us nor do us harm, and to turn on our heels after Allah has guided us, like someone the shaytans have lured away in the earth, leaving him confused and bewildered, despite the fact that he has companions calling him to guidance, saying, "Come with us!"?' Say: 'Allah's guidance, that is true guidance. We are commanded to submit to the Lord of all the Worlds.'"* (6:71) This in turn leads to the supreme example of Ibrahim's guidance to the Divine Unity by means of observation of natural phenomena. The situation of the Prophet Ibrahim, peace be upon him, corresponds to that of the Prophet Muhammad in that both of them reintroduced the worship of Allah into an environment where it had been entirely lost. He ends: *"I have turned my face to Him who brought the heavens and earth into being, a pure natural believer. I am not one of the idolaters."* (6:79)

This affirmation of One God and denial of idolatry is the core Message of all the Prophets and Allah takes this opportunity to outline the whole historical framework of prophetic guidance to humanity, mentioning seventeen Prophets by name and concluding thus: *"And some of their forebears, descendants and brothers. We chose them and guided them to a straight path. That is Allah's guidance, by which He guides whichever of His slaves He wills. If they had attributed partners to Him, all they did would have been of no avail. They are the ones to whom We gave the Book, Judgement and Prophethood. If these people reject it, We have already entrusted it to a people who did not."* (6:87-89)

Islam is simply a continuation of this process and the followers of Muhammad are the heirs of Nuh, Ibrahim, Musa and 'Isa. They are the standard-bearers of the ancient Prophetic way, the true human tradition – those who fight against idolatry and injustice and submit to the Lord of the worlds. Disbelief, ancient and modern, consists in ignorance of Allah and disobeying His harmonious laws. The *deen*, ancient and modern, consists in true recognition of Allah and sincere obedience to Him. Only Muslims have that now.

The Qur'an then addresses the inability of the unbelievers to comprehend the immensity of the nature of Allah and His Revelation to them: *"They do not measure Allah with His true measure when they say, 'Allah would not send down anything to a human being.'"* (6:91) First Allah warns them of the terrible shock in store for them when, too late, they realise their mistake: *"If you could only see the wrongdoers in the throes of death when the angels are stretching out their hands: 'Disgorge your own selves! Today you will be repaid with the punishment of humiliation for saying other than the truth about Allah, and for being arrogant about His signs.'"*(6:93)

Then after administering this painful goad to people's lifeless hearts, Allah proceeds in a magnificent effulgent passage of self-description to awaken them to the reality of His Existence: *"Allah is the Splitter of the seed and kernel, bringing forth the living from the dead, and the Producer of the dead out of the living. That is Allah, so how are you perverted? He is the Splitter of the sky at dawn, the Appointer of the night as a time of stillness and the sun and moon as a means of reckoning. That is what the Almighty, the All-Knowing, has ordained."* (6:95-96) In the face of this radiant outpouring no one with an open mind and heart could fail to see, but there is no cure for impenetrable bigotry: *"Clear insights have come to you from your Lord. Whoever sees clearly, it is to his own benefit. Whoever is blind, it is to his own detriment. I am not here as your keeper."* (6:104)

Allah now goes on to say that unfortunately there are many people in this state and that the only course is to abandon them and on no account to be influenced by anything they say or do: *"Follow what has been revealed to you from your Lord – there is no god but Him - and turn away from the idolaters."* (6:106) Then Allah gives an instance of how the evil influence of the unbelievers might be exerted to persuade people to eat what Allah has forbidden: *"Do not eat anything over which the Name of Allah has not been mentioned. To do so is wanton deviance. The shaytans inspire their friends to dispute with you. If you obeyed them you would be idolaters."* (6:122) Beware of manipulation by shaytan resulting from entering into a dialectic with the believers; do not allow yourselves to be derailed: *"This is the path of your Lord and it is straight. We have made the Signs plain for people who remember."* (6:126)

Following on from this the *sura* next gives us an exposition of the nature of human misguidance and of the specific forms it took among the Arabs to whom the Book was immediately addressed. This particularly concerns human arrogance and the tendency of the human being to arrogate to himself matters whose legislation in reality belongs to Allah alone – something, of course, especially prevalent in our own time: *"Those who attribute partners to Allah will say, 'If Allah had willed we would not have attributed any partners to Him, nor would our fathers; nor would we have made anything unlawful.' In the same way the people before them denied until they felt Our violent force. Say: 'Do you have some knowledge you can produce for us? You are following nothing but conjecture. You are only guessing.'"* (6:148)

Allah makes it clear that ignorant people have invented acts of worship and laws for which Allah did not sent down any authority and have begun to judge one another according to their own inventions. They have abandoned Divine Revelation for ignorant and short-sighted man-made innovations: *"Who could do greater wrong than someone who fabricates lies against Allah, thus leading people astray without any knowledge? Allah does not guide the people of the wrongdoers."* (6:144) People have made their own opinion the yardstick of good and evil and the inevitable result is spiralling corruption in every sphere of human existence.

Then Allah shows us in an extraordinarily comprehensive passage the basic ingredients of Divine guidance to humanity and that it truly is nothing but common sense and basic good behaviour: *"Say: 'Come and I will recite to you what your Lord has made unlawful for you: that you do not attribute any partners to Him; that you are good to your parents; that you do not kill your children because of poverty – We will provide for you and them; that you do not approach indecency, outward or inward; that you do not kill any person Allah has made inviolate – only when you have the legal right. That is what He instructs you to do so that perhaps you will gain understanding. That you do not go near the property of an orphan before he reaches maturity except in a good way; that you give full measure and full weight with justice – We do not charge any self except with what it can bear; that you are equitable when you speak even if a near relative is concerned; and that you fulfil Allah's contract. That is what He instructs you to do, so that perhaps you will remember. This is My Path and it is straight so follow it. Do not follow other ways or you will become cut off from His Way. That is what He instructs you to do. Perhaps you will be godfearing."* (6:151-153)

We can see from this that Allah's laws for us are not in any way an arbitrary imposition of His Will to govern our lives but are simple guidelines to keep human beings within parameters which ensure their well-being and keep them from self-destructive and anti-social behaviour. There is no place for capricious innovation, ignorant superstition or unjust despotism.

After this no one can claim that they have not received Allah's guidance: *"Nor can you say: 'If the Book had been sent down to us, We would have been better guided than them.' For a clear Sign has come to you from your Lord, and guidance and mercy. Who could do greater wrong than someone who denies Allah's Signs and turns away from them? We will repay those who turn away from Our Signs with the worst kind of punishment because they turned away."* (6:157) This threat of course applies to all those like the nationalists and secularists of our time who have jettisoned Revelation and Islam for other systems and ideologies. There is also a warning for those form sects within their *deen* to further their own positions and opinions: *"As for those who divide up their* deen *and form into sects, you have nothing whatsoever to do with them. Their case will go back to Allah and then He will inform them about the things they did."* (6:159)

The *sura* concludes with a complete restatement of the traditional Prophetic position and mankind's basic responsibility to worship Allah alone: *"Say: "My Lord has guided me to a straight path, an upright* deen, *the religion of Ibrahim, a man of pure natural belief. He was not one of the idolaters." Say: "My prayer and my rites, my living and my dying, are for Allah, the Lord of the Universe. He has no partner. So I have been commanded and I am the first of the Muslims." Say: "Am I to desire other than Allah as Lord when He is the Lord of everything?" What each self earns is for itself alone. No bearer of a burden can bear another's burden. Then you will return to your Lord, and He will inform you regarding the things about which you differed. It is He who appointed you regents on the earth and raised some of you above others in rank so He could test you regarding what He has given you. Your Lord is Swift in retribution. And He is truly Ever-Forgiving, Most Merciful."* (6:162-167)

Sura 7

Al-A'raf: The Ramparts

Surat al-A'raf deals basically with two subjects: the first is the Noble Qur'an itself but the main theme of the *sura* is the origin, history and destiny of the human race, particularly focusing on those who disavow and deny Divine Revelation.

The first is introduced by the words of Allah: *"It is a Book sent down to you – so let there be no constriction in your heart because of it – so that you may give warning by it and as a reminder to the believers. Follow what has been sent down to you from your Lord and do not follow any protectors besides Him."* (7:2-3) The constriction referred to was due to the bad reception that the idolaters gave to the one who desired to guide them and their refusal to accept what he brought.

The *sura* continues to discuss the Book in a number of places. One instance is: *"We have brought them a Book elucidating everything with knowledge, as a guidance and a mercy for a people who believe. What are they waiting for but for its divulgence?"*, (7:52-53) meaning: "Are they waiting for anything but Allah's Promise and Threat to be realised when the believers will win victory and be rewarded and the unbelievers will be defeated and receive their punishment?" Another instance is *"My Protector is Allah who sent down the Book. He takes care of the righteous"* (7:196) which gives good news to the Prophet, may Allah bless him and grant him peace, and the believers that Allah will protect and preserve him so that he can convey the Message. Allah also talks about the correct behaviour to be observed in respect of the Book: *"When the Qur'an is recited, listen to it and be quiet so that perhaps you will receive mercy."* (7:204)

The main theme is introduced by Allah's words: *"How many a city We have destroyed! Our violent force came upon them during the night, or while they were sleeping in the day. And their only utterance, when Our violent force came upon them, was the cry: 'Truly we have been wrongdoers!'"* (7:4-5) The destruction of the people who disobeyed the Messengers is something which runs through human history. *Surat al-A'raf* explains what befell the peoples of 'Ad, Thamud and Madyan, Nuh and Lut, and then moves on to Musa who brought a Book for the guidance of the people of Egypt and the tribe of Israel. The *sura* deals in some detail with the way Pharaoh and the Jews respectively rejected the guidance they had been brought. Now Revelation has returned for the last time to bring mankind out of the darkness into the light and as long as this world continues it is the duty of mankind to listen to it and learn from it because it alone can give them true guidance.

From the beginning the *sura* makes it clear that the final destiny of every human being depends on how they respond to the Divine guidance which comes to them: *"We will question those to whom the Messengers were sent, and We will question the Messengers. We will tell them about it with knowledge. We are never absent."* (7:6-7) It is on people's acceptance or rejection of the Divine Message that the Reckoning is based: *"The weighing on that Day is the Truth. As for those whose scales are heavy, they are the successful. As for those whose scales are light, they are the ones who have lost their own selves because they wrongfully refuted Our Signs."* (7:8-9)

After this general statement of the basic position the *sura* takes us right back to the beginning of the human story: *"We have installed you firmly on the earth, and granted you your livelihood in it. What little thanks you show! We created you and then formed you and then We said to the angels, 'Prostrate to Adam,' and they prostrated – except for Iblis. He was not among the prostraters."* (7:10-11) The account concentrates on the seduction of Adam by Shaytan which marks the starting point of human history on the earth and, in consequence, the repeated cycles of Divine guidance to man-kind.

In his complete innocence Adam had no defences against the deceptive trickery of Shaytan. The ironic thing about the whole event of Adam's enticement by Shaytan is that Adam already had the very things that Shaytan persuaded him he would gain from the forbidden tree, and it was his listening to Shaytan's whisperings which caused them to be removed. Shaytan's insinuation was that Adam and Hawwa were being deprived of angelic status and immortality by not eating from the tree; but it is clear from the prostration of the angels that Adam's status was in fact higher than theirs and that the Garden where he and his wife were living was the Abode of Immortality. So it can be seen that anxiety that you will not have what you need, anxiety about provision, almost always baseless, is something which goes right back to the very roots of human history and is an open gate for Shaytan to gain access to the human heart.

From the beginning Shaytan made it his business to dislodge mankind from the straight path of Allah's guidance by bombarding them from every direction: *"Because of the way that You misguided me, I will lie in ambush for them on Your Straight Path. Then I will come at them, from in front of them and behind them, from their right and from their left. You will not find most of them thankful."* (7:16-17) But it must always be remembered that his power is limited, like that of a radio transmitter, to transmission, and we can in fact choose whether to listen or not to listen. Shaytan has no physical power whatsoever over human behaviour.

The event of Adam's expulsion from the Garden is a mine of instruction for reflective minds. One essential point to realise is that the Christian doctrine of original sin, with its implication of a perpetual curse on the whole of mankind ever since, is a complete misreading of the event. Indeed, from one viewpoint exactly the opposite is true inasmuch as it was the springboard for all the Divine guidance to mankind that has flowed forth from Allah ever since and thus the source of all our blessings! What is certain is that it was an inevitable part of Allah's plan for the human race and the starting point of human history, and a necessary element in the fulfilment of the chief purpose of human life: the worship of Allah.

In any case, the result was that Adam and his wife descended to the earth and their descendants were exposed to the trials of this world to see whether they would reflect: *"He said, 'Descend as enemies to one another! You will have residence on the earth and enjoyment for a time,'"* (7:24). Every human being lives on the earth for a determined period and then returns to his Creator, who will ask him about how he spent his life. Was he a slave of Allah or a slave of Shaytan? *"In it you shall live and die, and from it you shall be brought forth."* (7:25)

This account of the story of Adam is directed to all his descendants throughout the ages and in the course of it they are addressed four times directly, three times in respect of clothing and once about following the Message: *"Children of Adam! We have sent down clothing to you to conceal your private parts, and fine plumage, but the garment of godfearing, that is best. That is one of Allah's Signs, so that perhaps you will remember."* (7:26) *"Children of Adam! Do not let Shaytan tempt you into trouble as He expelled your parents from the Garden, stripping them of their covering and disclosing to them their private parts."* (7:27) *"Children of Adam! Wear fine clothing in every mosque and eat and drink but do not be profligate. He does not love the profligate."* (7:30) *"Children of Adam! If Messengers should come to you from among you, recounting My Signs to you, those who are godfearing and put things right, will feel no fear and will know no sorrow."* (7:34)

Clothing is, of course, something unique to man – nothing else in existence covers itself in the same way we do – and this *ayat* shows that the wearing of clothes is absolutely basic to human existence and has more to do with modesty than with physical conditions. Natural modesty is both the reason for and the keynote of all the regulations concerning dress and the threefold mention of this subject here shows its importance in human life and tells us all we need to know about it. It is clear from these *ayats* that the purpose of clothing is to cover and conceal nakedness; and for this reason fear of Allah is a kind of garment since it lowers people's eyes and prevents them from looking at other people's private parts.

Given that this is the basis there are various ways that people go beyond the limits in respect of clothing. People sometimes use clothing to vaunt their social status in arrogance so that the measure of the person becomes the cost of the clothing they wear. Nowadays clothing is frequently used by members of both sexes to reveal rather than conceal their private parts, being made so tight and thin as to be almost non-existent! These are two of many different ways that clothing is used in a non-permissible fashion. The honour of a man does not consist in his clothes; nor does his value lie in what he wears.

It was Shaytan who disclosed to Adam and his wife the nature of their nakedness, stripping them of their innocence, and this has remained one of Shaytan's main gates to the corruption of the human being. He is a malicious enemy and can see us while we cannot see him. Yet he cannot mislead a sincere believer because, as the Qur'an makes clear, sincerity forms a protecting wall which Shaytan cannot breach; his traps only snare those who lack sincere belief. So the Arabs before Islam were duped by Shaytan into making people go around the Ka'ba naked, making it a matter of piety to do so – but Allah is too Exalted and Majestic to command something vile which is contrary to basic human nature: "*Do you say about Allah what you do not know? Say: 'My Lord has commanded justice.'*" (7:28-29)

Justice is balanced behaviour easily recognisable to all mankind, so why do we not submit to Him who created us and knows where this balance lies and to whom We will certainly return? "*'Stand and face Him in all the mosques and call on Him, making your* deen *sincerely for Him. As He originated you, so you will return.' One group He has guided; but another group deserved to be misguided.*" (7:29-30) False religiosity lies in the kind of extremist behaviour exemplified by this pre-Islamic practice. It frequently appears in the guise of those who say that monasticism and self-mortification are a necessary condition to connect people to their Lord. Such people make a virtue of tattered clothing, coarse food and repelling all the good things of life.

The teaching of Islam makes it clear that balance is needed in these things as in everything else. Submission to Allah is achieved first and foremost within the human individual. The most important thing is soundness of heart and overcoming selfishness and making humility and mercy inward realities. People should honour themselves as Allah has honoured them and therefore it is appropriate for people as worshippers of Allah to wear the best clothing and eat the best food they can properly afford: *"Children of Adam! Wear fine clothing in every mosque and eat and drink but do not be profligate. He does not love the profligate."* (7:31) And the Prophet, may Allah bless him and grant him peace, said, "Eat what you like and wear what you like as long as you do not err into two qualities: profligacy and arrogance."

The truth is that the impermissible aspect of food and clothing lies in profligacy in respect of them, not in the things themselves: *Say: 'Who has forbidden the fine clothing of Allah and the good kinds of provision He has produced for His slaves?'"* (7:32) The ascription of these things to Allah means that He is their source and desires His slaves to enjoy them within the limits He has prescribed. What Allah forbids is misuse of His blessing: *"Say: "My Lord has forbidden indecency, both open and secret, and wrong action, and unrightful tyranny, and that you attribute partners to Allah for which He has sent down no authority, and that you say about Allah what you do not know."* (7:33) The important thing is to have a sound basic human nature based on belief in Allah alone and not attributing any partners to Him. Islam is based on the natural form of man with respect to both creed and character and this has been the basis of Allah's *deen* since the beginning of human history.

Having taken us right back to the beginning and told us of the basic nature of our transaction with the Divine, the last of the four *ayats* referred to previously, addressed directly to us as the descendants of Adam, reminds us that the way to fulfil it is to follow the Messengers Allah has sent to guide us.

Then Allah informs us that failure to do so will result in endless regret: *"But as for those who reject Our Signs and are arrogant regarding them, they are the Companions of the Fire, remaining in it timelessly, forever."* (7:36) And this ushers in a passage about the final, timeless destiny of human existence either in endless bliss or in endless torment, depending upon whether or not we grasped the point of human existence and followed the Messengers in submission to Allah, or refused to do so and followed our own whims and desires, thinking we knew best. *"As for those who deny Our Signs and are arrogant concerning them, the Gates of Heaven will not be opened for them, and they shall not enter the Garden until a camel goes through the eye of a needle. That is how We repay the evil-doers. They will have Jahannam as a resting-place and above them smothering layers. That is how We repay the wrongdoers. As for those who believe and do right actions – and We do not charge any self beyond what it can bear – they are the Companions of the Garden. They shall remain in it timelessly, forever. We will strip away any rancour in their breasts. Rivers will flow under them and they will say, 'Praise be to Allah who has guided us to this! We would not have been guided if Allah had not guided us. The Messengers of our Lord came with the Truth.' It will be proclaimed to them: 'This is your Garden which you have inherited on account of what you did.'"* (7:39-43)

Part of the reward of the blessed and the punishment of the lost is that they remain aware of their life in the world and that their present state has resulted from it: *"The Companions of the Garden will call out to the Companions of the Fire, 'We have found what our Lord promised us to be true. Have you found what your Lord promised you to be true?' They will say, 'Yes!' Between them a herald will proclaim: 'May the curse of Allah be on the wrongdoers!'"* (7:44) So it is clear that as we live in this world we are simultaneously shaping our own eternal destiny. The wrongdoers deny the Resurrection and Judgement and attack and mock the believers and bar the way to the Truth, and by doing these things they actually create their own endless torment.

The *sura* takes its name from the men of the Ramparts (*al-A'raf*) who are now mentioned: *"Between them there will be a barrier wall and on the ramparts there will be men who recognise everyone by their mark."* (7:46) What is generally accepted among the commentators is that these are people whose good and evil actions are equal and who are waiting for their fate to be decided. However, there is another opinion: that they are those who call people to Allah and convey the Message of the Prophets and lead their communities to good. In the Next World they will be in a position to overlook the destinies of all mankind and give the greeting of peace to the People of the Garden and see the terrible end of the People of the Fire. The account of the Noble Qur'an about them makes this interpretation more likely. Here we notice how the meanings of the Qur'an interpenetrate and interweave, meeting all together in one thread which produces a great effect on the soul.

The Qur'an then reminds mankind that Allah is the Creator and Lord of all creation: *"Your Lord is Allah: He who created the heavens and the earth in six days and then settled Himself firmly on the Throne. He covers the day with the night, each pursuing the other urgently, and the sun and moon and stars are subject to His command. Indeed, to Him belong both creation and command. Blessed be Allah, the Lord of all the worlds."* (7:54)

Having focused our attention on our Creator, the Qur'an now returns to the theme of Divine guidance which provides the measure against which human destinies are decided. As often happens, a natural event is used to illustrate an inward reality: *"He it is who sends out the winds, bringing advance news of His mercy, so that, when they have lifted up the heavy clouds, We dispatch them to a dead land and send down water to it, by means of which We bring forth all kinds of fruit. In the same way We will bring forth the dead; perhaps you will remember."* (7:57) The constant renewal of Divine guidance to the human race is like rain for the dried-out earth, bringing it to life again after a drought, but unfortunately not everyone is receptive: *"Good land gives forth its plants by the permission of its Lord, but land which is bad only gives forth very meagrely. That is how We diversify the Signs for a people who are thankful."* (7:58)

This *ayat* leads into a long section of the *sura* which continues the main theme of the history of the human race and its relationship with Divine guidance, speaking of a whole series of peoples who rebelled against the Messengers sent to them and were consequently destroyed. This fills the time gap between the prehistoric time of Adam and the true historical era which begins with the time of Musa. Those mentioned are the peoples of the Prophets Nuh, Hud, Salih, Shu'ayb and Lut and Allah conveys to us in considerable detail that the whole history of mankind is one of constant renewal of Divine guidance and recurrent rejection of it by the people to whom it is addressed. At the end of this comes a summary of the entire subject: *"We have never sent a Prophet to any city without seizing its people with poverty and illness so that perhaps they would be humble. Then We gave them good in exchange for evil so that they increased in number and said, 'Poverty and illness were what our fathers suffered.' Then We seized them suddenly when they were not expecting it. If only the people of the cities had believed and been godfearing, We would have opened up to them blessings from heaven and earth. But they denied, so We seized them on account of what they earned."* (7: 94-96)

Then Allah makes it clear to us that we ourselves are not outside this historical process and that it has a direct relevance to our own situation: *"Are those who have inherited the earth after these people not guided by the fact that, if We willed, We could strike them for their wrong actions, stamping a seal upon their hearts so they could not hear?"* (7:100)

At this point the *sura* enters the era of modern history with Musa, peace be upon him, dealing firstly with his encounter with Pharaoh, which gives us an archetypal picture of human society and its political structure that continues to be relevant to us now, and secondly with his relationship with the tribe of Israel who, as we know, continue to follow the same misguided path in the world today with enormous repercussions for all mankind. Allah shows us here in detail how they came to be misguided and how that should serve as an example to us so that we do not go the same way.

A crucial aspect of this story which so epitomises the modern situation is the effect that living under the domination of idolaters had on the tribe of Israel. Musa told them not to despair of Divine help, saying: *"It may well be that your Lord is going to destroy your enemy and make you the successors in the land so that He may see how you behave."* (7:129) This also expresses Musa's fears for his people because they had been influenced by the idolatry which had surrounded them in Egypt. His fears proved justified because as soon as they were delivered from bondage, they immediately longed to worship idols. *"We conveyed the Tribe of Israel across the sea and they came upon some people who were devoting themselves to some idols of theirs. They said, 'Musa! Appoint a god for us just as these people have gods.' He said, 'You are indeed an ignorant people. What these people are doing is destined for destruction. What they are doing is of no avail.'"* (7:138-139) Allah warned them of the consequences of yearning for the very disbelief which they had just left: *"As for those who adopted the Calf, anger from their Lord will overtake them together with abasement in the life of this world. That is how We repay the falsifiers."* (7:152)

Inserted in the middle of this litany of Jewish misguidance and ingratitude to Allah is a striking passage in which we are transported right into the present and reminded of the renewed Divine guidance for our time at the hands of Allah's final Messenger, Muhammad, may Allah bless him and grant him peace. *"As for My punishment, I strike with it anyone I will. My mercy extends to all things but I will prescribe it for those who are godfearing and pay the* zakat, *and those who believe in Our Signs: those who follow the Messenger, the Unlettered Prophet, the one they find written down with them in the Torah and the* Injil, *commanding them to do right and forbidding them to do wrong, making good things lawful for them and bad things unlawful for them, releasing them from their heavy loads and the chains which were around them. Those who believe in him and honour him and help him, and follow the light that has been sent down with him, they are the successful. Say: 'O mankind! I am the Messenger of Allah to you all: of Him to whom the kingdom of the heavens and the earth belongs. There is no god but Him. He gives life and causes to die. So believe in Allah and His Messenger, the Unlettered Prophet, who believes in Allah and His words, and follow him so that perhaps you will be guided.'"* (7:156-159)

After this detailed exposition of how human beings lose sight of the truth despite Allah's continued guidance to them – which is, as we have seen, the hallmark of all human history – Allah takes us right back to the timeless core of human identity, showing us that recognition of the Divine Unity is the birthright of every single human being, independent of any historical circumstances. *"When your Lord took out all their descendants from the loins of the Children of Adam and made them testify against themselves: 'Am I not your Lord?' They said, 'We testify that indeed You are!' Lest you say on the Day of Rising, 'We were unmindful of this.' Or lest you say, 'Our forefathers attributed partners to Allah before our time, and we are merely descendants coming after them. Are You then going to destroy us for what those falsifiers did?'"* (7:172-173) It is clear from this that people's historical conditions, however adverse, can never serve as an excuse for their failure to recognise and submit to their Lord. Every human being has an innate capacity to know Allah.

Then having shown us this innate, supra-historical element of Divine guidance, Allah shows us the root cause of misguidance in the human being which is also independent of historical considerations: *"Recite to them the tale of him to whom We gave Our signs, but who then cast them to one side and followed Shaytan. He was one of those lured into error. If We had willed, We would have raised him through them. But he gravitated towards the earth and pursued his whims and base desires. His likeness is that of a dog: if you chase it away, it sticks out its tongue and pants, and if you leave it alone, it sticks out its tongue and pants. That is the likeness of people who deny Our Signs. So tell the story, so that perhaps they will reflect. How evil is the likeness of the people who deny Our Signs! They have done themselves great wrong. Whoever Allah guides is truly guided. But those whom He leads astray are the losers. We created many of the jinn and mankind for Jahannam. They have hearts they do not understand with. They have eyes they do not see with. They have ears they do not hear with. Such people are like cattle. No, they are even further astray! They are the unmindful."* (7:176-179) This applies to every individual and society who have received Divine guidance and then ignored or rejected it. Human beings cut themselves off from their own innate capacity to know the truth by their own tendency to deny the higher aspect of their own being in the pursuit of the immediate gratification of their appetites and lower desires.

The whole matter of human guidance and misguidance is now brought firmly into the present tense. *"Among those We have created there is a nation who guide by the Truth and act justly according to it. And as for those who deny Our Signs, We will lead them, step by step, into destruction from where they do not know. I will give them more time; My strategy is sure. Have they not reflected? Their companion is not mad. Have they not contemplated the realms of the heavens and the earth and the things that Allah has created, and the fact that it may well be that their fixed term has drawn near? In what discourse after this will they then believe? If Allah misguides someone, no one can guide him. We will abandon them to wander about blindly in their overweening insolence."* (7:181-186) And most importantly the last of these *ayats* indicates that the whole matter of guidance and misguidance is in Allah's hands while simultaneously making it clear that misguidance is merited by 'overweening insolence'.

Allah also makes clear to us here the difference between the nature of His own guidance and prophetic guidance so that we will not make the mistake of associating the Messenger with Him: *"They will ask you about the Hour: when is it due? Say: 'Knowledge of it is with my Lord alone. He alone will reveal it at its proper time. It hangs heavy in the heavens and the earth. It will not come upon you except suddenly.' Say: 'I possess no power to benefit or harm myself, except as Allah wills. Had I had knowledge of the Unseen, I would have gained much good and no evil would have touched me. I am only a warner and a bringer of good news to a people who believe.'"* (7:186-187) One of the characteristics of Islam is affirmation of the Prophethood and createdness of Muhammad and that divinity does not attach to him in any way. The same applies to all the angels and mankind and every other created being; anyone who claims otherwise is a liar.

And now, with perfect symmetry, *Surat al-A'raf* returns, as it began, to the subject of Adam: *"It is He who created you from a single self and made from him his spouse so that he might find repose in her."* (7:189) Here the context conveys a rebuke to

Adam's descendants. Instead being grateful to Allah, they associate others with Him. *"Do they make things into partner-gods which cannot create anything and are themselves created; which are not capable of helping them and cannot even help themselves?"* (7:191-192) They are rebuked for failing to use their intellect, worshipping something which is created: *"Those you call on besides Allah are slaves just like yourselves."* (7:194)

Allah warns us once more against his and our ancient enemy, showing us the weapon we have to wield against him: *"If an evil impulse from Shaytan pricks you, seek refuge in Allah. He is All-Hearing, All-Seeing. As for those who are godfearing, when they are bothered by visitors from Shaytan, they remember, and immediately see clearly."* (7:200-201)

Finally, Divine guidance has been made available to us just as it was to all our predecessors throughout history and it is up to us to follow him who brought it to us by paying careful attention to every aspect of the Qur'an and remembering our Lord and fulfilling our purpose as human beings by praising and worshipping Him: *"Say, 'I follow only what has been revealed to me from my Lord. This is clear insight from your Lord, and guidance and mercy, for a people who believe.' When the Qur'an is recited, listen to it and be quiet so that perhaps you will gain mercy.' Remember your Lord in yourself humbly and fearfully, without loudness of voice, morning and evening. Do not be among the heedless. Those who are with your Lord do not consider themselves too great to worship Him. They glorify His praise and they prostrate to Him."* (7:203-206)

Sura 8

Al-Anfal: Booty

Surat al-Anfal is the *sura* of Badr as *Surat Ali 'Imran* is the *sura* of Uhud, and just as the defeat of Uhud was unexpected so was the victory of Badr. Unexpected events, both good and bad, are the best gauge of people's true mettle and the most potent unmaskers of their hidden feelings. *Surat al-Anfal* was revealed after the victory of the Muslims at Badr to give us a correct understanding of the Divine Decree and its relationship with human effort. Allah makes it clear in the *sura* that the victory with which Allah had honoured the Muslims was Divine recompense for the steadfastness displayed by the Muslims during the preceding years of persecution and hardship and also that the men who plunged into battle were the instruments of realising the noble *ayat*: *"Allah has written, 'I will be victorious, I and My Messengers.' Allah is All-Strong, Almighty."* (58:21)

That is why the *sura* begins by ascribing all booty gained in battle to Allah and His Messenger and giving them jurisdiction over its distribution since the booty is the by-product of fighting whose intention is primarily to establish Allah's *deen*: *"Allah desired to verify the Truth by His Words and to root out the last remnant of the unbelievers."* (8:7)

It is clear that faith manifests itself in different ways at different times according to the particular exigencies of the moment. In this instance when the distribution of booty is in question we find: *"The believers are those whose hearts tremble when Allah is mentioned, whose faith is increased when His Signs are recited to them, and who put their trust in their Lord; those who establish the prayer and give of what We have provided for them. They are in truth the believers."* (8:2-4)

103

Here the signs of faith are remembrance, fear, recitation, trust and giving. At the end of the *sura*, we find true faith being described in a different way. The Almighty says: *"Those who believed and emigrated and did* jihad *in the way of Allah and those who gave refuge and help, they are in truth the believers."* (8:74) Here its signs are emigration, *jihad* and giving refuge and help. In another *sura*, Allah Almighty says: *"The believers are only those who have believed in Allah and His Messenger, and then not had any doubt, and fought their hardest with their wealth and themselves in the Way of Allah. It is those who are the truthful."* (49:15) In this instance the signs of faith are unwavering certainty and unceasing spending, and *jihad* with one's person and possessions. In yet another *sura* we find: *"The believers are those who believe in Allah and His Messenger and who, when they are with him on a matter of common concern, do not leave until they have asked him for permission."* (24:62) So the sign of true faith in this situation is asking the Prophet's permission to leave.

It can be seen from this that it is the nature of faith to manifest itself in various ways according to the demands of the particular situation faced by the believers concerned, and so when the Muslims were told to leave the booty to Allah's judgement, the response of the true believers was to realise immediately that their best interest lay in submitting to the Command of Allah.

However, when the Messenger of Allah suddenly told the Muslims that they had to confront the idolaters in battle, a group of them maintained that fighting at that time was a bad idea and that they should wait until it was possible to call out all the Muslims in Madina so that everyone could take part in the unexpected battle. *"Just as your Lord brought you forth from your house with truth, even though a group of the believers disliked it, arguing with you about the Truth after it had been made clear – as though they were being driven to their death with open eyes."* (8:5-6) But the Noble Prophet knew that Islam would be jeopardised if he did not immediately confront the challenge and was aware that Allah would never fail them in their hour of need. The situation was presented to all the fighters and they decided to meet the enemy.

The Prophet, peace and blessings be upon him, hoped that Allah would not let the Muslims return disappointed and Allah shows that He is entirely aware of the situation when He says: *"When Allah promised you that one of the two parties* (the caravan or the army) *would be yours and you would have liked it to have been the unarmed one,"* (8:7) desiring easy booty. However Allah had other ideas and wanted a quite different outcome to the fighting, so He ensured that the events led up to what He desired: *"So that He might verify the Truth and nullify the false, even though the evil-doers hate that."* (8:8)

Human nature is such that when they are taken unawares by something they think is beyond their capacity they take refuge in Allah and seek His help. That is what occurred when the Muslims saw the readiness of their enemy and the fact that they were far more numerous than themselves and much better armed: *"When you were calling on your Lord for help and He responded to you: 'I will reinforce you with a thousand angels, riding behind you.'"* (8:9) One angel would in fact have been enough to demolish the idolaters but Allah wanted to reassure His slaves by mentioning such a number: *"Allah only did this to give you good news so that your hearts would be set at rest. Victory comes from no one but Allah. Allah is Almighty, All-Wise."* (8:10)

During the Battle of Badr, the Prophet, peace and blessings be upon him, devoted much effort to making supplication saying: "O Allah, Your help is what You promised me! O Allah, if this group of believers is destroyed, You will no longer be worshipped on the earth!" He called on Allah with fervour and devotion, raising his arms so high that his cloak fell from his shoulders, while Abu Bakr was behind him saying, "Messenger of Allah, that is enough importuning of your Lord! Allah will fulfil what He promised you." Nevertheless the Messenger did not stop his supplication until Allah informed him of the defeat of the enemy.

Sometimes the paradox is pointed out between the anxiety of Abu Bakr in the Cave during the *hijra* when the Messenger was the one who reassured him, and his confidence on this occasion during the Battle of Badr when he was the one who reassured and calmed the Messenger. The reason for this is that during the *hijra* they had absolutely no means of protecting themselves and therefore the Prophet had absolutely no hesitation in relying on Allah's protection whereas at Badr there was an army with him and there was a danger of relying on that. So the Noble Prophet wanted to free himself of any claim to strength and power and sought refuge in supplication to Allah for victory, knowing that victory would come from Him alone.

And indeed Heaven intervened, making rain fall so that the sand became firm under their feet and granting the Muslims a deep restful sleep despite their anxiety. Allah strengthened the hearts of the Muslims and filled those of the idolaters with terror so they fought badly. Their lines were smashed by the heavy hammer of defeat, a possibility which had never occurred to them: *"That is because they broke with Allah and His Messenger. If anyone breaks with Allah and His Messenger, Allah is Severe in retribution."* (8:13)

It is vital to remember, however, that Divine help will not be secured by anyone who neglects normal means, and the first of these means is that courage which impels a man's feet towards something which exposes him to the danger of his own destruction out of desire for the Pleasure of Allah. It is to discard this world for love of the Next World. This is what is being referred to in the *ayat*: *"O you who believe! When you encounter those who disbelieve advancing in massed ranks into battle, do not turn your backs on them."* (8:15) Resist love for this life and seek that death which will give you true life!

The courageous few at Badr showed that the idolatrous horde was nothing but a mirage in the desert and the unbelievers were indeed nearly all either captured or killed. But how did this come about? Allah Almighty tells us clearly: *"You did not kill them, it was Allah who killed them; and you did not throw, when you threw, it was Allah who threw: so He might test the believers with this blessing from Him. Allah is All-Hearing, All-Knowing."* (7:17) The implacable plan laid out by the Divine Decree drew the tyrants of Makka on to their doom. Neither their numbers nor their arms were of any use to them, whereas the few believers who sought refuge with Allah and asked for His help won a tremendous victory.

✼✼✼✼✼

Surat al-Anfal contains six blunt commands to the believers which give us much food for reflection. There is no sense whatever of congratulation. Allah sets about readying the victorious Muslim army for the new political situation resulting from their victory by commending self-control, discipline and the conquering of any tendency to self-delusion. The first command tells them not flee the enemy and is followed by terrible threats for doing so even though none of the Companions fled or even thought of it. It would seem that the strong tone the Revelation took after the victory was to emphasise the role the Divine Decree played in it and to prevent the believers from attributing it to their own power.

Allah also describes the unbelievers very aptly using several different images and each time we find advice for the Muslims not to be like them but to be on a higher level. He describes the unbelievers, for instance, as being beasts without awareness or intelligence. Their lives are totally dominated by their lower appetites which blind them to any higher aspirations and make them deaf to anything they are told. If only they had listened and acknowledged what they were called to; but overwhelming pride kept them from responding. Before this incisive description, Allah has issued the second of His commands to the believers: *"O you who believe! Obey Allah and His Messenger, and do not turn away from him while you are listening. Do not be like those who say, 'We hear,' when they do not hear."* (8:20-21)

Then the Muslims are told what they should do: *"O you who believe! Respond to Allah, and to the Messenger, when He calls you to what will bring you to life!"* (8:24) and the instruction is hedged in by threats and warnings: *"Know that Allah intervenes between a man and his heart,"* (8:24) and *"Be fearful of trials which will not afflict solely those among you who do wrong. Know that Allah is Severe in Retribution."* (8:25) This is the comment on victory after fifteen years of ceaseless struggle! What does that indicate? Simply that He who has granted victory to His slaves refuses to allow them to indulge in any type of delusion or arrogance. It is Allah alone who has humiliated disbelief and its adherents and it is He who arraigns the victorious Muslims so that they do not become intoxicated by the wine of victory and start to attribute power to themselves.

Allah continues to drive the lesson home: *"Remember when you were few and oppressed in the land, afraid that the people would snatch you away. He gave you refuge and supported you with His help and provided you with good things so that perhaps you would be thankful."* (8:26) He reminds them of their previous humiliation and abasement so that any trace of self-elevation is effaced. Then He directs a further strong caution to them: *"O you who believe! Do not betray Allah and His Messenger, and do not knowingly betray your trusts. Know that your wealth and your children are a trial and that there is an enormous wage with Allah."* (8:27-28) How different this is from the way in which victory is usually acknowledged!

Victorious armies throughout the ages have returned vainglorious from the battlefield to a triumphant welcome from an adoring populace; flowers are scattered over them, their mistakes are forgiven and they can do no wrong. But the victors in the first great battle of Islam, which assured the continuance of Allah's worship on the earth for all time, were given none of these things. This should surely serve as a lesson to the blind orientalists who claim that 'Badr' was the first manifestation of the conquering spirit and aggression of Islam!

The context of the *sura* then returns to the situation of the Muslims before Badr and before the Hijra and it speaks of the machinations of the idolaters against Islam and its Prophet. By the command of his Lord, the Messenger of Allah says to them: *"Say: 'You will not be asked about the evil we did and we will not be asked about the evil you did.' Say: 'Our Lord will bring us all together and then will judge between us with the truth. He is the Judge, the All-Knowing.'"* (34:25-26) And what was the evil they had done? Unabating persecution of all the Muslims in general and, in the case of the Messenger, threatening him with imprisonment, murder or banishment. *"When those who disbelieve were plotting against you to imprison you or kill you or expel you: they were plotting and Allah was plotting, but Allah is the best of plotters."* (8:30)

If people are confused and unsure about what path to take, they should say, "O Allah, show us the Truth as true and make us follow it! Show us the false as false and make us avoid it!" But those tyrants said: *"O Allah! If this is really the Truth from You, rain stones down on us out of heaven or bring upon us a painful punishment."* (8:32) Then Allah makes it clear to them why they had been spared up to that time: *"Allah would never punish them while you were among them. Allah would never punish them while they sought forgiveness."* (8:33) It was not because they did not merit punishment; and now that the Prophet was no longer among them their days were numbered: *"But what is there to stop Allah from punishing them now when they bar access to the Sacred Mosque? They are not its guardians. Only the godfearing can be its guardians. But most of them do not know that."* (8:34) What they considered to be worship was merely "whistling and clapping" and part of idolatry. Only actions done for the sake of Allah alone can bring any real benefit, but the unbelievers put all their efforts into trying to fight against Allah and will never be successful: *"Those who reject spend their wealth to bar access to the Way of Allah. They will spend it. Then they will regret it. Then they will be overthrown."* (8:36)

So at Badr they were overcome and a crushing defeat was inflicted on them. Then the Messenger once more offered them the option of repenting and turning from disbelief and idolatry: *"Say to those who disbelieve that if they stop they will be forgiven what is past but if they return to it, the fate of the earlier peoples has already gone before."* (8:39) Those who persist in injustice will harvest only regret and be destroyed just like those who denied the Message in earlier times. There will be no quarter given by the Muslims: *"Fight them until idolatry is no more and the* deen *is Allah's alone ..."* (8:39) This *ayat* has never been abrogated.

The *sura* now returns to the subject of booty and makes clear the parameters within which it is permitted: a fifth must be devoted to good causes and the remaining four-fifths goes to the fighters: *"Know that when you take any booty a fifth of it belongs to Allah, and to the Messenger, and to close relatives, orphans, the very poor and travellers...."* (8:41) It is clear that gaining booty in the struggle to establish Islam, fighting against the enemies of Allah and His Messenger, has always been a major means of livelihood for Muslims in situations when the Muslim community is truly fulfilling its role of ensuring that *"the* deen *is Allah's alone..."* but it is vital that it should not become an end in itself and that it be collected and distributed as Allah has commanded.

The *Ayat* of Booty comes sandwiched between two matters which make the provenance of the booty absolutely clear. The first, as we have seen, is the description of the injustice and aggression of the unbelievers who expend their wealth to bar people from the Way of Allah, and the second is Allah's reaffirmation that the overwhelming victory of the Muslims was His doing. *"When you were on the nearer slope, and they were on the further slope, and the caravan was lower down than you. If you had had an appointment to meet, you would have broken the appointment. But it came about so that Allah might settle a matter whose result was foreordained, so that those who died would die on clear proof, and that those who lived would live on clear proof. Allah is All-Hearing, All-Knowing."* (8:42) The Battle of Badr was the Day of Discrimination, the Day when the two groups met, the group who worshipped Allah alone and the group who clung to idolatry. Allah raised up and confirmed His worshippers and crushed the idolaters.

Then after the presentation of the events of the battle, the sixth and last of Allah's commands to the believers in *Surat al-Anfal* referred to previously is given. It constitutes a complete formula for the achievement and maintenance of victory. Reaching the summit requires great effort but remaining there requires even more. The Almighty says: *"O you who believe! When you meet a troop, stand firm, and remember Allah repeatedly so that perhaps you may be successful. Obey Allah and His Messenger and do not quarrel among yourselves lest you lose heart and your momentum disappear. And be steadfast. Allah is with the steadfast. Do not be like those who left their homes in arrogance, showing off to people and barring them from the Way of Allah...* " (8:45-47) The necessary elements are standing firm in the face of the enemy, continual remembrance of Allah, obedience to Allah and His Messenger, avoidance of internal disputes, general steadfastness and avoidance of arrogance.

Standing firm in the face of the enemy requires a soul filled with certainty and self-sacrifice and the history of the early Muslims gives us many examples of this quality. Remembrance of Allah brings about in us awareness that we are certainly going to meet Him and will return to Him and ensures that we fight for His sake alone, undistracted by secondary anxieties. Obedience to Allah and His Messenger are absolutely indispensable to achieve and maintain victory. When they were fighting the Persians, 'Umar ibn al-Khattab used to advise his army to avoid acts of disobedience to Allah, telling them that it was not the stratagems of their enemy they needed to fear but their own acts of disobedience to Allah. Next comes avoidance of internal disputes. The Muslims today form a fifth of the world's population but internal disputes ensure that we remain in a state of perpetual abasement. There can be no steadfastness in people whose main occupation is the satisfaction of their appetites and immediate gratification of every desire which is the predominant condition of Muslims everywhere in the world today. Finally arrogance and self-aggrandisement have become the hallmark of Muslim leaders everywhere. That is the attitude of tyrants and their end will be the same: *"As was the case with the people of Pharaoh and those before them. They rejected Allah's Signs, so Allah seized them for their wrong actions. Allah is Strong, Severe in retribution."* (8:52)

✽✽✽✽✽

The Day of Badr was indeed a turning point in world history. The battle decided once and for all between Islam and idolatry. The supremacy of the idolaters was finished and it was simply a matter of time before that of the Muslims became completely dominant. The days of their blessings had only increased the idolaters in obduracy and arrogance and so they were removed from them: *"Allah coins a likeness of a city which was secure and at peace, its provision coming to it plentifully from every side. Then it showed ingratitude for Allah's blessings so Allah made it taste hunger and fear like enveloping garments for what they did."* (16:112) That is how Allah always deals with all who are ungrateful for His bounty and unthankful for His gifts: *"That is because Allah would never change a blessing He has conferred on a people unless they changed what was in themselves."* (8:53) Thankfulness secures blessings and preserves them. When the bonds of gratitude are untied, blessing flies off in all directions.

Such people only live up to an agreement if it is to their advantage to do so. If it is not useful for them, they break it. That is why the Almighty sent down: *"The worst of beasts in the sight of Allah are those who reject and do not believe, those with whom you make a treaty and who then break their treaty every time. They are not godfearing."* (8:55-56) The only thing which might wake them up is the blow of a painful defeat. That is why the Messenger was told: *"Strike the one you meet with a blow which will cause fear to those behind him! So if you come upon such people in war, make a harsh example of them to deter those coming after them so that perhaps they will remember. If you fear treachery on a people's part, revoke your treaty with them equally. Allah does not love treacherous people."* (8:57-58)

Injustice will only be eliminated by the sword and so the Muslims should carry the sword. Justice will only be achieved by killing so let the Muslims plunge into battle so that the Banner of Justice may be raised high! We are eager for peace and in its shadow we convey our message to all. But what can we do when our mouths are muzzled and the Path of Truth is blocked? Then there must be fighting.

Inequality of numbers does not remove the duty to fight. Allah is the Helper of the believer when he fights for His sake. When the believer strikes, He who has power over heaven and earth strikes with him. In that situation the believer is simply a cloak for the

Power of Allah, the Avenger who destroys His enemies. This is the meaning of the *ayat*: *"O Prophet! Spur on the believers to fight. If there are twenty of you who are steadfast, they will overcome two hundred; and if there are a hundred of you, they will overcome a thousand of those who reject, because they are a people who do not understand."* (8:65) This judgement is lightened when there is unexpected weakness or extenuating circumstances: *"Now Allah has made it lighter it for you, knowing there is weakness in you. If there are a hundred of you who are steadfast, they will overcome two hundred; and if there are a thousand of you, they will overcome two thousand with Allah's permission. Allah is with the steadfast."* (8:66)

Surat al-Anfal ends with verses which explain the ties that bind together the Muslim world and all its inhabitants, and make it a single body. When one part of is hurt, it all hurts. This tie is the common brotherhood of all Muslims. The *deen* is a mercy which connects all Muslims together and it is not permitted to sever this connection. The Muslims are in reality one body. Yet today the Muslims are divided into a hundred conflicting parts and in spite of their vast numbers and great wealth they have been reduced to humiliating impotence, unable even to defend themselves, let alone expand the *deen*.

In the same way the unbelievers, despite their various nations and apparent differences, are also in reality a single body and the Muslims must recognise this: *"Those who reject are the friends and protectors of one another. If you do not act in this way, there will be trouble in the land and great corruption."* (8:73)

The true Muslims are those who come together and devote their lives to combating disbelief by establishing Allah's *deen*, a task which is no less incumbent on the Muslims of this time than it was on the Prophet, may Allah bless him and grant him peace, and those with him, may Allah be pleased with all of them. *"Those who believed and emigrated and fought their hardest in the Way of Allah and those who gave refuge and help, they are in truth the believers. They will have forgiveness and generous provision."* (8:74) The only solution for our problems and the problems of today's world is to restore the sovereignty of Islam both among ourselves and in the world as a whole.

Sura 9
At-Tawba: Repentance

Surat at-Tawba or *Bara'a* was sent down fifteen months before the Messenger of Allah, may Allah bless him and grant him peace, died. In other words, it came over twenty-years after the beginning of the Revelation. The policy followed during most of that time in dealing with the enemies of Allah was: *"If they deny you, say, 'I have my action and you have your action. You are free of what I do and I am free of what you do.'"* (10:41) However, the enemies of Islam, both the idolaters and People of the Book, refused to allow the Message to be spread peacefully and came to blows with Islam in a fight which was bound to end in their defeat. They refused to acknowledge the truth and refrain from aggression, behaving like a fox who pretends to be dead in order to gain time and resume its treachery and killing. Individuals and groups formed coalitions hampering and attacking the Muslims. So the transgressors had to be fought to limit their harm. That is the meaning of the announcement which issued from Allah and His Messenger against those perfidious forces.

It is not correct to understand the words *"An announcement from Allah and His Messenger to mankind on the day of the greater pilgrimage"* (9:3) as being a declaration of war upon the entire human race! To do so would be to forget the exception which comes immediately after this general statement: *"except those among the idolaters you have treaties with, who have not then broken their treaties with you in any way, nor granted assistance to anyone against you."* (9:4) The Messenger, peace and blessing upon him, was instructed to give those people security and assurance and to let them return safely to their land: *"If any of the idolaters asks you for protection, give him protection until he has heard the Words of Allah. Then convey him to a place of safety. That is because they are a people who do not know."* (9:6) *Surat Bara'a* did not initiate aggression or start any war.

Let us look at the beginning of the *sura* again. What do we see? Islam gave its attackers a respite for four months so they could reflect and make amends for their error: *"Travel about in the land for four months and know that you cannot thwart Allah and that Allah will disgrace the rejectors."* (9:2) The respite is not because of weakness. The announcement was made on the Day of the Greatest *Hajj* which was the day when all the Arabs gathered together, believers and idolaters, people with a treaty and others without, so the matter would be completely clear to everyone and so there would be no excuse for anyone.

To make the matter even clearer and further disclose the inner reality of the idolaters and the foulness of their intentions the *sura* then says: *"How could any of the idolaters possibly have a treaty with Allah and with His Messenger, except for those with whom you made a treaty beside the Sacred Mosque? As long as they are straight with you, be straight with them."* (9:7) Look at the encouragement to be true to those who are true! But on the other hand how is it possible to keep a treaty with treacherous people who do not keep theirs? *"How indeed? For if they get the upper hand over you, they will respect neither kinship nor treaty. They please you with their mouths but their hearts belie their words. Most of them are wantonly deviant. They have sold Allah's Signs for a paltry price, and they have barred access to His Way. Truly what they have done is very evil. They respect neither kinship nor treaty where a believer is concerned. They are the people who go beyond all limits."* (9:8-10)

It appears that the Muslims felt some uneasiness about the consequences of taking this position. They knew that their enemies were strong and that their strength was what was encouraging them to clash with the Muslims and oppress them. The Noble Qur'an abhors this fear and gives orders to urge the Muslims to resist and punish the treacherous: *"...then fight the leaders of disbelief – their oaths mean nothing – so that perhaps they may relent."* (9:12) Then Allah offers further encouragement for the

Muslims to punish the treaty-breakers: *"Will you not fight a people who have broken their oaths and resolved to expel the Messenger, and initiated hostilities against you in the first place? Is it them you fear? Allah has more right to your fear if you are believers."* (9:13)

Surat Bara'a did not in fact alter the course of war in Islam. The Muslims always did and will continue to keep the peace with those who keep the peace with them and make war on those who make war on them, relying on full explanation and clear proclamation while rejecting any base action and disdaining abasement and humiliation. During the twenty-two years before the revelation of *Surat Bara'a,* Arab paganism was dealt in the wisest and most merciful manner. In Makka, Islam was an outlawed religion without any possibility of self-defence. After the *hijra* to Madina, the Muslims engaged in about thirty battles and expeditions against their enemies in the course of all of which only about two hundred unbelievers were killed. That is only a hundredth of the number slaughtered in one day by Christians in the St Bartholomew's Massacre in Paris, when their victims were their co-religionists!

For twenty-two years the Muslims were adjuring the unbelievers to use their intellects or at least to be fair even if they would not be logical. Listen to the tone of sincerity and love in the Words of the Almighty: *"Therefore call and go straight as you have been ordered to. Do not follow their whims and desires but say: 'I believe in a Book Allah has sent down and am ordered to be just between you. Allah is our Lord and your Lord. We have our actions and you your actions. There is no argument between us and you. Allah will gather us all together. To Him is the journey's end.'"* (42:15)

But these entreaties were not heeded and once the Muslims had firm authority they said to their enemies: "Leave us this land and go wherever you want. You are distressed at seeing Islam in the land and you plot against its followers as much as possible and you wait for disasters to befall it and are not content to remain in your homes with your disbelief. We will fight you, but we are protecting ourselves against your worship of idols. So go wherever you like and leave us alone."

117

The announcement also made the final split with all pre-Islamic religious practices: no idolater could make the *Hajj* after this time or go around the Ka'ba. *"It is not for the idolaters to frequent Allah's mosques, bearing witness against themselves of their unbelief. They are the people whose actions come to nothing. They will be in the Fire timelessly, forever. The mosques of Allah should only be frequented by those who believe in Allah and the Last Day and establish the prayer and pay the* zakat, *and fear no one but Allah."* (9:17-18)

❋❋❋❋❋

The Lord of the Worlds knew that the life of His Prophet would end little more than a year after the revelation of *Surat at-Tawba*, and it was therefore necessary for all contingencies to be covered so that Divine legislation was in place to cover all the needs of the future expansion of Islam. One element of this was how to deal with People of the Book such as the Byzantine communities to the North of the Arabian Peninsula as they came within the hegemony of Islam.

Islam is the unique connection between Allah and His slaves, and Allah has obliged the Muslims to convey its Message and to kindle its light before those who are ignorant. If People of the Book try to prevent the Message from being conveyed and to prevent others from responding to it they are to be fought. If they then submit to the authority of the Muslims the *jizya* tax is imposed upon them in return for protection within the Muslim polity: *"Fight those of the people who were given the Book who do not believe in Allah and the Last Day and do not forbid what Allah and His Messenger have forbidden and do not take as their* deen *the* deen *of Truth, until they pay the* jizya *with their own hands in a state of complete abasement."* (9:29) Because the truth of such people is that: *"They desire to extinguish Allah's light with their mouths. But Allah refuses to do other than perfect His light."* (9:32) Their rabbis and monks had ways of usurping people's property which took much more from them and gave far less in return than the Muslims.

The whole history of the *jizya* tax should be thoroughly re-examined. The system ensured centuries of peaceful co-existence between the various communities involved and its abandonment led to the blood-bath we have witnessed in our own time. In any case nearly all the people who acknowledged Islam nearby quickly became Muslim, in large areas of the Middle East, North Africa, Khorasan and other places. The Muslim treasury suffered owing to the great numbers who entered into the *deen* of Islam, but this was and remains the goal. Muhammad was sent as a guide to Allah, not as a tax-collector.

✻✻✻✻✻

The *Hajj* which Abu Bakr made with the people in 9 AH was an excellent preparation for the great *Hajj* which followed in 10 AH when the Prophet himself led it. On this preparatory occasion the way was swept clean: *"O you who believe! Idolaters are unclean, so after this year they should not come near the Sacred Mosque."* (9:28) Idolatry was finally done away with and the idolaters heard that their contracts were abrogated and that dealings after that day would involve fair retaliation. Paganism was conclusively brought to an end.

The Jews had been finally disarmed in the attack on Khaybar in 7 AH and, although they continued to cultivate their fields and trade in Madina and elsewhere, the important thing was that their military power had been broken. They still had their individual liberty and under its auspices one of their merchants even took the armour of the Prophet, peace and blessings be upon him, as a pledge in a transaction with him.

Delegations of Christians used to come to Madina, as indeed they previously had to Makka, to listen to the new Revelation. The hearts of some of them were expanded to the truth and they became Muslims. The Prophet, may Allah bless him and grant him peace, argued calmly with others about Islam's rejection of the divinity of 'Isa while still honouring him. Islam did not sense any danger from the Christians of Yemen or elsewhere.

The Christian danger came from the Byzantine empire, which set up a sharp barrier against the penetration of Islam to the north of the Arabian Peninsula after it had spread in the middle and south. Islam was basically friendly to the Christians and the Prophet, peace and blessings be upon him, commanded those who were victimised to emigrate to Abyssinia to a Christian king in whose realm they would not be harmed.

However, in spite of this friendliness towards Christian peoples, Islam was unambiguous in its denial of the Trinity and the divinity of 'Isa and Jibril, making it clear that they were simply righteous servants of Allah. This was continually stressed by the Revelation both in Makka and in Madina. The followers of the Messiah were asked to rectify their creed and proclaim that Allah was One and take judgements about what was lawful and unlawful from Him. The final Qur'anic statement about this is in this *sura*: *"They have taken their rabbis and monks as lords besides Allah, and also the Messiah, son of Maryam. Yet they were commanded to worship only one God. There is no god but Him! Glory be to Him above and beyond any partners which they attribute to Him!"* (9:31) The Qur'an makes it quite clear that the legislation of bishops and rabbis which is based on their opinion and not on the commands of Allah is a form of *shirk*, attributing partners to Allah.

The Byzantine state decided to close its doors to Islam and mobilised its defences to ensure that Islam should not emerge from within the Peninsula, so the Muslims had no alternative but to fight them. The Truth must have a community to represent it and defend it and ensure that the laws and rites of Allah continue in existence: *"Let there be a community among you who call to the good, and enjoin the right, and forbid the wrong. They are the successful."* (3:104)

But the Byzantines rejected the right of the Muslims to call people to the Truth and sent their armies to fight the Muslims at Mu'ta, Tabuk and elsewhere. So the Prophet, peace and blessings be upon him, realised the necessity of breaking down the barrier which the Byzantines had erected to prevent the spread of Islam and mobilised all the Muslims to confront the Byzantine threat, knowing that the future of Islam would depend on victory over them.

When war was declared on the Byzantine empire, it was the foremost power in the world, having recently crushed the Persians, and stood alone at the summit of world power, so it is not surprising that the weak Muslims and Hypocrites should have trembled at the idea of fighting them. Indeed it must have seemed an impossible task for anyone who did not have absolute reliance on Allah and certainty of the truth of Allah's promise to make Islam victorious over every other *deen*. That is why *Surat Bara'a* now devotes itself to disgracing the Hypocrites and waverers and to mobilising the forces of the believers so that they will perform their daunting duty: *"O you who believe, what is wrong with you that when you are told, 'Go out and fight for the Cause of Allah,' you sink down heavily to the earth? Are you happier with the life of this world than the Next World? Yet the enjoyment of the life of this world compared to the Next World is very small. If you do not go out to fight, He will punish you with a painful punishment and replace you with another people. You will not harm Him in any way."* (9:38-39)

Now that the threat of paganism and treacherous Judaism had been resolved the one remaining internal danger for the Muslims was the Hypocrites. The Expedition of Tabuk or of Hardship, which forms the background to this *sura,* was the occasion on which Allah's anger finally erupted against the Hypocrites and exposed their secrets, described their plots, and cautioned the believers against ever being deceived by them. It shows how hypocrisy reveals itself and how it can be combated so that the harm of the Hypocrites is minimised. *Surat Bara'a* also mobilises the community so that it will be ready to carry forward the Message after the death of its leader. The fight with the Byzantines was the touchstone which revealed the true mettle of the Muslim community.

The people of true sincerity were victorious because their connection to Allah was stronger than their connection to anything else and the need for this is made eloquently clear. *"Say: 'If your fathers or your sons or your brothers or your wives or your tribe, or any wealth you have acquired, or any business you fear may slump, or any dwelling-places which please you, are dearer to you than Allah and His Messenger and performing* jihad *in His Way, then wait until Allah brings about His command. Allah does not guide wantonly deviant people.'"* (9:24)

The Hypocrites reveal their lack of faith immediately the call to arms arrives: *"Those who believe in Allah and the Last Day do not ask you to excuse them from performing* jihad *with their wealth and their selves. Allah knows the godfearing. Only those who do not believe in Allah and the Last Day ask you to excuse them. Their hearts are full of doubt and in their doubt they waver to and fro."* (9:44-45) They use any excuse to avoid having to go out and fight: *"Among them are there some who say, 'Give me permission to stay. Do not put temptation in my way.' Have they not fallen into that very temptation? Jahannam encircles the unbelievers."* (9:49)

The truth is that Hypocrites hate Islam and long for its defeat and smile secretly at these feelings. *"If good happens to you it galls them. If a mishap befalls you, they say, 'We prepared ourselves in advance,' and they turn away rejoicing. Say: 'Nothing can happen to us except what Allah has ordained for us. He is Our Master. It is in Allah that the believers should put their trust.'"* (9:50-51)

Hypocrisy is the cancer of society and a society in which Hypocrites play a dominant role cannot succeed: *"Do not let their wealth and children impress you. Allah merely wants to punish them by them during their life in this world, and for their souls to depart while they are still rejectors."* (9:55) The real desire of the hypocrite is for wealth and power in this world; they thought that Islam would prove a means for them to acquire it.

That desire for personal gain showed itself plainly when charity was being distributed: *"Among them there are some who find fault with you concerning the collected* sadaqa. *If they are given some of it they are pleased, but if they are not given any of it they are angry."* (9:58) Then they insulted the Prophet. *"Among them are some who insult the Prophet, saying he is but an ear. Say, 'An ear of good for you, believing Allah and believing the believers, and a mercy for those among you who believe.' As for those who insult the Messenger of Allah, they will have a painful punishment."* (9:61)

The Hypocrites do not show themselves all at once. They increase and decrease, but their party continues to shelter doubters, lurkers and those who hate Islam and its followers. The Qur'an calls attention to their threat in various *suras*, but *Surat at-Tawba* pursues them into their hideouts and bolt-holes until they have nowhere to hide.

Fighting the Byzantines was no easy matter and if the Prophet had been weak on this occasion the enemies of Islam would have been emboldened against him, the Ka'ba would have been destroyed, the Book effaced, and the worship of the One God derided. The idolaters and Hypocrites hoped that Muhammad and his army would not return from the north of the Peninsula and that the Byzantine state would swallow them up. But Allah's Decree is inexorable: *"It is He who sent His Messenger with the Guidance and the* Deen *of Truth to exalt it over every other* deen, *even though the idolaters hate it."* (9:33)

The agitation of the Hypocrites was apparent during the preparations for the expedition: *"When a* sura *is sent down saying: 'Believe in Allah and do* jihad *together with His Messenger,' those among them with wealth will ask you to excuse them, saying, 'Leave us to be with those who stay behind.' They are pleased to be with those who stay behind. A seal has been stamped on their hearts so they do not understand. But the Messenger and those who believe with him have performed* jihad *with their wealth and their selves. They are the people who will have the good things, and they are the successful."* (9:86-88)

But in fact it was much better that they did stay behind. *"If they had really desired to go out, they would have made proper preparations for it, but Allah was averse to their setting out and so He held them back and they were told: 'Stay behind with those who stay behind.' Had they gone out among you, the only thing they would have added to you is confusion. They would have scurried about among you seeking to cause conflict between you, and among you there are some who would have listened to them. Allah knows those who do wrong."* (9:46-47)

The time had now come to deal firmly with Hypocrisy so that its true nature would be revealed and its evil deactivated. At the time of Uhud Allah treated them gently: *"What assailed you on the day the two armies met was by Allah's permission, and so that He would know the believers, and so that He would know the Hypocrites. They were told, 'Come and fight in the Way of Allah or at least defend yourselves.' They said, 'If we knew how to fight, we would certainly follow you.' They were closer to unbelief that day than to belief."* (3:166-167) But the Hypocrites did not respond to the opportunity they had been given.

Now, with the death of the Prophet approaching, it was necessary that the community should be made absolutely aware of the danger represented by hypocrisy, both inwardly and outwardly, so that all possible steps could be taken to eliminate it: *"The men and women of the Hypocrites are as bad as one another. They command the wrong and forbid the right and keep their hands tightly closed. They have forgotten Allah, so He has forgotten them. The Hypocrites are the people who are wantonly deviant. Allah has promised the men and women of the Hypocrites and the rejector the Fire of Jahannam, to remain in it timelessly, forever. It will suffice them. Allah has cursed them. They will have everlasting punishment."* (9:67-68)

Allah orders the Prophet to treat them in the same way as unbelievers and exposes their inner reality: *"O Prophet! Fight your hardest against the unbelievers and Hypocrites and be harsh towards them. Their refuge is Jahannam. What an evil destination! They swear by Allah that they said nothing, but they definitely spoke the word of unbelief and rejected faith after their Islam. They planned something they did not achieve and the only reason they were vindictive was that Allah and His Messenger enriched them from His overflowing favour."* (9:73-74)

Some people asked for wealth to enable them to give *sadaqa* and do *jihad*, but when they were given what they asked for they were miserly and revealed their true hypocrisy. *"Among them there were some who contracted with Allah: 'If He gives us of His favour, we will definitely give* sadaqa *and be among the righteous.' But when He did give them of His favour, they were miserly with it and turned away in aversion. So He has punished them by putting hypocrisy in their hearts until the Day they meet Him."* (9:75-77)

Society must be defended against malignant hinderers who sit and accuse people who give large amounts of *sadaqa* of ostentation and mock and insult people who can only give a little: *"As for the people who find fault with the believers who freely give* sadaqa, *and with those who can find nothing to give but their own effort, and poke fun at them ..."* (9:79)

The brazenness of the Hypocrites reached such a pitch that they even set about constructing a mosque from which to orchestrate their attack on Islam and to act as a gathering-point for malcontents from inside and outside Madina: *"As for those who have set up a mosque causing harm and out of unbelief, to create division between the believers, and in readiness for those who previously made war on Allah and His Messenger, they will swear, 'We only desired the best.' But Allah bears witness that they are truly liars."* (9:107) But Allah alerted His Messenger to it and the Muslims destroyed this mosque which was rightly called 'the Mosque of Harm': *"Do not stand in it ever. A mosque founded on fear of Allah from the first day has a greater right for you to stand in it. In it there are men who love to purify themselves. Allah loves people who purify themselves."* (9:108)

Thus as the beginning of the *sura* was concerned with purifying society of the affliction of idolatry the latter part is concerned with purifying the Muslim community of the cancer of hypocrisy. The end of the *sura* is devoted to the true believers and it is made clear that the basis of their contract with their Lord is a ceaseless and ongoing struggle to establish His *deen* on the earth: a contract which was also made with the followers of the previous Prophets: *"Allah has bought from the believers their selves and their wealth so that they will have the Garden. They fight in the Way of Allah, and they kill and are killed. It is a promise binding on Him in the Torah, the* Injil *and the Qur'an – and who is truer to his contract than Allah? Rejoice then in the bargain you have made: that is the great victory."* (9:111)

The unbelievers will never stop attacking the Truth and so *jihad* will always be an essential element of the *deen.* Allah says: *"O you who believe! Fight those of the unbelievers who are near to you and let them find you implacable. Know that Allah is with the godfearing."* (9:123)

At the end of *Surat al-Fath* we find this description of the believers: *"Muhammad is the Messenger of Allah, and those who are with him are harsh with the rejectors, merciful to one another."* (48:29) The final *ayat* of *Surat at-Tawba* shows how this gentle compassion and fearless courage are perfectly combined in the Messenger of Allah, may Allah bless him and grant him peace. He is the Prophet of Battles and the Prophet of Mercy, implacable in the fight against the enemies of Allah but at the same time full of compassion for all of Allah's creatures. *"Truly a Messenger has now come to you from among yourselves. Your suffering is distressful to him. He is deeply concerned for you, gentle and merciful to the believers. Then if they turn away, say, 'Allah is enough for me. There is no god but Him. I have put my trust in Him. He is the Lord of the Mighty Throne.'"* (9:128-129)

Sura 10
Yunus: Jonah

Surat Yunus is a Makkan *sura* and its main theme resembles *Surat al-An'am* and *Surat al-Isra'*, which is seeking to recognise Allah by looking into the cosmos and reflecting on His creation. The language used in the Makkan *suras* is primarily directed towards pagan listeners and is aimed at stimulating the intellect and kindling dormant reflection in order to propel people towards their Lord and encourage their reliance on Him. It is therefore suited to addressing the secularists and materialists and other non-believers of today.

Idolaters of all kinds are dominated by material existence and are preoccupied by working for this world alone, and this sickness is particularly apparent in modern civilisation. The civilisation of Europe and America – and it is a civilisation which has now been disseminated throughout the world – has no concern with Allah or our inevitable meeting Him.

The Qur'an affirms that the life we are living is a prelude to another existence in which we will be resurrected from the dead and that the people who recognise Allah here will be the ones who recognise Him there. It could also be said that there is only one existence, whose first part we experience here, where its keynote is personal responsibility and effort, and whose last part we will experience as the Judgement and Repayment of the first part. Contem-porary civilisation rejects this understanding.

In this life it is our duty to glorify Allah's praise and thank Him for the blessings He has given us and carry out the obligations He has imposed on us; in the Next Life glorification, praise and performance of obligations will be natural for us and unconnected to responsibility or effort: *"But as for those who believe and do right*

127

actions, their Lord will guide them by their belief. Rivers will flow under them in Gardens of Delight. Their cry there is: 'Glory be to You, O Allah!' Their greeting there is: 'Peace!' The end of their cry is: 'Praise belongs to Allah, the Lord of all the worlds!'" (10:9-10) All who are familiar with Allah here will be familiar with Him there and happy in His presence.

But as for those who deny Him here, what can they expect there? Preoccupation with the immediate present and complete disregard for what is beyond it is the custom of western civilisation and the *ayats* make the destiny of such people very clear: *"As for those who do not expect to meet Us and are content with the life of this world and at rest in it, and those who are unmindful of Our Signs, the refuge of such people is the Fire because of what they earned."* (10:7-8)

Materialist logic finds the Noble Qur'an and indeed all Revelation incomprehensible; that is because it is based on material existence and does not look towards Heaven at all except perhaps when reflecting on how to reach the planets! This is greatly deluded disbelief!

Surat Yunus begins by rejecting the materialist position: *"Those are the signs of the Wise Book. Do people find it so extraordinary that We should reveal to a man among them: 'Give warning to mankind and give good news to those who believe that they are on a sure footing with their Lord'? The rejectors say, 'This is downright magic!'"* (10:1-2) Belief is simple spontaneous acceptance of the way things are. Its springs are only muddied by ignorant philosophers and opinionated fools.

In this *sura* we see that there is a strong link between belief and righteousness. Belief must be accompanied by righteous actions. The Almighty says: *"That He may repay with justice those who believed and did right actions,"* (10:4) and *"But as for those who believe and do right actions, their Lord will guide them by their belief."* (10:9)

A little later Allah says: *"Those who do good will have the best and more!"* (10:26) The 'best' is the aggregate of clear belief and righteous action when they come together in witnessing and watchful obedience. It is made clear that the friends of Allah are those who possess both certainty and are actively godfearing: *"Yes, indeed! The friends of Allah will feel no fear and will know no sorrow: those who believe and are godfearing,"* (10:62-63)

Reflect on what the Prophet, may Allah bless him and grant him peace, is made to say: *"I fear, were I to disobey my Lord, the punishment of a Dreadful Day."* (10:15) The Almighty says: *"But as for those who have earned bad actions - a bad action will be repaid with one like it. Debasement will darken them. They will have no one to protect them from Allah,"* (10:27) and He says: *"Allah does not uphold the actions of corrupters."* (10:81)

The Islamic nation seeks neither to dishonour other nations nor to be accommodating to them. Bygone nations reaped what they sowed, so the Muslims are warned that they too are equally subject to the same process: *"We destroyed generations before you when they did wrong. Their Messengers brought them the clear Signs, but they would not believe. That is how We repay the evil-doers. Then We appointed you after them to be successors in the earth so We might observe how you would act."* (10:13-14)

The *sura* continues to stress this right to its very end: *"Say: 'O mankind! The truth has come to you from your Lord. Anyone who is guided is guided only to his own benefit. Anyone who is misguided is misguided only to his own detriment. I have not been set over you as a guardian.' Follow what has been revealed to you and be steadfast until Allah gives judgement."* (10:108-109)

The Prophet's task is to establish justice and show the Truth to be true and the false to be false. The *sura* describes a community which is neither proud nor profligate; a community which acknowledges its Lord and is acknowledged by Him, travelling along the Path He has laid down and confident of meeting Him; a community which avoids the behaviour of the Pharaohs, who are alluded to, and is not deluded by wealth or power; a community which rather fights tyranny and oppression, saying as Musa said when he was calling on his Lord: *"Our Lord, obliterate their wealth and harden their hearts so that they do not believe until they see the painful punishment."* (10:88)

If anyone were to ask us to describe the Lord who has obliged us to worship Him and to whom we shall return after our lives in this world end, the answer is to be found in *Surat Yunus*: *"Your Lord is Allah who created the heavens and the earth in seven days and then established Himself firmly on the Throne. He directs the affair. No one can intercede except with His permission. That is Allah your Lord, so worship Him. Will you not then remember?"* (10:3)

This general answer requires further elaboration which is provided by other *ayats* in the *sura*. There are billions of consuming mouths and digesting bellies. Who do you think provides for all their needs? Who made eyes to see and ears to hear? Who put all these intricate functions together in a single entity. How great is the power which fashioned all these billions of beings! *"Say: 'Who provides for you out of heaven and earth? Who has control over hearing and sight? Who brings forth the living from the dead and the dead from the living? Who directs the affair?' They will say, 'Allah.' So say, 'Will you not then be godfearing?'"* (10:31)

A farmer places one seed in the soil and a thousand seeds come from it. Who transforms foul tasting and malodorous mud into wheat or rice or barley which is sweet to eat and smell? Who transforms organic waste into flowers which display all the colours of the rainbow and from which so many sweet perfumes proliferate? *"That is Allah, your Lord, the Truth, and what is there after truth except misguidance? So how have you been distracted?"* (10:32)

Belief in Allah is an uncomplicated and natural thing. We must reflect on the attributes of Allah and not try to uncover His essence. We must know that Allah settled on His Throne in an appropriate manner without asking how He did so. We should reflect on His wise direction of the affairs of the universe which He created without partner or helper. The Creator has no need of the help of His creatures nor does the All-Powerful seek the help of the powerless. All mankind must recognise this and not direct their prayers to anyone except Allah. The Noble Qur'an censures the ignorant who do that: *"They worship, instead of Allah, what can neither harm nor benefit them. They say, 'These are our intercessors with Allah.' Say: 'Would you inform Allah of something about which He does not know either in the heavens or in the earth?' May He be glorified and exalted above the partners they attribute to Him!"* (10:18)

When people's faith is sound their connection to Allah is sound and when they reach the timeless realm of everlasting life their time in this world will be transformed into pleasant memories. Dozens of years in the life of individuals and dozens of centuries in the history of nations will be transformed into a few moments: *"On the day He gathers them together – when it will seem if they had tarried no more than an hour of a single day – they will recognise one another."* (10:45)

However, when the punishment for wrong-doing is long in coming, some people think that the delay means cancellation and not just deferment: *"If Allah were to hasten evil forpeople the way they try to hasten good, their term would already have expired for them. We abandon those who do not expect to meet Us to wander blindly in their overweening insolence."* (10:11)

This warning should be taken together with Allah's words in *Surat al-Kahf*: *"Your Lord is the Ever-Forgiving, the Possessor of Mercy. If He had taken them to task for what they have earned, He would have hastened the punishment to them. Instead, they have a promised appointment and they will find no refuge from it."* (18:58)

But in this *sura* He asks the wrongdoers why they were so anxious to hasten it, and whether it would not in fact be better to repent before they are punished and to take advantage of the deferment they have been granted: *"Say: 'Tell me, have you considered? If His punishment comes upon you by night or by day, what part of it will the evil-doers then try to hasten on?' And then when it actually comes about... 'Now do you believe in it? This is what you were trying to hasten on!'"* (10:50-51)

No one is able to escape the punishment of Allah on the Day when it comes in accordance with His decreed promise. How could they when all things belong to Allah? *"Yes indeed! Everything in the heavens and the earth belongs to Allah. Yes indeed! Allah's promise is true. However, most of them do not know."* (10:55) And the Almighty also says a little later on: *"Yes, indeed! Everyone in the heavens and everyone in the earth belongs to*

Allah. Those who call on other than Allah are not really following their partner-gods. They are only following conjecture. They are only guessing." (10:66)

All existence, animate and inanimate, is entirely subservient to Allah and His property, so where can a man flee with his sin? Who will give him shelter? *"They will ask you to tell them if this is true. Say: 'Yes indeed, by my Lord, certainly it is true and you can do nothing to prevent it.'"* (10:53)

Why do people find it extraordinary that the All-Merciful has chosen the Prophet to receive Revelation to and to convey His Message? Envy is the reason given: *"Has the Reminder been sent down to him out of all of us?"* (38:8) Another reason for people's anger is the Prophet's condemnation of paganism and its traditions. People who have inherited a system of multiple gods automatically reject monotheism, and the inheritors of a materialist philosophy who worship the here and now automatically reject any discussion of a life to come.

Surat Yunus is one of the *suras* which raises the banner of Allah's Unity and gives detailed evidence of Allah's existence and explains how the created universe indicates the immensity of Allah: *"It is He who appointed the sun to give radiance, and the moon to give light, assigning it phases so you might know the number of years and the reckoning of time. Allah did not create these things except with truth. He makes the signs plain for people who know."* (10:5)

The Arabs rejected the Revelation and their opposition to the Qur'an is mentioned three times in this *sura*. The first is when Allah says: *"When Our clear Signs are recited to them, those who do not expect to meet Us say, 'Bring a Qur'an other than this one or change it.'"* (10:15) In other words, "Say something else in which you praise our gods and confirm our traditions and circumstances!"

Allah tells the Prophet how to reply to their demand: "Say: *"It is not for me to change it of my own accord. I follow nothing except what is revealed to me."* (10:15) He had reached the age of forty without receiving any revelation or *deen* when suddenly the command of his Lord came and all he could do was convey it:

"Say: 'If Allah had willed, I would not have recited it to you nor would He have made it known to you. I lived among you for many years before it came. Will you not then use your understanding?'" (10:16)

The second time is when the Qur'an says: *"This Qur'an could never have been devised by anyone besides Allah. Indeed, it is confirmation of that which came before it and an elucidation of the Book which contains no doubt from the Lord of the worlds."* (10:37) After reading the Qur'an, an objective reader will be aware that Muhammad could not have invented a single word of it and that the Divine Voice permeates it as water permeates a growing plant. If the Qur'an was the words of a human being there would be nothing to stop people coming up with the same thing: *"Do they say, 'He has devised it'? Say: 'Then produce a sura like it and call on anyone you can besides Allah if you speak the truth.'"* (10:38)

They are told to seek the assistance of any human being or jinn who has a particular capacity for eloquence in composing a book like it or a similar *sura.* Centuries have passed since this challenge was made and no one has brought forward anything! *"No, the fact is that they have denied that which their knowledge does not embrace and the meaning of which has not yet reached them."* (10:39) They are even ignorant of the fact that their punishment has been deferred which might have made them repent.

No book has ever presented its thesis so fairly as this Book does. There is no disparagement and no compulsion. People of open feelings whose hearts are devoted to the Truth must respond to it. And as for others, what can you do with deaf people whose ears are so blocked by prejudice that they cannot hear or understand? Or blind people whose eyes are so impervious to light that they cannot see anything? *"Among them there are some who listen to you. But can you make the deaf hear, if they do not understand? Among them there are some who look at you. But can you guide the blind, if they do not see?"* (10:42)

The third time is when Allah says about the Qur'an: *"O mankind! An admonition has come to you from your Lord and also healing for what is in the hearts, and guidance and mercy for the believers."* (10:57) The Qur'an is the best teacher. It restrains vices, protects against uncertainty and doubt, gives rest from confusion, and gives access to both spiritual and material wealth.

This is why it says after that: *"Say: 'It is in the favour of Allah and His mercy, that they should rejoice. It is better than what people accumulate.'"* (10:58) If a man is given the Qur'an and then someone else thinks that he has been given better than it, he is labouring under a severe delusion.

The Qur'an covers all areas of life and undermined every objection which the unbelievers offered. The Prophet continued to recite the Qur'an to them in every kind of situation, and Allah informed His Prophet that all of this is witnessed and recorded. *"You do not engage in any matter or recite any of the Qur'an or do any action without Our witnessing you while you are engrossed in it. Not even the tiniest speck eludes your Lord, either in the earth or in heaven. Nor is there anything smaller than that, or larger, which is not in a Clear Book."* (10:61)

The end of the *sura* reaffirms what was said at the beginning about holding to the Revelation and relying on it. Allah says to the Messenger: *"Follow what has been revealed to you and be steadfast until Allah gives judgement. He is the Best of Judges."* (10:109)

The dispute between Muslims and others concerning the Qur'an is intense and we are certain that it is the Clear Truth. Some expressions are used whose true meaning is only understood by people with great knowledge of Arabic rhetoric. For instance Allah says to His Prophet: *"If you are in any doubt about what We have revealed to you, then ask those who were reciting the Book before you..."* (10:94) This must be taken in the context of the statement of the Prophet, "I do not doubt or question," and certainly does not refer to any doctrinal differences between Islam and its predecessors.

Belief in Allah's Unity is the bedrock of Islam and is not open to question or debate. This applies to the insinuations of the Jews mentioned in the *sura,* which they directed at the Prophets and Allah Almighty. These are not an occasion for doubt, nor is any question about them admissible: *"The Truth has come to you from your Lord, so on no account be among the doubters. And on no account be among those who deny Allah's Signs and so become losers. Those against whom the Words of your Lord are realised will not believe, even if every Sign were to come to them, until they see the painful punishment."* (10:94-97) The Reality of Allah's existence is absolutely independent of the deficiencies and short-comings of the limited human intellect.

✳✳✳✳✳

Human beings are continually susceptible to all kinds of crises in which they are aware of pain and incapacity; they are quick to turn to Allah in their search for a way out, begging Him to release them from their distress. But does the removal of the affliction leave us with the same intensity of faith we had in the time of our difficulty or does our ardour falter and become forgotten? Allah reminds us of this human tendency: *"When harm touches man, he calls on Us, lying on his side or sitting down or standing up. Then when We remove the harm from him, he carries on as if he had never called on Us when harm touched him. Thus We make what they have done seem good to the profligate."* (10:12)

This kind of behaviour shows lack of true understanding. We should remember the One who rescued us from our hardship and cling to Him in good times just as we did in bad for we are totally dependent on Him all the time.

Surat Yunus goes into this matter again in graphic detail: *"It is He who conveys you on both land and sea, so that when some of you are on a boat, running before a fair wind, rejoicing at it, and then a violent squall comes upon them and the waves come at them from every side and they realise there is no way of escape, they call on Allah, making their* deen *sincerely His: 'If You rescue us from this, we will truly be among the thankful.' But then, when He does rescue them, they become immoral in the earth without any right. O mankind! Your immorality is only against yourselves. There is the enjoyment of the life of this world and then you will return to Us and We will inform you as to what you did."* (10:22-23)

When they are drowning and disaster surrounds them on every side, people's hopes are cut off from everything except Allah. They see no place of refuge except in Him. They see no possibility of help except from Him. So why do we forget the Hand that helped us when we are safe again? Why do people revert to heedlessness and ingratitude? It is blatant fickleness and foolish short-sightedness!

People immersed in this world's delights to the exclusion of all else deserve what happens to them. They are struck down at the peak of their intoxicated absorption: *"The likeness of the life of this world is that of water which We send down from the sky and which then mingles with the plants of the earth, providing food for both people and animals. Then, when the earth is at its loveliest and takes on its fairest guise and its people think they have it in their grasp, Our command comes upon it by night or day and We reduce it to dried-out stubble, as if it had not been flourishing only the day before! Thus do We make Our Signs plain for people who reflect."* (10:24)

People have the right to turn to Allah when harm touches them; but Allah's right over them is that they should thank Him after their rescue, that their connection to Him should remain constant in times of ease, and that they should never think themselves independent of Him. The metaphor of cultivated land used in the *ayat* embraces all kinds of human projects and concerns. It is when people are completely caught up in the illusion of their permanence that the blow falls and they reap what they have sown.

Before the end of the *sura* Allah sums up all of these lessons in a passage overflowing with good counsel: *"Say: 'O mankind! If you are in any doubt about my* deen, *I do not worship those when you worship besides Allah. Instead I worship Allah who will take you back to Him, and I am commanded to be one of the believers. Turn your face towards the* deen *in pure natural belief, and on no account be one of the idolaters. Do not call on something other than Allah which can neither benefit nor harm you. If you do, you will then be one of the wrongdoers. If Allah afflicts you with harm, none can remove it except Him. If He desires good for you, none can avert His favour. He bestows it on any of His slaves He wills.*

He is Ever Forgiving, Most Merciful.'" (10:104-107)

This is the essence of Islam: to link yourself to Allah alone and to expect nothing from anyone besides Him. Attach your desire and fear to Him alone and deal with all people on this basis.

✳✳✳✳✳

In this *sura* Allah also mentions some of the stories of the earlier peoples, including the story of Yunus and his people which is mentioned very briefly indeed even though the *sura* takes its name from it. It may be that the reason for this is that it is an indication that the people of Makka would have the same fortunate fate as that which befell the people of Yunus.

Although the people of Makka put up intense resistance to Islam when it first appeared and led the battle against it for almost twenty years, they later entered Islam and became its sincere supporters and bore its banner. This corresponds to what happened with the people of Yunus: *"Why has there never been a city that believed whose belief then brought it benefit, except for the people of Yunus? When they had faith We removed from them the punishment of disgrace in the life of this world and We let them have enjoyment for a time."* (10:98)

The different stories deal with circumstances similar to those which were affecting the Prophet, peace and blessings be upon him, so that he might learn useful lessons from them and find appropriate replies to answer the unbelievers of his own time. For instance Nuh spent nine hundred and fifty years calling his people to the truth: *"Recite to them the story of Nuh when he said to his people, 'O my people! If my standing here and reminding you of the Signs of Allah has become too much for you to bear, know that I have put my trust in Allah. So decide, you and your gods, on your future and then it will no longer be a problem for you and you should do with me whatever you decide, granting me no reprieve. If you turn your backs, I have not asked you for any reward. My reward is only with Allah. I am commanded to be one of the Muslims.'"* (10:71-72) So the Prophet was able gain encouragement from what had happened with Nuh by realising that he had had to face even more obstinate resistance from his people.

After that Allah mentions other Messengers and then goes on to discuss the behaviour of Pharaoh and his people and then how the tribe of Israel responded to their guidance. The Pharaohs were destroyed because they disregarded the Truth and despised their people. The tribe of Israel trafficked with the Revelation, were insolent to Allah, and did not use the knowledge they were given. The followers of Muhammad should avoid these pitfalls and respond to his Message with devotion and direct themselves to Allah with sincerity.

Sura 11
Hud

Surat Hud begins, as many *suras* do, by speaking about the Noble Qur'an and then immediately makes very clear the intimate connection between the Revelation and the one who is bringing it: *"A Book whose verses are perfectly constructed and then made plain, coming directly from One who is All-Wise, All-Aware. 'Do not worship anyone but Allah! I am a warner and bringer of good news for you from Him. Ask your Lord for forgiveness and then turn in repentance to Him. He will let you enjoy a good life until a specified time, and will grant His favour to all who merit it. But if you turn your backs, I fear for you the punishment of a Mighty Day. You will return to Allah. He has power over everything.'"* (11:1-4)

The Qur'an is the cornerstone of Islam and its great proof and the secret of its immortality. The Messenger was given the task both of being the recipient of the Qur'an and also of conveying it to all mankind and it is clear that he found that to be a crushing burden. Abu Bakr once asked the Messenger of Allah, may Allah bless him and grant him peace, what had given him his white hairs. He replied, *"Hud* and its sisters turned my hair white."

So the question arises as to what it is about *Surat Hud* in particular that made it exceptionally burdensome. Some people have said that it is because it deals largely with the destruction of past nations who rejected Divine Guidance; but Allah recounts these things to His Prophet in other *suras*, *Surat al-A'raf* for instance, without it having had this effect.

Another suggested reason is that it was the failure of people to acknowledge the Messenger and their turning away from his Message which made his hair go white. That is unlikely. The

Messenger is too great to be shaken by the recalcitrance of the ignorant!

However, there is something in this *sura,* foreshadowed in the first two *ayats* quoted above, which is not to be found so much in other *suras,* and that is the great number of directives which touch the person of the Messenger himself and the many times when he is addressed directly in the second person singular, all of which served to make him acutely aware of his personal responsibility for conveying the Message.

This starts when Allah says: *"Perhaps you are tempted to leave out part of what has been revealed to you and your heart is constricted because they say, 'Why has treasure not been sent down to him or an angel not accompanied him?' You are only a warner and Allah is Guardian over all things."* (11:12) In this *ayat* alone the pronoun 'you' is repeated three times in a row and once separately. This happens dozens of times in the *sura,* the last example being in the final *ayat* of the *sura: "The Unseen of the heavens and the earth belongs to Allah and the entire affair will be returned to Him. So worship Him and put your trust in Him. Your Lord is not heedless of anything you do."* (11:123)

After the story of Nuh and his people and their destruction in the Flood, this *ayat* comes to address the Noble Messenger: *"That is some information from the Unseen which We reveal to you. Neither you nor your people knew it before this time. So be steadfast. The best end result is for the godfearing."* (11:49) The second person singular is once more used three times without any intervening pronoun, all directed to the Prophet, may Allah bless him and grant him peace, and adding at the end of them the command to be steadfast and *"The best end result is for the godfearing."*

In the course of the story itself, the flow of the narrative is interrupted by this *ayat: "Or do they say, 'He has fabricated it'? Say: 'If I have fabricated it, my crime is against myself but I am innocent of the crimes which you commit.'"* (11:35) Even though the Prophet is, of course, far removed from what is imputed to him nevertheless he is brought firmly into the picture and reminded of his responsibility.

The Noble Qur'an then recounts the story the people of 'Ad and how they attacked Hud and injured him. Then the Lord of the worlds says: *"When Our command came, We rescued Hud and those who believed with him by a mercy from Us. We rescued them from a harsh punishment."* (11:58) Then the Messenger of Allah himself is addressed: *"That was 'Ad. They refuted the Signs of their Lord and disobeyed His Messengers and followed the command of every obdurate tyrant."* (11:59)

The same thing happens in the subsequent account of Thamud. The Messenger of Allah, may Allah bless him and grant him peace, is addressed at the end of the story: *"Then when Our command came, We rescued Salih and those who believed with him from the disgrace of that day, by a mercy from Us. Your Lord is the All-Strong, the Almighty."* (11:66)

After the cities of the people of Lut were destroyed Allah says to His Prophet: *"When Our command came, We turned their cities upside down and rained down on them stones of hard baked clay, piled on top of one another in layers, each one earmarked by your Lord. They are never far from the wrongdoers."* (11:82-83) This *ayat* makes it clear that Allah's power to punish is not confined to the past and is a very real possibility for those who continue in the path of error without repenting.

Then after talking of the destruction of Madyan and the Pharaohs, Allah says to His Prophet: *"That is some of the news of the cities which We relate to you. Some of them are still standing, while others are now just stubble."* (11:100) This ties together all the accounts of the past communities which have made up the bulk of the *sura* and informs the Prophet that the whole matter has been addressed directly to him.

The use of the second person singular pronoun now increases exponentially so that in the final twenty-two *ayats* of the *sura* it occurs eighteen times, and that does not include the many accompanying commands. How could this have failed to have an overwhelming effect on the heart of the Message-bearer? Allah says: *"We did not wrong them; rather they wronged themselves. Their gods they called upon besides Allah did not avail them in any way when Allah's command came upon them. They increased them only*

141

in ruination. Such is the seizing of your Lord when He seizes the cities which do wrong. His seizing is painful, violent." (11:101-102)

The second person pronoun is again twice connected to 'Lord' when the repayment of the Rising is mentioned: *"As for those who are wretched, they will be in the Fire, where they will sigh and moan, remaining in it timelessly, forever, as long as the heavens and earth endure, except as your Lord wills. Your Lord does whatever He wills."* (11:106-107) It is mentioned a third time when the fortunate are mentioned: *"As for those who are glad, they will be in the Garden, remaining in it timelessly, forever, as long as the heavens and earth endure, except as your Lord wills, an uninterrupted gift."* (11:108)

Then Allah addresses the Prophet directly: *"So do not be in any doubt about what these people worship..."* (11:109) He reminds him of His prior decision to defer the repayment of all people until a promised Day: *"If it were not for a word which preceded from your Lord, it would already have been decided between them."* (11:110) So until this Day of Gathering occurs, the Message-bearer must openly proclaim what he has been ordered to convey and endure the pains of trials and long waiting.

Those who are with him must take him as a model in this prolonged steadfastness: *"Go straight as you have been commanded, and those who turn with you to Allah,"* (11:112) and *"Establish the prayer at both ends of the day and in the first part of the night. Good actions eradicate bad actions. This is a reminder for people who remember."* (11:114)

The use of the second person pronoun is reiterated even more as the *sura* approaches its end: *"If your Lord had willed, He would have made one nation of mankind but they persist in their differences, except for those your Lord has mercy on. That is the reason He created them, so the word of your Lord would be fulfilled: 'I will fill up Jahannam with the jinn and mankind all together.' We have told you all this news of the Messengers so that We may make your heart firm by means of it. The truth has come to you in this, and an admonishment and reminder to the believers."* (11:117-119)

Is this not a sufficient explanation of the words of the Noble Messenger, "*Hud* and her sisters turned my hair white"?

✻✻✻✻✻

Momentary acts of disobedience do not destroy a man's future hopes. They may be followed by a remorse which effaces the effects of any lingering gratification. Indeed they may well be the 'seed' which protects a person from falling into similar actions in the future and so ultimately be beneficial! The acts of disobedience which destroy individuals and nations are those which abide in the soul without being attended to, remaining there until they become an integral part of it.

When that happens, those actions become a part of society at large. They may even be transmuted into traditions or laws so that avoiding them seems wrong and forbidding them becomes a crime! Reflect on what Lut's people said to him: *"The only answer of his people was to say, 'Expel them from your city! They are a people who keep themselves pure!'"* (7:82) Purification had become something disapproved of and depravity was the accepted norm.

A corrupt society is one in which this phenomenon has occurred and in contemporary society there are all too many examples of it. The stories of past peoples occur throughout the Qur'an, and each of them contains an example of a particular social evil which has become generally accepted in it and shows how this leads to the destruction of the society concerned. In some *suras* several of these stories are grouped together - we already had an example of this in *Surat al-A'raf* - but *Sura Hud* is almost totally devoted to it.

Each time the stories are repeated different aspects are brought out and so in order to obtain a complete picture of the particular people concerned it is necessary to gather together all the various versions in one place, which requires considerable knowledge. However, *Surat Hud* contains the salient points of all the stories and some details, particularly with regard to the story of Nuh, which do not occur anywhere else.

There is a long account of the interaction between Nuh and his people in which it is clear that their besetting sin lay in their arrogant assertion that they had no need of guidance. They had invested their faith in the outward appearance of this world and declared themselves independent of Allah.

This is epitomised when Nuh's own son thinks that the mountain will give him greater protection than the Ark when his father implores him to come on board: *"It ran, carrying them in the midst of mountainous waves, and Nuh called out to his son, who had kept himself apart, 'My son! Come on board with us. Do not be with the unbelievers!' He said, 'I will go to a mountain for refuge. It will protect me from the water.' He said, 'There is no protection from Allah's command today except for him on whom He has mercy.' And the waves swept in between them and he was one of the drowned."*

This leads to the moving account of Nuh's plea to his Lord on behalf of his drowned son and brings home to us the implacable difference between belief and disbelief: *"Nuh called out to his Lord and said, 'My Lord, my son is one of my family and Your promise is surely the Truth and You are the justest of judges.' He said, 'Nuh, he is definitely not of your family. He is someone whose action is not righteous. So do not ask Me for something about which you have no knowledge. I admonish you lest you should be one of the ignorant.'"* (11:46-47)

This *ayat* has led some people to foolish and unacceptable speculation; but what is certain is that by his action in rejecting his father's offer to save him the flood Nuh's son rejected his relationship with him, and by asking for Allah's succour for him Nuh himself is in a way questioning the Divine Decree.

However Nuh immediately responds to Allah's admonishment: *"He said, 'My Lord, I seek refuge with You from asking You for anything about which I have no knowledge. If You do not forgive me and have mercy on me, I will be among the lost.' It was said, 'O Nuh! Descend with peace from Us and with blessings on you and the nations which shall issue from those who are with you."* (11:47-48) Throughout the succession of different prophethoods from the time of Nuh and Ibrahim to Musa, 'Isa and Muhammad, it is always made clear that the relationships created by the *deen* supersede blood relationships, and that love and hate for the sake of Allah is the basis of mutual connection or severance.

The next nation to be discussed are the people of Hud after whom the *sura* is named. Their besetting fault was rejection of their Prophet. They were not going to change their way of life for anything Hud said to them and preferred without any evidence to declare him insane. When Hud found himself alone before a people who were stubbornly resistant, he said: *"I have put my trust in Allah, my Lord and your Lord. There is no creature He does not grasp by the forelock. My Lord is on a straight path."* (11:56)

Divine punishment was not long in coming and only Hud and those with him escaped: *"When Our command came, We rescued Hud and those who believed with him by a mercy from Us. We rescued them from a harsh punishment."* (11:58) The gloomy tale ends with this verdict: *"That was 'Ad. They refuted the Signs of their Lord and disobeyed His Messengers and followed the command of every obdurate tyrant. They were pursued by a curse in this world and on the Day of Rising. Yes indeed! 'Ad rejected their Lord, so away with 'Ad, the people of Hud!"* (11:59-60)

When the word of Allah is realised against a people they become weaker than dust, no matter how strong and established they appear to be. Their strength does not help them in any way against Him in Whose hand is the dominion of the heavens and earth.

After 'Ad and their Prophet Hud we hear about Thamud and their Prophet Salih. Theirs was an arrogant society in which a rigid class structure had developed. As is frequently the case the majority of those who responded to the Prophetic call were from the lower echelons of society and for this reason the upper classes rejected Salih's teaching, as we learn in *Surat al-A'raf*: *"The nobles, among those of his people who were arrogant, said to those who were oppressed - those among them who believed, 'Do you know that Salih has been sent from his Lord?' They said, 'We believe in that with which he has been sent.' Those who were arrogant said, 'We reject Him in whom you believe.'"* (7:75-76)

This kind of bigotry can take many forms of which the racism and fanatic nationalism so prevalent in today's world are just two manifestations. Western assumption of superiority is another. Allah did not create people to make these empty claims. That is why He says in the story of Thamud: *"To Thamud [We sent] their brother Salih. He said, 'O my people! Worship Allah! You have no god but Him. He brought you into being from the earth and made you its inhabitants. So ask His forgiveness and then turn in repentance to Him. My Lord is Close, Quick to Respond.'"* (11:61) This address to Thamud is equally applicable to all the human beings whom Allah has brought into being on the earth.

But Thamud's bigotry blinded them to Allah's guidance when it came to them and their tyranny and arrogance caused them to reject and desecrate the clear sign Allah gave them in the form of the She-Camel and ensured the implacable inevitability of their destruction: *"Then when Our command came, We rescued Salih and those who believed with him, from the disgrace of that day, by a mercy from Us. Your Lord is the All-Strong, the Almighty. The Great Shout seized hold of those who did wrong and morning found them lying flattened in their homes. It was as if they had never lived there at all. Yes indeed! Thamud rejected their Lord. So away with Thamud!"* (11:66-68)

The next people to be examined are the community of the Prophet Lut who was the nephew of the Prophet Ibrahim. Their sexual deviation is, of course, notorious but what is extraordinary is the extent of its acceptance and even its legal endorsement in the world today when the so-called 'gay movement' has political influence of unprecedented magnitude. Far from being the abominated outrage it has always been known to be, homosexuality has become an accepted norm. How far human society has strayed from that Divine Guidance which is its only hope for sound survival!

The people of Lut were destroyed for their sexual deviance and Allah makes it clear that such behaviour brings Allah's punishment very near to anyone who indulges in it: *"When Our command came, We turned their cities upside down and rained down on them stones of hard baked clay, piled on top of one another in layers, each one earmarked by your Lord. They are never far from the wrongdoers."* (11:81-82)

146

After them come the people of Madyan who combined political and economic corruption. In *Surat al-A'raf* the emphasis was more on their political corruption in *Hud*; their economic deviance is more prominently exposed. In the former *sura* Allah says to them: *"Do not lie in wait on every pathway, threatening people, barring those who believe from the way of Allah, desiring to make it crooked. Remember when you were few and He increased you in number. See the end result of the corrupters!"* (7:86) In *Surat Hud*, on the other hand, the emphasis is clearly placed on their economic malpractice: *"And to Madyan [We sent] their brother Shu'ayb. He said, 'O my people! Worship Allah. You have no god other than Him. Do not give short measure and short weight. I see you prospering and I fear for you the punishment of an all-encompassing day. O my people! Give full measure and full weight with justice; do not diminish people's goods; and do not go about the earth corrupting it."* (11:84-85)

The people of Madyan rejected their Prophet's warning with a combination of mockery and scorn: *"They said, 'Shu'ayb, do your prayers instruct you that we should abandon what our fathers worshipped or stop doing whatever we want to with our wealth? You are clearly the forbearing, the rightly-guided!"* (11:87) They were people whose only measure was economic power: *"We see you as weak among us. Were it not for your clan, we would have stoned you. You are not esteemed by us!"* (11:91) But just as with every other nation who denied the guidance Allah sent to them, their destruction was ensured within a very short time: *"Away with Madyan, just as it was away with Thamud!"* (11:95)

The final people in the Qur'anic sequence of earlier peoples is the Egyptians of the Pharaohs at the time of the Prophet Musa who are only mentioned very briefly in this *sura*, which is significant because in a way they are different from the previous peoples in that with them we enter the era of recorded history. Their story is of course given in much detail in various other places throughout the Revelation and has great relevance to the time in which we live.

What must be obvious to all who have read this is that every single one of the fatal flaws which caused the destruction of the ancient peoples is now the flagrant practice of large portions of the human race. It can only be the scattered presence of true believers throughout the world that prevents the same fate occurring to the people of our time: *"We have told to you all this news of the Messengers so that We may make your heart firm by means of it. The truth has come to you in this, and an admonishment and reminder to the believers."* (11:120)

Surat Hud details the circumstances of past nations and their Messengers so that the Final Messenger may know that there is nothing new in Quraysh's denial of him. The struggle between truth and falsehood is ancient and unending but the final result always favours the believers and exalts the godfearing.

✵✵✵✵✵

The stories of the past nations which make up the bulk of *Sura Hud* are sandwiched between two sections speaking directly to the people to whom the Qur'an is addressed, the former outlining the general premises on which human success and failure are based and the latter detailing the consequences of going the same way as those before and showing the way to avoid their fate. Truly the Qur'an is as Allah has described it in the first verse of the *sura*: *"A Book whose verses are perfectly constructed and then made plain, coming directly from One who is Wise, Aware."* (11:1)

The Message has lost none of its urgent relevance and is as desperately needed by mankind today as it was 1400 years ago: *"'Do not worship anyone but Allah! I am a warner and bringer of good news for you from Him. Ask your Lord for forgiveness and then turn in repentance to Him. He will let you enjoy a good life until a specified time, and will give His favour to all who merit it. But if you turn your backs, I fear for you the punishment of a Mighty Day. You will return to Allah. He has power over everything.'"* (11:2-4)

Allah calls attention to the fact that not only is the origination of this universe out of nothing a marvel, but the fact that He continues to maintain it without neglecting a single atom of it for an instant is still more extraordinary. The existence of man and the

148

universe in which he lives is not without purpose. It provides a testing ground for our conduct. Allah says of this: *"It is He who created the heavens and the earth in six days – when His Throne was on the water – in order to test which of you is best in action."* (11:7)

After this brief discussion, Allah summarises basic human nature: *"If We let man taste mercy from Us, and then take it away from him, he is despairing, ungrateful; but if We let him taste blessings after hardship has afflicted him, he says, 'My troubles have gone away,' and he is overjoyed, boastful."* (11:9-10)

Then the stark choice facing man is put plainly and clearly: either accept the Divine Guidance you have been sent and reap its rewards or invest your hopes in this world and suffer the consequences: *"As for any who desire the life of this world and its finery, We will give them full payment in it for their actions. They will not be deprived of their due in it. Such people will have nothing in the Next World but the Fire. What they achieved in it will come to nothing. What they did will prove null and void. But as for those who have clear evidence from their Lord followed up by a witness from Him - and before it the Book of Musa came as a model and a mercy - such people believe in it. Any faction which rejects it is promised the Fire. Be in no doubt about it. It is the Truth from your Lord. Yet most people do not believe."* (11:15-17)

This primary division of the human race into believers and unbelievers is figuratively restated immediately before the stories begin: *"The likeness of the two groups is that of the blind and deaf and the seeing and hearing. Are they the same as one another? Will you not then remember?"* (11:24)

After concluding the account of the past nations Allah makes it clear that nothing has changed and that the people of this time are no different: *"So do not be in any doubt about what these people worship. They only worship as their forebears worshipped previously. We will pay them their portion in full, with no reduction."* (11:109) Nor will their eventual fate be different.

Then we are succinctly told what we must do to avoid this fate; and finally all that has gone before is beautifully summed up in the five final *ayats:*

"Your Lord would never have destroyed those cities wrongfully as long as their inhabitants were setting things right. If your Lord had willed, He would have made one nation of mankind but they persist in their differences, except for those on whom your Lord has mercy. That is the reason He created them, so the word of your Lord might be fulfilled: 'I will fill up Jahannam with the jinn *and mankind all together.' We have told you all this news of the Messengers to make your heart firm by means of it. The truth has come to you in this, and an admonishment and reminder to the believers. Say to those who do not believe: 'Do as you think best: that is what we are doing. And wait: we too are waiting.' The Unseen of the heavens and the earth belongs to Allah and the entire affair will be returned to Him. So worship Him and put your trust in Him. Your Lord is not heedless of anything you do."* (11:117-121)

Sura 12
Yusuf: Joseph

Yusuf's importance in the sight of Allah was already obvious when he was still a child. His elder brothers did not display any particular virtue or good character, and although he was younger than them he was closer than they were to his father and more loved by him. It seemed likely that the inherited mantle of Prophethood would fall on his shoulders. His father Ya'qub was the heir of Ishaq and Ishaq was the heir of Ibrahim. Would he be the next link in this chain? Then Allah informed him of his destiny in a dream: *"When Yusuf told his father, 'Father! I saw eleven bright stars, and the sun and moon as well. I saw them all prostrate in front of me.'"* (12:4)

Ya'qub understood what the dream presaged regarding the future of his young son and was afraid for him on account of the jealousy of his brothers. *"He said, "My son, do not tell your brothers your dream lest they devise some scheme to injure you. Shaytan is a clear cut enemy to man. Accordingly your Lord will pick you out and teach you the true meaning of events and perfect His blessing on you and on the family of Ya'qub..."* (12:5-6)

The chosen lad, however, could not escape the envy of his elder brothers and so he was ensnared by them, seized and thrown into the bottom of a well where he found himself in a limbo between life and death, hoping for deliverance but in fear of destruction. Then in that dire extremity Allah informed him that those bullying brothers of his who had plotted against him would one day fall into his hands so that he could rebuke them for what they had done. Now he was young and had been overpowered by them but then they would be in his power. They thought they had got rid of him; but how wrong they were! No one is able to reverse

Allah's decree. *"But when, in fact, they did go out with him and gathered all together and agreed to put him at the bottom of the well, We then revealed to him: 'You will inform them of this thing that they now do at a time when they are totally unaware."* (12:15)

Yusuf was given a premonition of what would only come true in Egypt many years later when, without recognising him, his brothers came to him seeking charity after he had become an important official there. *"So when they came into his presence, they said, 'Your Eminence! Hardship has hit us and our families. We bring scant merchandise, but fill the measure for us generously. Allah always rewards the generous giver.' He said, 'Are you aware of what you did to Yusuf and his brother in ignorance?'"* (12:88-89) Thus Yusuf's hour of extreme hardship and abasement at the bottom of the well presaged his rise to the very pinnacle of worldly power. How extraordinary and inexorable are the decrees of destiny!

His father's unceasing quest for him was also based on his absolute certainty about Allah's decree. When his elder brothers returned after they had carried out their plot, they said to Ya'qub, *"We went out to run a race and left Yusuf together with our things and then a wolf appeared and devoured him. But you are never going to trust us now, even if we really speak the truth."* (12:17) He said, *"It is merely that your lower selves suggested something to you which you did; but steadfast patience, that is beautiful. It is Allah alone who is my Help in face of what you describe."* (12:18) Unwavering patience results in abundant good, and both Yusuf and his father eventually realised their highest hopes.

❊❊❊❊❊

The story of Yusuf is an episode of real life history, not a made-up narrative contrived by a human being. Fictional literature is very widespread in our age and although its subject matter varies greatly it is always the product of its author's imagination. The heroes of the narrative act in the way the author dictates for them and speak the words he puts into their mouths. The responsibility, first and last, is that of the writer who gives rein to his thoughts and expresses his own principles and aspirations.

Real life history is quite another matter, in which the reality of events and people appear as Allah created them so that a true picture of existence results. That is why Allah says to His Prophet: *"We tell you the best of stories in revealing this Qur'an to you, though you were oblivious of it before it came."* (12:3) The Messenger of Allah had no active part in what Allah revealed to him; he merely received and transmitted exactly what came to him: *"This is news of the Unseen which We reveal to you. You were not with them when they decided what to do and devised their scheme."* (12:102)

As we can see from these two preceding *ayats*, the actual historical narrative of the story of Yusuf is both prefaced and concluded by several *ayats* which do not form part of the story itself but serve to put the story into the context of the Revelation as a whole. The final *ayat* makes the whole matter clear: *"There is instruction in their stories for people of intelligence. This is not a narration which has been fabricated but is confirmation of all that came before, an explanation of everything, and a guidance and a mercy for a people who believe."* (12:111)

The story of Yusuf is presented to us as an exemplary model of perseverance in accepting Allah's decree and conveying His Message, and of triumphing by that over all the obstacles which arise on the way by never giving up hope of Allah's generous disposition of existence.

The period of Yusuf's actual Prophethood began when he came of age which indicated by Allah's words: *"And then when he became a full-grown man, We gave him knowledge and right judgement too. That is how We recompense good-doers."* (12:22) Right judgement and knowledge are two things which Allah gives His Prophets. Allah says about Lut: *"We gave right judgement and knowledge to Lut and rescued him from the city which committed disgusting acts..."* (21:74) and He says about Musa: *"When he reached maturity and came of age, We gave him right judgement and knowledge. That is how We repay those who do good."* (28:14)

153

Yusuf, whose great-grandfather, grandfather and father were all Prophets, was sold as a slave and the people who sold him put no value on him, considering him a burden to be got rid of with the least possible delay! How extraordinary life's ups and downs are! A *'noble angel'* (12:31) sold as unwanted goods but sold into the highest echelons of society! *"The Egyptian who had bought him told his wife, 'Look after him with honour and respect. It is possible he will be of use to us or perhaps we might adopt him as a son.'"* (12:21)

From complete ignominy the offspring of Prophets was in one move transposed to a palace where he was destined to face another sort of test. Even in this early period of his youth, he had knowledge and fear of his Lord and was aware of the difficulties which would inevitably dog his path: *"And thus We established Yusuf in the land to teach him the true meaning of events. Allah is in control of His affair. Yet most of mankind do not know."* (12:21)

Yusuf valued the house which had given him shelter and took his responsibilities towards it seriously. The master of the house held a special place in his affection. He was not arrogant like the Pharaohs, but a man of honour and gentle courtesy. He loved Yusuf and acknowledged his noble breeding. In spite of the passage of time, Yusuf never forgot his noble origin and his religious inheritance. His forebears had been Prophets and he was determined to remain on their path of worshipping Allah, the One God, and doing good and abandoning wrong action.

While the governor of Egypt loved Yusuf like a son for his noble qualities, his wife loved him in a different way! Yusuf was a man of remarkable beauty. He is said to have been given half the beauty of the world. The woman had the place of a mother in his life and consequently was very close to him and had authority over him. She found herself falling passionately in love with Yusuf but he remained aloof and would not respond to her overtures.

Faith had refined his nature and purified his heart and his connection to Allah was strong. It did not occur to him to commit a base action. When the woman accosted him he remembered what he had inherited from his forefathers and also remembered to honour the master of the house who had given him shelter and honoured him: *"The woman whose house it was solicited him. She barred the doors and said, 'Come over here!' He said, 'Allah is my refuge! He is my Lord and has been good to me regarding where I live. Those who do wrong will surely not succeed."* (12:23)

This is a difficult but well-known test of faith and there is a *hadith* which states that those who pass it will form one of seven groups to whom Allah will give shade on the Day when there is no shade but His shade: "a man who refuses the advances of a noble and beautiful woman, saying, 'I fear Allah'." (al-Bukhari and Muslim) In this dangerous situation, Yusuf quite rightly proved himself to be someone in whom the fear of Allah was paramount. He rejected any misdoing out of hand, a fact which was later acknowledged by the governor's wife when she said, *"I tried to seduce him, but he resisted me."* (12:32)

Yusuf was a young man of healthy appetites, so it was not that he had no desire – but, as he later maintained, death itself would have been preferable to him than to have disobeyed Allah by giving way to it. There would have been no trial in it for him if he had been a man devoid of sexual desire: *"She wanted him and he would have wanted her, had he not seen the clear proof of his Lord. That happened so We might avert from him all evil and lust. He was one of Our chosen slaves."* (12:24) His faith overcame his desire and Yusuf continued to remember his Lord, which kept him from overstepping Allah's limits.

The governor came in while his wife was tugging at Yusuf's shirt as he tried to escape from her. The impudent wife, being aware of the predicament she was in, quickly said to her husband: *"How should a man whose intention was to harm your family be punished for what he did, if not with prison or painful punishment?"* (12:25) Yusuf cried out: *"It was she who tried to seduce me."* (12:26) So how was the case to be decided? *"A witness from her people then declared, 'If his shirt is torn in front, she speaks the truth and he is someone who has told a lie. If his shirt is torn at the back, then she has lied and he is someone who has told the truth.' When he saw the shirt torn at the back, he said, 'This has come from women's deviousness. Truly your deviousness is immense.'"* (12:26-28) It is on the basis of this *ayat,* among others, that circumstantial evidence is admitted in the *Shari'a.*

The governor's wife denied the charge in spite of the overwhelming evidence against her, but her unrestrained feelings made her very headstrong and when the rumours about her continued to spread, she decided on another approach, as if to tell those who were talking about her: If you had been in my place, you would have done the same thing! *"Some city women said, 'The governor's wife solicited her slave. He has fired her heart with love. We see her clearly to be at fault.'"* (12:30)

She gathered together the women who were criticising her and ordered Yusuf to come out to them during a meal she had prepared in which they were eating fruit and other things. When Yusuf appeared they were so overcome by the sight of him that they cut their hands with their knives and said, *"This is no man. What could this be but a noble angel!"* (12:31) Having made her point the governor's wife had no compunction about admitting her part in the affair: *"I tried to seduce him, but he resisted me. If he does not do as I command, he will be put in prison and be brought low."* (12:32)

The present atmosphere of permissiveness would condone her action and accuse Yusuf of sexual repression. How far we have come from basic morality and in how short a time! Virtue is condemned and vice is the accepted norm. But Yusuf, who personified honour and manliness, restrained himself and sought Allah's pleasure: *"He said, 'My Lord, prison is preferable to me rather than what they call on me to do. Unless You turn away their guile from me, it may well be that I will fall for them and so become a man of ignorance.' His Lord answered his plea and turned away from him their guile and deviousness. He is the All-Hearing, the All-Knowing."* (12:33-34) Yusuf voluntarily forsook the palace for the prison, sure of Allah's help and that justice would eventually be done.

Dreams play a crucial part in the story of Yusuf and there are three occasions when they occur. The first comes, as we have already heard, right at the beginning when Yusuf himself dreams that the sun, moon and twelve stars are prostrating. The second time dreams appear is at the beginning of his time in prison: *"Two servants entered prison along with him. One said, 'I dreamt that I was pressing grapes.' The other said, 'I dreamt that I carried bread upon my head and birds were eating it. Please tell us the true meaning of these dreams. We clearly see you are a righteous man."* (12:36)

A true dream is an intimation from the unseen world to which man is given access by a spiritual faculty he possesses. It can give a human being a power of perception unknown in normal human consciousness, enabling him to see what others are unable to see. Sometimes people see things that are happening simultaneously but a great distance away and sometimes others are given a premonition of something which is going to happen in the future. Sometimes people see things exactly as they occur or are going to occur and sometimes the event appears in the dream in a coded form.

The dreams of Yusuf's companions were clearly of the last type. As we know, one of Yusuf's gifts was the ability to interpret dreams: *"He said, 'No meal to feed you will arrive before I have informed you what they mean. That is part of what my Lord taught me. For I have left the religion of a people who are clearly not believers in Allah and are rejectors of the Afterlife. I hold fast to the creed of my forebears Ibrahim and Ishaq and Ya'qub. We do not attribute any partners to Allah ...'"* (12:37-38)

Yusuf gloried in the unitary faith he had inherited from his forebears which had been his constant support throughout all his tribulations. He was determined to communicate it to his fellow prisoners: *"My fellow-prisoners, are many lords better, or Allah, the One alone, the Conqueror?"* (12:39) This message is as relevant to us as it was to them. Nothing in existence has real power except Allah, so why are we so persistent in clinging to the illusion that other things have power over us? How strange it is that modern civilisation, which has uncovered so many wonders of existence and manifestations of Allah's power that should have moved people to acknowledge Him, has in many cases had the opposite effect! Mankind's connection to Allah has never been weaker. People do not think about their inevitable meeting with Him and they pay no attention to His Revealed Guidance. They are only concerned with material necessities and what will make their life on earth more comfortable.

Yusuf then explained the meaning of the two dreams: *"My fellow-prisoners, one of you will serve his lord with wine; the other will be crucified and birds will eat his head."* (12:41) He asked the prisoner who was going to be released to put in a word on his behalf with his master but the man forgot until he was reminded of him by the third dream in the story. The Pharaoh, whose servant he was, had a dream which alarmed him and which none of those around him were able to explain. The servant immediately thought of Yusuf and said he would be able to find out the meaning of the dream.

He went to visit Yusuf in the prison: *"O truthful Yusuf, tell us concerning seven fat cows which seven thin ones ate, and seven green ears of wheat and seven others which were dry, so that I may return to them and they may know."* (12:46) Yusuf explained the dream and the Pharaoh sent for him but Yusuf refused to come until his innocence had been acknowledged. So Yusuf's case was reopened and the women who knew what had happened were summoned. *"He asked, 'What was this past affair of yours when you solicited Yusuf?' Then they said, 'Allah forbid! We know no ill of him.' The governor's wife then said, 'The truth has now emerged. Indeed I tried to seduce him then and he is the one who has told the truth.'"* (12:51)

After Yusuf's wise interpretation of the dream the Pharaoh brought him close to him. It was evident that he was the best person to manage things in the famine years which the dream had foretold: *"He said, 'Entrust me with the country's stores. Truly I am a knowing guardian.' And thus We established Yusuf in the land so he could live in any place he pleased. We bestow Our mercy on anyone We will and do not allow to go to waste the wage of any of the people who do good."* (12:55-56) He allowed himself to seek the position because there was no one more qualified to do it. Although as a general rule it is not good to put oneself forward for a position of leadership, in this situation, when no one else is going to do the job properly, it becomes correct to do so.

The famine foretold by Yusuf's interpretation of the Pharaoh's dream duly occurred and appears to have extended from the Nile Valley to Syria so that people from as far away as that, including Yusuf's family, were forced to seek food from Egypt which alone had made the necessary preparations to meet the disaster: *"The brothers of Yusuf came into his presence. He recognised them but they did not know him."* (12:58)

He gave them a hospitable reception and enquired about their circumstances. After graciously granting what they sought, he asked them to bring his full brother with them the next time they came: *"They said, 'We will solicit our father for him. That is something we will surely do.'"* (12:61) Their father was alarmed at this request and said to his sons: *"How will my trusting him to your care be different from entrusting his brother before? But the Best of Guardians is Allah. He is the Most Merciful of the merciful."* (12:64) Eventually he agreed to let him go with them.

They arrived again before Yusuf who gave his full brother a special reception: *"Then when they entered into Yusuf's presence, he drew his brother close to him and said, 'I am your brother. Do not be distressed concerning all that they used to do.'"* (12:69) Yusuf must have known the circumstances of his brother when he uttered these words to console him. Then Yusuf devised a stratagem to force his brothers to leave his brother with him and oblige them to return to his father without him.

When Ya'qub learned what had happened, he cried out, *"Perhaps Allah will bring them all together. He is indeed All-Knowing and All-Wise."* (12:83) For all his understandable human grief, Ya'qub knew in the depths of his heart that Yusuf was alive and that he would finally return to him. The loss of a second son was a terrible blow: *"He turned himself away from them and said, 'What anguish is my sorrow for Yusuf!' And then his eyes turned white from hidden grief."* (12:84) But Ya'qub's faith in Allah was undiminished: *"My sons! Seek news of Yusuf and his brother. Do not despair of comfort from Allah. No one despairs of comfort from Allah but the people who reject faith."* (12:87)

Yusuf's brothers set out a third time for Egypt, their hearts broken, their situation desperate, and their abasement evident: *"So when they came into his presence, they said, 'Your Eminence! Hardship has hit us and our families. We bring scant merchandise, but fill the measure for us generously. Allah always rewards the generous giver."* (12:88)

After this demonstration of true humility on the part of his brothers, Yusuf revealed himself to them: *"He said, 'Are you aware of what you did to Yusuf and his brother in ignorance?' They asked, 'Are you Yusuf?' He said, 'I am indeed Yusuf, and this is my brother. Allah has acted graciously to us. As for those who fear Allah and are steadfast, Allah does not allow go to waste the wage of any people who do good.'"* (12:89-90)

One of Allah's natural laws had been demonstrated. *Taqwa* and steadfastness bring success, just as oxygen and hydrogen combine to produce water and the sum of the angles of a triangle is 180 degrees! Yusuf's brothers were made absolutely aware that Allah truly is in charge of His creation: *"They said, 'By Allah, Allah has favoured you above us. Clearly we were in the wrong.' He said, 'No blame at all will fall on you. Today you have forgiveness from Allah. He is the Most Merciful of the merciful."* (12:91-92) Great men do not harbour any rancour. After victory they have even greater magnanimity and humility towards Allah than they had before it. The same qualities were displayed by the Last Prophet when he conquered Makka.

Then Yusuf said to his brothers: *"Go with this shirt of mine and throw it over my father's face, and he will see again. Then come to me with all your families."* (12:93) The caravan set off from Egypt to Syria and suddenly those who were around Ya'qub heard him let loose a cry of joy. They did not know what had happened. They heard him say, *"I can smell Yusuf's scent."* (12:94) He added, *"You probably think I have become senile!"* The spiritual world is an extraordinary thing! How did the good news come to the heart of Ya'qub? How could he know what had happened? *"But when the bringer of the good news came, he threw it over his face and sight returned. He said, 'Did I not tell you before that I know things from Allah which you do not know?'"* (12:96)

After a few days the first dream was fully explained as the others had been previously but this time the explanation took on a physical form. *"Then when they entered into Yusuf's presence he drew his parents close to him and said, 'Enter Egypt safe and sound, if Allah wills.' He raised his parents up onto the throne. The others fell prostrate in front of him. He said, 'My father, truly this is now the meaning of the dream I had. My Lord has made it all come true. He was kind to me when He brought me out of prison and brought you from the wilds after Shaytan had caused dissent between me and my brothers. My Lord is kind to anyone He wills. Truly He is All-Knowing and All-Wise."* (12:99-100)

After the narrative has come to its triumphant conclusion, Allah reconfirms its factual nature to His Messenger, *"This is news of the Unseen which We reveal to you. You were not with them when they decided what to do and devised their scheme."* (12:102) He was certainly not with them so as to have been an actual witness of the events described, nor could he read so as to have gleaned them from a written source. It was pure Divine Revelation conveyed to him which he did not add to or change in any way. Nevertheless, many people still deny his Prophethood. In our time the unbelievers and People of the Book who attack him are legion and never cease their babbling. Let them continue! They will not stop the course of the Final Message:

"Say: 'This is my way. I call to Allah with inner sight, I and all who follow me. Glory be to Allah! I am not one of the idolaters!'" (12:108)

Sura 13
Ar-Ra'd: Thunder

At the beginning of *Surat ar-Ra'd* Allah addresses His Prophet: *"And what has been sent down to you from your Lord is the Truth..."* Many people deny this truth: *"but most people do not believe."* (13:1) Is there an excuse for the many who turn away from the truth and refuse to follow it? None whatever.

This introduces the two intertwining themes of this *sura*: the nature of faith and disbelief and the necessity of insight and intelligence in the believer; and how the natural world inevitably leads those with the necessary intellectual qualities towards faith. It implies there is enough evidence in the universe testifying to the divinity and immensity of its Maker almost to dispense with the need for Revelation at all! Intelligent appraisal of the heavens and earth makes it utter folly to deny their Divine Source and attribute power to the non-entities which people hold up as their gods.

We will leave till later the *ayats* which describe how Allah's signs appear in existence and examine the first of the two themes. The words of the first *ayat*, *"And what has been sent down to you from your Lord is the Truth",* are echoed in another *ayat* later in the *sura*: *" Is he who knows that what has been sent down to you from your Lord is the Truth like him who is blind?"* (13:19) Faith is therefore firstly equated with the capacity to see. After that the *ayat* goes on to enumerate the qualities of the believer, beginning with the words of the Almighty: *"It is only people of intelligence who remember: those who fulfil Allah's contract and do not break their agreement; those who join what Allah has commanded to be joined ..."* (13:19-21)

It is clear from the first words in this last *ayat* that the kind of sight which is being referred to is inner sight, which in turn leads to righteous action and finally results in the eternal reward of the Next World: *"It is they who will have the Ultimate Abode, Gardens of Eden which they will enter, and all of their parents, wives and children who were righteous. Angels will enter in to welcome them from every gate: 'Peace be upon you because of your steadfastness!'"* (13:22-24)

So what about those who reject faith? This *sura* provides many illustrations of the forms this denial took: *"Those who reject say, 'If only a sign could be sent down to him from his Lord!' You are only a warner. Every people has a guide."* (13:7) *"Those who reject say, 'Why has a sign not been sent down to him from his Lord?' Say: 'Allah misguides anyone He wills and guides to Himself all who turn to Him."* (13:27) *"Those who reject say, 'You are not a Messenger.' Say: 'Allah is sufficient witness between you and me, and so is anyone who has knowledge of the Book.'"* (13:43) Their blindness takes the form of first doubting and then denying the Messenger.

This is the obtuseness and stupidity of prejudice which blinds the heart and dulls the intellect. People who lack insight cannot have sound belief. People who are debarred from looking into themselves cannot recognise Allah in any meaningful way. The results of this blindness are indeed dire: *"Those who reject will not cease to be struck by disaster for their handiwork, or one will happen close to their homes, until Allah's promise comes about. Allah will not fail to keep His promise."* (13:31)

Sometimes the blindness of prejudice is overcome by recognition of the truth when it appears and sometimes it cannot be overcome: *"Those to whom We gave the Scripture rejoice at what has been sent down to you but some of the parties refuse to acknowledge part of it. Say: 'I have only been ordered to worship Allah and not to attribute any partners to Him. To Him I call and to Him I will return.'"* (13:36)

When Islam knocked at the doors of Egypt and Syria, it went swiftly to people's hearts and most Christians entered it in throngs and embraced it wholeheartedly. It is clear that Allah had handed over both spiritual and political power to the Muslims, replacing the deviations which had accrued in Christianity with clear judgement and guidance: *"And thus We have sent it down as a judgement in Arabic. If you followed their whims and desires after the knowledge that has come to you, you would have no protector or defender against Allah."* (13:37)

Nevertheless, there were some who clung to the past and would not open their eyes to the truth in front of them. It is a wonderful testimony both to the enlightened governance of Islam and to the enduring strength of irrational prejudice that the descendants of those people have survived into the present time!

✽✽✽✽✽

The Qur'an is made up of clearly articulated signs specifically dedicated to directing people to Allah; but the phenomenal world is also full of signs, though of a more passive, silent kind, which also clearly indicate Allah's existence. Both forms of evidence require a clear intellect and acute perception to grasp them. Heedlessness and stupidity never bring anything good. That is why one often reads in the Qur'an: *"Will you not then use your understanding?"* and *"Will you not then remember?"*

Surat ar-Ra'd is partly devoted to pointing out this aspect of the natural world and in many *ayats* it uses illustrations drawn from natural phenomena to awaken this dormant faculty of human perception. One such *ayat* is: *"In the earth are diverse regions side by side and gardens of grapes and cultivated fields, and palm-trees sharing one root and others with individual roots, all watered with the same water. And We make some things better to eat than others. There are signs in that for people who use their understanding."* (13:4)

Think about a single piece of land covered with grape vines. lemon trees, colocynth trees and thorn trees all watered by the same water and yet all differing in terms of fruit, taste, colour and use. Reflect on the worm feeding on the mulberry tree and making silk, and the bee feeding from the same tree and making honey, and the sheep feeding from the same tree and making droppings!

The Will of Allah has created millions of differentiated species and elements filling the entire universe with teeming forms of matter. The Qur'an describes the vast power of the Creator in proliferating the propagation of living things – human beings, animals, birds, fish, reptiles, insects and the other myriad forms of life. There are thousands upon thousands of species distributed throughout the land and sea and air; billions of individuals which breed and multiply, their embryos passing through clearly demarcated stages. Everywhere there is order: *"Allah knows what every female bears"* in the air or lair or earth or hospital *"and every shrinking of the womb and every swelling. Everything has its measure with Him, the Knower of the Unseen and the Visible, the Great, the High-Exalted."* (13:8-9)

The Doer of all this is the One who created the universe and nothing distracts Him from anything else. He adorned it with the stars and no star falls from its place, no planet leaves its orbit. The laws of the universe protect it from destruction. And man too is protected from the many dangers which threaten him continually. Do you see how the immune system defends us against invasive germs? These protective forces issue directly from Allah's command in every instance.

Surat ar-Ra'd exhorts us to reflect deeply on these things and to ask ourselves penetrating questions about the nature of existence: *"Say: 'Who is the Lord of the heavens and the earth?' Say: 'Allah.' Say: 'So why have you taken protectors apart from Him who possess no power to help or harm themselves?' Say: 'Are the blind and sighted equal? Or are darkness and light the same? Or have they assigned partners to Allah who create as He creates, so that all creating seems the same to them?' Say: 'Allah is the Creator of all things. He is the One, the All-Conquering.'"* (13:16)

Paradoxically, the universal diffusion of scientific knowledge, which has to some extent 'explained away' existence, has made people less inclined to ask themselves fundamental questions of this kind and has made them take for granted, and even hold in contempt, things which should inspire in them the highest wonder and reverence; and the Muslims are unfortunately not least among those espousing this obtuse vision of the world. This lack of respect has led to mankind to misuse the earth's natural resources in the most destructive way with only short-term gain in mind.

The air is made foul by clouds of chemicals which pollute the atmosphere and destroy its purity. The environment is also polluted by, among many other things, the storm of incessant noise emitted by all kinds of machinery and electronic equipment which makes silence almost impossible to find. The earth's water is increasingly also losing its purity so that vast quantities are now unusable and no longer support life as they used to do. Mankind is digging its own grave and speeding its irreplaceable inheritance, the planet earth, to an early end.

This is what we have made of what Allah has given us. But what are we in comparison with the vastness of the universe? A black hole discovered recently in a distant galaxy, the size of a pinpoint as seen from the earth, apparently contains thousands of millions of stars of greater magnitude than the sun and is so dense that nothing can escape it, not even light!

If that is what a hole in existence is like, then what of existence itself? And even more than that, what of the Creator of this vastness beyond imagination: *"Allah is He who raised up the heavens without any support which you can see and then settled Himself firmly on the Throne. He made the sun and moon subservient, each running for a specified term. He directs the affair. He makes the signs plain so that perhaps you will be certain about the meeting with your Lord."* (13:2)

That is existence on a macrocosmic level – but on a microcosmic level the marvellous intricate complexities are equally stupefying if we consider our own bodies, its cell structure with its countless cells separate yet connected and mutually supportive, its networked nervous system which permeates every part controlled from one point. Then there are the mysteries of the subatomic world with its appearing, disappearing wave/particles which nevertheless make up the solid forms of our day to day lives.

The list of marvels is endless. And everything affirms the Unity of its Source and reverberates with His praise:

"It is He who shows you the lightning, striking fear and bringing hope, and heaps up the heavy clouds. The thunder glorifies His praise, as do the angels, out of fear of

Him. He discharges the thunderbolts, striking with them anyone He wills. Yet still they argue about Allah while He is inexorable in His power!" (13:13-14)

Sura 14
Ibrahim: Abraham

"It is a Book We have sent down to you so that you may bring mankind out of the darkness into the light, by the permission of their Lord, to the path of the Almighty, the Praiseworthy. Allah is He to whom everything in the heavens and everything in the earth belongs." (14:1-2)

There are many kinds of darkness in this world: the darkness of ignorance, the darkness of delusion, the darkness of sin, the darkness of disobedience.

Allah informs people that this life is a preparatory stage leading to what comes after it and that those who prefer this life to the Next are sadly misguided; that those who turn their backs on Divine Guidance and dislike living in its light are completely lost. Darkness and light are images used to describe disbelief and faith throughout the Qur'an.

The same image is used in respect of Musa two *ayats* further on: *"We sent Musa with Our signs: 'Bring your people out the darkness into the light and remind them of the Days of Allah.' Surely there are signs in that for every steadfast, thankful one."* (14:5) It is clear that every prophetic mission involves a transition from ignorance to knowledge and from crookedness to rectitude, and the Book which was given to Prophet Muhammad, may Allah bless him and grant him peace, is full of rays of light which banish darkness and lead people to Allah Almighty and protect them from falling prey to all types of ignorance.

However, human beings throughout time have opposed the Divine Guidance revealed to them, resisted the Messengers who brought it and attempted to harm them, and done everything in their power to seduce the believers from the Truth. But true believers always stand their ground and do not give up: *"And why indeed should we not put our trust in Allah when He has guided us to our ways? We will be steadfast however much you harm us. Let all who have trust put their trust in Allah."* (14:12)

Bringing any community out from the darkness to the light cannot be achieved overnight. It requires a long time and our Prophet spent twenty-three years attaching his people to the Noble Qur'an until it had effaced their coarseness, ignorance and backwardness to the extent that in a very short time they were able to gain preeminence and leadership throughout the known world.

The Qur'an completely transformed them, culturally, politically, morally and in terms of knowledge. This gave them the upper hand when they met the enemies of Allah and ensured that they speedily attained a strong position in the earth and that Allah's promise to the believers was fulfilled: *"Those who rejected the Truth said to their Messengers, 'We shall drive you from our land unless you return to our religion.' Their Lord revealed to them, 'We will destroy those who do wrong. We shall give you the land to live in after them. That is the reward of those who fear My station and fear My threat.'"* (14:13-14)

One of the core themes of the whole Qur'an is the inevitable eventual destruction of the power structures of disbelief and their replacement by people who truly adhere to Allah's Message and Messengers. In the final analysis it is the people of Allah who prevail: *"They asked for Allah's decision, and every obdurate tyrant failed."* (14:15) Let our Islamic community which does not want to renew itself pay heed to this!

In every society there are always leaders, those who set the fashion, and others who follow them, and this applies in every facet of human life, politics, art, business - everything. Followers and followed are in fact the same, it is simply that the leaders are more adept at voicing or embodying the common aspiration of their particular societies. The hidden aspirations of the followers are realised by those whom they look up to as their leaders. This creates a loop of mutual deception which can have disastrous consequences when confronted by the truth.

For instance, in the Battle of Badr the idolaters looked up to Abu Jahl, the leader of disbelief, saying, "Abu'l-Hakam[1] cannot be touched!" and they all flocked to him as a sure security until he was surrounded by a forest of spears, but that proved no protection against the Muslim army fighting for Allah and he was killed!

This attitude can, and in many cases will, persist beyond the grave but there its true futility will be revealed: *"They will all parade before Allah and the weak will say to those who were arrogant, 'We followed you, so can you help us at all against the punishment of Allah?' They will say, 'If Allah had guided us, we would have guided you. It makes no difference if we are unable to stand it or we bear it with patience: we have no way of escape.'"* (14:21)

Allah describes these things to people so that followers may not be deluded by their leaders, or leaders by their followers. Nevertheless, deluded leaders continue to delude their populations and to exploit their trust and propel them to destruction. *"Do you not see those who have exchanged Allah's blessing for unbelief, and consigned their people to the abode of ruin, Jahannam, where they roast? What an evil abode!"* (14:28-29) The end is the same for the leaders who call to the Fire and the deluded people who respond to them.

Surat Ibrahim parallels *Surat ar-Ra'd* in its description of the nature of truth and falsehood. In *Surat ar-Ra'd*, Allah compares truth and falsehood to jetsam and flotsam and says in conclusion: *"That is how Allah portrays the true and the false. As for the froth, it is quickly swept away. But that which is of use to people remains behind in the ground."* (13:17) In *Surat Ibrahim* He uses different imagery, saying about truth: *"Do you do not see how Allah coins a likeness of a good word? A good tree whose roots are firm and whose branches are in heaven. It bears its fruit regularly by the permission of its Lord."* (14:24-25)

Truth is a firmly-rooted tree with many branches and good fruit, producing a flourishing civilisation for the one who knows it and is illuminated by it and seeks shade in its many lesser branches.

1. Abu Jahl, 'Father of Ignorance', was called 'Abu'l-Hakam' by the idolaters of Quraysh.

Falsehood is likened to a tree which has no roots: because it has no real basis it cannot last. *"The likeness of a corrupt word is that of a rotten tree, uprooted on the surface of the earth. It has no staying power."* (14:26)

The question is whether we will seek the shade of the Tree of Truth or fasten our hopes to something which has no future. Will we in truth return wholeheartedly to the entirety of Allah's Book and the *Sunna* of His final Messenger, or will we continue to allow ourselves to be deluded by the illusory power of Western scientific materialism? *"The likeness of those who reject their Lord is that their actions are like ashes scattered by strong winds on a stormy day. They have absolutely no power over anything they have earned. That is extreme misguidance."* (14:18)

❉❉❉❉❉

Surat Ibrahim speaks about two responsibilities which the believers have. The first is to make the establishment of the prayer and the payment of *zakat* their main concern, superseding all other social and economic interests. This is indicated by Allah's words: *"Say to My slaves who believe that they should establish the prayer and give from what We have provided for them, secretly and openly, before a Day arrives on which there will be no trading and no friendship."* (15:31) In other words, no business or social relationship will be of any use unless the prayer and *zakat* are established. The community which possesses the Divine Message must establish it firmly in the land so that the Word of Allah is uppermost and so that He continues to be remembered and glorified on the earth.

The history of all the Prophets indicates that the nations which they establish call upon Allah and not upon human beings, and make the strengthening of their connection to Allah the basis of their untiring activity. When divine teachings wane or disappear you see nations wallowing in over-indulgence of the bodily appetites, vying in increase of wealth and worldly reputation. If they weep at all it is only for the decline in their standard of living or because of a decrease in their means of attaining sensual gratification.

The world today is in desperate need of a community which will make itself an exemplar of the worship of Allah and speak about His glories and commands. Only the Muslim community can fulfil this need, but in order to do so it must regain its rightful place at the helm of world affairs and be master of all aspects of life. This is the second responsibility of the believers: the responsibility for making it clear that the people of belief are masters and not indigent slaves and that they have the reins of this world in their hands so that they may lead it in the direction they wish it to go.

This responsibility is shown in the following three *ayats,* in which the word 'you' is repeated five times in respect of certain blessings from Allah and which, as can be seen from the context, refers specifically to the believers. *"Allah is He who created the heavens and the earth and sends down water from the sky and by it brings forth fruits as provision for **you**. He has subjected the ships to **you** to run upon the sea by His command, and He has subjected the rivers to **you**, and He has subjected the sun and the moon to **you** holding steady to their courses, and He has subjected the night and the day to **you**. He has given you everything you have asked Him for. If you tried to number Allah's blessings, you could never count them."* (14:32-34) So Allah is saying that these things are specifically for the benefit of the believers.

When, however, believers stray from the Straight Path, their gifts, as it were, become frozen. They become subjugated on the earth instead of having it subjected to them. Instead of them helping Allah by means of what He has given them their necks are bowed in subjection before the enemies of Allah, who take advantage of the Muslims' impotence to advance and take hold of the reins of power and subdue the whole world to their disbelief to the extent that faith has almost vanished even in its own homelands.

In the time we live in, *jihad*, obligatory for the Muslims when confronted by the domination of unbelievers, requires mastery of land, sea and air, as well as the requisite knowledge of existence to be able to be of benefit to the whole of mankind. How can the Muslims claim anything of that? No scientific development which might enable the Muslims to restore the supremacy of Allah's

172

deen and achieve their proper place in the world can be laid at their door.

In fact what we find is that "those most hostile to the believers", the Jews, are at the forefront of scientific advance and wield power over existence as if they had control of the jinn of Sulayman! The difference is that the jinn of Sulayman were under the control of a believing man who made his power subservient to Allah, whereas most Jews today want to uproot Islam and create a world based on rebellion against Allah.

How vast the gap has grown between the two lines of descent from Ibrahim! One line has followed their own whims and desires and rejects both 'Isa and Muhammad. Those now have power. The other line inherited the Revelation but failed to protect it and now live in a state of perpetual humiliation. They are the Arabs in these barren days.

Allah's Messenger, Ibrahim, was a righteous reformer who travelled far and wide calling people to *tawhid*, finally bringing his wife, Hajar, and young son Isma'il, to the Hijaz where he made the great supplication recorded in this *sura*: *"Our Lord, I have settled some of my offspring by Your Sacred House in a valley with no cultivation. Our Lord, may they establish the prayer! Make the hearts of mankind incline towards them and provide them with fruits, so that perhaps they will be thankful."* (14:37)

The branch of the family of Ibrahim which descended from them were the Arabs. The other branch are the descendants of Ishaq, the father of Israel, by his wife Sara. Both of them were born when Ibrahim was old, which is why he said, *"Praise be to Allah who has given me, despite my old age, Isma'il and Ishaq. My Lord is the Hearer of supplications. My Lord, make me and my descendants people who establish the prayer. My Lord, accept this supplication."* (14:39-40)

It is abundantly clear from this that both Allah and His Messenger Ibrahim held both sons in equal esteem and that any claims the Jews make on the basis of the different social status of their mothers is entirely without foundation. The sons of Adam are equal; they only differ in *taqwa*.

Although the machinations of the enemies of Allah are endless and their scheming is evil and the plans which they lay out to strike at the truth may be cunning, that will never stop the believers if they follow Allah's Guidance: *"They concocted their plots, but their plots were known to Allah, even if they were such as to make the mountains vanish. Do not imagine that Allah will break His promise to His Messengers. Allah is Almighty, the Exactor of Revenge."* (14:46-47)

Allah stresses that the the wrongdoers will get their comeuppance in the end. Even if punishment does not befall them in this world, it is waiting for them in the Next World. *"Do not consider Allah to be heedless of what the wrongdoers do. He is merely deferring them to a Day on which their sight will be transfixed."* (14:42)

Surat Ibrahim began by telling us that Allah revealed the Book to His Final Prophet to bring us out of the darkness into the light, and it ends by confirming that transmission: *"This is a communication to be transmitted to mankind so that they may be warned by it and that they may know that He is One God and that people of intelligence may remember."* (14:52)

People of intelligence should respect their intellects and not worship illusions or bow to idols and so live in darkness. They have no choice but to follow the Messenger so that their way through this life may be illuminated for them and they may live in the bright light of Divine guidance.

Sura 15
Al-Hijr

"Alif. Lam. Ra'. Those are the signs of the Book and a clear Qur'an." (15:1) Inasmuch as the Divine Revelation is composed of written words, it is a Book, and inasmuch as it is recited Signs, it is a Qur'an. Both expressions refer equally to the Noble Qur'an.

"It may be that those who reject will wish they had been Muslims." (15:2) Those who fell short will wish they had been more diligent and those who rebelled may wish that they had been obedient. When the Great Veil is lifted those who frittered away their days and did not prepare for an everlasting future will be bitterly remorseful: *"Leave them to eat and enjoy themselves. Let false hope divert them. They will soon know."* (15:3)

The worship of this world and absorption in its pleasures has always been a human tendency but never has worship of this world been more pronounced than at the present time when the Next World has been almost reduced to the status of an unreality. To combat this Allah says to his Prophet: *"Do not direct your eyes longingly to what We have given certain of them to enjoy. Do not feel sad concerning them."* (15:88)

It will be seen that this last *ayat* comes right at the end of the *sura* and that it corroborates and is in accord with the *ayats* quoted above which came from the beginning. This indicates to us the unified theme of the whole *sura* – the true nature of this world and how human beings become intoxicated by it and absorbed in it to the point that it blinds them to the Next World and becomes the cause of their destruction.

Consequently we find near the beginning of the *sura* the *ayat.* *"We did not destroy any city but that it had a set time. No nation can advance its appointed time nor can they delay it."* (15:4-5)

175

This succinct statement is clarified and amplified later in the *sura* when we hear how the people of Lut, the people of Shu'ayb and people of al-Hijr were destroyed because of their love of this world.

Allah says about the people of Lut: *"By your life! They were wandering blindly in their drunkenness! So the Great Shout seized hold of them at the break of day. We turned the place completely upside down and rained down on them stones of hard-baked clay. There are certainly signs in that for the discerning."* (15:72-75) He says about the people of Shu'ayb: *"The people of the Thicket also were wrongdoers. We took revenge on them. They are both on a well-beaten track."* (15:78-79) And He says about the people of al-Hijr, from whom the *sura* takes its name: *"We brought them Our signs but they turned away from them. They hewed out houses from the mountains, feeling safe. But the Great Shout seized hold of them in the morning, and so all that they earned was of no use to them."* (15:80-84)

The Revelation then turns to those to whom it was directly addressed, who were mocking the Qur'an and the one to whom it was being revealed: *"They say, 'O you to whom the Remembrance has been sent down, you are clearly mad. Why do you not bring the angels to us if you are telling the truth?'"* (15:6-7) By saying this, those people are demonstrating their ignorance of the nature of creation and in effect denying the spiritual dimensions of existence, saying that there is nothing more to existence than the empirical universe their five senses are capable of perceiving.

Allah responds to them by showing them clearly the nature of the error they have made: *"We do not send down the angels except with the Truth – and in that case they would be granted no reprieve."* (15:8) The spiritual dimensions cannot be openly displayed in the material world which is simply not capable of sustaining the power and light that that would entail.

The exception, of course, is the Revelation itself which is, as we know, the Uncreated Word of Allah. In a kind of interjection at this point Allah affirms this in the famous *ayat* about the preservation of the Qur'an: *"Truly it is We who have sent down the Remembrance and We are its Preservers."* (15:9) This is rightly understood to mean that this final Revelation will endure as long as the heavens and the earth endure and that the enemies of the truth, however great their desire or power, will never be able to extinguish its light.

But it also indicates that Allah continues to make it possible for something which comes direct from Him to co-exist with this material dimension of existence. It is part of the wonder of the Qur'an that this fact also finds its echo near the end of the *sura* where we read: *"We have given you the Seven Oft-Repeated and the Magnificent Qur'an."* (15:87)

That denial of the spiritual world by the unbelievers is such that they would not believe it even if they saw it: *"Even if We opened up to them a door into heaven, and they spent the day ascending through it, they would still only say, 'Our eyesight is befuddled! Or rather we have been put under a spell!'"* (15:14-15) No amount of evidence would serve to convince them that there is more to existence than what they can see and feel.

So Allah now turns in the *sura* to the material universe itself and gives us a beautiful description of the universe and its secrets and its powers, all of which only serve to indicate its Maker. The Almighty says: *"We have placed constellations in heaven and made them beautiful for those who look. We have guarded them from every cursed Shaytan except for the one who listens stealthily, and he is followed by a clear flame of fire. As for the earth, We stretched it out and cast firmly embedded mountains in it and made everything grow in due proportion in it. And We put a livelihood in it for you and for those for whom you do not provide. There is nothing that does not have its store with Us and We do not send it down except in known measure."* (15:16-21)

The beginning of the *sura* details the blessings of existence, its treasures and wonders, but Allah summarises it all at the end of the *sura* when He says: *"We did not create the heavens and the earth and everything between them, except with truth. The Hour is certainly coming. So turn away in the most gracious way. It is your Lord who is the Creator, the All-Knowing."* (15:85-86)

The elements from which every human being is made up come from the earth: *"We created mankind out of dried clay made from fetid black mud."* (15:26) But that is not the whole story: *"When your Lord said to the angels, 'I am creating a human being out of dried clay made from fetid black mud. When I have formed him and breathed My spirit into him, fall down in prostration in front of him!'"* (15:28-29)

So the human being is composed of clay and Spirit, and the choice for the human being is whether to identify with the one or the other. The angels call us to the one and, as the *sura* makes clear, Shaytan does all he can to make us identify with the other: *"He said, 'My Lord, because of the way You misled me, I will make things on the earth seem good to them and I will mislead them all, every one of them, except Your slaves among them who are sincere.'"* (15:39-40)

The story of Adam and his enemy in the Garden is repeated several times throughout the Noble Qur'an but it is clear that the emphasis in this instance is on the physical substance from which Adam's body was created, since the words *"dried clay from fetid black mud,"* meaning mud with a foul smell, are repeated twice. So it is Adam's earthly origin which is in question here and his subsequent tendency, aided and abetted by Shaytan, to identify with it completely.

This makes people forget that this world is in fact a temporary residence, a bridge which man must cross to reach his everlasting destiny, which will be defined by the actions he did during his life in the world. We must remember too that Iblis does not have any real power over man. His only power is to mislead and deceive! He makes the poison appear attractive to those who take it. Allah, however, ends the passage by leaving us in no doubt of the results of allowing ourselves to be duped into thinking that this world is all that there is: *"Tell My slaves that I am the Ever-Forgiving, the Most Merciful – but also that My punishment is the Painful Punishment."* (15:49-50)

The *sura* then cites, as we noted earlier, three examples of past communities who in different ways allowed this world to veil them from the Life to Come. First it speaks of the people of Lut who were contemporary with the great Prophet Ibrahim and lived in the cities of Sodom and Gomorrah. As we know they became addicted to the unnatural practice of homosexuality to such an extent that it dominated their society. They became the slaves of their perverted sexual appetites. When completely free rein is given to the bodily appetites the heart is blinded to spiritual realities and trapped in this world so that it is deaf to any call to guidance.

This unfortunately applies to many people today in a world which openly advocates sensual gratification as a desirable and even praiseworthy goal of life. It is clear from history that the specific sexual perversion of the people of Lut, although known to exist, was always everywhere execrated and those who practised it could only do so in the greatest secrecy. Then the Americans and Europeans first condoned it, then legalised it, and finally have now acclaimed it! How many perversions will this civilisation endorse? But the punishment of Allah is waiting.

Examples of the marvellously unified nature of this *sura*, connecting the beginning of the *sura* to its end, have already been given. Another passage reinforces the general theme of the grave danger of love of this world: *"Do not direct your eyes longingly to what We have given certain of them to enjoy. Do not feel sad concerning them. And lower your wing to the believers. Say: 'I am indeed a clear warner.'"* (15:88-89) The *sura* concludes by returning to the very nub of the matter for human beings in the world: the necessity for sincere worship of Allah and the only certainty of human existence, its inevitable end:

> *"So glorify the praise of your Lord and be one of the prostrators. And worship your Lord until the Certain comes to you."* (15:97-99)

Sura 16
An-Nahl: The Bee

Surat an-Nahl was revealed at the end of the Makkan period when the idolaters' hostility towards the believers had become very fierce. A considerable length of time had passed and Islam had not apparently made any real headway, nor had anything happened to make the power of the idolaters seem any less strong. It was therefore an extremely difficult time for the fledgling Muslim community. The idolaters were taunting the believers with their lack of discernible success and with the fact that Allah's promised support had not materialised.

In that context, then, the *sura* begins by reassuring the believers that Allah is with them: *"Allah's command is coming, so do not try to hasten it"* (16:1), and ends by warning them against giving up hope so they do not become people *"who reject Allah after having believed ..."* (16:106), and consoling those who hold firm: *"But to those who emigrated after they were persecuted and then fought their hardest and were steadfast, to them your Lord is All Compassionate, Most Merciful."* (16:110) Finally it exhorts the Prophet and those with him not to let present appearances delude them but to remain steadfast: *"Be patient – but your patience is only by Allah. Do not be grieved by them and do not be dismayed by the plots they concoct. Allah is with those who are godfearing and with those who are good-doers."* (16:127-128)

The emigration referred to in the second *ayat* was not the emigration to Madina but the one made to Abyssinia by a group of the early Muslims in Makka when the unbelievers' persecution of the believers had reached intolerable proportions. It is evident that *Surat an-Nahl* was revealed at about the time it took place because the event is also referred to in an earlier *ayat*: *"As for those who emigrate for the sake Allah after being wronged, We shall give them good lodging in this world; and the reward of the Next World is much greater, if they did but know."* (16:41) Al-Bukhari relates a *hadith* about this subject.

Asma' bint 'Umays, who was one of those who came from Abyssinia to Madina, was once visiting Hafsa when 'Umar came in. He said to Asma', "We emigrated before you so, we are worthier of the Messenger of Allah than you are!" Asma' became angry and said, "No, by Allah, you were with the Prophet who was feeding the hungry among you and teaching the ignorant whereas we were despised exiles in far-away Abyssinia. We were injured and made fearful and it was all for the sake of Allah and His Messenger! By Allah, I will not eat or drink anything until I have told the Messenger of Allah what you said." When the Prophet came to Hafsa's house, Asma' said, "Messenger of Allah, 'Umar said such-and-such." He said, "And what did you say back to him?" She said, "I said such-and-such." The Messenger of Allah said, "No one is worthier of me than you are. He and his companions only made one emigration whereas you, the people of the boat, made two emigrations."

The second *ayat* of the *sura* introduces one of two main themes which interlace through it: *"He sends down the angels with the Spirit by His command to any of His slaves He wills: 'Give warning that there is no god but Me, so show fear of Me!'"* (16:2) The *ayat* is referring to the Qur'an itself, and interspersed throughout *Surat an-Nahl* are passages discussing various aspects of the Revelation. Here Allah calls Revelation a 'Spirit' because it gives life to individuals and nations. In another place, indicating the same thing, He says: *"In this way We have revealed to you a life-giving Spirit by Our command. You did not know what the Book was, nor belief ..."* (42:52)

The life-giving force of the Qur'an was certainly demonstrated historically by the unparalleled speed and energy with which the early Muslims came out of nowhere to take Islam to half the world where it has largely remained to the present day. And indeed the vigorous spread of Islam occurring now in Europe and elsewhere is continuing proof of the unceasingly revivifying nature of the Final Revelation.

The next reference to the Revelation concerns the different ways in which the unbelievers and the believers view it and the long-term consequences of their differing perception. First the unbelievers: *"When they are asked, 'What has your Lord revealed?' they say, 'Myths and legends of earlier peoples.' So on the Day of Rising they will carry the full weight of their own burdens and some of the burdens of those they misguided without knowledge. How evil is what they bear!"* (16:24-25)

Such people refuse to recognise the immediate provenance and relevance of the Revelation, consigning it to the past so that they feel safe in ignoring it. They are misguided themselves and they are the cause of misguidance for others. There is a *hadith* referring to people of this type which says: "Anyone who calls people to misguidance incurs the penalty of the sins of those who do so after them, without that decreasing their sins in any way." (Muslim, Abu Dawud, an-Nasa'i, At-Tirmidhi, Ibn Maja and Imam Ahmad ibn Hanbal; from Abu Hurayra)

The believers have a very different answer to the same question: *"And those who show fear of Allah are asked, 'What has your Lord sent down?' Their reply is, 'Goodness!' There is good in this world for the good-doers, and the Abode of the Next World is even better. How wonderful is the abode of the godfearing!"* (16:30)

These are the words of people who understand what the Qur'an entails. They know that the end result will be best for the godfearing in both this world and the Next. And their viewpoint leads them to action, for it is clear from the description that they are people who spend their lives in righteous action. They are people whose hearts have been brought to life.

The next reference is a reiteration of the core message of the Qur'an, in rebuttal of a statement by the idolaters which is practically a claim of Divine sanction for their idolatrous practices. Allah responds: *"We sent a Messenger among every people saying: 'Worship Allah and keep clear of false gods.'"* (16:36)

And then a little further on comes a reminder that the Revelation, though Divine in origin, is always delivered to us through the medium of a human being. *"We have only ever sent before you men to whom We gave Revelation – ask the People of the Reminder if you do not know – who brought clear signs and Revealed Books. And We have sent down the Reminder to you so that you may make clear to mankind what has been revealed to them, so that perhaps they will reflect."* (16:43-44) The *ayat* shows as well that Revelation is necessarily complemented by a Prophetic 'making clear' of it which, of course, takes the form of both words and actions. So from one point of view the *Sunna* of the Prophet is precisely this 'making clear' of Allah's Book.

The role that the Qur'an plays in the context of human history as a whole forms the basis of the next reference to it in this *sura*: *"We have revealed the Book only so that you may make clear to them the matters about which they differ, and as a guidance and a mercy to people who believe. Allah sends down water from the sky and by it brings the dead earth back to life. There is indeed a sign in that for people who hear."* (16:64-65)

It is clear from this that one of the main purposes of the Qur'anic Revelation is to correct the deviations and corruptions which have been introduced by past religious communities and are claimed by them to be part of Divine Guidance. The overt implication is that the Qur'an is the fulfilment and completion of the whole process of Allah's Guidance of mankind which has been going on since the very dawn of human history. The image of life-giving rain used in the second *ayat* is further confirmation of the life-giving quality of Revelation.

In an earlier reference (16:36) Allah reaffirmed the core Qur'anic message of Divine Unity and now He wonderfully summarises the Message as a whole in a single ayat: *"We have revealed the Book to you making all things clear and as guidance and mercy and good news for the Muslims. Allah commands justice and doing good and giving to relatives, and forbids indecency and doing wrong and tyranny. He admonishes you so that perhaps you may remember."* (16:89-90)

The essence of the Divine Message is absolutely free from any historical, cultural or geographic limitations and is quite simply a call to adopt the kind of basic, decent, correct human behaviour which every one knows in their heart of hearts to be right and to avoid those things which result from giving way to our lower appetites and worst characteristics.

The final direct reference in the *sura* to the Revelation is a group of *ayats* towards its end, the first of which is a practical instruction to the Muslims which has been followed by every Muslim when reciting the Qur'an ever since: *"Whenever you recite the Qur'an, seek refuge with Allah from the cursed Shaytan."* (16:98) The other *ayats* mainly concern objections raised against the Revelation by the unbelievers about the abrogation and replacement of certain ayats and accusing the Prophet of being taught what to say by a human being

Allah makes it clear that such people by their nature will never be convinced and that the Book is only of profit to those who believe in it: *"Say: 'The Purest Spirit has brought it down from your Lord with truth, to strengthen those who believe, and as guidance and good news for the Muslims.'"* (16:102) It will be noted that the word 'Spirit' here eloquently echoes the *sura's* first *ayat* concerning the Revelation, and by doing so draws all these disparate *ayats* into a coherent whole so that they can be seen as a single thread which appears at intervals throughout the *sura*.

❋❋❋❋❋

Now we come to the second of the themes mentioned earlier and that for which *Surat an-Nahl* is justly celebrated: its magnificent and beautiful evocation of the natural world as a manifestation of Divine generosity and blessing to us as human beings for which, in justice, we should be endlessly thankful but for which we all too often display arrogant ingratitude.

The subject is introduced by an affirmation of Allah first as the Creator of the universe and then as the Creator of man, mentioning our tendency, despite our most humble origin, to dispute our Lord's sovereignty: *"He created the heavens and the earth with truth. He is exalted above any partner they attribute to Him! He created man from a drop of sperm and yet there he is, an open challenger!"* (16:3-4)

Then in an extended passage of intense lyrical beauty Allah gives us a list of some of the many gifts He has bestowed on us without any effort on our part whatsoever. He starts with livestock which was, of course, an absolutely vital element in the lives of those to whom the Revelation was directly addressed: *"And He created livestock. There is warmth for you in them, and various uses and some of them you eat. And there is beauty for you in them in the evening when you bring them home and in the morning when you drive them out to graze. They carry your loads to lands you would never reach, except with great difficulty. Your Lord is All-Gentle, Most Merciful. And horses, mules and donkey, both to ride and for adornment. And He creates other things you do not know."* (16:5-8)

It is important to note that our enjoyment of these gifts is not merely a matter of the satisfaction of animal appetites but that there is an aesthetic element included as an essential part of human pleasure and it is also significant that these things and what follows all occur naturally. Things mentioned are the rain and the crops and fruit it makes possible, the workings of the universe, the huge variety of creatures, the oceans and all the benefits we get from them, and how the very physical geography of the earth is beneficial for us.

We can see why *Surat an-Nahl* has the alternative name of *Surat an-Ni'am* (Blessings) and an *ayat which* follows this list encapsulates it all: *"If you tried to number Allah's blessings, you could never count them. Allah is Ever Forgiving, Most Merciful."* (16:18) And the only thing Allah asks of us in return is to remember Him and thank Him for them, remembering that our thanks is a matter of action as well as words.

Despite this, unbelievers, while they avail themselves of all the gifts Allah has blessed them with, refuse to acknowledge the Giver and the result of their ingratitude will be everlasting regret. They ascribe divine powers to other things when in reality everything is totally subservient to Allah, and they fear them but not Allah.

"Everything in the heavens and the earth belongs to Him, and the deen *belongs to Him, firmly and forever. Why then do you fear other than Allah?"* (16:52)

Where blessings are concerned they refuse to acknowledge Allah, but when disaster strikes they turn to Him, only to turn away again immediately things improve. *"Any blessing you have is from Allah. Then when harm affects you, it is to Him you cry out for help. But when He removes the harm from you, a group of you attribute partners to your Lord, ungrateful for what We have given them. So enjoy yourselves. You will soon know!"* (16: 53-55)

A specific instance of human ingratitude is the desire for sons rather than daughters and the dreadful crimes this leads to. As we know, this is unfortunately just as much a feature of today's world as it was when the Qur'an was being revealed: *"When any of them is given the good news of a baby girl, his face darkens and he is furious. He hides away from people because of the evil of the good news he has been given. Should he keep it ignominiously or bury it in the earth?"* (16:58-59)

This attitude is shown to be even more stupid by the fact that, as the Prophet told us in more than one *hadith*, daughters bring us quite as much blessing and benefit as sons do, and in some respects more. In fact this human tendency has now been taken one step further, since many people do everything they can to avoid having any children at all!

Surat an-Nahl now gives us another list of Divine gifts, beginning again with beasts of the field: *"There is instruction for you in cattle. From the contents of their bellies, from between dung and blood, We give you pure milk to drink, easy for drinkers to swallow."* (16:66) The production of milk is, of course, a wonderful process with a most delicious and nourishing outcome but there is another element concerned in its usefulness for human beings which is not present in anything we saw in the list of blessings at the beginning of the *sura*. Human involvement is necessary for its extraction.

This in no way diminishes it as a blessing – in fact the human activity concerned if anything augments it – but unfortunately it does make it easier for human beings to claim credit for it themselves and to neglect to thank Allah who is their sole Provider. The other things mentioned in this passage are the produce of the date-palm and grape-vine, bees and honey, wives and children, permanent and temporary housing, wool, fur, leather, carpets, household utensils, clothing and armour. It will be noted that all these things require, to a greater or lesser extent, some kind of human activity in order for their benefit to be fully realised.

In the middle of this passage there is a section reaffirming Allah's power over existence, particularly in respect of provision, and His power to give it and withhold it, giving some illustrations to show how absurd it is for a human being to ascribe the blessings he receives to any other source. *"So why do they believe in falsehood and reject the blessings of Allah, and worship, instead of Allah, things that do not control their provision from the heavens or earth in any way, and are completely impotent?"* (16:72-73)

One of the purposes of our existence is to be grateful for what Allah has given us: *"Allah brought you out of your mothers' wombs knowing nothing at all, and gave you hearing, sight and hearts so that perhaps you would be thankful."* (16:78) But sadly most people, while taking the maximum advantage of what Allah gives them, refuse to show any gratitude: *"They acknowledge Allah's blessing and then deny it. Most of them are ungrateful."* (16:83) May Allah make us among those who are truly thankful for all the countless blessings He has given to every single one of us.

One *ayat* in this passage stands out because it is not something that requires any human participation nor does it apparently refer to provision: *"Do they not see the birds suspended in mid-air up in the sky? Nothing holds them there except Allah. There are certainly signs in that for people who believe."* (16:79) But this is one of the great *ayats* affirming Allah's Unity and the fact that He alone has absolute control over every aspect of existence at every moment. There is no movement and no stillness except by Allah's authority.

Thus it does in fact have a bearing on provision in that it demonstrates with clarity that in reality every single thing we receive comes to us exactly when and where Allah wills, regardless of anything we may or may not do to acquire it. It is particularly important for us, people of the 'scientific age', people steeped in things like the laws of aerodynamics and other scientific theories, to pay great attention to this *ayat* and be instructed by it. What applies to birds applies equally to aeroplanes!

The final part of the *sura* in a way ties together the two main themes in that perhaps the greatest of all of Allah's blessings to mankind is the Guidance He sends to us through His Messengers, and our gratitude or ingratitude for it is demonstrated by whether or not we accept and follow it. That is the measure against which our everlasting destiny will be decided: eternal reward or eternal punishment.

The whole motif of the *sura* is summed up in two *ayats*: *"Allah coins a likeness of a city which was safe and at peace, its provision coming to it plentifully from every side. Then it showed ingratitude for Allah's blessings and so Allah made it bear the robe of hunger and fear for what it did. A Messenger from among them came to them but they denied him. So the punishment gripped them while they were wrongdoers."* (16:112)

The *sura* ends by confirming that what the Prophet is calling people to is nothing other than Allah's *deen*, the primordial natural human Way given by Allah to Ibrahim, restored to its original purity: *"Then We revealed to you: 'Follow the religion of Ibrahim, a man of pure natural belief. He was not one of the idolaters'"* (16:123), and that those who are steadfast in following it will have the continual support and companionship of the Lord of all existence: *"Allah is with those who show fear of Him and with those who are good-doers."* (16:128)

Sura 17
Al-Isra': The Night Journey

The first *ayat* of this *sura* refers to the momentous Night Journey of the Prophet from Makka to Jerusalem and then through the Seven Heavens to the very Presence of Allah. After that one brief reference the subject matter of the *sura* turns to the history of the Tribe of Israel and what happened to them during their first period in Palestine, perhaps continuing from the earlier mention of the Furthest Mosque which is on the site of the great Temple of Solomon in Jerusalem. In any case a passage of this *sura* is now devoted to the history of the early Jews and this is reflected in the fact that it is also commonly known as *Surat Bani Isra'il*.

The Torah was given to the Jews to be the Divine basis not only of their religion but also of their state. Divine Law was supposed to be the basis of their system of governance and if properly applied would have brought order and not chaos, justice and not injustice. But the tribe of Israel had lived for a long time under the tyranny of Pharaonic despotism and it was not long before signs of it began to appear in their own system of government, causing corruption in the land, and for this reason they had to be disciplined.

The Noble Qur'an makes it clear that administrative and moral incapacity in a country's government will result in its downfall and in other people coming from outside to take it over and punish the perpetrators. The Almighty says: *"We decreed in the Book for the tribe of Israel"* - meaning in the scrolls of pre-eternal knowledge - *"'You will twice cause corruption in the earth and you will rise to a great height.' When the promised first time came, We sent against you slaves of Ours possessing great force, and they ransacked your houses, rampaging right through them, and it was a promise which was fulfilled."*(17:4-5)

189

The Jewish nation abandoned much of the Revelation they had been given and so they forfeited the Divine support which protected them. As the poet says:

You were given a kingdom and did not manage it well.
Those who do not manage a kingdom well
have it taken away.

Corruption and arbitrary confiscation of people's property are not conceivable in governance which really is based on Divine Revelation and there is no excuse for it, which is why the punishment of its people was so severe. The whole nation was brutally colonised by the Assyrians and many were transported to servitude in Babylon. The tribe of Israel suffered abasement and oppression until what was crooked became straightened and they returned to proper behaviour and they were once more reconciled with their Lord.

When that had taken place they once more regained the position and nobility they had lost: *"Then once again We gave you the upper hand over them and supplied you with more wealth and children and made you the most numerous group."* (17:6) So the retribution they suffered was not so much a punishment as a salutary lesson from Allah. They were obstinate people who had to be taught the hard way this basic principle of human existence: *"If you do good, you do it to your own benefit. If you do evil, you do it to your own detriment."* (17:7)

It is clear that the Jews were addicted to their vices and were very good at finding ways of justifying them. Therefore as soon as their circumstances improved again they were hankering after their old ways and injustices. Consequently before long the punishment was repeted, this time at the hands of the Romans and because they had failed to learn from what happened the first time it took them a very long time indeed to return.

It is evident from the Qur'an that the same fate awaits them again since once more they have abandoned the Torah and adopted the means of injustice and oppression: *"But if you revert to what*

*you did, We also will revert. We have made Jahannam a prison for
the rejectors of faith."* (17:8)

Then Allah ordained that the Muslims would imitate the Jews
and distort their Revelation according to their whims and desires
just as they had, and this, ironically, is what opened the way for the
tribe of Israel to re-establish their state on the land of the Arabs
who had abandoned the Qur'an and become the slaves of their
lower appetites.

So today's conflict between the Jews and the Muslims is a para-
doxical one, because it is the Muslims who have now abandoned
their Divine inheritance and become obsessed by racial considerations, and the Jews who raise the banner of the Torah and respect
the Sabbath. In other words, the struggle is between a true revelation with few supporters and a corrupted revelation whose people
venerate it.

We return to *Surat al-Isra* to note a feature unique to it, which
is that the word 'Qur'an' is repeated eleven times, something that
does not occur in any other *sura*. This may have a bearing on what
we have just mentioned about the nature of the present struggle
between the Muslims and the Jews. Let us now recall these *ayats*:

1. *"This Qur'an guides to the most upright way and gives
the good news to the believers, those who do right actions,
that they shall have an immense wage."* (17:9)

2. *"We have diversified things in this Qur'an so that they
might be reminded, but it only makes them shy away more."*
(17:41)

3. *"When you recite the Qur'an, We place an obscuring veil
between you and those who do not believe in the Next
World."* (17:45)

4, *"When you mention your Lord alone in the Qur'an, they
turn their backs, shying away."* (17:46)

5. *"We appointed the vision We showed you only as a trial
and temptation for the people, and the Accursed Tree in the*

Qur'an. We frighten them, but it only increases them in overweening insolence." (17:60)

6-7. *"... and also the recitation (qur'an) at dawn. The dawn recitation is certainly witnessed."* (17:78)

8. *"What We reveal in the Qur'an is a healing and a mercy to the believers but increases the wrongdoers in nothing but loss."* (17:82)

9. *"Say: 'If both men and jinn banded together to produce the like of this Qur'an, they could never produce anything like it, even if they backed each other up.'"* (17:88)

10. *"We have distributed throughout this Qur'an all kinds of metaphors for people, but most people spurn anything but unbelief."* (17:89)

11. *"We have divided up the Qur'an so that you may recite it to the people at intervals, and We have sent it down little by little."* (17:105)

Only in *Surat Bani Isra'il* is the name of the Qur'an given such peominence. The purpose of this, perhaps, is that the Muslims may understand that it is the Qur'an alone which is the foundation of their community and that it alone will enable them to regain dominion and leadership, remove love of this world and fear of death from their souls, and give them the courage they need to face the enemies of the Truth and re-establish the *deen* of Allah.

Ignorance can sometimes be deemed a mitigating excuse, but deliberate disregard of the Truth and arrogance towards it and preferring blindness to guidance are bound to incur devastating anger from Allah. In the past, as we have seen, Allah gave the idolaters power over the tribe of Israel because they did not show proper esteem for their Book. It is not surprising, then, that the Muslims were subjugated after they neglected the Qur'an and now have no standing or influence in the world.

The way to return is clear: there must be belief, law, morality, and correct action, all of which spring from the eternal fountain of the Qur'an. This alone will give the Muslims new life, a life which will make them once more the community of Revelation, able to restore the link between Heaven and earth. But it will not happen overnight. You cannot plant in the morning and expect to harvest in the evening. Everything has a time when it comes to fruition, regardless of whether a man is pleased or angry about it.

Allah has ordained a pattern for existence and we have to submit to that pattern and work within it, containing our impatience with steadfast adherence to the truth: *"Man prays for evil just as he prays for good. Man is ever impetuous."* (17:11) Regard for time and submission to it is mentioned in the very next *ayat*: *"We have made the night and day two signs. We blotted out the sign of the night and made the sign of the day a time for seeing, so that you may seek favour from your Lord and may know the number of years and the reckoning of time. We have made everything very plain."* (17:12)

Over the passage of time, some nations are raised up and others vanquished. The standing of the Jews rose and fell several times, as the beginning of the *sura* explains and every nation has its ups and downs in this way. But the responsibility for this lies with man himself. If he takes the right path he succeeds. If he deviates, he fails: *"Anyone who is guided is guided only to his own benefit. Anyone who is misguided is misguided only to his own detriment. No bearer of a burden can bear the burden of another ..."* (17:15)

This applies to both individuals and nations. The Noble Qur'an tells us in this regard that the appearance of luxury is the first manifestation of corruption in a nation and that the affluent are the pathogens which carry and transmit the destructive disease: *"When We desire to destroy a city, We send a command to the affluent in it and they become wantonly deviant in it and the Word is justly carried out against it and We annihilate it completely."* (17:16)

Societies which are based on Allah's Guidance bear its banner and remain strong as long as they keep away from luxury, pomposity, and hardness of heart. But when they turn to this world their days are numbered: *"How many generations We destroyed after Nuh! Your Lord is well able to be aware of and see the wrong actions of His slaves! For anyone who desires this fleeting existence, We hasten in it whatever We will to whoever We want. Then We will consign him to Jahannam ..."* (17:17-18)

The question is what people must do to escape such a fate. *Surat Bani Isra'il* now continues with two full pages giving us precise instructions about the actions which are necessary to save ourselves from the sorry fate of our predecessors, ensure our right guidance, and guarantee Divine protection for ourselves in the present and future.

First, as always, we are reminded of the central tenet of the Revelation, Allah's Oneness: *"Your Lord has decreed that you should worship none but Him ..."* and this is immediately followed by: *"and that you show kindness to your parents ..."* (17:23) The remainder of the *ayat* spells out the form which this kindness to parents should take. Its vital importance is indicated by the fact that it is coupled with the worship of Allah in the *ayat*.

No society can be strong unless it is united and no society can be united if its basic constituent, the family, is divided. So this instruction contains the key to continuing social strength. It is particularly important now, when the dominant ethos inculcates a very different attitude, one of disrespect for parents, whose effects can be seen in the social breakdown of Western society and which is rapidly spreading throughout the rest of the world.

Having laid a firm foundation it is necessary to make sure that other people within one's orbit have what they need: *"Give relatives their due, and the destitute and the traveller ..."* (17:24) This reveals an inherent flaw in the much vaunted social welfare systems of the world today. By removing individual responsibility for taking care of others' needs and replacing it by government aid, the modern state weakens the fabric of society.

In expenditure as in other things the Qur'an calls people to the middle way, in this case with a particularly vivid image: *"Do not keep your hand chained to your neck or extend it to its full extent lest you sit there blamed and destitute."* (17:29)

As is becoming more and more obvious, birth control is not the magic answer to all the world's social problems: *"Do not kill your children out of fear of being poor."* (17:31) Sexual promiscuity, on the other hand, which is condoned to the point of approval in the world today, is proving a social bane of epidemic proportions whose harmful medical and social consequences are becoming daily more visible: *"And do not go near to fornication. It is an indecent act, an evil way."* (17:32)

Another extraordinary facet of the modern world is that this century has probably seen more unjust killing than any previous period in human history and yet the widespread abolition of capital punishment has removed the only possibility of taking life in a just way. *"Do not kill any person Allah has made inviolate, except by legal right. If someone is wrongly killed We have given authority to his next-of-kin. But he should not be excessive in taking life: he will be helped."* (17:33)

The advice now moves to the vital sphere of economic transactions and we are instructed to respect the orphan's property, to fulfil contracts, and to be scrupulous with regard to weight and measures. This has an inner dimension because we will be held to account for all our actions: *"Hearing, sight and hearts will all be questioned."* (17:36)

Finally we are warned against the arrogance of considering ourselves the masters of existence, which is certainly the besetting human sin of this time: *"Do not strut arrogantly about the earth. You will certainly never split the earth apart nor will you rival the mountains in height."* (17:37)

These instructions provide a comprehensive agenda for a healthy and vigorous human society and if put into practice will set right each individual and society as a whole: *"That is part of the wisdom your Lord has revealed to you."* (17:39) Allah would never allow any nation which adhered to these principles to be overcome.

The passage ends, as it began, with a warning against doing anything to compromise the Divine Unity: *"Do not set up another god together with Allah and so be thrown into Jahannam, blamed and driven out."* (17:39) So these words of admonition begin with the Unity of Allah and end with His Unity because no heart which is subject to anything other than Allah has any hope of success. The cornerstone of the whole edifice is pure belief in Allah.

Following on from this the *sura* now proceeds to illustrate the unitary nature of Allah's existence. *"We have diversified things in this Qur'an so that they might be reminded, but it only makes them shy away more. Say: 'If there had been other gods together with Him as you say, they would have sought a way to the Master of the Throne.' Glory be to Him! He is exalted above what they say in greatness and sublimity! The seven heavens and the earth and everyone in them glorify Him. There is nothing which does not glorify His praise, but you do not understand their glorification. He is All-Forbearing, Ever-Forgiving."* (17:41-44)

Whether we look outward at the unimaginable vastness of the universe with its uncountable galaxies, stars and planetary bodies or inward at the equally amazing intricacies of molecular and atomic structure with its never-ending display of moving particles, we find the same phenomena occurring. Some scientists have described what they have found in both arenas in terms of an endless dance with everything in it in motion, rising or setting, ascending or descending, moving to a particular kind of music in which there is neither chaos nor cacophony. Every second that passes testifies to the Vastness of the Creator of the universe and articulates the extent of His Power and affirms His Unity. This is what is meant by "glorification" and everything in existence has a different way of expressing it.

Yet many people give the lie to what the very cells of their bodies are continually affirming, and the *sura* proceeds to speak about such unbelievers and idolaters who abandon Allah and turn other things into gods instead of Him. They are oblivious and lost. They do not want to hear about Allah. They think that the Messenger is mad and they do not believe that there is any life other than this one.

The odd thing is that almost all contemporary scientists, the people who have unveiled and discovered such marvels, also fall into this category: *"They say, 'What! When we are bones and crumbled dust, will we then be raised up as a new creation?' Say: 'It would not matter if you were rock or iron or indeed any cre-*

ation that you think is harder still!' They will ask, 'Who will bring us back again?' Say: 'He who brought you into being in the first place.' They will shake their heads at you and ask, 'When will it come?' Say: 'It may well be that it is very near.'" (17:49-51)

Later in the *sura* the unbelievers' rejection of the Resurrection and Judgement is again mentioned: *"Anyone whom Allah guides is truly guided. But for those He leads astray you will find no protector besides Him. We will gather them on the Day of Rising flat on their faces, blind, dumb and deaf. Their resting place is Jahannam: whenever the Blaze dies down, We will increase it for them. That is their repayment for rejecting Our signs and saying, 'What, when we are bones and crumbled dust, will we then be raised up as a new creation?' Do they not see that Allah, who created the heavens and the earth, has the power to create the like of them, and has appointed fixed terms for them of which there is no doubt? The wrongdoers still spurn anything but unbelief."* (17:97-99)

So it can be seen from this that worldly cleverness and true intellect are by no means the same thing; and that when intellect is lacking, a man looks but does not really see, listens but does not really hear. This prevents him from responding to Allah's guidance and leads to denial of His existence and the encounter with Him.

❋❋❋❋❋

The second half of the *sura* is largely devoted to the Prophet, may Allah bless him and grant him peace, and his relationship with his people. He is concerned for them and longs for them to be guided. Most of them fail to recognise him as Allah's Messenger.

Allah retells the story of the creation of Adam and of Iblis's refusal to recognise him and of His permitting Iblis to mislead any of the sons of Adam who would listen to him. But the descendants of Adam should reject the promptings of Iblis since Allah has poured His blessings onto them, which should make them profoundly grateful: *"We have honoured the children of Adam and conveyed them on land and sea and provided them with good things, and favoured them greatly over many We have created..."* (17:70)

But human resolve is weak and Shaytan is both cunning and extremely persistent in his assault on us; the fact is that most people succumb to it and prefer short-sighted short-term gratification to the infinitely greater reward of the long-term everlasting goal.

Muhammad, the Messenger of Allah, did everything he could to establish that Allah is One and that He sustains all existence but he was told, "Our idols are more worthy of esteem!" His people challenged him to bring a miracle to prove his truthfulness: *"'Let him bring us a sign like those sent to earlier peoples.' None of the cities which We destroyed before them believed. Will they then believe?"* (21:5-6)

They were very specific about what they wanted: *"They say, 'We will not believe you until you make a spring gush from the earth for us; or have a garden of dates and grapes, which you make rivers come pouring through; or make the sky, as you claim, fall down on us in lumps; or bring Allah and the angels here as a guarantee; or possess a house made out of gleaming gold; or ascend up into heaven, and even then we will not believe in your ascent until you bring us down a book which we can read.' Say: 'Glory be to my Lord! What am I but a human messenger?'"* (17:90-93)

Yet such things do not in fact bring people to believe: *"Nothing has prevented Us sending you signs except the fact that the earlier peoples denied them."* (17:59) The fact is that if Allah had yielded to their request for these things, belief still would not have entered their hearts, as He says in another place: *"Even if We opened up to them a door into heaven, and they spent the day ascending through it, they would only say, 'Our eyesight is befuddled! Or rather we have been put under a spell!'"* (15:14-15)

Blindness of the heart caused by prejudice, envy, stupidity, greed and egotism cannot be dispelled by any outward demonstration. It is so deep-rooted that it even survives death: *"On the Day We summon all people with their Records, those who are given their book in their right hand will read their book and they will not be wronged by even the tiniest shred. Anyone who is blind in this world will be blind in the Next World and even further off the path.*" (17:70-71)

Muhammad, peace and blessings be upon him, knew that the Revelation he brought contained the healing for every sickness, however deeply ingrained, and he refused to allow even the most hostile rejection to distract him from conveying Allah's Final Message to humanity.

Occasionally his deep compassion and concern for those to whom he had been sent and his eagerness for their guidance almost led him to overstep the mark: *"They were really near to inveigling you away from some of what We have revealed to you, hoping you would fabricate something against Us. Then they would have taken you as their intimate. Had We not made you firm, you would have leaned towards them a little. "* (17:73-75)

Another time, too, their ceaseless persecution of the believers almost succeeded in its aim: *"They were very near to scaring you from the land in order to expel you from it. But had they done so they would only have remained there a short time after you."* (17:76) Soon after this the Messenger emigrated to Madina and so Allah saved him from their plots; and not long after that Islam was victorious and he returned to Makka triumphant. Allah kept His promise.

Muhammad was Allah's final word to people and the last brick by which the edifice of Prophethood as a whole was completed. The People of the Book were aware that a Prophet would come, and in the Revelations sent to them they were told to expect him and confirm him when he came.

Those among them who were open-hearted were quick to recognise the truth when they heard and saw it and to follow the Prophet who brought and demonstrated it. Allah says:

> *"With Truth We have revealed it and with Truth it has come down. We have sent you only to bring good news and to give warning. We have divided up the Qur'an so you may recite it to the people at intervals and We have revealed it little by little. Say: 'Believe in it or do not believe. Truly, when it is recited to them those who were*

given knowledge before it fall on their faces in prostration, saying, 'Glory be to our Lord! The promise of our Lord is truly fulfilled!'" (17:105-108)

Sura 18
Al-Kahf: The Cave

Phenomenal existence indicates Allah's Existence, and Revelation provides guidance to Him. Both are needed for sound belief: study of Existence and reflection on the Revelation. *Surat al-Kahf* combines both elements by taking actual historical events and demonstrating the Divine Unity through them, and disclosing them as archetypal examples for human beings of every generation.

It contains the story of some young men who went to the Cave which gives the *sura* its name; the story of a debate between two unnamed men, one of whom was the wealthy owner of a garden and the other of whom was poor; the story of Musa with al-Khidr; and a general account of the life of Dhu'l-Qarnayn. The stories are divided by marvellous passages guiding to Allah and preparing people to meet Him.

Before these historical events are broached, there is a brief introduction confirming the Revelation and its Message of good news and warning, refuting the Christian heresy, consoling the Prophet and stating the purpose of our earthly life; then two *ayats* introduce the subject of the Cave.

These ten *ayats* have a special significance which take them beyond the context of the *sura* as a whole: Abu'd-Darda' reported Allah's Messenger as saying, "If anyone learns by heart the ten *ayats* at the beginning of *Surat al-Kahf*, he will be protected from the Dajjal (Antichrist)." There is a hidden dimension to the Qur'an independent of its linguistic meaning which makes it effective in other ways and the Prophet mentioned many *ayats* whose recitation in different situations would bring Allah's help to the reciter.

The People of the Cave were young men who believed in the One God and knew that all other gods were non-entities which could neither help nor harm anyone. Their, people, however, did believe in other gods and so they found themselves completely at odds with them: *"These people of ours have taken gods apart from Him. Why do they not produce a clear authority concerning them! Who could do greater wrong than one who fabricates a lie against Allah?"* (18:15)

Eventually they were forced to flee to a cave to escape from the injustice and hostility of their people. Allah desired to make their action a lesson whose usefulness would continue to the end of time. Political oppression and the persecution of faith is an ever-recurring theme in human history. Indeed it is necessary so that Allah's help to the believers and the frustration of the unbelievers can be demonstrated! Their story is not a unique case in history.

What makes the story of these particular young men so remarkable is the way Allah rescued them from their predicament. Rather than take them out of their society He removed their society from them by making them sleep right through it! When they woke up more than three hundred years later their oppressors were already ancient history!

They were not immediately aware of what had happened, thinking that only a few hours had passed, and only found out when one of them went to buy some food. They were still concerned about the persecution of their faith: *"If they find out about you, they will stone you or make you revert to their religion and then you will never have success."* (18:20) But the people of the time in which they had woken up revered and honoured them.

The whole incident shows us Allah's absolute Power over existence, His awareness of and minute concern for those who truly believe in Him, and that no believer of any age should despair of Allah's help: *"Say: 'Allah knows best how long they stayed.' The Unseen of the heavens and the earth belongs to Him. How perfectly He sees, how well He hears! They have no protector apart from Him, nor does He share His rule with anyone. Recite what has been revealed to you of your Lord's Book. No one can change His*

Words. You will never find any sanctuary apart from Him." (18:26-27)

People fall into two groups regarding the Revelation: one group believes in it and follows the Messenger while the other turns away from the Truth and follows its own whims and desires. Allah instructs His Prophet to hold to the first group: *"Restrain yourself patiently with those who call on their Lord morning and evening, desiring His Face"* (18:28); and to avoid the second: *"And do not obey anyone whose heart We have made heedless of Our remembrance, and who follows his own whims and desires and whose affair has burst all bounds."* (18:28)

The onus is on the individual to chose which of the two groups they will belong to: *"Say: 'It is the Truth from your Lord. So let anyone who wills believe and anyone who wills reject.'"* (18:29) After clearly stating the individual responsibility, Allah graphically describes the punishment of the latter group and the reward of the former: *"We have made ready for the wrongdoers a Fire whose billowing walls of smoke will encircle them. If they call for help, they will be helped with water like seething molten brass, scalding their faces. What a noxious drink! What an evil repose! But as for those who believe and do right actions, We shall not let the wage of the good-doers go to waste. They will have Gardens of Eden with rivers flowing under them. They will be adorned in them with bracelets made of gold, and wear green garments made of finest silk and rich brocade, reclining there on couches under canopies. What an excellent reward! What a wonderful repose!"* (18:29-31)

This description is followed by the second story about two gardens in this world. Their owner, a wealthy unbeliever, refused to listen to the sincere advice of a poor believer concerning them: *"Cite the example to them of two men. To one of them We gave two gardens of grape-vines and surrounded them with date-palms, putting between them some cultivated land."* (18:32) The rich man considered that his property made him superior to the other: *"I have more wealth than you, more people under me."* (18:34) This attitude comes from falsely attributing permanence to this world: *"I do not think that this will ever end. I do not think the Hour will ever come."* (18:35)

This is, of course, the dominant viewpoint of our time; but it is not the truth. The truth is: *"What is with you comes to an end. But what is with Allah goes on for ever."* (16:96) This world is: *"...like water We send down from the sky and the plants of the earth combine with it. But then it becomes dry chaff scattered by the winds. Allah has complete power over everything."* (18:45) It is not that wealth is wrong in itself but it must never be allowed to distract its possessor from understanding the truth of existence, something which it is all too prone to do: *"Wealth and sons are the embellishment of the life of this world. But, in your Lord's sight, right actions which are lasting are better in reward and a better basis for hope."* (18:46)

The poor believer warns the other about his presumptuous claims, counselling him to attribute his blessings to their true Source: *"Why, when you entered your garden, did you not say, 'As Allah wills. There is no strength but in Allah'? Though you see me with less wealth and children than you, it may well be my Lord will give me better than your garden and send down on it a fireball from the sky so that morning finds it a sliding heap of dust."* (18:39-40) But his earnest, well-meant advice falls on deaf ears.

What he predicts takes place, and because the rich man had invested everything in this world, he is left with nothing but regret and despair: *"'Oh, if only I had not attributed any partner to my Lord!' There was no group to come to his aid, besides Allah, and he was not given any help."* (18:42-43)

The relevance of this story to our own time is so clear that it needs no pointing out. Modern civilisation has created generations of people of this kind whose consciousness is totally entrapped in this world, unable to see anything beyond it. The Next World scarcely enters into their frame of reference at all, and when it does it is only to consider any idea or discussion of it to be a kind of superstition which intelligent people do not dwell on or think about.

The Messenger of Allah, may Allah bless him and grant him peace, pointed out the proper balance that must be achieved in relation to wealth: "If one is concerned with the Next World, Allah will put wealth in his heart and reunite him and force this world to be subject to him. If one is concerned with this world, Allah will put its poverty before him and disunite him and will only give of this world what is decreed for him and he will remain poor in the morning and the evening. No one advances to Allah with his heart but that Allah makes him the hearts of people incline to him with love and mercy and Allah hastens every good to him."

Allah reinforces the teaching of this story by evoking the end of the world and the reality of human accountability: *"The Day We make the mountains move and you see the earth laid bare and We gather them together, not leaving out a single one of them. They will be paraded before your Lord in ranks. The Book will be set in place and you will see the evil-doers fearful of what is in it. They say, 'Alas for us! What is this Book which does not pass over any action, small or great, without recording it?' They will find there everything they did, and your Lord will not wrong anyone."* (18:47-49)

This discussion continues until the third story in the *sura* which is about Musa, the Prophet of the Tribe of Israel, and another Prophet, one of the righteous slaves of Allah, called al-Khidr. The story illustrates a universal truth which might be summed up by the words: "If you knew the Unseen, you would choose to leave things as they are." In this life we do what we think is right but sometimes the results of what we do surprise us by bringing harm, which is difficult for us to comprehend, and sometimes the opposite is true. The most fitting thing is for a man simply to submit to the Decree.

Allah says elsewhere: *"It may be that you hate a thing when it is good for you, and it may be that you love a thing when it is bad for you. Allah knows and you do not know."* (2:216) This does not mean we should not act rationally or that it is permissible to act contrary to the *Shari'a* because good sometimes results. It is just that things are not always what they appear to be and that Allah brings about what He wants in whatever way He desires.

The story of Musa with al-Khidr is a special case included in the Revelation to make this matter clear. It cannot be taken as a licence by anyone to do anything against the *Shari'a*. Both men were Messengers of Allah conveying the Message from their Lord with which they were entrusted. The time of Revelation has ended, so if anyone commits a reprehensible action and then claims that he was given permission to do so by Allah he is a liar and must be punished for what he did – and for his claim as well.

The story begins by pointing out two qualities which are needed for the achievement of any worthwhile goal: firm resolve and great steadfastness. That is made clear by the *ayat*: *"When Musa said to his servant: 'I will not give up until I reach the meeting-place of the two seas, even if I must press on for many years.'"* (18:60) It means he would not give up in his quest even it took years! Strength and piety alone are not enough: they need the two supplementary qualities to enable them to bear fruit.

Musa and al-Khidr met. Musa said to him in great humility: *"May I follow you on condition that you teach me some of the right guidance which you have been taught?"* (18:66) Al-Khidr replied that following him would entail a kind of trial that Musa, notwithstanding all his great inner and outer strength, would not be able to tolerate. *"He said, 'You will not be able to bear with me. How indeed could you bear patiently something you have not encompassed in your knowledge?'"* (18:67-68)

Musa nevertheless took on the challenge and promised to be steadfast and obey; but he failed at the first hurdle when he found his companion making a hole in the ship they had embarked upon. He could not stop himself from objecting to this inexplicable action! The same occurred when al-Khidr killed a young boy and again when he rebuilt a wall belonging to some people who had refused them hospitality. On the surface each of the actions was completely wrong.

Before they parted company al-Khidr explained each of the three actions to Musa. Each of them involved unseen circumstances which, once disclosed, made complete sense of what had been done. The boat was holed to stop it being commandeered by a tyrannical king. The boy was killed to save his righteous parents from his evil. And the wall was rebuilt to safeguard the future of two orphans.

The important thing is that al-Khidr did not act of his own will but by Allah's command. He says: *"'I did not do it of my own accord.'"* (18:82) If anyone were to undertake such actions on their own initiative, they would violate the laws of Allah and corrupt the earth and be held responsible for it. The Unseen Worlds belong to their Lord and He can oblige whomever of His slaves He wishes to do whatever He wishes. But those who follow their own whims and desires and commit aggression against others are not safe from punishment.

People ask whether al-Khidr was better than Musa in the sight of Allah. The reply is "No." Musa was one of the five Messengers with resolve from whom Allah took covenants to guide mankind. They are Nuh, Ibrahim, Musa, 'Isa and Muhammad. No people are better than these. Al-Khidr's ascendancy in this instance does not make him superior to Musa. Ascendancy in a particular instance does not necessarily imply absolute pre-eminence. A man's standing is the result of many different gifts and other factors which come together in his person, not of one particular gift which especially distinguishes him.

The fourth and last of the stories of *Surat al-Kahf* is about an inspired leader named Dhu'l-Qarnayn who possessed both sovereignty and wisdom. He is an example of piety and righteousness, combining great political power with great fear of Allah. There are various suggestions as to the exact historical identity of Dhu'l-Qarnayn, with Alexander the Great high on the list of possibilities, but it is not in fact important whether he was king of Greece, Persia, China or somewhere else.

The important thing is that Allah opened the way for him to great worldly power and he took full advantage of the opportunities he was granted. He had an immense kingdom in the administration of which he made use of all the knowledge, faith and wisdom with which Allah had endowed him: *"They will ask you about Dhu'l-Qarnayn. Say: 'I will relate an account of him to you.' We gave him power and authority on the earth and granted him a way to everything. So he followed a way."* (18:83-85)

He travelled west towards the setting sun as far as it was possible to go and found a people there of whom some were good and some were evil, and Allah revealed to him: *"'You may either punish them or else you may treat them with gentleness.' He said, 'As for anyone who does wrong, we will punish him and then he will be returned to his Lord and He will punish him with a dreadful punishment. But as for anyone who believes and acts rightly, he will receive the best of rewards."* (18:83-85)

This is the good policy of a just ruler. Then he travelled equally far to the East, where he found a backward people who had nothing to shelter them from the sun.

In the other journey mentioned in the Qur'anic account he arrived at a place between two mountains where there was another backward people who were living under the continual threat of attack: *"They said, 'O Dhu'l-Qarnayn! Yajuj and Majuj are causing corruption in the land. Can we, therefore, pay tribute to you in return for your making a barrier between us and them?'"* (18:94)

Dhu'l-Qarnayn refused their money but asked them to help him in constructing a great wall: *"Just give me a strong helping hand and I will build a solid barrier between you and them."* (18:95) The engineering genius of Dhu'l-Qarnayn became evident as he built a huge wall of iron, brass and rock which the people's enemies were unable to surmount or breach: *"So they were unable to climb over it, nor could they make a breach in it. He said, 'This is a mercy from my Lord.'"* (18:97-98)

Such technical prowess used to be the hallmark of the early Muslims but now expertise in such matters is in the hands of unbelievers. The Muslim skill in innovation has unfortunately passed from the things of this world to matters of the *deen*, which has left us in a state of intellectual and ethical confusion that is disastrous both for this life and for the Next!

The identity of Yajuj and Majuj is also the subject of much discussion – but again that is not in fact the important point. They are part of the 'legions' of Allah restrained by the action of Dhu'l-Qarnayn only, as we discover elsewhere in the Qur'an, to be released before the end of the world: *"When Yajuj and Majuj are let loose and rush down from every slope, and the True Promise is very close, the eyes of those who rejected will be transfixed."* (21:96-97)

Surat al-Kahf concludes by rounding out the ideas raised in its introductory *ayats*. At the beginning of the *sura*, the Christian heresy of attributing a son to Allah is forcefully repudiated: *"It is a monstrous utterance which has issued from their mouths."* (18:5) Here we find: *"Do those who reject imagine that they can take My slaves as protectors instead of Me? We have prepared Jahannam as hospitality for the rejectors!"* (18:102)

Also at the beginning of the *sura*, Allah tells us: *"We made everything on the earth adornment for it so that we might test them to see whose actions are best."* (18:7) At the end we find: *"Say: 'Shall I inform you of the greatest losers in their actions? People whose efforts in the life of this world are misguided while they suppose that they are doing good.' Those are the people who reject their Lord's signs and the meeting with Him..."* (18:103-105)

There follows a seminal *ayat* about the countlessness of Allah's Words, showing that they go far beyond the texts of the Revealed Books and implying that all existence is in reality nothing other than the Speech of Allah. *"Say: 'If all the sea were ink to write down the words of my Lord, it would run out long before the words of my Lord ran out, even if We brought the same amount of ink again.'"* (18:109)

The *sura* ends with one of those wonderful *ayats* which sum up the entire Revelation:

> *"Say: 'I am only a human being like yourselves. It is revealed to me that your God is One God. So let him who hopes to meet his Lord act rightly and not associate anyone with the worship of his Lord.'"* (18:110)

Sura 19
Maryam: Mary

Surat Maryam is unusual in the Qur'an in that it is phonetically unified in a very distinct way: the first four-fifths of its *ayats* end in the letter *ya'* in the accusative and doubled, and the last fifth in the letter *dal* in the accusative and doubled. This gives the *sura* an unmistakable identity and makes it immediately recognisable when recited.

Another distinguishing feature of the *sura* is the number of times that mercy is mentioned in it. It begins with it: *"Remembering your Lord's mercy to His slave Zakariyya"* (19:2) and the word is repeated several times in the course of the *sura*. The name of Allah, ar-Rahman (the All-Merciful), is repeated sixteen times:

1. *"I seek refuge from you with the All-Merciful,"* (19:18)

2. *"I have made a vow of silence to the All-Merciful and today I will not speak to any human being."* (19:26)

3. *"Father, do not serve Shaytan. Shaytan was disobedient to the All-Merciful."* (19:44)

4. *"Father, I am afraid that a punishment from the All-Merciful will afflict you, and turn you into a comrade of Shaytan."* (19:45)

5. *"Among those We guided and picked out, when the Signs of the All-Merciful were recited to them they fell on their faces, weeping, in prostration."* (19:58)

6. *"Gardens of Eden which the All-Merciful has promised*

to His slaves in the Unseen. His promise always comes true." (19:61)

7. *"Then We shall drag out from every sect the one among them most insolent towards the All-Merciful."* (19:69)

8. *"Say: 'As for those who are astray, let the All-Merciful prolong their term.'"* (19:75)

9. *"Has he surveyed the Unseen or has he made a contract with the All-Merciful? No indeed! We shall write down what he says and prolong the punishment for him."* (19:78-79)

10. *"That Day We will gather the godfearing to the All-Merciful with due ceremony."* (19:85)

11. *"They have no right of intercession. None do but those who have made a contract with the All-Merciful."* (19:87)

12. *"They say, 'The All-Merciful has got a son.' They have devised a monstrous thing!"* (19:88-89)

13. *"Their ascribing a son to the All-Merciful."* (19:91)

14. *"It is not fitting for the All-Merciful to have a son."* (19:92)

15. *"There is no one in the heavens and the earth who shall not come as a slave to the All-Merciful."* (19:93)

16. *"As for those who believe and do right actions, the All-Merciful will give them His love."* (19:96)

It is clear that mercy must be a theme of *Surat Maryam,* and indeed the first half of the *sura* speaks about people to whom Allah shows mercy in a particular way and the second half is mostly about people who reject Allah's mercy.

Surat Maryam was revealed in Makka before the emigration to Abyssinia. It speaks about the miraculous birth and infancy of 'Isa son of Maryam, placing it within the context of the story of

Zakariyya and his son Yahya. The connection between the two events was noted previously in *Surat Ali 'Imran*. The birth of Yahya was also miraculous because his father Zakariyya was a very old man and his mother was barren. Just as Allah's power revived an old man and made a barren woman fertile so it also made it possible for a virgin to give birth.

Zakariyya's ardent wish for a child when it seemed impossible, and the apparent lack of contentment with Allah's decree that it implies, stemmed from his desire for sound spiritual leadership for the Tribe of Israel. He had relatives who aspired to the leadership but were unfit for it so he asked Allah to give him a son who would be equal to the task: *"I fear my relatives when I am gone, and my wife is barren, so give me an heir direct from You to be my inheritor and the inheritor of the family of Ya'qub; and O Lord, make him pleasing to You."* (19:5-6)

Allah gave him Yahya, who was conceived after three nights of glorification, praise and devotion to worship: *"He came out to his people from the Upper Room and gestured to them to glorify Allah in the morning and the evening. 'O Yahya, take hold of the Book with vigour.' We gave him judgement while still a child."* (19:11-12)

The *sura* continues with a full account of the birth of 'Isa, mentioning Maryam's distress, how Allah consoled her, the slander of the Jews against her, and how the words of 'Isa in the cradle provided striking proof of his mother's innocence: *"He said, 'I am the slave of Allah. He has given me the Book and made me a Prophet. He has made me blessed wherever I am and directed me to pray and give* zakat *as long as I live."* (19:30-31) However, as is well known, the birth of 'Isa in this manner gave rise to a false belief: that because he did not have a human father, his father must be God Himself - may He be glorified and exalted! This led to the even greater heresy of ascribing divinity to 'Isa.

Allah makes it clear that there was no question of fatherhood at all: *"It is not for Allah to have a son. Glory be to Him! When He decides on something, He only says to it, "Be!" and it is."* (19:35) Allah is One and Indivisible and 'Isa is His slave and Messenger like the other Messengers: *"'Allah is my Lord and your Lord, so worship Him. This is a straight path.' The parties differed among themselves. Woe to those who reject because of their presence on a terrible day! How clear will be their hearing, how perfect their sight, on the Day they come to Us! Whereas today the wrongdoers are clearly misguided."* (19:36-38)

Their spurious positions about 'Isa will be resolved on *"the Day of Bitter Regret when the affair will be resolved."* (19:39) On that day it will clear to all that all that is other-than-Allah are His creatures and subject to Him.

The *sura* then speaks of Ibrahim, peace be upon him, concentrating on his relationship with his father and his compassionate concern for him. In the dialogue between them the nature of the call to right guidance and of the resistance to it is demonstrated. Ibrahim begs his father four times in a manner full of gentleness and courtesy to abandon the idols and submit to Allah. The last of his entreaties is: *"Father, I am afraid that a punishment from the All-Merciful will afflict you, and turn you into a comrade of Shaytan."* (19:45). What a contrast there is between this and the harshness of his idolatrous father's response: *"Do you forsake my gods, Ibrahim? If you do not stop, I will stone you. Keep away from me for a good long time."* (19:46)

Ibrahim left his father and people, and Allah showed mercy to him and appointed Prophethood in his progeny: *"When he had separated himself from them, and what they worshipped besides Allah, We gave him Ishaq and Ya'qub, making each of them a Prophet."* (19:49) After that the *sura* mentions a number of Prophets and the blessings which Allah bestowed on them. The Prophets are the cream of humanity who are sent by Allah to acquaint people with Him and their behaviour is a model for people to follow.

There is no doubt that those who lived with and learned from them were affected by their contact with them in a unique way which made them higher and purer than other people. That is why Muhammad, the Imam of the Prophets, says: "The best of generations is my generation and then those after them and then those after them."

The human tendency to fall away is very strong, however, and before long people lost sight of the prophetic light and fell into darkness: *"An evil generation succeeded them who neglected the prayer and followed their appetites. They will plunge into the Valley of Evil."* (19:59) The prayer is the touchstone of human society; it keeps people's souls attached to their Lord and prevents them from becoming entrenched in wrong action of any kind.

Abandoning it cuts people off from Allah and makes them easy prey for the shaytans, opening the way to vices of every kind. But those who hold fast to Divine Guidance will be safe: *"...except those who turn in repentance and believe and act righteously. They will enter the Garden and they will not be wronged in any way."* (19:60)

The people who reject the mercy of the Divine Guidance they have inherited from their predecessors become blind to the true nature of existence: *"Man says, 'When I am dead, will I then be brought out again alive?' Does not man recall that We created him before when he was not anything? By your Lord, We will collect them and the shaytans together. Then We will assemble them around Jahannam on their knees. Then We will drag out from every sect the one among them most insolent towards the All-Merciful."* (19:66-69) This is the archetypal form of the unbelievers of every age.

They look only to outward appearances: *"When Our clear Signs are recited to them, those who reject say to those who believe, 'Which of the two parties has the better position and the finer gathering?'"* (19:73) But worldly superiority is no safeguard against Allah: *"How many generations We destroyed before them who had finer furnishings and better appearance!"* (19:74)

They hide behind mockery: *"Have you seen him who rejects Our Signs and says, 'I will certainly be given wealth and children there.' Has he surveyed the Unseen, or has he made a contract with the All-Merciful?"* (19:77-78) But they will eat their words when the implacable reality of what they held in mockery actually occurs. *"No indeed! We shall write down what he says and prolong the punishment for him. We shall inherit from him the things he speaks of, and he will come to Us all alone,"* (19:79-80)

The *sura* returns to the crucial importance of affirming the absolute Unity of Allah and terrible reality of the Christian error in saying what they say about 'Isa: *"They say, 'The All-Merciful has got a son.' They have invented a monstrous thing. The heavens are all but rent apart and the earth split open and the mountains brought crashing down, at their ascribing a son to the All-Merciful! It is not fitting for the All-Merciful to have a son."* (19:88-92)

What they say indicates a complete misunderstanding of the true nature of existence, and as is clear from this *ayat* it has cataclysmic cosmic reverberations. If they knew the universal implications of their heresy they would cease immediately to voice it!

Allah Almighty hates people attributing partners to Him and it is the only thing that can never be forgiven. Allah's love is reserved for those who wholeheartedly proclaim His Unity and then live their lives accordingly, following the guidance of His Messengers: *"As for those who believe and do right actions, the All-Merciful will give them His love."* (19:96) And Allah's love brings with it the love of everything else in existence.

In a well-known *hadith* related by Abu Hurayra the Messenger of Allah, may Allah bless him and grant him peace, said, "When Allah the All-Glorious loves a slave, He calls to Jibril and says, 'I love so-and-so, so love him.' So Jibril loves him. Then he calls out in Heaven, saying: 'Allah loves So-and-So, so love him!' so the people of Heaven love him. Then He places acceptance for him in the earth.'"

Sura 20
TaHa

The Noble Qur'an was sent down as Revelation from Heaven and its origin is evident in its contents. It has no rival in its uncompromising affirmation of the Absolute Unity of Allah. The force of its expression compels people to acknowledge their Lord, lets their hearts drink in His Majesty, floods their intellects with His Light, and shows them the Next World without a veil.

It was hearing the first few *ayats* of this *sura* which transformed 'Umar ibn al-Khattab in one moment from being one of the most hostile opponents of the Revealed Message into one of its strongest supporters. But hearts which are hardened by prejudice and wrongdoing remain deaf and blind.

The Prophet had always been known for his absolute truthfulness and trustworthiness and he naturally expected that his people would listen to the Revelation he had received. But their fanatical adherence to their inherited traditions led them to reject what he had brought and made them ascribe it to forgery and madness.

When a noble man is suspected of something of which he is innocent, he is inevitably distressed, and so at the beginning of this *sura* Allah revealed some *ayats* to alleviate the distress of His Messenger and to confirm him in his Divinely appointed role: *"We did not send down the Qur'an to you to make you sorrowful, but only as a reminder for those who fear, a Revelation from Him who created the earth and the high heavens, the All-Merciful, established firmly on the Throne."* (20:2-5)

Conveying the Divine Message to coarse deniers is an onerous task. One means that Allah employs to make the load bearable for His final Messenger is to tell him of the equally difficult situations faced by the Prophets and Messengers before him. *"Has not the story of Musa reached you? When he saw a fire and said to his family, 'Wait here. I can make out a fire. Maybe I will bring you a brand from it, or I will find guidance at the fire.'"* (20:9-10)

As we know, the story of Musa and his encounter and travails with the Tribe of Israel are repeated many times in the Qur'an. The version we find in *Surat TaHa* is a particularly full account and takes up almost the whole *sura*. It covers in detail Musa's election by Allah, his early life, his encounter with Pharaoh and the magicians of Egypt, his flight from Egypt with the Tribe of Israel, and his difficulties with them and the Golden Calf.

Every time the story appears different aspects of it emerge. Each version has details which are not included in any other version. In this one, for instance, Musa talks of the various uses of his staff when he is asked about it by Allah: *"He said, 'It is my staff. I lean on it and beat down leaves for my sheep with it, and I have other uses for it.'"*

There are also the words with which Musa describes his Lord here, when he is telling Pharaoh about Him. *"He asked, 'Who then is your Lord, Musa?' He said, "Our Lord is He who gives to each thing its created form and then guides it.' He asked, 'What about the previous generations?' He said, 'Knowledge of them is in a Book with my Lord. My Lord does not misplace nor does He forget. It is He who made the earth a cradle for you and threaded pathways for you through it and sent down water from the sky, by which We have brought forth various different types of plants."* (20:49-53) This description is unique to this *sura*. No other version includes it.

Another thing is the words the magicians used to justify their belief in Allah and how they clung to it when Pharaoh threatened them with a horrible death. *"'We have put our trust in our Lord so that He may forgive us our mistakes and the magic which you forced us to perform. Allah is better and longer lasting.' As for those who come to their Lord as evil-doers, they will have Jahannam where they will neither die nor stay alive. But those who come to Him as believers, having performed right actions, they will have the highest ranks."* (20:73-75) There is also the

217

extremely interesting account of the Samaritan's role in the manu-facture of the Golden Calf, which appears nowhere else.

The story of Musa is followed by a description of the Last Day and its aftermath which is sufficient to strike terror in all but the most deadened and hardened heart, from: *"They will ask you about the mountains. Say: 'My Lord will scatter them as dust. He will leave them as a barren, level plain on which you will see no bend or bump"* to His words: *"Faces will be humbled to the Living, the All Sustaining, and anyone loaded down with wrongdoing will have failed."* (20:105-110)

This description is followed up by an *ayat* explaining what Allah intends by it: *"Accordingly We have revealed it as an Arabic Qur'an and We have distributed threats throughout it so that perhaps they may be godfearing or it may spur them into remembrance."* (20:113)

It will be noted from the *ayat* that Allah wants people to remember. Remembrance is a constant theme of the Qur'an as a whole and it is a special theme of this *sura* in which the matter of remembrance and its opposite, forgetfulness, are mentioned in eleven places:

1. *"We did not reveal the Qur'an to you to make you miserable, but only as a **reminder** for those who fear."* (20:2-3) Revelation is a reminder and one of its objects is to erase heedlessness and forgetfulness.

2. *"I am Allah. There is no god but Me, so worship Me and establish the prayer to **remember** Me."* (20:14) Establishing the prayer means performing it in a group in rows and preparing physically and spiritually to glorify and greet Allah. According to *hadith*, "Putting the rows straight is part of establishing the prayer."

3. Musa said after praying for Harun to share with him in bearing the burden of the Message: *"Let him share in my task, so that we can glorify You much and **remember** You much, for You are watching us."* (20:32-34)

4. Allah then says to Musa: *"Go, you and your brother, with My Signs and do not slacken in **remembering** Me."* (20:42)

5. Then He makes the goal of his mission to awaken Pharaoh from his lack of true awareness: *"But speak to him with gentle words so that perhaps he may **remember** or show some fear."* (20:44)

6. Musa describes Allah's knowledge of beings before and after time: *"He said, 'Knowledge of them is in a Book with my Lord. My Lord does not misplace nor does He **forget**.'"* (20:52)

7. When the Samaritan described the Calf which he made he said: *"This is your god and Musa's god, but he **forgot**."* (20:88)

8. Commenting on the story of Musa and his people, Allah says to His Prophet: *"Thus do We give you news of what has gone before and We have given you a **reminder** direct from Us. Those who turn away from it will bear a heavy burden on the Day of Rising."* (20:99-100)

9. The *ayat* quoted above: *"Accordingly We have revealed it as an Arabic Qur'an and We have distributed threats throughout it so that perhaps they may be godfearing or it may spur them into **remembrance**."* (20:113)

10. Then Allah says about the expulsion of Adam from the Garden: *"We contracted with Adam before, but he **forgot**. We did not find that he had a firm resolve."* (20:115)

11. Then comes this general warning to individuals and communities: *"But if anyone turns away from My reminder, his life will be a dark and narrow one and on the Day of Rising We will gather him blind. He will say, 'O Lord, why have You gathered me blind when before I was able to see?' He will say, 'Just as Our Signs came to*

*you and you **forgot** them, in the same way you too are **for-gotten** today.'"* (20:124-126)

So it can be seen that throughout its entire length *Sura TaHa* is concerned with the danger of heedlessness of Allah and with calling people back to remembrance of Allah and the inevitability of their meeting with Him. There is no fear for someone who forgets temporarily; since he can swiftly be made to remember. What is feared is that forgetfulness might become woven into the fabric of the heart so that it turns into an impervious covering which blinds the inner eye and makes a man fuel for Jahannam.

The archetypal story of forgetfulness and remembrance is the story of Adam and this is retold in *Surat TaHa*. In this version of it Adam's eating from the Forbidden Tree is attributed to forgetfulness: *"He forgot. We did not find that he had a firm resolve."* (20:115) Then His Lord reminded him and he repented and regained a high station with Allah.

This story is repeated day after day in the lives of his descendants. Forgetfulness overwhelms us and a fall ensues! It is remembering that sets us back on our feet. But if people refuse to heed the reminders which come to them they condemn themselves by their obstinate forgetfulness to a miserable fate. *"But whoever turns away from My reminder, his life will be a dark and narrow one and on the Day of Rising We will gather him blind. He will ask, 'O Lord, why have You gathered me blind when before I was able to see?' He will say, 'Just as Our Signs came to you and you forgot them, in the same way you too are forgotten today."* (20:124-126)

We look at the end of the *sura* and we see, as in so many other *suras*, that there is a clear connection with its beginning. It addresses the people who had caused the Messenger of Allah to feel distress and warns them of the fate which befell their predecessors: *"Are they not guided by the many generations We destroyed before them, among whose dwelling-places they walk about? There are signs in that for people of sound intellect."* (20:127)

They were destroyed for their refusal to listen to the truth when it was presented to them. They can only expect the same if they act in the same way: *"And were it not for a word which preceded from your Lord, and a specified term, it would inevitably have already taken place."* (20:129) There is an inexorable and unchanging pattern to existence.

At this point the Prophet, may Allah bless him and grant him peace, and by extension all the believers, are given a remedy for the distress caused by the obstinate rejection of the unbelievers: *"So be steadfast in the face of what they say and glorify the praise of your Lord before the rising of the sun and before its setting. And glorify Him during part of the night and at both ends of the day, so that perhaps you will be pleasing."* (20:130)

This resembles the end of *Surat al-Hijr*, where the feeling of distress is actually mentioned together with the advice: *"We know that your breast is constricted by what they say. So glorify the praise of your Lord and be one of the prostrators."* (15:97-98) If the heart is filled with remembrance of Allah there is no room for sorrow. The best way to oppose the enemy is to love the Friend. *"Is it not by remembrance of Allah that hearts are made still?"* (13:28)

Looking at what other people have is not conducive to peace of mind: *"Do not direct your eyes longingly to what We have given certain of them to enjoy, the flower of the life of this world, so that We may test them by it."* (20:131) Sometimes the unbelievers and rebels have the amplest portion of this world and seem to take the most enjoyment in it. But as we saw in the previous *sura* such appearances belie the reality of the situation: *"How many generations We destroyed before them who had finer furnishings and better appearance!"* (19:73-74)

In the life of the Prophet, may Allah bless him and grant him peace, it is related that 'Umar ibn al-Khattab, may Allah be pleased with him, was deeply grieved when he saw the marks on the skin of the Messenger of Allah from the twigs of the coarse bed. on which he slept. 'Umar thought of the luxuries which Khusraw and Caesar enjoyed and expressed the desire that the

Prophet should have a better material situation. The Prophet, peace and blessings be upon him, pointed out that those rulers had their pleasure in this world only. The truth of the matter is: *"Your Lord's provision is better and longer-lasting."* (20:131)

The way to gain that provision is to call people to the worship of Allah and be constant in it yourself: *"Command your family to pray, and be constant in it. We do not ask you for provision. We provide for you. And the best end result is gained by fear of Allah."* (20:132) Most people, Muslims included, are almost totally preoccupied with the provision which is guaranteed them by Allah but about which they almost worry themselves to death, losing sight of the obligations whose observance in fact ensure the very thing they are so concerned about!

The final *ayats* are once more addressed to the unbelievers, warning that time will inevitably show that the truth was with the Messenger of Allah and those who follow him:

"Say: 'Everyone is waiting expectantly, so wait expectantly. Soon you shall soon know who are the Companions of the Right Path and who is rightly guided.'" (20:135)

Sura 21
Al-Anbiya': The Prophets

Surat al-Anbiya' was one of the last *suras* to be revealed in the Makkan period. Its name derives from the fact that in the second half of it the names of sixteen Prophets are mentioned together with brief references to their lives. But the first half of the *sura* concerns the same theme in that it is devoted to the nature of Prophet-hood in general and how the Prophetic Message is received in the human communities to which it is sent.

One of the main functions of Prophethood is to remind heedless mankind of their Heavenly origin and destiny: *"Mankind's Reckoning has drawn very close to them, yet, heedlessly, they turn away. No fresh **Reminder** comes to them from their Lord but that they listen to it as an entertainment. Their hearts are distracted."* (21:1-3) *"We have revealed to you a Book containing your **Reminder**. Will you not then use your understanding?"* (21:10) *"We have revealed to you a Book containing your **Reminder**. Will you not then use your understanding?"* (21:50)

The Prophets are sent to remind mankind that their lives have purpose: *"We did not create Heaven and earth and everything in between them as a game"* (21:16); and that this life is a time of testing: *"We test you with both good and evil as a trial. And you will be returned to Us"* (21:35), and that we are accountable for every action we do: *"We will set up the Just Balance on the Day of Rising and no self will be wronged in any way. Even if it is no more than the weight of a grain of mustard-seed, We will produce it. We are enough as Reckoner."* (21:47)

Though the Prophets are sent by Allah they are necessarily human beings. They must be human beings so that they can be imitated and learned from by other human beings. Their bodies are subject to the same accidents as the rest of us, and they too are tested and have to strive in the face of the difficulties of ordinary human existence: *"We have only ever sent before you men to whom We gave Revelation. Ask the people of the Reminder if you do not know. We did not give them bodies which did not eat food. They were not immortal."* (21:7-8)

Yet the fact that the Prophets are human blinds many people to their Divinely-appointed function: *"Those who do wrong confer together secretly, saying, 'Is this man anything but a human being like yourselves?'"* (21:3) Consequently such people cast about frantically, seeking explanations for the Prophetic Message within the framework of ordinary human experience: *"Furthermore they say, 'A muddled jumble of dreams!' and, 'He has fabricated it!' and, 'He is a poet!'"* (21:5)

This makes them unable to appreciate the Reminder they are being given and their disparagement reveals itself in sarcastic scepticism: *"They say, 'When will this promise come about if you are telling the truth?'"* (21:38) The truth is not open to question, but they are: *"He will not be questioned about what He does, but they will be questioned."* (21:23)

When the Promised Day arrives it will be their turn to be questioned. *"'Do not run away! Return to the life of luxury you enjoyed and to the places where you lived, so that you can be interrogated!' They said, 'Alas for us! We were indeed wrongdoers!'"*(21:13-14) But at this point their regret will be of no avail: *"'If those who reject faith only knew of the time when they will not be able to keep the Fire away from their faces or their backs, and they will not be helped! No, it will come upon them suddenly, confounding them, taking them completely by surprise, and they will not be able to ward it off. They will be granted no reprieve."* (21:39-40)

Another aspect of the Prophetic Reminder is the call to human beings to recognise the Divine Hand at work in the world surrounding them: *"Do those who reject not see that the heavens and the earth were sewn together and then We unstitched them? And We made from water every living thing."* (21:30) This is, of course, an astonishing *ayat* in the light of present-day theories about the origin of the universe.

"We placed firmly embedded mountains on the earth, so it would not move under them, and put broad valleys as roadways in it, so that perhaps they might be guided. We made the sky a preserved and protected roof, yet still they turn away from Our Signs. It is He who created night and day and the sun and the moon, each one swimming in a sphere." (21:31-33) The indications of Divine workmanship and presence are there for all to see – but how few people do!

No discussion of Prophethood would be complete without a reiteration of the core of the Prophetic Message: *"We sent no Messenger before you without revealing to him: 'There is no God but Me, so worship Me.'"* (21:25) And *Surat al-Anbiya'* reinforces it with further argument: *""Everyone in the heavens and the earth belongs to Him. Those in His Presence do not consider themselves too great to worship Him and do not grow weary of it. They glorify Him by night and by day, without ever flagging. Or have they taken gods out of the earth who can bring the dead to life? If there had been any gods except Allah in heaven or earth, they would both be ruined. Glory be to Allah, Lord of the Throne, above what they describe!"* (21:19-22)

The *sura* also refutes the trinitarian heresy by stating that 'Isa and Jibril are: *"...honoured slaves! They do not precede Him in speech and they act on His command. He knows what is in front of them and what is behind them. No one can intercede except those with whom He is pleased, and even they are apprehensive out of fear of Him. Were any of them to say, 'I am a god apart from Him,' We would repay him with Jahannam ..."* (21:26-29)

❋❋❋❋❋

Then the *sura* begins to discuss specific Prophets, usually mentioning particular incidents or aspects of their lives as well. It does not take them in the chronological sequence usual in the Qur'an. It begins with a brief mention of Musa and Harun before proceeding to Ibrahim although, of course, Musa and Harun were descendants of Ibrahim and lived many generations after him.

The *ayats* about Ibrahim concentrate on an incident in his youth when he smashed the idols of his people to prove they had no power, hoping to show by dramatic example what his words had been unable to convey: *"We heard a young man refer to them. They call him Ibrahim."* (21:60) He left the largest idol intact in order to be able to make his point even more effectively: *"No, this one, the biggest of them, did it. Ask them – if they are able to talk!"* (21:63)

His people were forced to acknowledge the validity of his argument but blind prejudice prevailed and Ibrahim was sentenced to be burned alive. Allah saved Ibrahim from the fire by taking away its power to burn: *"We said, 'O Fire, be coolness and peace for Ibrahim!'"* (21:69) He then established Ibrahim and his family in a new place which would prove a blessing to all mankind, moving the centre of the civilised world from the mouth of the Euphrates to the Mediterranean basin: *"We delivered both him and Lut to the land which We had blessed for all beings. And besides that We gave him Ishaq and Ya'qub and made both of them righteous men."* (21:71-72)

Lut was the nephew of Ibrahim and his trouble with and escape from his people is next to be mentioned. Then there is a reference to Nuh and his escape from the fate of drowning suffered by the rest of his people. Da'ud and Sulayman, two of the Prophets of the Tribe of Israel, are now mentioned together with the gifts they received from their Lord. The *sura* also mentions Ayyub and the removal of his affliction. Isma'il, Idris, and Dhu'l-Kifl, too, were steadfast in enduring the difficulties they were faced with and Allah delivered them.

Yunus to some extent brought difficulty upon himself, but he too was rescued by Allah after his repentance. Then we come to Zakariyya whose need for a son was fulfilled by Allah in the form of Yahya. And the last to be mentioned is the son of Maryam. Allah says of all of them: *"They vied with each other in good actions, calling out to Us in yearning and in awe, and humbling themselves to Us."* (21:90) Apart from this the common factor in all cases is the fact of Allah's deliverance of each of them from the particular difficulties which faced him.

This brings us to the theme of the last part of the *sura*. The first part of the *sura* was chiefly concerned with people who rejected the Prophetic Reminder, but the last part also speaks of those who accept it and act accordingly: *"As for anyone who does right actions and is a believer, truly his striving shall not go unthanked."* (21:94) Those who follow the Prophets benefit through them from Allah's deliverance and support: *"We wrote in the Zabur, after the Reminder: 'It is My righteous slaves who will inherit the earth.'"* (21:105)

In the in the Next World, while the rejectors of faith are experiencing the unimaginable torment of the Fire, the believers: *"...will be far from it. They will not hear the slightest hint of it and they will remain timelessly forever amidst all that their selves desire. The Greatest Terror will not upset them, and the angels will welcome them: 'This is your Day, the one that you were promised.'"* (21:101-103)

The *sura* ends with a wonderful confirmation of the last of Allah's Messengers, Muhammad ibn 'Abdullah who brought the final Divine Reminder to mankind.

> *"Certainly there is a transmission in this for people who worship. We have only sent you as a mercy to all the worlds. Say: 'It is revealed to me that your God is One God. So are you Muslims?' If they turn their backs, then say: 'I have informed all of you equally and I do not know if what you have been promised is near or far. He knows what is said openly and He knows what you hide. For all I know it may be a trial for you and you will have enjoyment for a time.' Say: 'O Lord, judge with Truth! Our Lord is the All Merciful, the One whose help is sought in the face of what you describe.'"* (21:106-112)

Sura 22
Al-Hajj (Pilgrimage)

Surat al-Hajj bursts open with a truly awe-inspiring evocation of the events of the Last Day: *"O mankind, fear your Lord! The quaking of the Hour is a terrible thing. On the day they see it, every nursing woman will be oblivious of the baby at her breast, and every pregnant woman will abort the contents of her womb, and you will think people are drunk when they are not drunk, but Allah's punishment is so severe."* (22:1-2)

This terrible warning is followed by a call to the human intellect to reflect on the reality it refers to: *"O mankind! If you are in any doubt about the Rising, know that We created you from dust, then from a drop of sperm, then from a clot of blood, then from a lump of flesh, formed yet unformed, so We might make it clear to you. We cause what We will to stay in the womb until a specified time and then We bring you out as children so that you can reach your full maturity."* (22:5)

Doubt about the Resurrection points to a failure in understanding the underlying processes of life itself and to thinking of it simply as a dramatic future event rather than as something which is in fact indicated by many events in our everyday lives. Every day, indeed every moment, is a kind of resurrection. Conception, foetal development and the birth process are a particularly vivid example of Allah's power transforming something from one stage of existence to another. The Resurrection is simply the same thing taken a stage further.

Another example is the growth of plants out of the earth: *"And you see the earth dead and barren; then when We send down water upon it it quivers and swells and sprouts with luxuriant plants of every kind."* (2:5) We see nothing strange in this phenomenon, which we witness everyday of our lives – yet how marvellous it is! There is no logical reason to suppose that the Power which brings it about is not equally capable of bringing us back into existence again after death: *"That is because it is Allah Who is the Real and gives life to the dead and has power over everything; and the Hour is coming without any doubt; and Allah will raise up all those in the grave."* (22:6-7)

Materialists, however, who say they do not believe in anything beyond the reach of their five senses, think that all life is simply the result of chance evolutionary development and will end in nothingness. Unfortunately this is now the dominant view of most scientists and they spare no pains in propagating it as widely as possible: *"Among the people there is one who argues about Allah without knowledge or guidance or any light-giving Book, turning away arrogantly, to misguide people from the Way of Allah."* (22:8-9)

There are also agnostics or what might be called 'armchair believers'. So long as it is convenient and easy for them to do so they believe, but the moment it becomes inconvenient or difficult for them their faith vanishes into thin air: *"Among the people there is one who worships Allah right on the edge. If good befalls him he is content with it, but if a trial befalls him he reverts to his former ways, losing both this world and the Next. That is indeed sheer loss."* (22:11) They rush here and there, turning to anything they think will help.

Allah challenges those who turn to other than Him by saying that if they really think there is no Afterlife they should kill themselves to escape their problems. *"Anyone who thinks Allah will not help him in this world and the Next should stretch a rope up to the ceiling and then hang himself. Let him see whether his stratagem gets rid of what enrages him."* (22:15) But the truth is that all mankind will be returned to Allah and will discover the true meaning of their life: *"As for those who believe and those who are Jews and the Sabaeans and the Christians and the Magians and the idolaters, Allah will distinguish between them on the Day of Rising. Allah is Witness of all things."* (22:17)

After this long introduction, *Surat al-Hajj* begins to describe the conflict between belief and disbelief, between those who bear the Banner of Truth and those who bear the Banner of Falsehood. The struggle between these two is a major factor in human life on earth and through it the wrongdoers and righteous become distinct from one another.

Love cannot develop between one who believes in Allah and one who denies Him; and they will inevitably be at odds with one another. The believers are charged with calling the deniers to the Truth and making the Path of Right Guidance clear to them. That was the behaviour of our Prophet, may Allah bless him and grant him peace, until Allah gave him victory over his enemies. That is the nature of the conflict which exists between the people of belief and the people of disbelief: *"Here are two rival groups who disputed concerning their Lord."* (22:19)

It is related in a *hadith* that this *ayat* was revealed about the Battle of Badr which marked the beginning of the victory of the warriors of the Truth over the warriors of misguidance. It must, however, be remembered that the battle took place after fifteen years of patient proselytising during which the Muslims endured much injury and harm.

This matter is further clarified by *ayats* a little further on in the *sura* which make it clear that Prophets in all ages have passed through the same pattern, and that the houses which they built for the worship of Allah were only established after bitter fighting by the beleaguered believers. *"Allah will defend those who believe. Allah does not love any thankless traitor. Permission is given to those who are fought against because they have been wronged - certainly Allah has the power to come to their support - those who were expelled from their homes unrightfully merely for saying: 'Our Lord is Allah.' If Allah had not driven some people back by means of others, monasteries, churches, synagogues and mosques, where Allah's Name is much invoked, would have been pulled down and destroyed."* (22:38-40)

The Prophets and their followers only fight to protect and establish Allah's *deen* and not for any other end, and because of this Allah makes them victorious: *"Those who, if We establish*

them firmly on the earth, will establish the prayer and pay the
zakat, *and command the right and forbid the wrong. The end
result of all affairs is for Allah to decide."* (22:41) The followers
of the Messengers do not seek money or rank. Their goal is to
establish a just society in which people recognise their Lord and
worship Him.

Within these *ayats* which speak about fighting we find the passage about the *Hajj* from which the *sura* derives its name. It mentions the rites and waymarks of the ancient practice and informs
the idolaters that they have completely deviated from the *deen* of
Ibrahim whom they claim as the source of their tradition. They
betray his legacy even as they claim to guard it. They debar the
true followers of Ibrahim, those who believe in the Divine Unity,
from the Ancient House and so as well as despising the Truth they
are unjust to its followers: *"Those who reject and bar access to the
way of Allah and to the Sacred Mosque which We have appointed
for all mankind – equally for those who live near it and those from
far away – whoever desires to profane it with wrongdoing, We
shall make them taste a painful punishment."* (22:25) People who
act in this way must be fought.

Anyone who reflects on the rites of *hajj* will see that they constitute a great public demonstration of faith in Allah and submission to Him unparalleled by any other human activity or celebration. Nowhere else do human beings regularly gather in such numbers with a unified purpose and act together in such a harmonious
way over so many days.

It is said that from space all human movement over the surface
of the earth would appear random and chaotic except the annual
journey and gathering of the Muslims for the *Hajj,* which would
be the one visible regular pattern of movement as people come
together from every point of the compass mass together in one
spot and once again disperse back to their point of origin.
*"Announce the Hajj to mankind. They will come to you on foot
and on all kinds of lean animals, coming by every distant road so
that they can be present at what will profit them and mention
Allah's Name on specified days over livestock He has provided for
them. Eat of them and feed the poor and needy."* (22:27-28)

The *Hajj* with its rites was initiated by Ibrahim in the distant past: *"When We located the position of the House for Ibrahim: 'Do not attribute any partners to Me...'"* (22:26) The Ka'ba was established as a focus for believers in Allah's Unity and all the rites of *hajj* and *'umra* are a massive affirmation of unitary belief: *"Have done with the defilement of idols and have done with telling lies. Be people of pure natural belief in Allah, attributing no partners to Him. He who attributes partners to Allah, it is as though he had fallen from the sky and the birds had seized him and carried him away or the wind had dropped him in some distant place."* (22:30-31)

One of the practices is ritual sacrifice: *"We have appointed the sacrificial animals for you as one of the sacred rites of Allah. There is good in them for you, so mention the Name of Allah over them, standing in rows; then when they collapse on their sides, eat of them and feed both those who ask and those who are too shy to ask..."* (22:36) There is no superstitious element to the sacrifice: *"Neither their flesh nor their blood reaches Allah but your fear of Him does reach Him."* (22:37) And the same applies to all the other rites of *hajj*: *"That is it. Whoever honours Allah's sacred rites, it comes from the fear of Allah in their hearts."* (22:32)

❋❋❋❋❋

Trials have accompanied human life since it began. Anyone who calls people to truth and goodness necessarily finds himself confronted by those who call to falsehood and evil and who want to thwart his efforts and make him deviate from his path. The war between the two always continues for a period, during which the utmost striving is required. The Divine Wisdom sometimes permits a temporary defeat of the Truth in this war and mosques are occasionally destroyed or put to other uses.

We cannot see the future, so the Muslims should persevere and be steadfast. They will have the final word and they should listen to Allah's solace to His Prophet: *"If they deny you, the people of Nuh denied before them, and those of 'Ad and of Thamud, and the people of Ibrahim, and the people of Lut, and the companions of*

Madyan; and Musa too was denied. I allowed time to the rejectors but then I seized them, and how terrible was My denial!" (22:42-43)

Then the consolatory tone continues as Allah reveals that His reckoning of time is quite different from the ordinary human scale. One generation may witness defeat and then several further generations pass before another generation comes which witnesses victory: *"They ask you to hasten the punishment. Allah will not break His promise. A day with your Lord is the same as a thousand years in the way you count."* (22:47)

The task given to the Messenger is simply to convey the clear Message so that no one at all will be able to say he did not know the truth: *"Say: 'O mankind! I am only a clear warner to you.' Those who believe and do right actions will have forgiveness and generous provision. But those who strive against My signs, and try to thwart them will be the Companions of the Blazing Fire."* (22:49-51)

Shaytan is the inveterate enemy of the truth and will go to any lengths to prevent people hearing the Divine Message and do everything he can to discredit it. But even then people whose hearts are sound will not be influenced and only people already veering in his direction will be diverted by him. *"We did not send any Messenger or any Prophet before you without Shaytan inserting something into his recitation while he was reciting. But Allah revokes whatever Shaytan inserts and then Allah confirms His signs – Allah is All-Knowing, All-Wise – so that He may make what Shaytan inserts a trial for those with sickness in their hearts and for those whose hearts are hard - the wrongdoers are deeply hostile – and so that those who have been given knowledge may know it is the truth from their Lord and believe in it and their hearts may be humbled to Him. Allah guides those who believe to a straight path."* (22:52)

Shaytan's inventions can involve creating dissension about what was said and represent an attempt to obliterate the truth by those who defend the false. We all have experience of destructive rumours and things said by liars which are enough to undermine a mountain. But Allah will thwart their schemes and expose their lies and make the Truth emerge from the battle unharmed and unsullied.

The *sura* returns to the theme of fighting and assures those who are killed in the Way of Allah of their reward from Him in the Next World and His continued support in this world. *"Those who emigrate in the Way of Allah and then are killed or die, Allah will provide for them handsomely. Certainly it is Allah who is the best Provider. He will admit them by an entrance which is pleasing to them. Allah is All-Knowing, All-Forbearing. That is so. And if anyone inflicts an injury the same as the injury done to him and then is again oppressed, Allah will come to his aid. Allah is Ever-Pardoning, Ever-Forgiving."* (22:58-60)

That is because Allah continually supports and sustains the whole of existence: *"Do you not see that Allah sends down water from the sky and then in the morning the earth is covered in green? Allah is All-Subtle, All-Aware. Everything in the heavens and everything in the earth belongs to Him. Allah is the Rich beyond need, the Praiseworthy."* (22:63-64) The *ayats* continue to discuss the all-encompassing Power of Allah and the fact that He alone is in reality worthy of worship: *"They worship besides Allah something for which no authority has come down and something of which they have no knowledge. There is no helper for the wrongdoers."* (22:71)

When the command to perform the *Hajj* was revealed, the Messenger, may Allah bless him and grant him peace, told people, "Take your practices from me." Their practices and actions were explained to them, showing that the *Hajj*, as we said, was a great demonstration of unitary faith in which Allah alone is extolled, so that the pure faith which fills the heart becomes visible in a prayer which fills the valleys and resounds to the horizon.

The *Hajj* is a splendid demonstration of the power of Allah's *deen* and the sign of the overthrow of idolatry. That is why Allah says here: *"We have appointed for every nation a rite that they observe, so let them not dispute with you about the matter. Call the people to your Lord. You are guided straight. If they do argue with you, say: 'Allah knows best what you are doing.'"* (22:67-68)

The impotence of the idolaters is definitively illustrated by Allah: *"O people! A likeness has been coined, so listen carefully to it. Those you call upon apart from Allah cannot create a single fly, even if they were to join together to do it. And if a fly steals something away from them, they cannot even get it back from it. How feeble are both the seeker and the sought!"* (22:73)

Surat al-Hajj ends with a glorious passage summing up the Message of Islam and the task of the believers:

"O you who believe, bow and prostrate and worship your Lord, and do good, so that perhaps you may be successful. Fight your hardest for Allah with the striving worthy of Him. He has chosen you and placed no constraint on you in the deen, *the religion of your forefather Ibrahim. He named you Muslims before and also in this, so that the Messenger might be witness against you and you might be witnesses against all mankind. So establish the prayer and pay the* zakat *and hold fast to Allah. He is your Protector, the best Protector, the best Helper."* (22:77-78)

Sura 23
Al-Mu'minun (The Believers)

There is a strong connection between actions and their consequences. So the future outcome of good will inevitably be good
even if its present is unsettled, and the future outcome of evil will
inevitably be bad even if its present is deceptively pleasant. Most
people, however, are solely concerned with the immediate present
and completely caught up in it in it. *Surat al-Mu'minin* was
revealed to lift people's aspirations to the Next World and to give
the believers solid reassurance about their future happiness. The
unbelievers face nothing but endless misery.

The *sura* opens with this good news: *"It is the believers who
are successful: those who are humble in their prayer; those who
turn away from worthless talk; those who actively pay* zakat ..."
(23:1-4) 'Umar ibn al-Khattab, may Allah be pleased with him,
said, "When Revelation descended on the Messenger of Allah,
may Allah bless him and grant him peace, a humming sound could
be heard near his face similar to the humming of bees. One day
Allah sent down Revelation on him and he was in that state for
some time. Then it lifted from him and he recited: *'It is the believers who are successful ...'* and the nine following *ayats*. Then he
said, 'Anyone who acts on these ten *ayats* will enter the Garden.'
Then he faced the *qibla* and raised his hands and said, 'O Allah,
increase us and do not decrease us! Honour us and do not abase
us! Give to us and do not deprive us! Prefer us and do not prefer
others to us! O Allah, be pleased with us and make us pleased!'"

These ten *ayats* form a compendium of actions and attitudes
whose implementation ensures success for those who hold to
them. In the middle of this *sura* we find the same idea repeated in
slightly different form: *"Those who are filled with fear of their*

236

Lord, those who believe in the Signs of their Lord, those who attribute no partners to their Lord, those who give what they have given, their hearts fearful of their return to their Lord such people are truly racing towards good things, and they are the first to reach them." (23:57-61)

Again actions and attitudes are combined in such a way that their performance leads to guaranteed success. As for unbelieving people, their behaviour in this world is shown in the accounts of past nations presented in this *sura* and the misery of their eternal destiny is described in detail at the end.

Our life in the Next World will be the implacable recompense of our actions in this one, the result of the specified term we spend as human beings on the face of the earth. This period is described in a manner which encourages belief in Allah and awareness of His vast power: *"We created man from the purest kind of clay; then made him a drop in a secure receptacle."* (23:12-13)

How is the body created from earth? How is a shapeless lump transformed into a perfect human form? How are the characteristics of a palm tree placed in the date-stone and the characteristics of man in a drop of sperm? How does the genetic coding unfold over time, turning a helpless baby into a full-grown human being? The questions are endless and the scientists do not have the answers. And after this profusion of life is the inevitability of death: *"Then subsequently you will most surely die. Then on the Day of Rising you will be raised again."* (23:15-16)

The *sura* then takes us back into the distant past and recounts the ingratitude of earlier peoples for Allah's bounty and their refutation of His Guidance and denial of His Messengers. It mentions Nuh and his people and Hud and his people in some detail and then informs us that they were not isolated cases. *"Then We raised up other generations after them. No nation can advance its appointed time, nor can they delay it. Then We sent Our Messengers one after another, at intervals. Each time its Messenger came to a nation they called him a liar so We made them follow one another too and turned them into myths and legends. Away with people who have no faith* (23:42-44)

Did the Messengers ask more of people than they were able to do? By no means! They simply asked people to abandon foul things in favour of pure things and to do good: *"O Messengers! Eat of the good things and act rightly. Truly I know everything you do. This faith of yours is a single faith and I am your Lord, so fear Me."* (23:51-52) And Allah confirms that it is within our capacity: *"We do not charge any self except with what it can bear. With Us there is a Book which speaks the Truth. They will not be wronged."* (23:62)

Then after Musa and 'Isa came the Final Message as the seal to all previous Messages, universal Divine Guidance for the whole of humanity until the end of time. Yet Muhammad at first fared no better than his predecessors since the Arabs first rejected Islam and denied its Prophet; this despite the fact that they knew better than anybody how truthful and trustworthy he was. Indeed his uncle and protector Abu Talib said in a poem he composed about the situation as it was happening:

They know that our son is not a liar
　　and he is not accused of speaking falsely.

The Qur'an says of them: *"Do they not ponder these Words? Has anything come to them that did not come to their ancestors, the earlier peoples? Or is it that they do not recognise their Messenger and therefore disacknowledge him? Or do they say, 'He is a man possessed,' when he has brought the truth to them? But most of them have hatred for the truth."* (23:68-70) They would pay dearly for their hatred of the Truth.

Their leaders held forth in their assemblies, abusing Islam and mocking its teachings and harming the weak Muslims and violating their rights. But within a very short time they had suffered a humiliating defeat in the Battle of Badr and the corpses of those same men were rotting at the bottom of a well. Allah continues: *"He has brought the truth to them. But most of them have hatred for the truth. If the truth were to follow their whims and desires, the heavens and the earth and everyone in them would have been brought to ruin. No indeed! We have given them their reminder, but they have turned away from their reminder."* (23:70-71)

A man's suffering can be a purification for him and raise his rank, and that applies to believers, as is stated in a famous *hadith*: "A Muslim is not afflicted by worry, sorrow, discomfort or fatigue, even a thorn which pricks him, without that expiating some of his errors for him." Suffering can also act as a kind of instruction, bringing back the one who undergoes it into a state of balance when he has gone beyond the limits. But some people do not learn whatever happens to them: *"If We did have mercy on them and removed the harm afflicting them, they would still obstinately persist in wandering blindly in their overweening insolence."* (23:75)

Quraysh, the Prophet's tribe, were extremely obdurate in their unbelief for a very long time, taking exactly the same position as past peoples had taken with their Messengers: *"And yet they say the same as earlier peoples said. They say, 'When we are dead and turned to dust and bones, shall we then be raised up again? We and our forefathers were promised this before. This is nothing but the myths of earlier peoples!'"*(23:82-84)

Allah drives home to such people the illogicality of the position they have taken: *"Say: 'To whom does the earth belong, and everyone in it, if you have any knowledge?' They will say: 'To Allah. 'Say: 'Will you not then be reminded?' Say: 'Who is the Lord of the Seven Heavens and the Lord of the Mighty Throne?' They will say: 'Allah.' Say: 'Will you not then be godfearing?' Say: 'In whose hand is the dominion over everything, He who gives protection and from whom no protection can be given, if you have any knowledge?' They will say: 'Allah's.' Say: 'How then have you been bewitched?' The fact is that We have given them the truth and they are liars."* (23:84-90)

These questions were originally directed at the idolaters of Makka, who worshipped idols, even though they knew that they had not created anything and could not send provision or have any real effect on their lives. But they are equally applicable to anyone who pollutes unitarian belief by either openly dividing the Godhead into parts as the Christians do or by attributing to other things attributes that in reality belong to Allah alone.

The fact is that the Qur'an insists on the absolute Oneness of Allah which makes anything other than Him totally subservient to Him. *"Allah has no son and there is no other god accompanying Him, for then each god would have gone off with what he created and one of them would have been exalted above the other. Glory be to Allah above what they describe, Knower of the Unseen and the Visible! Exalted is He above the partners they attribute to Him!"* (23:91-92)

Here as in other places Allah tries to break through the obtuseness of the unbelievers by reminding them that their life in this world is not everlasting and that they will not have another chance to correct it: *"Until, when death comes to one of them, he says, 'My Lord, send me back again so that perhaps I may act rightly regarding the things I failed to do!' No indeed! Those are merely words he utters. Before them there is an interspace until the day they are raised up."* (23:99-100)

This belated and unavailing request to return to the world in order to make amends is repeated a dozen or more times in the Noble Qur'an and it is repeated twice in *Surat al-Mu'minin:* once, as we have seen, by an individual at the moment of death and once by people on the Day of Judgement. *"'Were not My signs recited to you, and did you not deny them?' They will say, 'O Lord, our miserable destiny conquered us. We were misguided people. Our Lord, remove us from it! Then if we revert again, we will definitely be wrongdoers.'"* (23:105-107)

There is no one who has not at some time experienced that dreadful feeling of knowing that they have done something that they would have done anything not to have done and wishing it were possible to return to the time before it happened. Allah is telling us, in a way that anyone should be able to understand, the terrible remorse that will be felt by those who failed to get the point of this existence: to believe in Him and follow His Messenger. *"'Did you suppose We created you as a game and that you would not return to Us?' High Exalted be Allah, the King, the Real."* (23:115-116)

Allah will confront them with their mockery of the believers, those they accused of being out of touch with the 'real world', whose success will now be apparent: "*"There was a group of My slaves who said, "Our Lord, we have believed. So forgive us and have mercy on us. You are the Best of the Merciful." But you made a mockery of them and so they made you forget to remember Me while you were laughing at them. Today I have rewarded them for being steadfast. They are the ones who are victorious.'"*(23:110-112) This is the success referred to in the first *ayat* of the *sura*.

The unbelievers, on the other hand, will never succeed however powerful or prosperous they might appear to be:

> "*Anyone who calls upon another god together with Allah has no grounds for doing so at all and his reckoning is with his Lord. Truly the rejectors have no success. Say: 'O Lord, forgive and have mercy! You are the Best of the Merciful.'*" (23:117-118)

Sura 24
An-Nur (Light)

Light is one of the Names of Allah. *Surat an-Nur* is given this name because it contains the noble *ayat*: *"Allah is the Light of the heavens and the earth ..."* (24:35) All light of whatever kind has its source in Allah. Indeed everything depends for its existence on Allah alone. Phenomenal being is like a shadow whose existence cannot be detached from the body which casts it. If the body goes, the shadow vanishes.

The entire universe only exists and endures because Allah brings it into existence and sustains it. The light of day when the sun rises and at night when the moon appears issues in reality from Allah. Every atom in the universe vibrates with unceasing praise of its Creator because it subsists by Him and indicates Him.

On the day when the idolaters rejected and injured the Messenger of Allah, may Allah bless him and grant him peace, in Ta'if, he said, "I seek refuge in the Light of Your Face which illuminates the darkness and by which this world and the Next are put right, from Your anger falling on me or Your wrath descending on me. You have the right to be satisfied until You are pleased. There is no power nor strength except by Allah." And he used to say when night came: "O Allah, all praise is for You. You are the Light of the heavens and the earth and those who are in them. Praise be to You. You are the Sustainer of the heavens and the earth and everything in them."

Further explanation of the *Ayat* of Light will come later. Meanwhile we will return to the beginning of the *sura: "A sura We have sent down and imposed. We have sent down clear signs in it so that perhaps you may remember."* (24:1) No other *sura* in the Qur'an begins in quite this uncompromising way, because the basic subject matter of the *sura* is the vital issue of the personal relationship between men and women which lies at the heart of every human society.

The "sending down of clear signs" refers to a number of clear directives contained in the *sura,* mainly on this subject. The expression is repeated three times in all during the course of the *sura* to emphasise the importance of these judgements: *"We have sent down clear signs to you, and the example of those who passed away before you, and an admonition for the godfearing."* (24:34) *"We have sent down signs making things clear. Allah guides anyone He wills to a straight path."* (24:46)

The injunctions include the punishments for illicit sexual intercourse on one hand and for scandalmongering about it on the other; the limits governing informal social intercourse between the sexes and within the household; the obligation to ask permission before entering people's houses; and the houses in which one is permitted to eat and with whom. The fundamental importance of these matters is obvious when we consider that they lie right at the very heart of every human community, and therefore if they are not in order their harmful effect automatically spreads right through the social fabric.

The firm instructions ensure a society based on chastity and purity and establish a firm protective wall around those private forbidden acts whose consequences are so destructive for society as a whole. These limits have been almost entirely abandoned in the contemporary world and the deplorable result is that in most countries society is literally rotten to the core, a rottenness which is revealed daily on every television and in every newspaper and which threatens the continuation of human civilisation as we know it.

Religion has been forced to abdicate from its restraining role in education and Islam has fared little better than other traditions in this respect in spite of the clarity of Allah's directives on the subject.

Surat an-Nur begins by confirming the punishment for fornication and for the crime of slandering chaste women. The law of mutual cursing[1] is also explained in cases where no other evidence is available. And it is made clear that these things are in fact a manifestation of Allah's wisdom and His generosity to us.

It is appropriate in this place to mention the story of 'The Lie'. It is an incident which disclosed the rancour in the hearts of the hidden enemies of Islam. It exposes the incalculable damage done by those who dissemble and then slander innocent women and encourage the heedless and naive to spread the gossip. That is what the chief hypocrite, 'Abdullah ibn Ubayy, did when he forged the lie about 'A'isha, the Mother of the Believers, and attacked her honour and left her saying "I thought that sorrow would break my heart."

The Messenger, peace and blessings be upon him, was overwhelmed and bewildered by this sudden affliction until Allah confirmed the innocence of his wife in the Revelation in *ayats* which will be recited until the end of time.

The event teaches us lessons which must never be forgotten: *"Why, when you heard it, did you not, as believing men and women, instinctively think good thoughts ..."* (24:16) *"People who love to see filth being spread about concerning those who believe will have a painful punishment both in this world and the Next ..."* (24:19) *"Those who accuse women who are chaste, but who are careless though believing, are cursed in both this world and the Next ..."* (24:23) These *ayats* tell us exactly how to act in order to scotch such rumours when we are faced with this all too common occurrence – but unfortunately so many people fail to learn.

The *sura* next turns to the correct behaviour to be observed when entering other people's houses. Their inhabitants have a right to privacy which must be respected by asking their permission and greeting them and waiting to receive their explicit permission before entering. This asking of permission is later expanded to include also those who move around from room to room within the house. This degree of respect is practically unique in the annals of human civilisation. Modern civilisation certainly has no such restraints and people's private affairs are all too often made public

---

1. A form of divorce which takes place when a husband accuses his wife of adultery and she denies it. They each swear oaths that they are telling the truth, followed by a curse on themselves if they are lying. This dissolves the marriage.

property with extremely pernicious consequences both on an individual and a social level.

Pursuant to the encouragement of sexual probity and keeping the appetites in check, the *sura* confirms the importance of lowering the eye and guarding the private parts and gives specific instructions as to what constitutes modesty in terms of both dress and general appearance.

Modesty in dress, general appearance, and demeanour, both for men and women, has always been an invariable constituent of every great religious tradition. One of the most remarkable and horrifying achievements of the last century has been the complete and unprecedented jettisoning of almost every constraint on human modesty although it was in fact foretold by the Messenger of Allah in several *hadiths*. It is true that certain sections of society in some periods of history were infamous for their flagrant immodesty but there has never been a time in human history when the human body was flaunted as much as it now is and when natural modesty was so completely disregarded.

These matters take up about two-thirds of the *sura*, but *Surat an-Nur* takes its name, as we said earlier, from the *ayat* in the middle of it which mentions the Divine Light which never diminishes. We shall now return to this *ayat* to explain a little of what it means.

In it Allah produces a metaphor for His Light and says: *"Allah is the Light of the heavens and the earth. The likeness of His light is that of a niche in which there is a lamp, the lamp inside a glass, the glass as if it were a brilliant star..."* (24:35) A 'niche' is a hollowed recess in a wall in which a lamp is placed. The glass around the lamp is for protecting and enhancing its light and preventing smoke. The simile made here is of a lamp which burns a special oil: the finest possible kind of olive oil which is almost luminous even if no fire touches it. The glass is transparent and radiant "as if it were a brilliant star."

The question is whether this metaphor applies to Allah's Light in existence as a whole or to Allah's Light in the heart of the believer. Al-Ghazali favours the first meaning and says: "The light referred to is that outward light by which everything appears: that

245

light by which things are made manifest and reveal Him and are revealed by Him. It is the essence of light and no light is above it. He made one of His Names 'the Light': this indicates His disassociation from non-existence and the emergence of all things from the darkness of non-existence to the light of existence."

The second meaning, which makes the analogy allude to the light in the heart of the believer, refers the symbol to the heart of the gnostic which sees by the Light of Allah and is protected by the translucent *Shari'a.* Another possible interpretation is that the Light is the Qur'an, since the Qur'an is referred to as a Light elsewhere: *"So believe in Allah and His Messenger and the Light that We have revealed."* (64:8) *"O Mankind! A clear proof has come to you from your Lord. We have sent down a clear Light to you."* (4:174)

Many volumes have been written in explanation of this great *ayat* and the fact is that it is one of those *ayats* of the Qur'an whose meanings are endless both in terms of breadth and depth, so it is not possible here to do more than hint at one or two of the possible directions to take when reflecting upon it.

The following *ayat* seems to extend its meaning to include places where Allah is remembered, and the hearts of those who do the remembering. And from there – from the brightest possible light – Allah takes us to the deepest possible darkness: *"...the darkness of a soundless sea which is covered by waves above which are waves above which are clouds, layers of darkness, one upon the other. If he puts out his hand, he can scarcely see it. Those to whom Allah gives no light to, there is no light for them."* (24:40) Such is the state of those who deny Allah's light, for without it there is truly nothing but absolute darkness.

The *sura* then goes on to discuss the immense power of Allah and encourages those with intelligence to look into phenomenal being. Such reflection strengthens belief and doubles its light: *"Do you not see that everyone in the heavens and the earth glorifies Allah, and the birds with their outspread wings? Each one knows its prayer and glorification. Allah knows all that they do. The kingdom of the heavens and the earth belongs to Allah; and the final destination is to Allah."* (24:41-42) Does this not impress on you that you are inextricably part of existence, all of which glorifies the praise of its Lord, acknowledging His blessings and majesty? *"There is surely a lesson in that for people with eyes."*(24:43)

It might be asked at this point what the *Ayat* of Light has to do with the social legislation and domestic injunctions which precede and follow it. There is of course nothing haphazard about anything in the Qur'an, and the positioning of this great *ayat* is particularly significant. Allah is telling us that His Light is not some theoretical abstract quality but is present in our most intimate moments, inseparable from our daily lived experience. *"He is with you wherever you are"*, as He tells us in another passage and in the end it is only this knowledge which keeps those who believe in Him within the limits He has in His Mercy prescribed for us.

This same connection is made repeatedly elsewhere when Allah ends an *ayat* of *Shari'a* with Names of His: *"Those who swear to abstain from sexual relations with their wives can wait for a period of up to four months. If they then retract their oath, Allah is **Ever-Forgiving**, **Most Merciful**. If they are determined to divorce, Allah is **All-Hearing**, **All-Knowing**."* (2:226-227) Here four of Allah's Names are used in confirmation of another decree concerning family life. In this way the Qur'an connects belief with action, and matters of daily life with the Divine Presence.

The connection between the *Shari'a* and belief in Allah's Oneness is firm and the connection between action and belief has not changed, yet in our times there are apostates who go to a source other than Islam when they make laws and who give judgements based on other than Revelation. Such people regard *Surat an-Nur* with particular annoyance because it forbids fornication, immodesty and decadence. The *sura* is very explicit about them: *"They say, 'We believe in Allah and in the Messenger and we obey.' Then after that a group of them turn away. Such people are not believers. When they are summoned to Allah and His Messenger so that he may judge between them, a group of them immediately turn away."* (24:47-48)

These people, who can be found throughout the Muslim world, make an outward display of Islam while all the time steadily eroding its ordinances to the point that they have now been almost completely eliminated. Their first and last goal is that Islam should not retain any power at all over people's lives and that the earth should be delivered over lock stock and barrel to the New World Order.

Allah then says: *"The reply of the believers when they are summoned to Allah and His Messenger so that he can judge between them, is to say, 'We hear and we obey.' They are the successful ones. Those who obey Allah and His Messenger and have awe of Allah and fear Him, it is they who are the victorious."* (24:51-52) There is an ancient and on-going war between these two groups: a group who dislike any form of religion and who resort to all sorts of devices to undermine it and thwart its goal, and a group who call people to their Lord and seek to draw together all areas of society by implementing of Islam in its entirety.

The state of the Muslims at this time is unprecedentedly debilitated and material and spiritual defeats encompass us on all sides. But in *Surat an-Nur* Allah opens up to us the doors of victory, as He has done for all our predecessors: *"Allah has promised those of you who believe and do right actions that He will make them the successors in the land as He made those before them the successors and will firmly establish for them their* deen.*"* (24:55)

This will obviously require continuous and strenuous effort on our part but we cannot content ourselves with anything less. Look at what the Messenger and his Companions did. They remained for about a quarter of a century fighting Arab paganism until they defeated it, and then gathered the rest of the Arabs and attacked both the Romans and Persians at the same time! Within a very short time Islam was governing the greater part of the world.

The *sura* also explains the means to this astonishing achievement: *"They worship Me, not attributing any partner to Me"* (24:55), and *"Establish the prayer and pay* zakat *and obey the Messenger, so that perhaps you may have mercy shown to you."* (24:56) This is what our glorious predecessors did and by it they gained the power which enabled them to rule the world for ten centuries. The same means are available to us and if we truly take hold of them and put them to use we too will find Allah's promise true: *"Do not imagine that those who reject are able to thwart Allah upon the earth."* (24:57)

And if we fail to do this we will have to answer to Allah for what we considered more important to do instead:

"Everything in the heavens and the earth belongs to Allah. He knows what you are engaged upon. The Day when they are returned to Him, He will inform them of all that they did. Allah has knowledge of everything." (24:64)

Sura 25
Al-Furqan (The Discrimination)

We do not know the names of all the Messengers who were sent by Allah to mankind; but we do know for certain that they ended with a Messenger whose Book contains the quintessence of all their teachings, and that Allah decreed that it should remain in force until the Day He inherits the earth and all those on it and in it. That Messenger's name is Muhammad ibn 'Abdullah, may Allah bless him and grant him peace eternally, and his Book is the Qur'an: *"Blessed be He who has sent down the Discrimination to His slave so that he may be a warner to all beings."* (25:1)

He, like us, was a man, but in him all the glories of humanity met together and the banner of universal Messengership was given to him alone. The right guidance of the entire world is contained in the Message he brought and only someone utterly bereft of goodness impedes people from following it.

Allah Almighty first sets out the first aspect of discrimination, which is to recognise the Creator of the universe, who created all the other criteria which man uses for discrimination. So the source of all discrimination is Allah Almighty: *"He to whom belongs the kingdom of the heavens and the earth. He has no child and He has no partner in the Kingdom. He created everything and determined it most exactly."* (25:2)

Surat al-Furqan gathers together a considerable number of the doubts and objections which the enemies of Islam use in their attempts to refute its Message. They are listed here in the order in which they appear, together with some appropriate comments.

- *"Those who reject say, 'This is nothing but a lie he has fabricated and other people have helped him to do it.'*

250

They have brought injustice and falsehood.'" (25:4) This accusation was also levelled against many of the earlier Messengers. The truth of what they brought was clearly demonstrated and so was that of the Final Messenger. As for the others who are supposed to have helped him, neither hide nor hair of them has ever been produced!

• *"They say, 'Myths and legends of the peoples of the past which he has had transcribed and which are read out to him in the morning and the evening.'"* (25:5) There are many details in the Qur'anic accounts of past peoples which occur in no other source; and what of the vast majority of the Revelation, which has nothing to do with peoples of the past?

• *"They say, 'What is wrong with this Messenger, that he eats food and walks in the market-place? Why has an angel not been sent down to him so that it might be a warner along with him?"* (25:7) The Prophet never made any claim to be anything other than a human being - indeed it is essential for his task that he is one - and so it is ridiculous to criticise him for eating. Ironically, we know that an angel was sent down to him with the Revelation. The rejectors' demand is simply proof that they are totally ignorant of the nature of the angelic realm.

• *"The wrongdoers say, 'You are only following a man who is bewitched.' See how they coin likenesses for you since they are misguided and cannot find a way."* (25:8-9) This shows that the unbelievers are unable to understand the nature of Prophethood and have no way of defining it within the framework of their own experience.

• *"Those who do not expect to meet Us say, 'Why have angels not been sent down to us or do we not see our Lord?' They have become arrogant about themselves and are inordinately insolent."* (25:21-22) The matter of the angels has been mentioned above. Another implicit motive is that the demand absolves those concerned from having to follow the Message since they know they are asking for an impossibility.

• *"Those who reject say, 'Why was the Qur'an not sent down to him all at one time?'"* (25:32) Why was the Qur'an sent down in instalments according to events? The answer is given by Allah: *"It is so that We may fortify your heart by it. We have recited it distinctly, little by little."* (25:32) The Qur'an is guidance for a developing human community and therefore it was revealed as and when it became necessary.

• *"When they see you they only make a mockery of you, 'Is this the one Allah has sent as a Messenger? He might almost have misled us from our gods had we not stood by them steadfastly!"* (25:41-42) This statement is a clear acknowledgement that the Qur'an unsettled the idolaters. Its patent truthfulness unveiled the falsehoods of the idolaters and they were almost persuaded to accept it. It shows that disbelief is more often than not a matter of blind prejudice and sheer pigheadedness. Allah describes such people in graphic terms. They are worse than animals: *"Have you seen him who has taken his whims and desires to be his god? Will you then be guardian over him? Do you suppose that most of them hear or understand? They are like cattle – indeed, they are more astray!"* (25:43-44)

• *"When they are told to prostrate to the All-Merciful, they say, 'And what is the All-Merciful? Are we to prostrate to something you command us?' And it only makes them run away the more."* (25:60) Pride and blind adherence to ancestral custom are the greatest obstacles to Islam. Shaytan used almost identical words in refusing to obey Allah and bow before the first human being, and his followers have always taken the same line down the centuries.

This, then, is what the unbelievers say about the Messenger and his Message; but how does Allah deal with them in this *sura*? We find that He takes basically two lines of approach. The first is to alarm them by recounting what happened to earlier nations who were punished. Accordingly the *sura* recounts the fate of Pharaoh and the end of 'Ad and Thamud and the people of ar-Rass, and it also mentions the destruction of the people of Lut, the ruins of whose cities the people of Makka were themselves familiar with[1]: *"They themselves have come across the city which was rained on by an evil rain. Did they not then see it? But they do not expect to be resurrected."* (25:40)

This technique of striking fear sometimes has an effect; but the other approach which Allah takes often has a greater and longer lasting effect, and that is to stimulate the intellect into reflection. In *Surat al-Furqan* there are several *ayats* of this type. The first of them concerns the phenomenon of the shadow: *"Do you not see how your Lord stretches out the shadow? If He had willed He could have made it stationary. Then We appoint the sun to be its guide."* (25:46) Sometimes our shadow is twice our height and at other times it shrinks to almost nothing. It reflects the movement of the earth around the sun and the rotation of the earth on its own axis. Its movement is so precise that it is possible to tell the time by it. So many lessons inward and outward from something so close to us!

Night and day, sleep and wakefulness, rain and plant growth, salt and fresh water, the sky with its panoply of the sun, moon and stars – all these varied things which are within the daily experience of every human being are food for reflection which can lead an intelligent and enquiring mind to grasp the existence of Allah. But how few people take advantage of the opportunity they offer! *"We have diversified it for them so that they might remember but most people spurn anything but unbelief."* (25:50)

As we have seen, the great majority of *Surat al-Furqan* is devoted to discussing the unbelievers. But it ends with a wonderfully comprehensive description of the believers, the 'servants of the All-Merciful'. It brings together ten qualities which charac-

---

1. Being located on the route between Makka and Syria.

terise those who accept the Last of Allah's Messengers and follow the Guidance which he brought. Although these qualities are mentioned individually in many other *suras*, nowhere else do we find such a complete picture of a believing human being.

Having previously highlighted pride as the dominant characteristic of the unbeliever, Allah begins by pointing out that the believer is characterised by humility: *"The slaves of the All-Merciful are those who walk lightly on the earth and, who, when the ignorant speak to them, say, 'Peace.'"* (25:63) The believer is aware that he only has a life tenancy on the earth, that he is just passing through. He does not want to control and dominate the earth, for he knows that everything in the heavens and the earth belongs to Allah. The unbelievers want disputation and conflict; the believer avoids useless confrontation.

"Those who pass the night prostrating and standing before their Lord." (25:64) This obviously does not mean that the believer gets no sleep at all. Sleep is necessary to restore the body and give it strength. However, as the Qur'an makes clear in many places, one of the qualities of a believer is that he devotes some of the night to his Lord and it is clearly most important not to sleep through the time of the Dawn Prayer.

"Those who say, 'Our Lord, avert from us the punishment of Jahannam. Its punishment is inescapable pain.'" (25:65) This indicates the true believer's vivid awareness of the reality of the Unseen World. For him the Fire is not an abstract threat but an ever-present danger which has an active effect on his life.

"Those who, when they spend, are neither extravagant nor mean, but take a stance midway between the two." (25:67) Miserliness is base and prodigality is foolish. In expenditure, as in the rest of his life,the believer is characterised by balance.

"Those who do not call on any other god together with Allah and do not kill anyone Allah has forbidden - except by legal right - and do not fornicate." (25:68) Murder and fornication proliferate in societies where the pure worship of Allah alone is abandoned. The unrestrained expression of the lower appetites is punishable in this world and the Next: *"Anyone who does that will receive an*

evil punishment and on the Day of Rising his punishment will be doubled." (25:68-69)

"Those who do not bear false witness and who, when they pass by worthless talk, pass by with dignity." (25:72) The believer is truthful in all circumstances and does not involve himself in obscenity, gossip or scandalmongering.

"Those who, when they are reminded of the Signs of their Lord, do not turn their backs, deaf and blind to them." (25:73) The heart of the believer is constantly awake and therefore responds to the recitation and the contents of the Qur'an. How often the Qur'an is now treated as background music to other apparently more important activities!

"Those who say, 'Our Lord, give us joy in our wives and children and make us a good example for the godfearing.'" (25:74) The believer hopes to find true enjoyment and sweetness in the company of his immediate family and seeks to implement the tenets of his faith so as to be a model to be followed.

"Those shall be recompensed for their steadfastness with the Highest Paradise, where they will meet with welcome and with the greeting of 'Peace'. They will remain in it timelessly forever. What an excellent lodging and abode!" (25:75-76) This is the highest position in the Garden, the greatest reward. May Allah make us among its inhabitants, by His Pardon and Forgiveness.

Sura 26
Ash-Shu'ara' (The Poets)

The contents and themes of *Surat ash-Shu'ara'* are similar to several other *suras* revealed in the middle Makkan period. The resistance of the people of Makka to the Revelation is compared with the way past nations rejected their Messengers. But it is stylistically remarkable for the brevity of its *ayats* which gives it a particularly powerful resonance in recitation.

It was most important for the Prophet to be informed of the fate met by earlier Messengers at the hands of their people because of the excessive degree of his concern for his own people. His desperate desire to see his fellow Makkans gain safety from eternal destruction knew no bounds, to the point that it endangered his health: *"Perhaps you will destroy yourself with grief because they will not become believers."* (26:2)

The whole *sura* is really Allah's means of telling His Messenger that what is happening is part of an inevitable pattern that He has imparted to existence. If Allah so willed, everyone would have instant faith: *"If We willed We could send down a Sign to them from Heaven, before which their heads would be bowed low in subjection."* (26:4) But a complete process is necessary so that people's complete freedom to believe or not to believe will not be jeopardised. This process will provide guidance for future generations.

As we are told many times throughout the Qur'an, the signs are there in existence for all to see. *"Have they not looked at the earth and seen how We have made every kind of beneficial species grow in it? There is certainly a sign in that; yet most of them are not believers. Truly your Lord is the Almighty, the Most Merciful."* (26:7-9) The last two *ayats* constitute a refrain which punctuates the *sura*, being repeated eight times in all. This again adds to the rhetorical impact of the *sura* when it is recited.

The Prophets' sole task is to bring guidance to human beings. They have the purest hearts of all people and, the greatest sincerity. They seek no material gain or recompense from anyone. Nuh speaks for all of them when he says to his people: *"'Will you not be godfearing? I am a faithful Messenger to you, so fear Allah and obey me. I do not ask of you any wage for it. My wage rests on no one but the Lord of the Worlds."* (26:105-109) Nonetheless, all of them were treated harshly. Some of them were even killed while performing their duty.

Surat ash-Shu'ara' mentions a group of the previous nations: Musa with Pharaoh, Ibrahim with his people, and also the stories of 'Ad and Thamud, the people of Lut and the People of Madyan. In each case the Message is presented in the same impeccable way free of any bias and in each case the Message is rejected with the same obduracy and delusion.

We look first at the story of Musa and notice Pharaoh's question about Allah. His use of the word "What?" means that he is asking about Allah's Essence, which is something that is impossible to know. We do not know our own essence, let alone that of our Creator. Musa responds by redefining "all the worlds": *"Pharaoh said, 'What is the Lord of all the worlds?' He said, 'The Lord of the heavens and the earth and everything between them if you knew for sure.' He said to those around him, 'Are you listening?' He said, "'Your Lord and the Lord of your forefathers, the earlier peoples.'" Said Pharaoh, 'This Messenger who has been sent to you is mad ...'"* (26:23-27)

Then a day was appointed for Musa to present what he had in competition with Pharaoh's magicians. The populace was asked to attend the contest. We notice that although they are told what to do if the magicians win, their position in the event of the magicians being defeated is not defined: *"The people were asked, 'Are you all assembled so we may follow the magicians if they are the winners?'"* (26:39-40) Apparently following Musa was not a possibility for them! When Musa won and the magicians realised that what he had was true and believed in him, Pharaoh was furious and said: *"Have you believed in him before I have given you per-mission? He is your chief who taught you magic. But you will soon know! I will cut off your alternate hands and feet and I will crucify every one of you."* (16:49)

The magicians, because they understood magic, knew that what Musa had done was beyond the scope of any magic and therefore they were certain that he was speaking the truth. For that reason nothing Pharaoh said had any effect on them. But Pharaoh himself remained deluded and obdurate and stupidly asked how they could believe without his permission – as if their consciences belonged to him!

After some time Musa decided to leave Egypt with his people to flee from slavery and torture. Pharaoh mobilised his army and went out after them to bring them back. The two parties ap-proached each other until they were in sight of one another. The Jews said, *"We will surely be overtaken!"* (26:61) Musa told them: *"Never! My Lord is with me and He will guide me."* (26:62) The Red Sea blocked their way and it seemed certain they would be captured. Musa struck the sea with his staff and the waters split to the right and the left and opened up a dry path by which the Israelites passed to the other shore. Pharaoh tried to follow them with his army but the waves crashed down on them from either side, drowning everyone of them.

The One who guided Ibrahim gave him simple belief without excess or deviation. This is brought home to us whenever we read the books of the theologians and examine their complicated argu-ments. The reality of faith has nothing to do with those things. Ibrahim says about his Lord: *"He who created me and guides me; He who gives me food and gives me drink; and when I am ill, it is He who heals me; He who will cause my death, then give me life; He who I sincerely hope will forgive me my mistakes on the Day of Repayment."* (26:78-82) These words of Ibrahim are a true exposi-tion of unitary belief.

In the story of Nuh we notice that contempt for the poor and the weak begins very early in human history. The rich despise the poor and the strong disdain the weak. It appears as if the seeds of class conflict have existed since the dawn of humanity. The poor are naturally the first people to follow the Prophets because they perceive their justice and nobility. That alienates the great, which is why they said to Nuh: *"'Why should we believe you when the lowest people follow you?' He said, 'What do I know about what they have been doing? Their reckoning is the responsibility of my Lord alone, if you were but aware. I am not going to chase away the believers. I am only a clear warner.'"* (26:111-115)

When the Message was presented to the idolaters in Makka, they also disdained the poor and asked the Prophet, peace and blessings be upon him, to exclude the poor and weak, but he refused. Allah said, confirming his action, *"Do not chase away those who call on their Lord morning and evening, seeking His Face."* (6:52)

However, the story of faith and disbelief is not one of a struggle between different classes, between rich and poor. Both rich and poor people believed in Muhammad and the prayers join them together in even rows, wiping out any distinction in the eyes of Allah. Each of them is tested by Allah in a different way.

Perhaps the stories which have the closest resemblance to modern times are those of 'Ad and Thamud. 'Ad belonged to the people of the Amalekites, who were very tall and strong and whose shrewdness and intelligence were proverbial. But they were arrogant about their physical and mental prowess, seeing themselves as superior to all other people of their time. Then they started to flaunt their power and went to excess in the way that they lived, thinking that they could do whatever they wished to whoever they wished. Whenever a weak person fell into their hands, they assaulted him without fear of retaliation. No one could anything about it.

Their Prophet Hud said to them: *"Do you build a tower on every headland, just to amuse yourselves, and construct great fortresses, hoping to live for ever, and when you seize, seize as tyrants do? So fear Allah and obey me."* (26:128-131) The towers which they built are said to be waymarks which marked the roads in those desert wastes. It is also said that they were plastered castles and fortresses. It is also said that they were water reservoirs.

Today we find Europeans and Americans following a similar way, building skyscrapers and tall buildings and remembering their appetites while forgetting the commands of their Lord. When they made war they developed the atom bomb with all its concomitant universally destructive consequences! When they quarrelled they did not care about any humiliation and deprivation endured by their enemies.

Allah's anger against 'Ad and Thamud and those similar to them is on account of their lack of acknowledgement of Allah, their forgetting of the fact that they will meet Him, and their rejection of Him and His Messengers.

Then the *sura* mentions the people of Lut and their abhorrent sexual practices. It is an extraordinary thing that modern civilisation, faced by a catastrophe of unprecedented proportions in which millions of lives are threatened, rather than condemn fornication and the sexual deviance which has played such a large part in it, simply tries to find ways of continuing down the same path safely!

There appears to be no understanding at all that the prevalence and acceptance of homosexual practices is a sign of deep and destructive imbalance in human society: *"Of all beings, do you make approaches to males, leaving the wives Allah has created for you? You are a people who have gone beyond the limits."* (26:165-166) Allah destroyed those towns for what they used to do and "there is no changing the pattern of Allah".

The last of these ancient narratives mentioned in *Surat ash-Shu'ara'* is that of the Prophet Shu'ayb and the People of the Thicket or Madyan, to whom it was said: *"Fill up the measure. Do not be skimpers. Weigh with a level balance. Do not diminish people's goods and do not go about the earth, corrupting it."* (26:181-183) Their wrongdoing took the form of blatant economic injustice.

Islam contains the remedy for every one of the sins, sicknesses, and injustices which brought about the downfall and destruction of those earlier peoples and which are all without exception widespread in the world today. Its universal Message to all creation makes it the heir of all the previous religions since the scattered remnants of the People of the Book have forgotten – or neglected –

what they received from Allah. So let us remember that Muhammad has an eternal universal Message which includes all the warnings and lessons given to past generations, and that the Revelation which he brought contains Allah's Guidance for mankind until the end of time.

"Put your trust in the Almighty, the Most Merciful. He who sees you when you stand up to pray and your movements with those who prostrate. He is the All-Hearing, the All-Knowing."(26:217-220)

Sura 27
An-Naml (The Ant)

Surat an-Naml begins with a brief characterisation of the believers and the unbelievers. The believers receive guidance and good news and the unbelievers ruin and loss. This brief preamble is expanded upon at the end of the *sura,* but not before four stories from the past have been retold: those of Musa and Pharaoh, Thamud, and the people of Lut very briefly; and that of Sulayman and the Queen of Sheba in considerable detail – indeed it is the only time this story is told in the Qur'an. The *sura* also contains a brief allusion to the Beast which will emerge before the Last Day.

Let us first look briefly at these stories. The particular incident in the life of Musa concentrated on in this *sura* is the occasion when Allah spoke to Him from the Burning Bush and confirmed him as a Messenger. Important features of that event were the two miraculous signs of his staff turning into a snake and of his hand turning pure white, which Pharaoh later repudiated. This is to be contrasted with the story of Sulayman when the Queen accepts the signs which he puts before her.

Before turning to the story of Sulayman, it is worth mentioning the Words of Allah: *"There is no creature crawling on the earth or flying creature, flying with its wings, who are not communities just like yourselves ..."* (6:38) Those communities live and communicate with one another in their own languages. This communication is quite distinctive and it is within the capacity of human beings to learn its secrets. Much research has been done in recent years and a great deal is now understood about the forms animal communication takes and how very sophisticated it is.

Allah gave Sulayman instinctive understanding of the languages of the birds and insects and so he was able to grasp exactly what they were saying: *"We have been taught the speech of birds and we have been given everything. This is indeed clear overflowing favour."* (27:16)

He was able to understand the words spoken by an ant to its community: *"'O ants! Go down into your dwellings so that Sulayman and his troops do not crush you unconsciously.' He smiled, laughing at its words and said, 'O Lord, keep me thankful for Your blessing with which You blessed me and my parents, and keep me acting rightly, pleasing You; and admit me, by Your mercy, among Your righteous slaves.'"* (27:18-19)

The *sura* then goes on to mention the news which the hoopoe brought to Sulayman about Bilqis, the Queen of Sheba who worshipped the sun. The hoopoe was amazed when it saw that they were pagans who worshipped other than Allah: *"... they are not guided and they do not prostrate to Allah, He who brings out the hidden in the heavens and the earth, and knows what you conceal and what you make known..."* (27:24-25) Sulayman wrote a letter to this queen in which he stated: *"In the Name of Allah, All-Merciful, Most Merciful. Do not rise up against me, but come to me in submission."* (27:30-31)

Bilqis hesitated in giving her reply to this. She wanted to make sure that Sulayman was not simply one of those kings who seek wealth and power but really was one of those who guide people to Allah and are above worldly things. When her delegation came to Sulayman bearing presents and gifts, he perceived her intention. He said to the delegation: *"Would you give me wealth when what Allah has given me is better than what He has given you? Rather it is you who delight in your gift."* (27:36)

He wanted to show the queen a miraculous sign by which she would know his truthfulness. He asked those who were sitting with him: *"Which of you will bring her throne to me before they come to me in submission?"* (27:37) One of them brought the throne by the power of Allah to Jerusalem from the Yemen in a split second. Sulayman recognised the magnitude of what had occurred and declared, *"This is part of my Lord's favour to test me to see if I give thanks or show ingratitude. Whoever who gives thanks only does so to his own gain. Whoever shows ingratitude, my Lord is Endlessly Rich, Generous."* (27:38)

Bilqis looked at her throne in astonishment. She was asked, *"'Is your throne like this?' She said, 'It is very similar to it.'"* (27:42) This answer indicates her intelligence. Then she saw from the state of Sulayman that he truly was a Messenger from Allah and she had faith in him and declared: *"I submit with Sulayman to the Lord of all the worlds..."* (27:44)

This is an extraordinary story with many different layers of meaning. Not the least of its lessons, as was already mentioned above, is the contrast between the way in which the queen reacted to Sulayman and the way that Pharaoh, another ruler, received the Prophetic signs presented to him by Musa.

After the story of Sheba comes a mention of Thamud who compare with 'Ad in their arrogance and insolence. When Salih came to them to call them to Allah, they saw him as a bad omen and plotted to kill him: *"They said, 'Let us make an oath to one another by Allah: that we will fall upon him and his family in the night and then say to his protector, "We did not witness the destruction of his family..."'"* (27:49)

It appears that instead of killing him they killed the she-camel which Allah had created as a miracle for him. Then they tasted painful retribution: *"They hatched a plot and We also hatched a plot but they were not aware. And see what was the result of all their plotting! We utterly destroyed them and all their people. These then are their houses, in ruins because of the wrong they did..."* (27:50-53)

Then comes the story of Lut and the depraved cities whose people had perverted their natural form and delighted in their perversion, indulging it publicly in their assemblies and gatherings. When Lut tried to deter them they determined to expel him, so deeply entrenched was the depravity of their souls and their society: *"And Lut when he said to his people, 'Do you commit depravity knowing full well what you do? Do you come with lust to men instead of women? You are a people who are deeply ignorant.' The only response of his people was to say, 'Drive them out of your city! They are a people who keep themselves pure!'"* (27:54-56)

The reaction of homosexuals today is exactly the same thousands of years later! They have not changed and they have not learned. Allah destroyed their cities and those who advocate their perversion will not escape retribution.

Looking again at the beginning of the *sura*, we find that it paves the way for the mention of these events and warns of their end: *"As for those who do not believe in the Next World, We have made their actions seem good to them and they wander about blindly. Such people will receive an evil punishment and will be the greatest losers in the Next World."* (27:4-5)

After Allah has recounted the ends of some of the nations who denied their Messengers, He proclaims: *"Say: 'Praise belongs to Allah and peace be upon His slaves, those He has chosen...'"* (27:59) Praise belongs to Allah for destroying these evildoers and purifying the earth of them as He says in *Surat al-An'am*: *"So the last remnant of the people who did wrong was rooted out. Praise belongs to Allah, the Lord of the Universe!"* (6:45)

Freeing the earth from injustice and making the pillars of truth firm is precisely the task of the noble Prophets and those who follow them. When they succeed in realising their goal, praise and thanks are due to Allah. But when disbelief and injustice are dominant the believers have no option but to persevere until the *deen* is for Allah alone.

The basis and goal of the whole matter is that affirmation of Allah's Oneness which lies at the heart of all the Divine Messages. It is the incessant human tendency to attribute partners to Allah which allows corruption and injustice first creep into and then to dominate human society. For this reason the Qur'an is absolutely adamant in its insistence on the Divine Unity, and here in *Surat an-Naml* it directs a series of rhetorical questions to unbelievers in another attempt to show them the utter unreasonableness of their position.

- *"He Who created the heavens and the earth and sends down water for you from the sky by which We make luxuriant gardens grow – you could never cause their trees to grow. Is there a god together with Allah? No indeed, but*

they are people who consider others equal to Him!"
(27:60) The whole process of the growth cycle is completely beyond human control and the coming together of all the factors which make it possible is so complex that even the scientists admit that it could not have come about by chance. So why are people so prone to attribute things to sources other than their true Source?

• *"He Who made the earth a stable dwelling place and appointed rivers flowing through its midst and placed firmly embedded mountains on it and set a barrier between the two seas. Is there a god together with Allah? No indeed, but most of them do not know!"* (27:61) The stability of the earth and everything on it so that it does not shake or tremble really is an astonishing thing because the earth has three intrinsic movements: its revolution around its own axis, its orbit around the sun, and its movement with the rest of the galaxy through space. In spite of this triple movement and the incredible speeds involved, the glass of water in your hand does not shake! And the whole matter of salt and fresh water which we take entirely for granted is in truth an extraordinary phenomenon which should impel us to see the Divine Hand at work.

• *He who responds to the one in dire need when he calls out to Him and removes the evil affliction, and who has appointed you as deputies on the earth … Is there a god together with Allah? How little it is that you remember."*
(27:62) The fact that people in great difficulty almost always turn to Allah in their hour of need, and that in most cases relief comes, should ensure belief in Divine Providence; yet nearly everyone almost immediately forgets.

• *"He who guides you in the darkness of land and sea and sends out the winds bringing advance news of His mercy. Is there a god together with Allah? Allah is exalted above what they associate with Him!"* (27:63) The truth is that trade, agriculture and travel – on land, sea and air – is dependent on Allah who controls all aspects of existence. He even created the stars in a manner which allows us to find our way even in total darkness in the middle of the sea. In spite of all this, man attributes this to forces of natures which he thinks he can control.

• *"He who originates creation and then reproduces it and provides for you from out of heaven and earth. Is there a god together with Allah? Say: 'Bring your proof if you are truthful.'"* (27:64) There can be no proof for the non-existence of Allah; and of course none has ever been produced.

Lack of faith is an emotional position, not a rational one. It is a delusion which is based on a false understanding of the nature of existence and it has no basis in rational thought. The prevailing materialist philosophy, for all its scientific justifications, is in reality exactly the same as ancient paganism: *"Those who reject say, 'When we and our fathers are turned to dust will we then be produced again? We have been promised this before, we and our fathers. This is nothing but the myths and legends of earlier peoples.'"* (27:67-69)

The Prophet Muhammad had to contend with this false world view and give people a clear and vivid understanding of the Next World. He founded a civilisation based on belief in Allah alone, bound by Divine Revelation and focused on the Day of Judgement. The implementation of Islam produces a community based on the worship of Allah in which the effect of awareness of the reality of the Next World can be seen in every sphere of society.

Surat an-Naml reveals one of the signs which will appear before the coming of the Last Day. A beast will emerge from the animal world which Allah will inspire with speech and which will itself remind mankind of their Lord: *"When the Word is justly carried out against them, We shall produce a beast from the earth which will speak to them: 'Truly mankind had no certainty about Our Signs.'"* (27:82)

The *sura* ends by mentioning the Next World and the Final Reckoning, which is based implacably on what we have done with our lives in this world:

"*Those who perform good actions shall obtain better than them and will be safe from terror on that day. Those who perform bad actions will be tossed head-first into the Fire: 'Have you been repaid for anything other than what you did?'*" (27:89-90)

Sura 28
Al-Qasas (The Story)

Surat al-Qasas is a very good example of how Allah uses the same story in different places to bring out various aspects of its meaning. The first half of the *sura* is almost exclusively devoted to retelling the story of the earlier part of the life of Musa. This was covered in the previous two *suras* and also in great depth in *Surat TaHa* and *Surat al-A'raf,* as well as being mentioned in several other places.

Apart from mentioning certain details not found anywhere else, which we will point out later, this narrative is here used very specifically to reassure the believers at the time when the Prophet and his Companions were being forced to leave the land of their birth to face what must have seemed a very uncertain future.

This message of reassurance in the face of the incessant persecution and hostility they had encountered for more than ten years on account of their faith in Allah and His Messenger was badly needed, and Allah makes it clear here that so long as they continue on the Path they have chosen the future will indeed belong to them in the same way as it did to Musa and his followers: *"We desired to show kindness to those who were oppressed in the land and to make them leaders and to make them the inheritors and to establish them firmly in the land..."* (28:5-6)

Although these words refer to the past, they put renewed confidence into the hearts of the Muslims and the message was reinforced at the end of the *sura* when Allah told the Prophet, peace and blessings be upon him, that he would certainly return to his birthplace: *"He who has imposed the Qur'an upon you will most certainly bring you home again."* (28:85)

"Pharaoh exalted himself arrogantly in the land and divided its people into factions, oppressing one group of them by slaughtering their sons and letting their women live. He was one of the corrupters." (28:4) This particular Pharaoh was most likely to have been Rameses II whose kingdom extended from the Congo to the Danube, which may have been partly what led him to make such extravagant claims about himself and behave in such a despotic way. The *ayat* also shows that the policy of 'divide and rule' has a long history!

As we said above this recounting of Musa's story contains details not mentioned anywhere else. For instance his birth and what happened with his mother is expounded in a much fuller way here than in *Surat TaHa*. Her emotional state is given considerable prominence: *"Musa's mother felt a great emptiness in her heart and she almost divulged him; only We fortified her heart so that she would be a true believer."* (28:10)

Another thing is the transaction between Pharaoh and his wife after Musa is rescued from the water, when she says: *"A source of delight for me and for you; do not kill him. It may well be that he will be of use to us or perhaps we could adopt him as a son."* (28:9) This gains in significance when we discover in another place that this woman was one of those especially favoured by Allah: *"Allah has coined a likeness for those who believe: the wife of Pharaoh when she said, 'My Lord, build a house in the Garden for me in Your Presence, and rescue me from Pharaoh and all his deeds and rescue me from the wrongdoing people.'"* (66:11)

In *Surat TaHa* we are simply told that Musa killed someone whereas here we are given a detailed account of the incident. He witnessed a quarrel between a member of his tribe and an Egyptian: *"The one from his party asked for his support against the other from his enemy. So Musa hit him, dealing him a fatal blow."* (28:14) Musa was extremely strong, but he did not imagine that his blow would prove fatal. When he realised what had happened he called to Allah: *"He said, 'O Lord, I have wronged myself. Forgive me.' So He forgave him ..."* (28:15) The following day the same man asked for his help again and he realised that he was a troublemaker. The whole episode meant that he had to flee Egypt and seek refuge in Madyan.

We learn that Musa found welcome, shelter and a wife in Madyan, which is very interesting and encouraging in the context of the move being undertaken by the Muslims from Makka to Madina. Musa moved from the tyranny and injustice of the Pharaonic system to one of justice and fairness. He had besought Allah, *"O Lord, I am truly in need of any good You have for me,"* (28:24) after his desperate flight from Egypt, and the answer came in the offer of marriage, shelter and fair contract: *"He said, 'I would like to marry you to one of these two daughters of mine on condition that you work for me for eight full years. If you complete ten, then that is up to you. I do not want to be hard on you. You will find me, Allah willing, to be a righteous man.' He said, 'That is agreed between me and you. Whichever of the two terms I fulfil, there should be no bad feeling towards me. Allah is Guardian over what we say.'"* (28:28)

Musa's sojourn in Madyan was clearly a time of retrenchment and consolidation for him prior to his return as Allah's Messenger to Egypt.

The story of his noticing the fire and finding the Burning Bush is very similar to other accounts except that here the exact location of the Bush is specified: *"But when he reached it a voice called out to him from the right hand side of the valley in the part which was full of blessing, from out of the bush, 'O Musa! I am Allah, the Lord of all the worlds.'"* (28:30)

The detailed account really ends at this point and the story of Musa's return to Egypt with Harun and his encounter with the Pharaoh, which is described in detail in *Surat al-A'raf, TaHa and ash-Shu'ara'*, is passed over very lightly here; but the salient point about Pharaoh is clear: *"He and his troops were arrogant in the land without any right. They thought that they would not be returned to Us. So We seized him and his troops and flung them into the sea. See the end result of the wrongdoers!"* (28:39-40)

One thing more, however, is mentioned here and nowhere else which is that Pharaoh asked his minister Haman to build an observatory: *"Pharaoh said, 'O Nobles! I do not know of any other god for you apart from Me. Haman, kindle a fire for me over the clay and build me a lofty tower so that perchance I may be able to climb up to Musa's god! I consider him to be a blatant liar.'"* (28:38)

This is not so far-fetched as it might sound. Eminent astronomers have been heard to say that their exhaustive search of the universe has revealed no trace of the Divine Presence and it is quite clear that this way of thinking has gained much popular credence. This dissemination of the materialist world view is particularly corrupting to the human spirit, which is perhaps why Allah says of Pharaoh and his like: *"We made them leaders, summoning people to the Fire, and on the Day of Rising they will not be helped. We pursued them with a curse in this world and on the Day of Rising they will be hideous and spurned."* (28:41-42)

The *sura* then moves from past to present and addresses the Last Prophet directly: *"You were not on the western side when We gave Musa the command. You were not a witness. Yet We produced further generations and their lives were long-drawn-out. Nor did you live among the people of Madyan and recite Our Signs to them, yet We have sent you news of them."* (28:43-44)

Allah's signs were given to His Final Prophet in the form of the Qur'an but his people asked for miracles like those which accompanied the message of Musa. Musa's miracles, however, had no effect: *"But when the truth did come to them from Us they said, 'Why has he not been given the same as Musa was given?' But did they not previously reject what Musa was given? They say, 'Two sorceries which reinforce each other.' And they say, 'We reject each one of them.'"* (28:48)

Some of the People of the Book, on the other hand, did recognise the truth when it came, perceiving that it simply confirmed them in their faith: *"Those to whom We gave the Book before this believe in it. When it is recited to them they say, 'We believe in it; it is the truth from our Lord. We were already Muslims before it came.' They will be given their wage twice over because they have been steadfast..."* (28:52-54)

About such people the Messenger of Allah, may Allah bless him and grant him peace, said: "Three kinds of people will be given their reward twice over. If a man of the People of the Book who believes in his Prophet meets me and then believes in me, follows me, and affirms my Prophethood, he will have two rewards. If a man has a slavegirl and feeds her well, then teaches her well and then sets her free and marries her, he will have two rewards. If a slave carries out what is due to Allah Almighty and due to his master, he will have two rewards."

West Asia and North Africa were full of People of the Book during the time of Roman rule; the vast majority of them entered Islam after learning of it and were convinced of its truth. But the Prophet's own people rejected it first and declared war on the new *deen*. The Messenger was distressed by this but Allah told him: *"You cannot guide those you love, rather Allah guides those He wills."* (28:56)

It is said that this *ayat* was revealed about Abu Talib whom the Prophet strongly wanted to become Muslim. Abu Talib knew that his nephew was truthful but his fear of tribal disapproval stopped him from becoming Muslim. He said:

> I know that the religion of Muhammad
>   is the best religion for mankind.
> Were it not for censure or fear of abuse,
>   you would have seen me openly embrace it.

The same fear was expressed by others: *"They say, 'If we follow the guidance with you, we shall be forcibly uprooted from our land." Have We not established a safe sanctuary for them, to which produce of every kind is brought, provision direct from Us? Yet most of them do not know."* (28:57) They have not learned the lesson of history: *"How many a city We have destroyed which lived in insolent ingratitude! There are their houses, never again inhabited after them, except a little. It was We who were their Inheritor."* (28:58) Then injunctions follow which encourage people to follow the Truth and caution them against the appetites of this world: *"Anything you have been given is only the enjoyment of the life of this world and its finery. What is with Allah is better and longer lasting. So why do you not use your understanding?"* (28:60)

So many people are veiled by the glitter of this world from the truth! What is worse, the people in power propagate this misconception among those they rule and all too often the ruled accept what they are told without question. But that will not excuse them. *"The Day when He summons them He will say, 'Where are they, those you claimed to be My partners?' Those against whom the Word has been justly carried out* [meaning the leaders] *will say, 'Our Lord, those people whom we misled, we only misled them as we too were misled. We declare our innocence to You. It was not us they were worshipping!'"* (28:62-63)

After this Allah gives us a concrete example of someone who was corrupted by vast wealth which dazzled many of those around him: the story of Qarun. Qarun's wealth was so great that the keys to his strongboxes alone required several men to carry them! He was wealthy beyond imagination. Money in itself is neither good nor bad. It becomes a cause of praise or blame according to the way it is used. A knife in the hands of a killer is a murder weapon but in the hands of a butcher it is a means to wholesome provision. For this reason Qarun was told: *"...Seek the Abode of the Next World with what Allah has given you, without forgetting your portion of this world. And do good as Allah has been good to you. And do not seek to cause corruption in the earth. Allah does not love people who cause corruption."* (28:77)

There are wealthy people who spend generously from what they have and seek out people's needs in order to satisfy them. They welcome the poor and give them more than they ask for. They thank Allah for what He has given them and for His help in obtaining it. They do not see wealth as a reason for exultation or as a means of vaunting themselves over others. It is a test from Allah and they see it in that light and are very careful to spend it in a way that is pleasing to Him.

But Qarun attributed his wealth to his own abilities and flaunted it in front of other people: *"He said, 'I have only been given it on account of knowledge I possess.' Did he not know that before him Allah had destroyed generations with far greater strength* than him and far more possessions? The evildoers will not be questioned about their sins." (28:78)*

The Messengers of Allah have included both wealthy and poor men. Some of them were kings and others had barely sufficient for their needs. But those who were wealthy were neither niggardly nor prodigal and those who were poor were neither incapable nor contemptible.

The trial of wealth proved difficult for various civilisations in the past and in the modern world it is a source of great affliction. It has produced a loathsome system based on great disparity between rich and poor and it does nothing to ameliorate it but on the contrary oppresses those who suffer by it.

The remedy for this is found in the teachings of Islam which puts the earth in order by following the Divine Guidance and gives the true perspective which prevents such imbalances from occurring: *"That Abode of the Next World, We grant it to those who do not seek to exalt themselves in the earth or to cause corruption in it. The successful outcome is for the godfearing."* (28:83) We must realise that human society will never be right without Allah's *deen* and no individual can be right without a sound heart. The *Shari'a* must be placed alongside true faith in the Last Day and the righteous action which inevitably accompanies it.

It is shameful that there are some so-called 'religious' people whose conduct belies their professed faith. They do not implement the laws they are commanded to carry out. They say that it is sufficient merely to affirm the Unity of Allah. This attitude has gained currency among the masses of the Muslims, who think that action is an optional extra! They believe that as long as a person believes in Allah he will be saved whatever he does. This idea has infected the nation of Islam for generations. Only belief coupled with right action will restore Muslims to their rightful place.

Surat al-Qasas ends by addressing by stressing the necessity of upholding the Revelation and acting on it:

"You did not expect to have the Book imposed upon you. It is nothing but a mercy from your Lord. Do not, then,

lend support to the rejectors. Do not let them debar you from Allah's Signs after they have been revealed to you. Call people to your Lord and no account be among the idolaters. Do not call on any other god together with Allah. There is no god but Him. All things are passing except His Face. Judgement belongs to Him. To Him you will be returned." (28:86-88)

Sura 29
Al-'Ankabut (The Spider)

The nature of this world is that it is a trial through which we have to pass: a trial whose results become apparent when we move beyond it - success or failure; the Garden or the Fire! The severity of the trial varies according to people's natures and capacities. People's troubles correspond to their aspirations. Someone whose job is to till the fields for cultivation is not the same as someone whose job is to return the world and bring it to the worship of Allah.

If we look at the world at the time when Muhammad came, peace and blessings be upon him, we find confusion everywhere. The vast mass of people were worshipping idols under all sorts of pagan systems. The Jews claimed to be the Chosen People and better than everybody else, distracted by their claim from faith, reform and calling other people to the truth. The Christians who had deified the human 'Isa and the angelic Jibril, had made the True God into one of three, saying, "Together they make one god." Darknesses piled one on top of the other.

Into this dense darkness came Muhammad, peace and blessings be upon him, and he was told, "It is your task to disperse all these dark clouds and lead all people to their Lord Whom they have forgotten. What a terrible trial! A single man was responsible for putting the whole world in order and changing its course and restoring all humanity to the path of true faith!

But he relied on Allah and rose to the challenge and around him gathered Companions who were "fierce against the unbelievers and merciful to one another". With them he faced exile, hardship and continuous battles. He had to fight entrenched tradition and great powers but did not waver or cease until people had entered the *deen* of Allah in droves.

Surat al-'Ankabut opens with an *ayat* which makes this trial aspect of existence clear: *"Alif. Lam. Mim. Do people suppose they will be left to say, 'We believe,' and not be tested? We tested those before them so that Allah might know those who told the truth from the liars."* (29:1-3)

In some respects the world today is similar to that which confronted the Prophet. The vast majority of people are caught up in worship of this world and refuse to acknowledge their Lord in any real way. Nowhere is Allah's *deen* established in its entirety. It is therefore the responsibility of the followers of Muhammad to confront their traditional enemies, to bring the masses back to the worship of Allah alone, and to bear the burdens that this will entail: *"Anyone who fights hard against the enemy, is fighting entirely for his own benefit. Allah is Rich beyond need of any being."* (29:6) But at the end of the *sura* we find a promise from Allah: *"As for those who fight hard in Our way, We will guide them to Our paths. Truly Allah is with the good-doers."* (29:69)

Faith in Allah is not easy. It requires a person with strong broad shoulders and firm resolve: *"There are some people who say 'We believe in Allah' and then, when they suffer harm in Allah's cause, take people's persecution for Allah's punishment; but if help comes from your Lord they say, 'We were with you.' Does Allah not know best what is in everybody's breast?"* (29:10) Such people seek to pluck the fruits of faith without putting in any effort. To instruct them the *sura* mentions that Nuh continued to call his people for 950 years!

Some people affirm that the struggle is for nothing. To teach them, the Qur'an recounts that Ibrahim said to his people: *"Have they not seen how Allah brings creation out of nothing, then reproduces it? That is easy for Allah. Say: 'Travel in the earth and see how He brought creation out of nothing. Then later Allah will bring about the next existence."* (29:19-20)

Others are overcome by bestiality and fulfil their sexual appetites in an abominable way, deviating from the natural human pattern of sex within the bond of marriage. Lut said to them: *"You*

are committing an obscenity not perpetrated before you by anyone
in all the worlds. Do you lie with men and waylay them on the
road and commit depravities within your gatherings?" (28:28-29)

This has of course been a major cause of the AIDS epidemic.
The reason is that people have rejected the framework which
Divine Guidance allows for the fulfilment of the sexual appetite,
which makes permitted sexual intercourse an act of worship and
sets up barriers to prevent us straying into forbidden territory.

The *sura* proceeds to list other nations which rebelled against
Allah and refused to follow His Path. What did He do to them?
*"We seized each one of them for their wrong action. Against some
of them We sent a sudden squall of stones; some were seized by the
Great Shout; some We caused the earth to swallow up; and some
We drowned..."* (29:40)

All of them saw their own situation as unassailable. They all
believed that they had everything under control. But in reality they
were extremely vulnerable. Allah makes a striking metaphor of
their self-deception from which the *sura* takes its name: *"The likeness of those who take protectors besides Allah is that of the spi-
der which makes itself a house. But no house is flimsier than a spi-
der's house, if they did but know."* (29:41)

The People of the Book fall into two categories: one category
do not begrudge us to the right to life, worship and calling people
to Islam. Instead they leave us alone. They are neutral and they do
not break treaties. The other category harass us, our Book and our
Prophet and strive to disgrace us and pull down our banner. It is
our right to protect ourselves against them and take measures! No
rational person would oblige us to trust them!

Surat al-'Ankabut contains general guidance about how to deal
with both categories: *"Argue with the People of the Book only in
the kindest way — except with those of them who do wrong — saying, 'We believe in what has been revealed to us and what was
revealed to you. Our God and your God are one, and we submit to
Him.' In the same way We have revealed the Book to you, and
those to whom We gave the Book believe in it; and some of these
people believe in it as well. Only the rejectors of faith repudiate
Our Signs."* (29:46-47)

If a commission of impartial scholars were to re-examine the relations between East and West over the course of history, they would discover that it was not the Muslims who were responsible for the bloody wars between them either in earlier or in later times. The Byzantines were the aggressors in the early days of Islam. Then their descendants resumed the attack in the course of the Crusades, but they were forced to retreat after many years of attack and retreat.

They resumed their onslaught once more in modern times, beginning with Napoleon's assault on Egypt. Then the French attacked all the states of the Maghrib, the English attacked the Nile Valley, and Italy attacked Libya. The Islamic world fell into the hands of the People of prior Scripture. The Muslims were not the aggressors in any of these wars.

Today the masses of Muslims want to live according to their *deen* but they are denied the possibility of doing so by the neo-colonialist governments which rule them. The generality of the Muslims believe in every line in their Book and want to act by it, but they are prevented from doing so by people who in fact negate what the Prophet brought. *"You never recited any Book before it, nor did you write one down with your right hand. If you had, the negators would have voiced their doubts. No, it is clear Signs reposited in the hearts of those who have been given knowledge. Only the wrongdoers repudiate Our Signs."* (28:48-49)

The trial caused to the Muslims by the injustices of the People of the Book and their followers is severe. They have launched a universal assault to turn the Muslims away from their *deen* and have narrowed it down to the point that its social, economic and legal impact has been almost completely eliminated.

Surat al-'Ankabut repeats the specious argument often put forward by the pagans when they asked Muhammad for miracles and were told: "The miracle you desire is found in the form of this Book whose *ayats* you hear." *"They say, 'Why have no signs been sent down to him from his Lord?' Say: 'The Signs are in Allah's hands. I am only a clear warner.' Is it not enough for them that We have revealed to you the Book which is recited to them? There is* certainly a mercy and a reminder in that for people who believe." (29:50-51)

The Qur'an is an abiding miracle that will endure until the end of time and it can be seen in the spiritual and social effects it produces. It has protected our community in every crisis and will continue to do so. No book has the same power of bringing about a connection between a man and his Lord. The Qur'an has produced generation after generation of human beings who have been connected to their Lord by an unbreakable tie which has produced social justice and luminous spirituality. That is one aspect of the miracle of the Noble Book.

However, there has been a long-running series of battles between Truth and falsehood; and the cost has been heavy. Impatient believers ask: "When will victory come?" Arrogant unbelievers taunt: "Where is that with which you threaten us?" *"They ask you to hasten the punishment. If it were not for a stipulated term, the punishment would have already come to them. It will come upon them suddenly when they are not expecting it."* (29:53)

Trials have been the lot of the Muslims from the beginning. Many of the first Muslims had to leave behind everything they had in Makka when they emigrated to Madina, and did not know how they were going to support themselves. Allah relieved them of their anxiety: *"How many creatures do not carry their provision with them! Allah provides for them and He will for you. He is the All-Hearing, the All-Knowing."* (29:60) The Muhajirun found everything they needed and more besides. The faith which the Qur'an creates has produced marvels and continues to do so.

Although there are many who have become ensnared by the modern world and deluded by its materialist philosophy, denying anything beyond it, there are still Muslims who believe in this world and the Next and know that our existence here is temporary and fleeting. In the Next World sight will be sharper and hearing keener and life more intense: *"The life of this world is nothing but a game and a diversion. The Abode of the Next World - that is truly Life if they did but know."* (29:64)

The *sura* closes by telling us the two possible outcomes of the trial outlined in the opening *ayats*:

"Who could do greater wrong than someone who fabricates lies against Allah or denies the truth when it comes to him? Is there not shelter in Jahannam for the rejectors? As for those who fight hard in Our way, We shall guide them to Our paths. Truly Allah is with the good-doers." (29:68-69)

Sura 30
Ar-Rum: The Byzantines

In describing the relationship between Islam and Christianity we note that the Noble Qur'an does not equivocate or dissemble in its affirmation of Divine Unity and its rejection of polytheism. Allah is One. He did not beget and was not begotten. He is One and is not a compound of two elements, as water, for example, is a compound of oxygen and hydrogen. The statement that Allah is the both the Father and the Son is rejected: *"Allah is One God."* (4:171) No second or third can be a god. The second and third are creatures of Allah Almighty: *"Say: 'Is it other than Allah that you order me to worship, you people of arrant ignorance?' It has been revealed to you, and to those before you: 'If you associate others with Allah, your actions will come to nothing and you will be among the losers.' Rather worship Allah and be among the thankful."* (39:64-66)

These *ayats* of the Qur'an were revealed in Makka. Islam from its very beginning defined its position in relation to the Trinity. On the other hand, on the political side, we notice that in the beginning Islam had good relations with Christians and that when the Prophet's Companions were being persecuted, he indicated to them that they should emigrate to Abyssinia which was a Christian kingdom at that time; and they went there believing that 'Isa and his mother were among the righteous servants of Allah.

Then came the defeat of the Byzantines at the hands of the Magian Persians. The Muslims were grieved for them and the idolaters gloated over it. The defeat of the Christians was very severe and extensive and they lost Egypt, Yemen and Syria and were forced to pay humiliating tributes. Everyone was sure that the sun of Byzantium had set and its future was dim.

The sole voice to contradict that assessment and challenge it was that of the Noble Qur'an in Makka. It proclaimed with certainty that the defeat was a temporary setback and would be reversed in a few years: *"The Byzantines have been defeated in the land nearby, but after their defeat they will themselves gain victory in a few years time. The affair is Allah's, both beforehand and afterwards. On that day, the believers will rejoice in Allah's help. He grants victory to whomever He wills. He is the Almighty, the Most Merciful. That is Allah's promise. Allah does not break His promise. But most people do not know."* (30:2-6)

These *ayats* are discussing a geopolitical reality in which the Christians had been humiliated and the Persians had gained the upper hand. No one doubted it. But the Revelation goes on to explicitly state that this situation would be turned round within as many years as could be counted on one's fingers. Time proved the truthfulness of the Qur'anic prophecy. The strange thing is that instead of that causing them to commend Islam, the Greeks simply maintained that Muhammad had said that because he hated the Persians! They refused to acknowledge that this prophecy was a Divine miracle whose truthfulness had been irrefutably proved.

We do not need their testimony and we only relate what occurred to indicate the basic political position of the Muslims towards the Christians. It is clear that the reason for that is that the Christians are more likely to embrace the unitary belief of Islam than other people and indeed that was shown by what happened after the Islamic conquests. Man's natural patterning triumphed and Christians entered Islam in droves. The masses preferred to abandon abstruse contradictions and spontaneously accepted the clear logic of Islam. Their hearts opened to Islam and they embraced it voluntarily, not by force.

The basic tenets of the idea of man's natural patterning have already been mentioned in *Surat al-A'raf* but the whole matter is explained in greater detail in *Surat ar-Rum*, which makes clear that Islam is the natural form of man, the instinctive life pattern adopted by upright human nature. It is the impulse which frees the liberated intellect from the shackles of animal appetites in its search for the Truth, protecting it from its perverse whims and desires: *"So set your face towards the* Deen, *as a natural pure believer, Allah's natural pattern on which He made mankind. There is no changing of Allah's creation. That is the upright* deen – *but most people do not know."* (30:30)

The Source of Life to whom the living are directed in the Heavens and earth transcends all forms of association and can only be described in terms of glory and praise. Human beings, jinn and angels prostrate in submission to Him. There is no corner or hidden place in the world concealing any being capable of contending with His power: *"So glory be to Allah when you enter the night and when you enter the morning. Praise belongs to Him in the heavens and the earth, in the afternoon and when midday comes."* (30:17-18)

The word of *tawhid* is also called the Formula of pure sincerity because it purifies faith of any taint of *shirk* and makes everyone other than Allah His slave, ennobled if they show humility towards Him and destroyed if they are rebellious towards Him. *"He brings out the living from the dead and brings out the dead from the living and brings the earth back to life after it was dead. In the same way you will be brought out."* (30:19)

The Almighty wished to test all human beings in this world so that after the life-span written for them He could bring them back to question them about what they had done. In order that they should have every opportunity not to be misguided, He set up signs for them bearing witness to His Presence, distributed them throughout Heaven and earth and then called our attention to them in His Mighty Book. In this *sura* He mentions six in a row and a seventh on its own. He says:

> *"Among His signs is that He created you from dust and here you are, human beings dispersed throughout the earth!"* (30:20)

> *"Among His signs is that He created spouses for you from yourselves so that you might find repose with them. And He has placed affection and mercy between you. There are certainly signs in that for people who reflect."*
> (30:21)

"Among His signs is the creation of the heavens and the earth and the variety of your languages and colours. There are certainly signs in that for all beings." (30:22)

"Among His signs is your sleep by night and by day and your seeking of His unbounded favour. There are certainly signs in that for people who can hear." (30:23)

"Among His signs is that He shows you the lightning striking fear and giving hope, and sends down water from the sky and by it gives back life to the earth when it was dead. There are certainly signs in that for people who use their intellect." (30:24)

"Among His signs is that heaven and earth stand fast by His command. Then, when He summons you with a call out from the earth, you will at once emerge." (30:25)

"Among His signs is that He sends the winds, bearing good news, and to give you a taste of His mercy, and to make the ships run by His command, and to enable you to seek of His unbounded favour so that perhaps you may show thanks." (30:46)

Everyone whose senses are awake in this existence will perceive that the Qur'an speaks about Allah in the best and most truthful manner. The atmosphere of knowledge evoked by the Qur'an awakens faith and counteracts the poison of atheism but many people merely *"know something of the outward of the life of this world, but are heedless of the Next World."* (30:7) They are especially numerous and conspicuous at the present time. The reason for their spread is the concealment of true Revelation because its bearers have failed to embody it and convey it. But the predominance of material philosophies denying the Next World cannot truly convince thinking minds or satisfy the yearning of man's natural patterning.

The naturally upright soul recognises its Lord and His beneficence strengthens it. It will return to recognition of Allah provided the person concerned protects himself from the tricks of Shaytan.

However, the fruit may be spoiled, the embryo marred, by sickness of the heart. People can be overcome by selfishness, schism and neglect of the truth, but the Qur'an does not abandon them to destruction. In fact it encourages them to return to their truly natural form: *"turning in repentance towards Him. And be fearful of Him and establish the prayer. Do not be among the idolaters, those who make divisions in their* deen *and form into sects, each faction exulting in what it has."* (30:31-32)

Discord and disunion among human beings result from affirmation of the lower self and the politics of envy. This happens among both people of religion and worldly people and is generally accompanied by self-satisfaction and self-righteousness. This has always been widespread among human communities and unfortunately still is. It has nothing to do with the differences of opinion which are expressed in the *ijtihad* of the great Imams of *fiqh* and the schools which developed from them. Legitimate disagreements in *fiqh* do not constitute divisions in the community. They are simply different ways of understanding secondary or marginal branches of knowledge and the people who express them are all rewarded, both those who are correct and those who err. Anyone who tries to distort such disagreements into partisanship and hostility has gone astray.

❋❋❋❋❋

After these *ayats* relating to the natural patterning of the properly functioning human being, there is a discussion about trials in good times and bad. Crises inevitably come to people from their Lord; but when He makes them happy again they immediately forget their earlier difficulties and are ungrateful for the renewal of Allah's blessing to them. *"When harm touches people they call on their Lord, turning in repentance towards Him. But then when He lets them taste mercy from Him a group of them at once make others co-partners with their Lord, thus showing ingratitude for what He has given them. 'Enjoy yourselves – you will soon know.'"* (30:33-34) This is a sign of heedlessness and false-heartedness.

How often people exult in the blessings they have and take them for granted, forgetting the thankfulness due to the Lord for them and then, when their health deteriorates or their wealth disappears, become overwhelmed by despair and overcome by despondency! That is because they think they have lost something they have an absolute right to and that it may never return. They ignore the fact that giving and withholding are part of the inevitable nature of existence. *"When We give people a taste of mercy, they rejoice in it, but when a bad thing happens to them on account of what they have done, they fall at once into despair. Do they not see that Allah expands the provision of anyone He wills and also restricts it? There are certainly signs in that for people who believe."* (30:36-37) We must be thankful in good times and steadfast in bad, and content with the Divine Decree.

Allah Almighty says: *"Give relatives their due, and the poor, and travellers. That is better for those who desire the pleasure of Allah. Such people are the successful."* (30:38) The discord between rich and poor has ground on in the world since the beginning of human history and the modern doctrines of capitalism and socialism continue to keep people following the same fruitless path of conflict and envy as that trodden by all their predecessors. Both groups suppose that life can only be fulfilled at the price of the complete ruination of the other, making the class war a bounden duty of the human species: *"Corruption has appeared on the land and in the sea through what people's own hands have earned to let them taste something of what they have done so that perhaps they might return."* (30:41)

The brotherhood of mutual assistance and mercy nurtured by true faith is the only viable restraint upon the excessive greed of the wealthy and the sterile resentment of the poor. *"So turn your face towards the Upright* Deen, *before there arrives from Allah a Day which cannot be turned back. On that day they will be split apart. Whoever rejected, their rejection was to their own detriment. Whoever acted rightly were making things easy for themselves."* (30:43-44)

Included in this discussion about the trials of good times and bad are some words about the eternal conflict between truth and falsehood, belief and disbelief. While the Messenger was conveying the Message of Allah and having to overcome the endless succession of obstacles which the idolaters placed in his path, he was told by way of encouragement, *"Before you We sent Messengers to their people, and they came with the clear signs to them, and then We took revenge on those who did evil; and it is ever incumbent on Us to help the believers."* (30:47)

The Community (*Umma*) which purports to follow Muhammad now constitutes a fifth of the inhabitants of the earth and yet it has suffered all these military, cultural and social defeats. What has reduced it to this level? The truth is that the Muslims have lost most of the characteristics of the natural human patterning which provide the basic moral and political strength of Islam and so they now possess no certainty, unity or civilisation. If you compare the Muslims in the world today with the people who do not acknowledge Allah and His Messenger you will find active energy on the part of the non-Muslims and torpid stagnation on the part of the Muslims.

While Muslims are being attacked in Bosnia and driven from their land in Palestine, the masses in the Nile Valley and Morocco are smiling with stuffed bellies, stupidly seeking amusement! Is this brotherhood in the *Deen*? Of course it is not. Islam is in fact only supported by a residue of befuddled and disfigured souls.

A community like this has no future. Allah divided the Tribe of Israel in the past and gave the pagan idol-worshippers power over them because there is no way that false religiosity can be victorious. Yet change is possible, and when the Muslims put their affairs in order the victory that now seems so distant will draw near for them. As things stand our Community merely mirrors the existing political, economic and social chaos in the world and Allah will certainly not give us His assistance under these circumstances unless we show a real resolve to put our house in order.

There is an *ayat* in this *sura* which indicates that Islam will last until the end of time and this necessarily implies a Community which will always be adhering to it and sacrificing themselves for it. *"Those given knowledge and belief will say, 'You have lingered in Allah's Book until the Day of Rising. And this is the Day of*

Rising, but you did not know.'" (30:56) We do know that we have
the last of the Messages and are the last Community and that after
us there is only the Last Hour. Will we reunite, renew our lives and
restore our glories? If we do, we have Allah's assurance of success. *"Therefore be steadfast. Allah's promise is true. Do not let
those who have no certainty disquiet you."* (30:60) Steadfastness
is the key to success in the struggle which will be followed by victory.

Sura 31
Luqman

Surat Luqman begins by mentioning those who go good and the rewards prepared for them. Then it mentions the evildoers and the trouble they make for Islam: *"But there are some people who trade in distracting tales to lead astray from the way of Allah without any knowledge and to make a mockery of it. Those, for them there is humiliating punishment."* (31:6) This *ayat* refers specifically to an-Nadr ibn al-Harith who used to buy books containing the history of the Persians kings and read them to Quraysh in their nightly gatherings and meetings. He used to say, "This is better than what Muhammad recites to you!"

Some commentators think that the *ayat* was sent down about singing. Singing about worldly matters is blameworthy. Every kind of discourse which distracts from the Truth and diverts people from following it is fruitless. The *ayats* then reconfirm the recompense of those who do good: *"For those who believe and do right actions there are Gardens of Delight, to remain in them timelessly forever. Allah's promise is true. He is the Almighty, the All-Wise."* (31:8-9)

The *sura* returns to this theme in a slightly different way in its middle part, beginning from the words of the Almighty: *"Whoever submits his face to Allah and does good has grasped onto the firmest handhold. With Allah is the end result of all affairs."* (31:22) As it promises good to the good-doers, it promises evil to the evildoers: *"Anyone who rejects, do not let his rejection make you sad. To Us is their return and We will inform them about the things that they were doing."* (31:23)

The *sura* also speaks early on of the Creator in a way befitting His glory and praise and asks about the partners which people attribute to him. Who are they then? Where is what they have created? The gibberish of the idolaters resembles the delirious rantings of someone with a fever, having neither weight nor substance. It returns later to the same theme, telling of the incomparable greatness of Allah and making it clear that His Words are beyond being counted. *"If all the trees on earth were pens, and all the sea, with seven more seas besides, were ink, the Words of Allah still would not dry up. Allah is Almighty, All-Wise."* (31:27) Yet this inconceivable vastness, of which the universe we inhabit is but a tiny part, is nothing to Him. *"Your creation and rising is only like that of a single self. Allah is All-Hearing, All-Seeing."* (31:28)

The major part of *Surat Luqman*, however, is devoted to the words of the sage whose name it bears. It is related that Quraysh asked the Prophet, may Allah bless him and grant him peace, about Luqman, wanting to learn more about him, and this *sura* was revealed to him in response to their request. It contains the nub of his wisdom in the form of advice he gave to his son which was full of profound benefit. Luqman the Sage had more insight into the truth than all the Greek philosophers whose names are so famous. Their philosophy consists of abstruse thought and abstract concepts, whereas Luqman summarised the eternal truth in the most succinct manner for the benefit of his son and also left it as a noble legacy for all subsequent generations.

It is one of the vagaries of human nature that people find it burdensome to be grateful for the favours people do for them. We want existence to serve us while remaining free from any obligation. Many people do good for us and we grab it avidly and then turn our backs without a word of thanks! We treat our Lord with the same ingratitude and our lives our tainted by this idiocy which even animals disdain. *"Truly man is ungrateful to his Lord."* (100:6)

The truth is that gratitude to Allah for the blessings of existence and sustenance lies at the very core of the relationship of each human being with their Lord. That is why the *ayats* about Luqman begin by mentioning it: *"We gave Luqman wisdom: 'Be thankful to Allah. Anyone who is thankful is only thankful to his own gain. Anyone who is ungrateful, Allah is Rich beyond need, Praiseworthy.'"* (31:12) Allah is Rich beyond need of His creatures. If His slave thanks Him for His favour, it simply indicates correct understanding and opens the door to increase. If he does not do so he merely harms himself.

The advice of Luqman to his son begins with the foundation of all knowledge, the recognition of the Unity of Allah: *"O my son, do not make any others co-partners with Allah. Associating others with Him is a terrible wrong."* (31:13) And this is immediately followed by advice concerning parents, since they are the outward source of human existence and it is vital for the health of any society that children show great honour and respect for their parents without allowing that to blind them to the fact that they have come from Allah and will return to Him. In our time, however, there is neither respect for parents nor knowledge of our Divine Source. Modern secular civilisation does not care about parents. When they are old, their children often deposit them in an old people's home where they are left alone and ignored. How can a society lay any claim to civilisation when it treats its old people with such scant respect and refuses to acknowledge its own Creator?

Luqman's advice to his son continues by laying the foundations of all right action: *"O my son! Establish the prayer and command the right and forbid the wrong and be steadfast in the face of all that happens to you. That truly shows firm resolve."* (31:17) That one counsel alone would be sufficient for a whole lifetime of right action. The advice concludes with Luqman warning his son against all forms of pride, the fountainhead of all the destructive vices of the heart, ending with practical ways of eliminating it: *"Be moderate in your tread and lower your voice. The most hateful of voices is the ass's bray."* (31:19) All the advice taken together, although comparatively brief in extent, contains all that a human being needs and is such that, if put into practice, it is sufficient to enable someone to live a complete and fulfilled life. The Noble Qur'an mentions it so that we may benefit from the wisdom it contains; and certainly wisdom is what the believer seeks.

The *sura* then returns to a previous theme and reaffirms the need for thankfulness. *"Do you not see that Allah has made everything in the heavens and the earth subservient to you and has showered you with blessings, outwardly and inwardly? There are some who argue about Allah without knowledge or guidance or any illuminating Book."* (31:20)

Having restated the inexorable reality that every individual human being is answerable for their own actions – *"No father will be able to compensate for his son, and no son able to compensate for his father, in any way"* (31:33) – *Surat Luqman* ends with a comprehensive *ayat* contrasting the absolute nature of Divine Knowledge with the limited possibilities of human cognition. *"Truly Allah has knowledge of the Hour and sends down the abundant rain and knows what is in the wombs. No soul knows what it will earn tomorrow and no soul knows in what land it will die. Allah is All-Knowing, All-Aware."* (31:34)

Sura 32
As-Sajda: Prostration

Surat as-Sajda is devoted to one of the major themes of the Qur'an, which it presents in a very concise yet comprehensive way: the universal nature of the Divine Message and the results of its acceptance or rejection by those to whom it is addressed. It is a Makkan *sura* and starts by confirming that the Qur'an is a restatement of Divine Guidance to a community who previously had no access to it. *"What! Do they say, 'He has fabricated it'? No indeed! It is the truth from your Lord to warn a people to whom, before you, no warner came, so that perhaps they may be guided."* (32:3)

The Qur'an makes it clear that the source of the Message is none other than the Source of all existence. *"Allah it is Who created the heavens and the earth and everything between them in six days, then seated Himself upon the Throne. You have no protector or intercessor but Him."* (32:4) He has direct, instantaneous control of everything in existence though it may be a process which seems to us to take a very long time in its unfolding. What to us is an age is no time at all in the sight of Allah. Allah wills and acts. Then in our world there are obliteration and rebirth, defeats and victories, and all the panoply of lengthy history. *"He directs the affair from Heaven down to earth. Then it rises back up to Him in a Day whose length is a thousand years by your reckoning. That is the Knower of the Unseen and the Visible, the Almighty, the Merciful."* (32:5-6)

Integral to Allah's plan was the creation of man, the only creature granted the possibility of conscious recognition of its Creator. *"He who has created all things in the best possible way. He started the creation of man from clay; then produced his seed from an extract of base fluid; then formed him and breathed into him of*

His spirit and appointed for you hearing, sight and hearts. How little thanks you show!" (32:7-9) But so many human beings become engrossed by the earthy aspect of their beings and lose sight of the spirit. *"They say, 'When we have become one with the earth, will we then be created all anew?' In fact they reject the meeting with their Lord."* (32:10-11)

On the Last Day they will regret this rejection of their true nature: *"If only you could see the evildoers hanging their heads in shame before their Lord, 'Our Lord, we have seen and we have heard, so send us back again and we will act rightly. Truly we now have certainty.'"* (32:12) Too late! The time for sowing has finished and the time for reaping has come. Only those who had faith and accompanied it by right action will prosper, people *"...whose sides eschew their beds as they call upon their Lord in fear and ardent hope. And they spend of that with which We have provided them."* (32:16) But their reward is more than worth the effort. *"No soul knows the delight that is hidden away for it in recompense for what it used to do."* (32:17) The key lies in the physical act of prostration from which the *sura* takes its name. That is the primary form faith that takes in the life of the believer.

The two groups are very different. *"Is he who believes like him who is degenerate? They are not the same."* (32:18) But the true nature of the difference will only become clear in the Next World. *"As for those who believe and do right actions, they will have the Gardens of Safe Refuge as hospitality for what they used to do. But as for those who are degenerate, their refuge is the Fire."* (32:19-20)

The Muslims in the past confronted the mass of misguided materialists who disdained worship from within the protected frontiers of the *Dar al-Islam*, but today they are controlled and infiltrated by them, dazzled by the magic of their technology and cowed by their military might. We must be steadfast in this confrontation. We must be prepared to pay the price demanded of us. Above all we must cease to be blinded by their technological prowess and truly rely on Allah as our predecessors did. If we do then we will become part of Allah's plan to punish these wrongdoers. *"Who could do greater wrong than he who is reminded of the signs of his Lord and then turns away from them? We shall take revenge on the evildoers."* (32:22)

Then Allah reminds His Prophet that the Messengers before him also encountered obduracy and endured hardships. He should be steadfast as they were steadfast: *"We gave Musa the Book – be in no doubt about the meeting with him. We made it a guidance for the Tribe of Israel. We appointed leaders from among them, guiding by Our command, whenever they were steadfast and certain of Our signs."* (32:23-24) Leadership is never fully achieved until the leaders have both steadfastness and certainty.

It was said to our Prophet that he would certainly meet Musa. It may be that this meeting takes place after death or it may refer to the Night Journey, but in either case the meeting will certainly happen. Ibn 'Ashur said in his *tafsir* that meeting here means *jihad* and it is as if Allah is saying to his Prophet, "Just as Musa endured the stratagems of Pharaoh and the tribulations of his people, you too will meet with the same from your opponents and from your people." But their end will also be the same. *"Does it not serve to guide them how many generations before them We destroyed, among whose dwelling places they still walk? There are certainly signs in that. Will they not then hear?"* (32:26)

The fact is that in these days the Muslims are in almost the same position they were in at the beginning and are encountering outer persecution and inner discord on an unprecedented scale. Look at the tragedy of the Balkans and India and elsewhere on the one hand and the troubles of the Gulf, Afghanistan and Algeria on the other. Nowhere do we see Islam established in its entirety. The judgements, practices and laws of the Qur'an have been buried and had earth heaped up on top of them with little or no resistance on the part of the Muslims. And the enemies of Islam have nothing but disdain for it. Nonetheless the hope of the true Muslims in Allah remains undimmed and He will judge between His slaves with the Truth. *"They say, 'When is this victory coming if you speak the truth?' Say: 'On the day the victory comes the belief of those who rejected will not benefit them. They will be granted no respite. So turn away from them and wait. They too are waiting.'"* (32:28-30)

Sura 33
Al-Ahzab: The Confederates

Surat al-Ahzab contains the Divine account of the Battle of the Ditch, which took place at Madina in 7 AH, but the greater part of it is devoted to social instructions for the rapidly expanding Muslim community. In this context the Prophet, peace and blessings be upon him, is addressed directly five times in his quality as guide and leader of the community and the believers are addressed six times. Each time the Prophet is addressed there are implications which involve the entire community.

The first of these direct addresses is: *"O Prophet! Show fear of Allah and do not obey the rejectors and the hypocrites. Allah is All-Knowing, All-Wise. Follow what has been revealed to you from your Lord. Allah is aware of everything you do. And put your trust in Allah. Allah is enough as guardian."* (33:1-3) The command and prohibition directed to the Messenger of Allah, may Allah bless him and grant him peace, are a further confirmation of him, as you might say to someone who is already in the lead, "Do not slacken off." It is urging him to continue to show fear of Allah and to be firm against disbelief and hypocrisy. His course is to follow the Revelation sent down to him. One of his names was 'he who trusts', so when he is commanded to do this, it means he should simply continue to do what he was already well-known for. And of course these instructions do not just apply to him alone but also to all who follow him.

However, these *ayats* do not stand on their own; in fact, they are a precursor to a general instruction to the Muslims concerning their social relationships, with specific reference to adopted children. As we know, the Prophet himself, may Allah bless him and grant him peace, had adopted Zayd ibn Haritha before the Revelation came and he was known as Zayd ibn Muhammad.

These *ayats* make it clear that adoption does not create a true family tie in either a literal or a legal sense. Allah says: *"Allah has not allotted to any man two hearts within his breast; nor has He made those of your wives you equate with your mothers' backs your actual mothers; nor has He made your adopted sons your actual sons. Those are just words coming from your mouths, but Allah speaks the Truth and He guides to the Way. Call them after their fathers. That is juster in Allah's sight. And if you do not know who their fathers were, then they are your brothers in the* Deen *and people under your patronage..."* (33:4-5) The child's natural father must be acknowledged but if he is not known the brotherhood of Islam replaces the missing connection.

An exception is made in the case of the deep spiritual connection between the Prophet and the believers. *"The Prophet has closer ties to the believers than their own selves, and his wives are their mothers..."* (33:6) Muhammad, peace and blessings be upon him, is the spiritual father of this community. He is the most eager of people for their guidance and deliverance. He is the embodiment of Islam which brought them out of the darkness to the light. On that basis the Messenger of Allah said, "There is no believer to whom I am not closer than anyone else in this world and the Next. If you wish you may recite: *'The Prophet has closer ties to the believers than their own selves.'* If any believer dies and leaves money, it goes to whatever legal heirs he has. But if anyone leaves a debt or a needy family, I am the one to come to. I am his guardian." (al-Bukhari) Before this *ayat* was revealed, the Prophet, peace and blessings be upon him, used to refrain from offering the funeral prayer for someone in debt if he died without leaving enough to settle his debt. After this *ayat* was revealed he began to take on the debts of the poor who died and care for the poor orphans.

Just as the Prophet is considered to be the father of the believers, his wives are the 'Mothers of the Believers'. As a consequence, it was unlawful to marry any of them. They were the transmitters of the Revelation and the teachings to the community. They provided it with an excellent model.

The second time the Prophet is addressed it concerns his wives. *"O Prophet, tell your wives, 'If it is the life of this world and its finery you desire, then come and I will give you all you need and let you go with kindliness.'"* (33:28) The household of a Prophet is not like that of a king. It is a household which is content with simple provision and there is no place in it for opulence or luxury. The Messenger, may Allah bless him and grant him peace, was not controlled by his stomach. There was no place in his life for a lot of worldly goods and comforts. But most of his wives came from wealthy backgrounds and in their former lives had been used to all the comforts and trappings of wealth. That is why, when it seemed after the Battle of the Trench and its aftermath that there was a real possibility of having more, they soon gathered to ask him for more maintenance and more comforts. The Revelation came to explain the situation to them.

The household of the Prophet had to be content with simple sufficiency, even though its master was the leader of the community and as such had access to the great wealth which was beginning to flow into Madina. Their duty was to bear the burdens of his position with him and be occupied with prayer, *jihad* and seeking the Next World. It was a choice between either being content with this life or divorce. *"But if it is Allah and His Messenger and the abode of the Next World you desire, Allah has prepared, for those among you who do good, an enormous wage."* (33:29) The Mothers of the Believers without exception preferred the life of simple sufficiency to leaving the Prophet's house.

The third time the Prophet is addressed it is the whole of mankind who are included. *"O Prophet! We have sent you as a witness, and a bringer of good news and warner, and as a caller to Allah by His permission, and as a light-giving lamp."* (33:45-46) Before Muhammad there was no universal prophethood extending to all humanity. Each Prophet had been sent to his own people exclusively. The sun that rose over all the earth was the sun of the Final Message. The Noble Qur'an was both the basis of the Message and its miracle. The Qur'an is addressed to every human being from the day of its revelation up until the Last Hour. Muhammad's task was to convey it, teach it and provide the perfect model of its teaching in action. Then he will be a witness against his people that he conveyed it to them, and his community will be witnesses against the rest of mankind by their holding to the Clear Book and its teaching and passing it on as they received it. The question is whether the Muslims have performed that task of theirs or not.

The first generations certainly brought Islam to the attention of the world and exemplified it with their actions in an excellent fashion; but the poison of earlier communities soon permeated the being of the Muslims and now they have put Divine Guidance to one side in their lands and corruption predominates and heedlessness is the rule. Indeed it might now be said that the Muslims are in fact obstacles to the *deen* and actually impede its establishment!

Conveying the Message of Muhammad, may Allah bless him and grant him peace, today requires precise knowledge and deep understanding of the techniques of the enemies of Islam and also strategic and tactical skill as well as great courage. This business will only be put right now by the same thing that made it happen in the first place.

The fourth time Allah addresses the Prophet in *Surat al-Ahzab* is clearly specific to him in that it concerns the women he is permitted to marry but it does make clear at the same time that first cousins are within the permitted degree for every Muslim. *"O Prophet! We have made lawful for you your wives you have given dowries to, and what your right hand owns that Allah has given you as booty; and the daughters of your paternal uncles and the daughters of your paternal aunts, and the daughters of your maternal uncles and the daughters of your maternal aunts, who have emigrated along with you; and any believing woman who gives herself to the Prophet if the Prophet desires to marry her – exclusively for you, not the believers as a whole..."* (33:50)

It is well-known that no Muslim may have more than four wives. When a man with ten wives became Muslim the Prophet commanded him to keep four and divorce the rest. An exception was made by Allah in the case of the Prophet alone and even in his case it was limited. *"After that no women are lawful to you nor may you exchange them for other wives, even though their beauty might be pleasing to you, with the exception of what your right hand owns. Allah is watchful over everything."* (33:52)

Polygamy is a system which is compatible with noble character, the needs of human nature and the legitimate desire for progeny and, contrary to popular opinion, has very little to do with sexual licence. It in fact makes demands on men which force them out of the nuclear family mould that has proved so emotionally destructive, and requires of them an even-handed maturity very rarely seen in the world today. It was an established practice in the lives of many of the previous Prophets and in many earlier civilisations. Western civilisation with its inhibiting Romano-Christian moral background is unable to tolerate such beneficent social amplitude, although the current debate on the subject would suggest that its great wisdom is beginning to seep through as an answer to some of the moral chaos which short-sighted, man-made legislation has brought about.

The final address to the Prophet is clearly directed to all the women of the community. *"O Prophet! Tell your wives and daughters and the believing women to draw their outer garments closely round themselves. That makes it more likely that they will be recognised and not be harmed. Allah is Ever-Forgiving, Most Merciful."* (33:59) The following *ayat* explains the reason for this directive. In Madina, as elsewhere, there were young men who loitered about hoping to catch a glimpse of a desirable female form. So the believing women were instructed to be very careful about preserving their modesty and not to let the wind or rapid walking allow their figures to become openly revealed, in order to prevent as far as possible the provocation of illegitimate sexual desire. The culprits themselves are also addressed. *"If the hypocrites, and those with sickness in their hearts, and the rumour-mongers, in Madina do not desist, We will set you onto them. Then they will only be your neighbours there a very short time. They are accursed people. Wherever they are found, they should be seized and relentlessly put to death."* (33:60-61)

The wisdom of this instruction could not be seen more plainly than in today's world where the flagrant immodesty of women's dress is an inescapable enticement which is without doubt a contributory factor to the atmosphere of sexual tension which has brought about a level of sexually induced crime unprecedented in human history.

In addition to these direct addresses made to the Messenger, may Allah bless him and grant him peace, there are six direct addresses to the believers in this *sura*. The first of them is in the context of the Confederates' attack on Madina which became known as the Battle of the Ditch. It was a very tight situation. Armies of unbelievers advanced on Madina from all over the Peninsula, seeking to storm it and they were supported by the hypocrites and Jews inside Madina. The Muslims were caught in a vice, struggling for their very survival. *"When they came at you from above you and below you, when eyes swerved aside and hearts were in the mouths and you were thinking unworthy thoughts about Allah. At that time the believers were tested and severely shaken."* (33:10-11)

The Muslims gathered in defence of their city behind a ditch which they had dug on the advice of Salman al-Farisi, and were running this way and that, plugging. any gaps and reinforcing areas where the situation seemed particularly threatening. If it had not been for the sincerity of their reliance on Allah, the defenders would never have been able to stand firm; but as it was they did not waver. *"When the believers saw the Confederates they said: 'This is what Allah and His Messenger promised us. Allah and His Messenger told us the truth.' It increased them in nothing but belief and submission. Among the believers are men who have been true to the contract which they made with Allah. Some of them have fulfilled their pact by death and some are still waiting to do so, and have not changed in any way at all."* (33:22-23) The understanding of people with faith is not the same as that of those who seek worldly gain!

Their firm stand was rewarded by help from Allah. Their attackers were overcome by despair when cold winds blew their tents away and overturned their pots and they decided to leave. *"Allah returned those who rejected in their unabated rage, and they did not achieve any good at all. Allah saved the believers from having to fight. Allah is All-Strong, Almighty."* (33:25) The

Prophet, may Allah bless him and grant him peace, said after what happened, "Praise belongs to Allah alone, Whose promise was true, Who exalted His army, and defeated the Confederates alone." After the Battle of the Ditch the Confederates were aware that Madina could not be taken and did not try to attack it again.

The second time the believers are addressed it is with one of the most comprehensive instructions in the whole Qur'an. *"O you who believe, remember Allah repeatedly and glorify Him both morning and evening."* (33:41-42) This is a communal as well as an individual responsibility. The Muslim community possesses the Divine Message which must be protected and defended. This Message is based on having a connection with Allah, establishing His devotional practices, and being certain that we will meet Him. These principles are not now commonly held in any nation. The energy of the entire world is basically devoted to raising people's standard of living and increasing their comfort in the life of this world. The Next World has been relegated to the status of a joke. The religions of the past have failed to make people recognise Allah and prepare to meet Him and this world is filled with worship of material existence.

Only if our community raises the banner of worship, will it be worthy of His words: *"It is He Who calls down blessing on you, as do His angels, to bring you out of darkness into the light, and to the believers He is utterly Merciful."* (33:43) The prayer of Allah and His angels is for a community which remembers Allah and is remembered by Him and makes that its duty. The Muslims achieved this for generations during which they were the foremost community in the world. But then they forgot Allah and so He has made them forget themselves and now they are trodden underfoot.

The third direct address is a judgement of *fiqh*: *"O you who believe! When you marry believing women and then divorce them before you have slept with them, there is no waiting-period for you to reckon for them..."* (33:49) Even the minor details of marital dissolution are taken care of by the Revelation. This shows us the importance of those things in the social life of the Muslim community. If there is disharmony at the level of the family the stability of the whole community is put at risk.

The fourth direct address concerns the correct behaviour to be observed when invited to the household of the Prophet. The believers loved the Messenger of Allah more than they loved themselves. That moved them to want to be with him often. But there were also those who had spare time and did not know how to spend it and others who just wanted the vicarious pleasure of being in the presence of the great. So Allah spelled out the behaviour required of guests. "*O you who believe! Do not go into the Prophet's rooms except after being given permission to come and eat, not waiting for the food to be prepared. But when you are called go in, and when you have eaten disperse and do not remain wanting to chat together...*" (33:53) While this is specific to the household of the Prophet and was revealed because he himself did not want to have to ask people to leave, it is clearly good advice to follow in any similar situation.

It is immediately followed by instructions about communicating with the Prophet's wives in the domestic situation. "*When you ask his wives for something, ask them from behind a screen. That is purer for your hearts and their hearts. It is not for you to cause injury to the Messenger of Allah, or ever to marry his wives after him. To do that would be dreadful in Allah's sight.*" (33:53) While it is evident from the context that this is specific to the household of the Prophet, it nevertheless clearly enshrines a general principle. A woman inside her own house can remove her outer garments and the informality of the situation opens the way to an unacceptable degree of familiarity. Therefore the same kind of care must be taken by all who find themselves in a comparable situation in the presence of other people's wives and womenfolk.

As we know from many recent incidents many people try to harm Islam by causing injury to the Messenger. During his lifetime this was done in a variety of ways by "the hypocrites and those with sick hearts," who tried to sow doubt in the hearts of the Muslims by saying things against the Prophet. Allah tells his Messenger to ignore them. "*Do not obey the rejectors and the hypocrites, disregard their abuse of you, and put your trust in Allah.*" *(33:48)* And He says about such people, "*Those who cause injury to Allah and His Messenger, Allah's curse is on them in this world and the Next. He has prepared for them a humiliating punishment. Those who cause injury to believing men and believing women, without their having justly earned it, have burdened themselves with slander and clear wrongdoing."* (33:57-58) It appears to be one of the laws of nature that righteous people become targets of abuse and slander.

The fifth direct address warns the believers themselves not to become a party to such behaviour. *"O you who believe, do not be like those who caused injury to Musa. Allah absolved him of what they said and he was highly honoured in Allah's sight."* (33:69) As we know from many *ayats* in the Qur'an and many statements of the Prophet, may Allah bless him and grant him peace, as much destruction is wrought upon the Muslim community by the tongues of those within it as by the guns of its enemies from without – if not more. This is directly followed by a sixth instruction to the believers, telling them how their tongues should be employed. *"O you who believe! Show fear of Allah and speak words which hit the mark. He will make your actions right for you..."* (33:70-71)

In the course of going through the various types of injury which the noble Prophet suffered, comes an instruction to the believers which was good news to him, bringing him solace, confirmation and elevation, and has formed an important and integral part of the life of every Muslim ever since. *"Allah and His angels call down blessings on the Prophet. O you who believe! Call down blessings on him and ask for complete peace and safety for him."* (33:72-73)

Surat al-Ahzab ends with a famous *ayat* which states at once the purpose and criterion of human life, showing how the human being is fundamentally different from anything else in existence. It makes clear both the individual and social responsibilities implicit in the Divine Message and the crucial consequences of taking them on or rejecting them. *"We offered the Trust to the heavens and the earth and the mountains and they refused to take it on and shrank from it. But man took it on. He is truly wrongdoing and ignorant. So that Allah might punish the men and women of the hypocrites, and the men and women of the idolaters, and turn towards the men and women of the believers. Allah is Ever-Forgiving, Most Merciful."* (33:72)

Sura 34:
Saba': Sheba

Surat Saba' is the fourth of the *suras* that begin with praise of Allah. Praise combines lauding, thanking and exalting Allah Almighty. He is the Master of the heavens and the earth and everything in them. The proceeds of this world return to Him and He will judge them with His justice and mercy. He possesses comprehensive and all-encompassing knowledge: *"He knows what goes into the earth and what comes out of it, and what descends from Heaven and what ascends into it."* (34:2) He knows every seed placed in the depths of the earth and every fruit which comes out, every drop which descends from heaven and every flutter of a wing which rises into it. All the dimensions of existence are a single page to Him and nothing is hidden from Him.

When a dust storm blows up on earth, He knows the exact movement of each dust-particle in it and where it will settle! When a solar storm erupts on the sun, He knows when it rises and abates and the exact effect it will have on the atmosphere, electromagnetic forces and radio waves. And in addition to this there is the ascent of spirits and angels in other dimensions of existence about which we know little: *"The Knower of the Unseen, not even the weight of the smallest particle eludes Him, either in the heavens or in the earth. Nor is there anything smaller than that, or larger, which is not in a Clear Book"* (34:3)

Surat Saba' resembles *Surat al-Furqan* in that it examines the objections of the unbelievers and refutes them one by one. The first of these is the unbelievers' dismissal of the Resurrection. *"Those who reject say, 'The Hour will not come to us.' Say: 'On the contrary! By my Lord, it will come to you...'"* (34:3) The truth is that dismissing the Resurrection is extreme stupidity. What is there to prevent the Creator from regenerating creation? Since He

was capable of bringing it into being in the first place what is there
to stop Him doing so again? When did people become independent
of His power? Allah makes them grow, awakens them, feeds them
and fills them up every day. But the human intellect is sometimes
blind to the most self-evident truths.

The Resurrection is a reality, and those who deny this will certainly come to know the truth of it. Everyone will receive his just
repayment: the good-doer good and the evil-doer evil. The People
of the Book who took a stand against Muhammad and refused to
follow him will realise that in doing so they were in fact denying
Allah and rejecting the Message that they should have supported
and adopted .

Denial of the Afterlife is an iniquity which spread among the
ancients and moderns. People in the world today do not give a
thought to the Next World and are only concerned with the physical world. That comes from their ignorance of Allah and their worship of themselves. Re-emphasising the danger of their shortsight-
ed understanding, the *sura* returns to their cynical rejection of the
truth. *"Those who reject say, 'Shall we direct you to a man who
will tell you that, when you have completely disintegrated, you
will then be recreated all anew? Has he forged a lie against Allah
or is he mad?' No indeed! Those who do not believe in the Next
World are in punishment and far astray."* (34:7-8)

Belief in the Next World, however, does not denote denial of
this world and the *sura* evokes a few examples from the past to
show how the two are perfectly compatible provided the correct
perspective is preserved. Ignorant religiosity even reckons that
backwardness in this world is necessary for advancement in the
Next World. This is certainly not the case. Faith produces intelligent activity, not stupid indolence. First, the example of Da'ud is
brought forward. *"We gave to Da'ud unbounded favour from Us,
'O mountains and birds! Echo with him in his praise!' And for him
We made iron malleable. 'Make full-length coats of mail, measur-
ing carefully the links. And act rightly, all of you, for I see the
things you do.'"* (34:10-11)

So Da'ud, peace be upon him, integrated both the worlds in his
actions: singing the blessings and glories of Allah and using iron

in the manufacture of weapons, armour and household utensils. Faith implies intelligent understanding of this existence and making the most of what it offers while preparing oneself for the permanent reality of the life to come. In this context the *sura* goes on to show that Sulayman, peace be upon him, created a very highly developed civilisation in this world by means of the powers with which Allah endowed him. *"And to Sulayman We granted power over the wind: a month's journey in the morning and a month in the afternoon. And We made a fount of molten brass flow out for him. And some of the jinn worked under his supervision by the permission of his Lord...They made for him anything he willed: high arches and statues, huge dishes like cisterns, great built-in cooking vats."* (34:12-13)

We can see from this that statues were not forbidden in the *shari'a* of Sulayman son of Da'ud. They became forbidden because people began to adopt them as objects of worship instead of Allah. Humanity has a perpetual tendency to idolatry which no amount of scientific knowledge is able to dispel. There is no doubt that statues in many places of worship continue to be objects of adoration for vast numbers of the world's population. However, the main lesson to be learned from these *ayats* is that Da'ud and Sulayman were Prophet-Kings whose power and activity in this world certainly did not distract them from their obligations of worship. That is why Allah says in the *sura*: *"'Work, family of Da'ud, in thankfulness!' But very few of My slaves show thanks."* (34:13)

To counterbalance this the *sura* continues by warning us of the danger of allowing success in this world to blind us to the reality of the Next, mentioning first the great Yemeni civilisation of Sheba (Saba') from which the *sura* takes its name. *"There was also a sign for Sheba in their dwelling place: two gardens – on the right and on the left. 'Eat of your Lord's provision and be thankful to Him. A bountiful land and a most forgiving Lord.'"* (34:15) Here was a great civilisation which forgot the Source of its prosperity, lost sight of the Next World, and suffered the consequences. *"But they turned away; so We unleashed against them the Flood of Arim and exchanged their two gardens for two others containing bitter things and tamarisk and a few lote trees. We paid them back with that for their rejection. Are any so repaid but the unthankful ?"* (34:17)

"Do you not see those who exchanged Allah's blessing for unbelief, and moved their people to the abode of ruin?" (14:28) When Allah's blessing is taken away, unity, health and security vanish and the opposites of these states justly replace them. *"They wronged themselves, so We made them into legends and scattered them without a trace. There are certainly signs in that for each and every steadfast, thankful man."* (34:19)

Surat Saba' shows that most people fail the test of worldly blessings and returns continually to the theme of the dangers inherent in wealth in this world. *"We never sent a warner into any city without the affluent people in it saying, 'We reject what you have been sent with."* (34:35-35) Wealth was a trial for the earlier peoples and it remains a trial for people today. Instead of those who have it spending what they have been given in a way which is pleasing to Allah, they use it to gain advantage over the poor and weak. In dialectical opposition to them socialist ideologies have grown up, seeking social equality and economic justice but ignoring Allah's guidance which alone can bring balance and justice to human society. *"It is not your wealth or your children that will bring you near to Us, except in the case of people who believe and act rightly. Such people will have a double recompense for what they did. They will be safe from all harm in the High Halls of Paradise."* (34:37)

In this way most of mankind have fallen into Shaytan's net. Only those who keep their eyes firmly fixed on the Next World escape his clutches. *"Iblis was quite correct in his assessment of them, and so they followed him, with the exception of a group of the believers. Over them he wields no authority except to enable Us to know him who believes in the Next World from him who is in doubt about it. Your Lord is Preserver of everthing."* (34:20-21)

By dint of persuasive arguments and warnings about what is to come Allah does everything He can to deter readers of the Qur'an from going the same way as those before them. Where does wealth in this world come from? *"Say: 'Who provides for you from the heavens and the earth?' Say: 'Allah. It is certain that either one or the other of us, we or you, is following guidance or clearly astray.'"* (34:24) Sometimes wealth and power dazzle even people who do not have it. *"If only you could see when the wrongdoers, standing in the presence of their Lord, cast accusations to and fro at one another! The downtrodden will say to the powerful, 'If it were not for you, we would have been believers!' And the powerful will say to the downtrodden, 'Did we debar you from the guidance when it came to you? On the contrary, it is you who were the evildoers.'"* (34:31-32)

So although there is nothing wrong with wealth and power in this world *per se* it is only beneficial in the context of firmly held faith in Allah and the Next World. It can never be a goal in itself and indeed presents to the human being grave dangers.

The basis of the prophetic message is belief in Allah and deep reflection on the meaning of existence. *"Say: 'I exhort you to do one thing alone – to stand up for Allah in pairs and individually and then reflect. There is no madness in your companion. He is only a warner come to you ahead of a terrible punishment.'"* (34:46) The dormant intellect must be awakened and the signs of the Lord in the universe understood. The Prophet himself has no interest in the acquisition of wealth. *"Say: 'I have not asked you any wage – any wage is yours. My wage is with none but Allah. He is witness over everything.'"* (34:47)

The *sura* ends with a reminder to people who have invested everything in this world of the implacable reality of their inevitable destiny. *"If you could only see when they are terrified, and there is no way out, and they are seized from a nearby place."* (34:51) Then they will have no choice but to believe. *"They will say, 'We believe in it,' but how can they reach out for it from a long way off?"* ((34:52) If people had used their intellects, they would have recognised Allah and followed the Messengers. Now it is too late and they will find that their short-sighted desire for wealth and power in this world and their doubt about what the Messenger brought them from Allah has cut them off from true fulfilment in the Next just as it has done throughout the history of the human race. *"A barrier will be set up between them and the thing that they desire, just as was done with their kind before. They too were in a state of crippling doubt."* (34:54)

Sura 35
Fatir: The Bringer-into-being

Surat Fatir is the last of those *suras* which begin with praise of Allah although, of course, praise of Allah, with which the whole of existence resounds, is to be found liberally scattered throughout all the *suras* of the Qur'an. Praise of Allah voiced by man is one of the enduring righteous actions. Praise of Allah should resound through our lives as it resounds through the rest of existence. *"Praise belongs to Allah, the Bringer-into-being of the heavens and the earth, The Maker of the angels as messengers, possessing wings – two, three or four..."* (35:1)

The Bringer-into-being is the Creator and the angels are subtle bodies of light which can take on different forms. Their business is good-doing, obedience, knowledge, and provident intervention in human affairs, and they abide in the Heavens. They carry out the will of Allah in respect of His creatures. There are angels for worship and glorification; others for death; others for life and birth; others for recording and guarding. There are angels concerned with every aspect of existence and the powers with which Allah has provided them are very disparate. The *ayat* here gives them two, three or four wings. But it is clear from the *hadith* that sometimes they have hundreds or even thousands of wings. *"He adds to creation in any way He wills. Allah has power over all things."* (35:1)

Surat Fatir resembles *Surat an-Nahl* in that it enumerates Allah's blessings and shows how Allah's favour is manifested by giving existence and sustenance to everything in creation. But it begins by declaring an unequivocal law. *"Whatever mercy Allah opens up to people no one can withhold, and whatever He withholds no one can afterwards release. He is the Almighty, the All-Wise."* (35:2) It is essential for human beings to recognise this law.

They imagine that the fountain of the good things they take so much for granted flows quite independently of Allah, and attribute give power to non-entities which have no real existence. They are like someone who fears a fawn but has no fear of a lion. So to preserve us from this self-delusion Allah immediately reminds us of our obligation to Him. *"O mankind! Remember Allah's blessing to you. Is there any creator other than Allah providing for you from the heaven and the earth? There is no god but Him. How then have you been perverted?"* (35:2)

Deep adherence to this belief is a necessary component of true faith, and forgetfulness of it, by Muslims as well as non-Muslims, is a kind of idolatry prevalent everywhere today which makes people afraid of flies and forgetful of their Creator. This is what allows the earth's tyrants to flourish and keeps the tyrannised in perpetual subjection. So to ensure that we get the point Allah gives us a further forthright reminder. *"O people of mankind! Allah's promise is true. Do not let the life of this world delude you and do not let the Deluder delude you about Allah. Shaytan is an enemy to you so treat him as an enemy. He summons his party so they will be among the people of the Searing Blaze."* (35:5-6)

Allah revealed this Book to Muhammad to bring people out of the darkness into the light but many were at first deaf to the guidance. *"If they deny you, Messengers before you also were denied. All matters return to Allah. "* (35:4) Most people are idolaters and unable to accept the Divine Unity and the inevitable accountability it implies, and so the Messenger encountered obduracy and opposition from his people. This is reiterated later in the *sura. "If they deny you, those before them also denied. Their Messengers came to them with clear signs, and written texts and the Illuminating Book. Then I seized hold of those who rejected. And how absolute was My denial!"* (35:25-26)

But this seizing does not necessarily take place immediately. Allah often defers it, to give sleeping people time to wake up and stupid people time to come to their senses: *"If Allah were to take mankind to task for what they have earned, He would not leave a single creature crawling on it, but He is deferring them until a specified time. Then when their time comes, Allah sees His slaves.*" (35:45) He knows who will benefit from the delay and repent and who will remain deluded and incur His anger. Such people often consider this deferral to be a sanction for their actions and so Divine forbearance only increases them in blindness to the truth: *"And what of him whose evil action appeals to him so that he sees it as something good? Allah misguides whoever He wills and guides whoever He wills. So do not let yourself waste away out of regret for them. Allah knows what they do."* (35:8) The Prophet was deeply saddened by the disbelief of those who rejected and he expended enormous effort in reminding people and trying to make them see; but in the end his task was simply to deliver the Message – not to put belief in people's hearts.

Then mankind are addressed directly by their Lord a third time. The first time was to remember Allah's blessings, the second not to be deluded by this world, and the third is a stark reminder that, though we are completely dependent upon Him, Allah has no need of us at all. *"O mankind! You are the poor in need of Allah and Allah is the Rich beyond need, the Praiseworthy. If He willed He could remove you and bring about a new creation. That is not hard for Allah."* (35:15-17) Nothing is difficult for Allah. He could obliterate the world, along with whatever and whoever is in it, and just as easily bring another purer and more godfearing world into existence. The fact that He does not shows that things are as He wants them to be and that there is great wisdom in existence being as it is.

The *sura* then proceeds to describe how Allah brings His creatures into existence and sustains them. He releases the winds to bring the clouds to give the earth water, changing it in the process from salt to sweet. From earth and water He created man, whom the whole world serves, to serve Him. Allah has not left us to discover this on our own but has Himself made sure that we and every previous people have been unequivocally told about it. *"We have sent you with the truth, bringing good news and giving warning. There is no nation to which no warner came."* (35:24) But so many, so many of mankind have failed to understand. The signs are there for all to see – but how few appreciate them! *"Do you not see that Allah sends down water from the sky and through it*

We bring forth fruits of varying colours? And in the mountains there are streaks of white and red of varying shades, and rocks of deep jet black. And mankind and beasts and livestock are likewise of varying colours. Only those of His slaves with knowledge have fear of Allah. Allah is Almighty, Ever-Forgiving." (35:27-28)

True belief clearly requires an intelligent investigating intellect. The *Deen* can only learned by a believing intellect and a heart which is firmly attached to Allah and His Messenger. The first Muslims fulfilled these criteria and were more successful than any previous people in spreading the *Deen,* but gradually the Muslim community went the way of its predecessors. Allah says: *"Then We made those of Our slaves whom We chose inherit the Book. But some of them wrong themselves; and some of them are ambivalent; and some of them outdo each other in good by the permission of Allah. That is the great favour."* (35:32) One group have wronged themselves with rebellion and neglect, a second group are ambivalent and content with whatever good or bad deeds are easy for them, and another group have done their utmost to gain the pleasure of Allah. Unfortunately in our time the first two groups greatly predominate and because people's hearts have become heedless the promise of Allah's reward and the threat of Allah's punishment has not been sufficient to keep them straight.

The Muslims will never succeed in conveying the Message if they come to this *ayat* and those like it and say: "Allah has made the community of Muhammad the inheritors of every Book which He has revealed. Their wrongdoers will be forgiven, the ambivalent among them will be given an easy reckoning and those of them who excel will enter the Garden without reckoning, as has been reported from Ibn 'Abbas." Statements such as these tend to corrupt people, encouraging a kind of wishful thinking which leads to indolence and inactivity.

Worse still, it can lead people to follow their forebears and turn away from Divine Guidance. *"They swore by Allah with their most earnest oaths that, if a warner were to come to them, they would be better guided than any other nation. But then when a warner did come to them, it increased them in nothing but aversion, being arrogant in the land and plotting evil. Evil plotting envelops none but those who do it. Do they then expect anything but the pattern of the earlier peoples? You will not find any changing the pattern of Allah. You will not find any alteration in the pattern of Allah.*" (35:42-43)

This claim on the part of misguided people to be open to guidance is repeated three times in the Noble Qur'an – here in *Fatir*, and in *Surat al-An'am* and in *Surat as-Saffat* – which suggests that it is something that human beings are prone to do. This is, of course, specifically referring to the Arabs of the *Jahiliyya* who used to claim that if they did receive Divine Guidance they would follow it far better than the Jews and Christians – which certainly, in the event, turned out not to be the case, at least not without a great deal of obstinate and violent resistance. In the end it must be said without equivocation that our righteous predecessors carried the Revelation in all directions and by their behaviour and character became models which encouraged other people to embrace it.

However, it was not very long before the Muslims once more became dominated by their impatient natures and deviated from the Path of Allah. They neglected the instructions of the Qur'an and immersed themselves in following their lower appetites. Now we find Muslims glorying in the fact of belonging to different nation states created by colonial powers precisely in order to cause division between them and rejecting Allah's laws for man-made legal systems which can only bring social disorder and moral chaos.

They have turned their backs on the legacy they received from the Messenger of Allah and the early Muslims, so how can they expect anything other than the humiliation and degradation they have been experiencing for so long now? They have gone the way of all the communities before them and have inevitably suffered the same fate. *"Have they not travelled in the land and seen what was the end of those before them, who were far greater than them in strength? Allah cannot be thwarted in any way, either in the heavens or in the earth. Truly He is All-Knowing, All-Powerful."* (35:44)

Sura 36
Ya Sin

Ya and *Sin* are two letters which appear at the beginning of some *suras* of the Qur'an. As is the case with so many of them, they are immediately followed by a reference to the Qur'an itself. *"By the Wise Qur'an. Truly you are one of the Messengers, on a Straight Path."* (36:1) This is an oath attesting to the truthfulness of the Message. It is extraordinary in that it ties together the Message, the Messenger and its implementation, showing that they are in a way one thing, inseparable from one other. We have access to Allah's Guidance only through the Messenger of Allah who himself clarifies and exemplifies it and ensures that it is put into practise exactly as Allah intended in a situation where it is sorely needed. *"The Sending-down of the Almighty, the Most Merciful, so that you may warn a people whose fathers were not warned and who are therefore heedless."* (36:5-6)

Surat Ya Sin is known as the "Heart of the Qur'an" and there are many *hadiths* and traditions attesting to the great blessing it contains. It is recommended that one recite it frequently, particularly at the time of death when it is said to ease the soul's departure from this world. As far as its structure is concerned, it can be said to consist of a preface and three sections. The preface is a discussion about the Qur'an and those who hear it and either reject or affirm it, and the three subsequent sections consist of different kinds of evidence attesting to its truth.

The first of these sections is a personal testimony, the affirmation of the truth by a trusted member of the community, which is contained in a brief historical narrative about a town, resembling Makka, whose inhabitants, like the Makkans, rejected the Divine Message when it came. Then one man from the city calls his fellow citizens by the clear testimony of his own faith. The second

317

section cites the evidence pointing to the presence of a Creator which can be seen in the universe by all whose hearts and minds are open to it. The third section is a direct reminder of human accountability and its consequences in the Next World, and of Allah's power over all existence. The overall theme is a call to Allah's Unity, reflection on His Power and preparation for the inevitable meeting with Him and its everlasting aftermath.

✽✻✽✻✽

Physical miracles are not sufficient on their own to bring illumination to the heart. Those who inherited devotion to idols were not weaned from their worship by the staff of Musa or the miraculous cures of 'Isa, may Allah's peace be upon both of them. They also needed a Book which stimulated their intellects and removed their illusions, provided, of course, that it was truly understood. But there are always people who live in a world of barriers and shackles, imprisoned behind walls, who cannot understand the truth no matter how clearly it is presented to them. *"We have put iron collars around their necks reaching up to the chin, so that their heads are forced back. We have placed a barrier in front of them and a barrier behind them, blindfolding them so they do not see."* (36:9) Blind adherence to tradition creates generations of this petrified type who are good for nothing. Warning cannot help them. It can only help people with open hearts and open ears. *"You can only warn those who heed the Reminder and fear the All-Merciful in the Unseen. Give them the good news of forgiveness and a generous wage."* (36:11)

This prefatory passage is followed by the first of the three sections referred to above, each of which provides a different kind of evidence for the truth of the Revelation. *"Make an example for them of the city's inhabitants when the Messengers came to it..."* (36:13) The name of the town is not important but what does concern us are the events which transpired in it after the arrival of these Messengers from Allah.

Some of the people thought that the Messengers had come to dispossess them of their power and commandeer their wealth.

They could only see them as a threat and a bad omen. *"They said, 'We see an evil omen in you. If you do not stop, we will stone you and you will receive a painful punishment at our hands.' They said, 'Your evil omen is in yourselves. Is it not just that you have been reminded? No, you are an unbridled people!'"* (36:18-19) Ever since the time of Nuh the enemies of the Prophets have always thought that they sought power and that their call was merely a means to a private end. But at the same time Allah always creates men with intense love for the Truth who are prepared to sacrifice everything for it and fight to the utmost to see it prevail.

This town was no exception and there was a man there determined to apprise his people of two vital truths: that Messengers are selfless people who do not seek rank or wealth; and that the One to Whom they call is the Truth Itself and anything other than that is illusion without substance and can neither harm or help anyone. *"O my people! Follow the Messengers! Follow those who do not ask you for any wage and who themselves are guided. Why indeed should I not worship Him who brought me into being, Him to whom you will be returned?"* (36:20-22) However, this faithful adviser failed to convince the misguided. The story does not mention whether he was killed or died but after he went to his Lord and to the honour He had prepared for him, he said in sorrow for their state: *"If only my people knew how my Lord has forgiven me and made me one of the honoured!"* (36:26-27)

His people suffered the inevitable consequences of their refusal to pay heed to his sincere counsel. *"We did not send down on his people after him any troop out of heaven nor would We send one down. There was but one Great Blast and they were extinct."* (36:28-29) The laws of existence are inexorable and rejection of Divine Guidance has a painful result: the humiliation and denial that the Messengers encounter must be paid for by the people who inflict it, and the punishment becomes harsher with the severity of the crime. That is why the Almighty says: *"What anguish for the slaves! No Messenger came to them without their mocking him. Do they not see how many generations before them We destroyed and that they will not return to them?"* (36:30-31) These laws have not changed and our own civilisation would do well to remember that. The future of the civilisation in which we live is in severe jeopardy because it refuses to remember Allah and to live within His laws. It is digging its own grave with unprecedented vigour.

The second section of this blessed *sura* brings a different kind of evidence for the truth of the Revelation which has its source in the natural phenomena that surround all of us every day. *"A sign for them is the dead land We bring to life and bring forth grain from it of which they eat. We place in it gardens of dates and grapes and cause springs to gush forth in it."* (36:33-34) We give the earth the worst of what we have and it gives us in return the best of what it has! Farmers say that the best melons are those whose fertiliser is pigeon droppings, and excreta of all kinds is spread all over the fields which produce corn and wheat, cotton and linen, and all the endless types of fruits and produce which we take so much for granted. And Who is the continual source of all this good? *"Glory be to Him who created all the species, from what the earth produces and from themselves and from things unknown to them."* (36:36)

We are then taken from the earth up into heaven for a brief look at the astronomical order. Darkness covers the globe when the rays of the sun withdraw from it, all by the control of Allah. *"A sign for them is the night: We peel away the day from it and there they are in darkness."* (36:37) From their very similar sizes as seen from the surface of the earth, ideal for the functions they so perfectly fulfil, the sun and moon appear as if they were in a single orbit. These things, to which we give scarcely a thought, are daily miracles. Even the slightest variation in them would make life on the earth impossible. *"And the sun runs to its resting place. That is the decree of the Almighty, the All-Knowing. And We have decreed set phases for the moon, until it ends up looking like an old palm spathe. It is not for the sun to overtake the moon nor for the night to outstrip the day; each one is swimming in a sphere."* (36:38-40)

We return again to the earth to look at the seas and the ships which sail them. *"A sign for them is that We carried their ancestors in the laden ship. And We have created for them the like of it in which they sail."* (36:41-42) The area covered by the oceans is four times larger than that covered by land and its realm is far vaster and more populous than the land. It has its own unique ecosystems, quite distinct from those of the land, and its own laws. For instance creatures living in it are subject to precise laws which affect their breathing, swimming, diving and feeding in ways quite different from their land-based cousins. Its strangeness is always felt by people adrift on its back and when people are exposed to its perils they are more liable to call on Allah to save them than at any other time.

These three previous pieces of evidence from the natural world are followed by others at the end of the *sura. "Have they not seen how We created for them by the work of Our Hands livestock which are under their control? We have made them tame for them and some they ride and some they eat."* (36:71-72) You look at the thousands of meat departments in the supermarkets and the count-less butchers' shops and stalls with all the vast amounts of meat they purvey day by day and see the millions buying and consum-ing it with never a thought for the One Who created the animals from which it comes and made them available to us. Look at this heedlessness of Allah and see how forbearing He is!

The third section of the *sura* contains discussion about the Resurrection and the Reckoning. They are part of the very bedrock of human existence but modern civilisation ignores them, criticises those who talk about them, and tries to persuade people that their end will be that of animals – without meaning or consequence. Death and the Last Day are similar in that they both come unan-nounced without people having time to prepare for them. *"And they say, 'When will this promise come about if you are telling the truth?' What are they awaiting but one Great Blast to seize them while they are quibbling. They will not be able to make a will or to return to their families."* (36:48-50) As a *hadith* says: "The Last Hour will occur while two men are spreading a garment between them and they will not have time to sell it or fold it up. The Last Hour will come when a man has taken the milk of a she-camel but before he can drink it. The Last Hour will come when a man has raised a morsel of food to his mouth but before he can eat it." (Related by al-Bukhari)

After the annihilation of the Last Hour people will be gathered to their Lord for the Reckoning faced with the unalterable consequences of their earthly lives. *"The Trumpet will be blown and suddenly they will emerge from their graves towards their Lord. They will say, 'Alas for us! Who has raised us from our resting-place? This is what the All-Merciful promised. The Messen-gers were telling the truth.'"* (36:51-52) There follows a marvellous description of the people of the Garden which contains the *ayat* often described as the "heart of the heart of the Qur'an": *"'Peace!' A word from a Merciful Lord."* (36:58)

We are reminded of our basic commitment as human beings. *"Did I not make a contract with you, O tribe of Adam, not to worship Shaytan, who truly is a clear-cut enemy to you, and to worship Me? This is a Straight Path. He has led huge numbers of you astray. So will you not use your intellects?"* (36:60-62) – and of the terrible truth that everything is recording what happens and will relay it when the time comes. *"Today We seal up their mouths and their hands speak to us, and their feet bear witness to what they have earned."* (36:63) No defence will be possible in the face of such overwhelming evidence.

Finally evidence for the Resurrection is given first by means of a logical premise: *"He makes likeness of Us and forgets his own creation, saying, 'Who will give life to the bones when they are decayed?' Say, 'He will bring them to life who originated them in the first place. He has total knowledge of each created thing'"* (36:78-79) – and secondly by taking an example from nature: *"He who produces for you fire from the green trees which you then use to light your fires."* (36:80) The Qur'an directs our attention to a scientific reality in the process of existence. It is that we breathe and take oxygen from the air and then return it as carbon dioxide. The plants breathe in the carbon dioxide and release oxygen. The carbon dioxide gas which the plants take in is combined and solidified in their essence to form stems, branches and leaves, and in time it becomes firewood.

These natural processes are among the signs of Allah Who brings forth the living from the dead and the dead from the living. This process is evident in the plants which He produces alive from the "dead" elements of the earth over a period of time. *"Glory be to Him who has the dominion over all things in His Hand, Him to whom you will be returned."* (36:83)

Sura 37
As-Saffat: Those in Ranks

"By those drawn up in ranks and the warners crying warning and the reciters of the Reminder." (37:1-3) This is a description of the escort which accompanied the Revelation when it was being revealed to the heart of the Seal of the Messengers, may Allah bless him and grant him peace, led by the Trusty Jibril, upon whom be peace, and surrounded by noble angels. It is an oath to corroborate the Great Reality which lies at the heart of the Qur'an: the Oneness of Allah the All-Glorious.

Although Jibril is responsible for the Revelation, many angels descend with it to honour the Message and extol its importance: *"He sends down the angels with the Spirit by His command to any of His slaves He wills: 'Give warning that there is no god but Me, so fear Me!'"* (16:2) They also drive away the parasitic shaytans from the reports of Revelation so they are unable to interrupt its transmission. There is also a reference to this in *hadith*: "When Allah decides the matters in heaven the angels beat their wings out of humility to His word, like a chain on stone," meaning the flutter of their wings is heard like the sound of a metal chain on stone: *"Thus when the terror has left their hearts they will say, 'What did your Lord say?' They will say, 'The Truth. He is the All-High, the All-Great.'"* (34:23)

The One God is described as the *"Lord of the heavens and the earth and everything in between them, Lord of all the Easts."* (37:5) referring to the places where the sun rises, which vary according to the time of year. The beginning of the *sura* contains two realities: the first is *tawhid* and the second is the Resurrection. Both of these were rejected by the idolaters: *"When they were told, 'There is no god but Allah,' they were arrogant. They said, 'Are we to abandon our gods for a mad poet?'"* (37:35-36) But denying the truth is of no avail. The truth necessarily imposes itself. In affirming the Reckoning, the Qur'an depicts two of the events of the Rising, presenting them first in this world so that perhaps the deniers may take note: *"And call them to a halt. They will be asked: 'Why are you not helping one another?' No indeed! Today they come in absolute submission. They confront each other, questioning one another. They say, 'You used to come at us from a position of power.' They say, 'No, the truth is that you were not believers."* (37:24-29)

Leaders and their followers will argue in the Next World and each will blame the other. The weak will say, "You deceived us with your strength and power." The powerful will say to them, "You were stupid and did not see the Truth!" They will both bear the responsibility. *"On that day they will be partners in the punishment. That is how We deal with evildoers."* (37:33-34) That is the first picture.

You see the features of the second in the words of the Almighty: *"They will turn and face each other, questioning. One of them will say, 'I used to have a friend who would say to me, "Are you one of those who say that it is true: that when we have died and become dust and bones, we will face a reckoning?"' He will say, 'Are you looking down?' So he will look down and see him in the middle of the Blazing Fire, and say, 'By Allah, you almost ruined me!'"* (37:50-56) This is a spectacle witnessed all too frequently in this world. Each friend tries to attract the other to his way of thinking. Were it not that the believer was strong, he would slip and be lost. That is why he will say when he sees his companion in the midst of the Fire: *"'If it were not for the blessing of my Lord, I would have been one of the arraigned. Are we not going to die, except for our first death? Are we not going to be punished?' This is the Great Victory. It is for the like of this that all workers should work."* (37:57-61)

Bringing an event of the Unseen to the attention of people in the visible world is common in the Qur'an. We saw another example of this kind of exchange between the people of the Garden and the Fire in *Surat al-A'raf* (7:44). Here you see the joy of salvation that infuses the believer when his faith saves him from the evil end which swallowed up his companion. He will enjoy the delights of the Garden together with his brothers but will recall a man who used to deny Allah and the last Day and will want to learn what his situation is. When he sees him, his awareness of the deliverance and bliss he has will be doubled.

Then Allah says, *"Is that a better kind of hospitality or the tree of az-Zaqqum? We have made it an ordeal for the wrongdoers. It is a tree that emerges from the base of the Blazing Fire. Its fruit are just like the heads of shaytans."* (37:62-65) The tree of *az-Zaqqum* is mentioned in a number of places in the Qur'an. It is found in *Surat al-Waqi'a* where Allah says: *"Then you, O misguided, O deniers, will eat from the tree of Zaqqum and fill your bellies with it and drink scalding water on top of it."* (56:51-52) In *Surat ad-Dukhan*, Allah Almighty says: *"The Tree of az-Zaqqum is the food of the sinful, bubbling in the bellies like molten brass as boiling water bubbles up."* (44:43-46) In *Surat al-Isra'*: *"The Accursed Tree in the Qur'an."* (17:60)

It is said that it is one of the trees of the desert which appears in arid places. and has a disagreeable smell and small poisonous leaves with lethal sap. If the sap touches a man's skin, he usually bloats up and dies from it. This is by way of metaphor. The trees of Hell will not be luxuriant and shady with a good crop of delicious fruit. They will have a foul taste and appearance similar to the desert trees that people know. Allah made the Tree of *az-Zaqqum* the food of the people of the Fire: *"They will eat from it and fill their bellies with it. Then they will have a boiling brew on top of it."* (37:66-67)

Why this painful punishment? *"They found their fathers misguided and they are following hard on their heels."* (37:69-70) It is blind imitation and ignorant following of custom and tradition that leads to this painful punishment. The reality is that most people cling to what they have inherited in exactly the form they receive it and attack any claim or system which disagrees with what they have without even thinking of critically examining either their own beliefs or what they are being offered. In their fanaticism and injustice they kill those who oppose them, or they concoct a conspiracy to eliminate their ideas: *"Most of the ancients before them went astray though We sent warners to them. See then what was the end result of those who were warned."* (37:71-73)

In the middle of *Surat as-Saffat* six earlier Messages are mentioned in the Revelation to the Messenger, peace and blessings be upon him, to comfort him and strengthen his heart. The first is that of Nuh who endured long affliction for the sake of Allah. Then there is that of Ibrahim who was the one "who named us Muslims before" (22:78)[1]. Then comes that of Musa who received the Book which presented the *Deen* as creed, law, and governance which gives it a certain resemblance to the Message of Muhammad. Those three are the roots and the three others are branches coming from them. Lut founded a new branch from Ibrahim, whose nephew he was. Ilyas and Yunus, were both among the Prophets of the Tribe of Israel. Their book is the Torah which was revealed to Musa.

It is telling that the story of Nuh here begins with its ending! He continued to call on his people for nine hundred and fifty years and met only with obstruction and constriction. When he was aware of defeat, he cried, *"Lord, I am overcome, so help me!"* (54:10) and salvation came. The story here in *Surat as-Saffat* begins with this supplication: *"Nuh called out to Us, and what an excellent response We gave! We rescued him and his family from the terrible plight and made his descendants the people who survived, and We left the later people to say of him: 'Peace be upon Nuh among all beings!'"* (37:75-79)

Ibrahim espoused the creed of *tawhid* for which Nuh had striven before. He presented overwhelming evidence to his people of how wrong they were to worship idols. Allah begins the account of his struggle thus: *"He took a look at the stars and then said, 'I am sick.' So they turned their backs on him. He turned surreptitiously to their gods and said, 'Do you not eat? What is wrong with you that do you not speak?'"* (37:88-92) The *ayat* recounts that he thought about what he could do to demonstrate the falsehood of this idol-worship. So he feigned illness and they left him on his own. He went to the idols in their temple and reduced them to firewood: *"He broke them into pieces, except the biggest one,*

---

1. Some scholars also consider Allah Almighty to be the Namer in this *ayat.*

so that they would have it to consult!" (21:58) He hung the axe round the neck of the largest idol to make it seem that it was the one which had smashed his fellow gods. It is clear that Ibrahim used this example in order to disgrace the fools among his people and show up their pathetic notion of worshipping wood or stones which had no power whatsoever.

Perhaps the most significant and moving incident in this account is the story of Ibrahim's relationship with his son and his son's with him, especially when we consider Ibrahim's earlier relationship with his own father. In his old age and after much supplication, Ibrahim was given a son who then grew into a fine young man who was the delight of his father's eyes. Then Allah revealed to Ibrahim that he was to sacrifice the boy to Him. *"When he was of an age to work with him, he said, 'My son, I saw in a dream that I was sacrificing you, so what do you think of it?'"* (37:102)

What was the situation of this old man when he was ordered to sacrifice the son whom he loved more than anything else on earth? Anyone would be grieved at the thought of his being killed, but how was it when he himself was the one who was obliged to do it? And yet Ibrahim was the slave, Messenger, and close friend of Allah. He only knew how to live in the pleasure of Allah and was unable to disobey Him in any command, however arduous. He spoke to his son about it, and the righteous lad did not lessen the certainty and truthfulness of his father: *"He said, 'O father, do as you are ordered to. You will find me, Allah willing, one of the steadfast.'"* (37:102)

The father submitted in respect of his son and the son in respect of himself. When he began to carry out the command and placed the knife against the boy's throat, deliverance came and a substitute was provided as a ransom: *"We called out to him, 'O Ibrahim! You have confirmed the vision. This is the way We recompense good-doers.' This was indeed the ultimate trial."* (37:104-106) The story shows that the Divine testing of man is serious and that it never ceases, and that faith is not simply words on the tongue but means steadfastness and submission.

We pass over other stories in the *sura* until we reach the words of the Almighty: *"Ask them for their true opinion: Does your Lord have daughters while they have sons?"* (37:149) This is the second command to ask for an opinion. The first instruction was: *"Ask them for their true opinion – are they stronger in structure or other things We have created? We created them from sticky clay."* (37:11) This asking for an opinion follows a discussion of the horizons of existence and its Easts and Wests clarifying the vast expanse of the *Malakut* and the immensity of the Creator. It is clear that the idolaters' idea of divinity was inadequate and narrow. They did not measure Allah as He should be measured. They compared him to a father of daughters. They themselves were disgusted to have a daughter born to them and would bury her alive. In spite of that they considered the angels female and then ascribed them to Allah: *"Or did We create the angels female with them as witnesses?"* (37:150)

The Arabs used to claim that if they were given a Scripture as the Jews and Christians had been, they would be better than them: *"If we had only had a Reminder from the earlier peoples, we should certainly have been sincere slaves of Allah!"* (37:167-169) But when Allah gave them the Book, they mostly rejected it. As we know, after great difficulty the Prophet succeeded in conveying the Message and then the world was conquered by its power and wisdom. But all too soon the people of the Revelation deviated from its guidance with the consequences which we know. However, the situation remains the same. It is only those who hold fast to the Divine Guidance brought by the Messengers and then stick to it through thick and thin who will win in the end. *"Our Word has already preceded to Our slaves, the Messengers that they would certainly be helped. It is Our army which will be victorious."* (37:171-173)

Sura 38
Sad

"Sad. By the Qur'an holding the Reminder." (38:1) He says in another *ayat*: *"We have sent down to you a Book containing your Reminder."* (21:10) The Reminder is something which removes forgetfulness and heedlessness and brings about awareness and wakefulness: *"We have made the Qur'an easy to remember. But is there any rememberer there?"* (54:40) But there are those who are arrogant towards the truth. When it is offered to them, pride takes hold of them. Their end is destruction, however long it is in coming!

"They are amazed that a warner should have come to them from among themselves. The rejecters say, 'This is a lying magician. Has he turned all the gods into One God? That is indeed an astonishing thing!'" (38:4-5) The Messenger was told this to make him steadfast and to console him: *"Be steadfast in the face of what they say and remember Our slave Da'ud, who possessed true strength. He truly turned towards his Lord."* (38:17) That is something worth thinking about. Did Da'ud and Sulayman suffer for the sake of their mission in any way that the Messenger, may Allah bless him and grant him peace, could use as an example for his own situation?

There were Prophets who were kings and Prophets who were servants, and it might be imagined that those who were kings had lighter burdens and that those who were weak and poor were the ones who were more exposed to afflictions. But Allah explained to His Prophet that all of them were the same in respect of affliction and that the most afflicted people of all mankind are the Prophets, regardless of their different portions in respect of worldly things. Da'ud and Sulayman were both Prophets who were kings and

330

Allah makes it clear that they endured great troubles in the course of their Missions.

The story of Da'ud begins with the words of the Almighty: *"Has the story of the litigants come down to you? They climbed up to the Upper Room and came in on Da'ud and he was alarmed by them. They said, 'Do not be afraid. We are two litigants, one of whom has acted unjustly towards the other, so judge between us with truth..."* (38:21-22) The one who was wronged describes his story: *"This brother of mine has ninety-nine ewes and I have only one. He said, 'Let me have charge of it,' and got the better of me with his words."* (38:23) The wrongdoer was silent in the face of this, clearly admitting his guilt.

Da'ud said: *"He has wronged you by asking for your ewe together with his ewes. Truly many partners act unjustly to one another."* (38:24) Da'ud was aware that this story was in fact being aimed at him. He had many wives but in spite of that he proposed to a girl when it was clear that someone else wanted to marry her. When he appeared, the chances of the other man disappeared. How could he compete with someone who was both Prophet and king? He added her to his wives and the other man left with nothing. The Lord of the Universe was not pleased with what had happened. He made Da'ud aware of his mistake. *"Da'ud inferred that We had put him to the test. He therefore begged forgiveness from his Lord and fell down prone, prostrating, and repented. So We granted him forgiveness for that and he has nearness to Us and a good homecoming."* (38:24-25)

Da'ud was one of the rich who are thankful to Allah and was well able to cope with the expansion Allah had granted him which allowed him to do whatever he liked. But he should not have proposed to a woman to whom another man had already proposed. Even if he had proposed first, it would still have been better for him to forgo his due. But in any case, Allah made him aware of his error and pardoned him. Then the divine instructions follow which raise him to the station befitting him: *"O Da'ud! We made you a khalif in the earth, so judge between people with truth and do not follow your own desires, letting them misguide you from the Way of Allah."* (38:26) This Prophet-King erred but washed away his error with his tears. He slipped up but the pain of doing so returned him to Allah in accepted repentance. Did his kingdom and his rank protect him from experiencing such trials?

In some ways the denial and rejection experienced by Muhammad, may Allah bless him and grant him peace, were easier to bear than that affliction. Allah elevated Muhammad by a Book whose pages contain the definitive and final Revelation and contains teachings which, if followed, will protect people from making mistakes and which guide people to Allah and to embracing the Truth: *"Shall We make those who believe and do right actions the same as the corrupters of the earth? Shall We make the godfearing the same as the dissolute? It is a Book We have sent down to you, full of blessing. So let people of intellect ponder its Signs and take heed."* (38:28-29)

The Jews accused their Prophet of adultery and murder and claimed that he committed adultery with the wife of Uriah and plotted to kill him so that he could have his wife after her husband had been killed. But the Qur'an clears him completely of all such slanderous imputations. The Prophet Kings were not a group of people who dissipated the good things which were given to them this world. They spent what they possessed for the Cause of Allah, to please Allah.

We find that Sulayman equipped an army to fight the kingdom of Sheba and its queen Bilqis but did not go ahead when she stopped worshipping the sun and entered into the worship of Allah the One and became Muslim: *"Do not rise up against me, but come to me in submission."* (27:31)

In this *sura* Allah Almighty says: *"We gave to Da'ud Sulayman. What an excellent slave! He truly turned towards his Lord."* (38:30) Sulayman used to inspect his horses to be certain of their readiness. Sometimes this would require a great deal of time but he knew that the training of horses for *jihad* was an act of worship which merited attention and interest: *"When swift horses, champing at their bits, were displayed before him in the afternoon, he said, 'I put the love of good things above the remembrance of my Lord until the sun disappeared behind its veil. Return them to me!' And he set about slashing through their shanks and through their necks."* (38:31-33) I wish that my people loved the implements of war in this fashion! Then we would be saved from the immense humiliation which has befallen us when hands are empty of weapons.

Sulayman was a great king. What we realise when we look at him is that he gained his kingdom through righteous service, humble slavehood, quick repentance, and deep understanding. His Lord described him as possessing all these attributes when he said that he was *"an excellent slave!"* (38:30). His insight was opened to the name of Allah, the Abundant Giver, and he saw all creation rejoicing in bounteous divine gifts. He saw both pious and impious seeking Allah's gifts and he longed for a share of this limitless ocean: *"My Lord, forgive me and give me a kingdom which no one after me will be allowed. Truly You are the endless Giver of gifts."* (38:35) The truth is that when one looks at the endless outpouring of Allah, yearning knows no limit. The sea of Divine Generosity overflows and does not diminish.

Sulayman desired a kingdom greater than that of any other king – then or in the future – and Allah granted his request. *"So We made the wind subservient to him, to blow at his command, softly, wherever he directed it to go, and the* shaytans, *every builder and diver."* (38:36-37) Sulayman continued to rule this kingdom and govern it until death came to him and he fell from his throne. He had jinn and men under his command. Allah promised him even more in the Next World than he had received in this world: *"He has nearness to Us and a good homecoming."* (38:40)

Sura Sad contains a narrative of yet another Prophet among the men of wealth and actions who was afflicted by a calamity which took away both his health and his wealth. This was Ayyub, peace be upon him: *"Remember Our slave Ayyub when he called on his Lord, 'Shaytan has afflicted me with exhaustion and torment.'"* (38:41) Shaytan wanted to make him have a bad opinion of Allah and be angry about what had befallen him.

In *Surat al-Anbiya'* we find: *"And Ayyub when he called out to his Lord, 'Great harm has afflicted me and You are the Most Merciful of the merciful.'"* (21:83) This shows that Shaytan desired to exploit the trial by which Allah was testing His sincere slave Ayyub to unsettle him and weaken his faith in his Lord. But when he reached the limit of his endurance Allah showed him the way out of his desperate state. *"Stamp your foot! This is a cool washing-place and water to drink."* (38:42)

Allah healed Ayyub of what had afflicted him inwardly and outwardly and restored to him all he had lost and much more. *"We gave him back his family and the same again with them, as a mercy from Us and a reminder for people of intelligence."* (38:43) It means that people of intellect will benefit from these lessons and remain secure in their relation to Allah in spite of the trials and tribulations which are inevitable for all who aspire to take the path to Allah. These three examples also show that no amount of wealth is able to fend off life's difficulties if Allah desires to test us by them.

The *sura* then proceeds to mention the names of six further Prophets. First come Ibrahim and his son Ishaq and his grandson Ya'qub, whom it describes as *"possessors of true strength and inner sight"*. This description tells us that righteousness is a question of strength and insight – not of weakness and stupidity as the people of this time would have us believe. It is humanity's most noble possibility. *"We purified their sincerity through sincere remembrance of the Abode. In Our eyes they are among the best of chosen men."* (38:46-47) The remaining three are Isma'il, al-Yasa'a and Dhu'l-Kifl, all of whom are great Prophets and among the highest examples of human perfection.

The theme of remembering and reminding pervades the whole *sura* and indeed the Prophetic examples which have been cited are part of it. *"Remember Our slave Da'ud, possessor of strength."* (38:17) The stories are there as a reminder and inform us that a good remembrance is a blessing which Allah grants to His righteous slaves. By it He raises their worth and makes their wage endure. It could be said that remembrance is a lifeline for all human beings. What is necessary is that a Muslim seek the Face of Allah by His actions rather than acting to please mortal men. If Allah accepts what he does, He will love him and put love for him in people's hearts and praise of him on their tongues but above all He will make such men the means of reminding others of Himself.

Continuing with this theme Allah Almighty tells us of the benefits of paying heed to the Reminder and the consequences of not doing so. *"This is a Reminder. For the godfearing there is a good homecoming: Gardens of Eden, whose gates are open to them. They recline in them, calling in them for abundant fruit and drink."* (38:49-51) As for the enemies of Allah and the opponents of the Message, their reward will be of a very different kind. *"This! Whereas for the inordinate there is an evil homecoming: Hell, where they will roast. What an evil resting-place!"* (38:55-56)

Taking up another common Qur'anic theme, the *sura* speaks of the events of the Last Day and the conversation which will take place between the followers and their leaders. Allah says to the people of Hell: *"Here is a crowd hurtling in along with you. There is no welcome for them. They will certainly be roasting in the Fire."* (38:59) It appears that those "hurtling in" are the followers and those who refused to welcome them are their leaders. They do not welcome them although they supported them in their disbelief. *"They will say, 'On the contrary, it is you who have no welcome. It is you who brought it upon us. What an evil place to settle!'"* (38:60)

The tyrants will remember this world and recall what they did to the believers they persecuted. *"They say, 'How is it that we do not see men whom we used to count among the worst of people? Did we make them objects of our ridicule? Did our eyes disdain to look at them?'"* (38:62-63) All the hidden resentment which people felt in this world will find its expression in the Next World in endless bickering. *"All that most certainly is true – the squabbling of the people of the Fire."* (38:64)

As so often happens with the *suras* of the Qur'an, the end of the *sura* is tied to its beginning. *"Say: 'I am but a warner. No god is there but Allah, the One, the All Conquering.'"* (38:65) This refers back to the words of the unbelievers about the Messenger of Allah at the beginning of the *sura*: *"This is a lying magician. Has he turned all the gods into One God?"* (38:4-5) There is only one Master of existence. Everything other than Him worships Him. Muhammad, may Allah bless him and grant him peace, affirmed this reality in the most sublime way but even so most people are heedless. *"Say: 'It is momentous news. Yet you are turning from it! I knew nothing of the Highest Assembly when they were in debate. Revealed to me is only that I am a clear warner.'"* (38:67-70) The Messenger says to people, "From where could I gain knowledge of a conversation which took place in the Highest Assembly? I receive only what comes to me from Allah."

Allah chose Muhammad and revealed this Book to his heart so that it might explain the reality of *tawhid* and refute all varieties of polytheism. Mankind have one Lord and they and everything else will inescapably return to Him. *"Say: 'I do not ask you any wage for it, nor am I a man of false pretension. It is but a reminder to all the worlds. You will certainly know its truth after a while.'"* (38:86-88)

Sura 39
Az-Zumar: The Companies

The word *'zumar'* means different companies of people and is only used in the present *sura* which bears this name. The *sura* contains various references to several disparate groups of people, and each group is compared with another until all the groups in the *sura* have been examined in this way. It centres on the way each group approach *tawhid* and and the consequences which that has for them.

Idolatry is a sin which is widespread among the people of every time. Are you not astonished at an intelligent man who worships a stone? Are you not astonished at a pilot who thinks that his safety depends on a horseshoe? The vagaries of human nature are innumerable but one of them which is all too common is having a bad opinion of Allah. It is vital for us to have a good opinion of our Creator and to ascribe absolute perfection to Him. Neverthe-less we insist on ascribing obscure partners to Allah and making images of them which we worship and then say: *"We only worship them so that they can bring us close in nearness to Allah."* (39:3) These idols are nonentities invested with meaning by delusion. They should be thrown into a corner of the rubbish heap.

The question of Divinity is much higher than such triteness. If Allah had made anything a medium between Him and His creation, He would have chosen a far higher thing: *"If Allah had desired to have a son, He would have chosen, out of what He has created, whatever He willed. Glory be to Him! He is Allah the One, the Conqueror."* (39:4)

There is no intermediary standing between man and his Lord. The human being's connection to Him is direct and immediate. Each and every man can speak directly to his Lord at any time and in any place. If it had so happened – to posit an impossibility – that

337

Allah had decided to have a son, He would have chosen from His creation a noble angel, and that chosen individual would in any case be a creature, not a Creator, a subject, not a Master.

Divinity is the summit of existence and all creatures are merely the locus of humble worship. But the idolaters – whether pagans or People of the Book – fail to understand this reality and do not recognise the difference between creature and Creator. Faith is only made valid by a deep conviction of the absolute unity of God and by the explicit realisation that everything other than Him is His slave. The Noble Qur'an is *par excellence* the Scripture which deals most exhaustively with this topic and reinforces the heart in its affirmation. *Surat az-Zumar* repeatedly points out the invaluable blessing we have in Allah's Book.

> *"The sending down of the Book is from Allah, the Mighty, the Wise. We have sent down to you the Book with truth. Therefore worship Allah, making the* deen *sincerely His alone."* (39:1-2)

> *"Allah has sent down the Supreme Discourse, a Book consistent in its frequent repetitions. The skins of those who fear their Lord tremble at it and then their skins and hearts yield softly to the remembrance of Allah."* (39:23)

> *"We have coined all kinds of examples for people in this Qur'an, so that perhaps they may remember – an Arabic Qur'an with no distortion in it, so that perhaps they may be godfearing."* (39:29)

> *"We have sent down to you the Book for mankind with truth. So those who are guided are guided to their own good..."* (39:41)

> *"Follow the best that has been sent down to you from your Lord, before the punishment comes upon you suddenly when you are not expecting it...."* (39:55)

The beginning of *Surat az-Zumar* contains some *ayats* concerning Allah, the Creator, and about how His creative power manifests itself in the creation of the heavens and the earth, of man and of the animals. This paves the way for the subsequent comparisons between the various classes of people, clarifying their secrets and different motivations.

The first of these comparisons is a very fundamental one, mentioned in many places in the Qur'an, between the grateful and the ungrateful. *"If you are ungrateful, Allah is rich beyond any need of you, and He is not pleased with ingratitude in His slaves. But if you are grateful, He is happy with that in you. No bearer of a burden can bear that of another..."* (39:7)

The fact is that human beings are immersed in the blessings of Allah – they live on His earth, breath His air and eat what He has provided. Then they forget that and take it completely for granted, treating it as if they had not been given any favour whatsoever! When they are in difficulty they pray fervently for deliverance but once they are delivered from their plight they soon forget. *"And when the waves hang over them like canopies, they call on Allah, making their* deen *sincerely for Him. But then when He delivers them safely to the land, some of them are ambivalent. Only a treacherous ungrateful man repudiates Our signs."* (31:32)

Thankfulness for blessing is a sign of sound insight and of an upright nature. Our Prophet said about the secret of his striving in worship, "Should I not be a grateful slave?" What is required of people is to recognise the provenance of the blessings they enjoy, and not to use them as a means of disobeying Him from Whom they have come.

The second comparison is in the words of the Almighty: *"What of him who is obedient through the night, prostrating and standing, mindful of the Next World and hoping for the mercy of his Lord? Say: 'Are they the same – those who know and do not know?'"* (39:9) It is clear that the other side of the comparison is elided, implying: Is someone who is obedient at night the same as someone who sleeps through it? Or is someone who is busy worshipping at night the same as someone who is busy with amusement and looking for illicit pleasure? We will see that in these comparisons one side or the other is often elided to stress the importance of what is mentioned. In this case the object is to encourage rising to pray at night.

The noble Messenger said, "You must pray at night. It was the custom of the righteous before you and it is an act which brings you near to your Lord, expiates bad actions, prevents sin, and repels illness from the body." Regarding sincerity of intention to rise in the night, Abu'd-Darda' related that the Prophet, may Allah bless him and grant him peace, said: "Whoever goes to his bed with the intention of rising to pray at night, if his eyes overcome him until morning what he intended is still written for him and his sleep is *sadaqa* for him from his Lord."

The third comparison is between two further groups. The first are the godfearing who do good, who are sincere in their *deen* and walk in the footsteps of their Prophet and model themselves on him. He says: *"Say: 'I fear, if I disobey my Lord, the punishment of a dreadful Day.'"* (39:13) They restrain their appetites and submit themselves to Allah. The others are those who only work for the life of this world and live only to satisfy their appetites, forgetting the encounter with their Lord and dedicating their lives to the present. Allah says about those: *"Say: 'The real losers are those who lose their selves and their families on the Day of Rising. Is not that clear loss?'"* (39:15)

Thousands upon thousands of people put all their effort into advancing themselves and their families in this life and boosting their wealth and rank to the greatest possible extent. But when the Day of Resurrection comes, they will be gathered naked and barefoot and what they earned will be of no use to them at all. This is all summarised in the words of the Almighty: *"Those who shun the worship of false gods and turn towards Allah will have good news. So give good news to My slaves: those who listen well to what is said and follow the best of it. They are the people Allah has guided; they are the people of intellect."* (39:17-18)

The fourth comparison mentions one of the two parties and omits the other because it is understood from the context. The Almighty says: *"Those against whom the word of punishment is realised ... can you save those who are in the Fire?"* (39:19) This means: "Is someone who acts badly and so deserves humiliation like someone who is godfearing and deserves honour? No one can save anyone against whom the word of your Lord is realised." The other side in the comparison is defined when Allah says: *"But those who show fear of their Lord will have high-ceilinged halls, and more such halls built one above the other, and rivers flowing under them."* (39:20)

The fifth comparison resembles the previous one in eliding one of the two sides: *"Is he whose breast is opened to Islam, and who therefore is illuminated by his Lord...? Woe to those who hearts are hardened against the remembrance of Allah!"* (39:22) The words imply: "Is someone whose breast is opened to the Truth like someone whose breast is constricted by the truth and dislikes to enter into it and act by it?" When the breast is opened, a man turns eagerly to action, as al-Busiri says:

> When guidance releases the soul,
> the limbs act in obedience.

But those who deviate from Allah find the prayer heavy and *zakat* burdensome and flee from *jihad*. The following *ayat* explains this fifth comparison: *"Allah has sent down the Supreme Discourse, a Book consistent in its frequent repetitions. The skins of those who fear their Lord tremble at it and then their skins and hearts yield softly to the remembrance of Allah."* (39:23) The Noble Qur'an is the source of the Wise Reminder and Straight Guidance, protection against falsehood and connection to the Truth.

The sixth comparison in which again one side is missing is found in the noble *ayat*: *"Is someone who tries to shield himself with his face from the worst of the torment on the Day of Rising...? The wrongdoers will be told, "Taste what you have earned."'"* (39:24) The meaning is: "Is someone who guards his face against the punishment of the Rising by faith and good action like someone who sets his face up to receive this punishment by his rejection and injustice?" The natural tendency of human beings is to protect their faces but the encompassing punishment will come to them suddenly so that they will be unable to repel it. The following *ayat* adds that the punishment will also be hastened for them in this realm: *"So Allah made them taste disgrace in the life of this world; and the punishment of the Next World is far greater, if they only knew."* (39:26)

The seventh comparison is between *tawhid* and short-sighted stupidity, between those who seek the Pleasure of their Lord and those who seek the pleasure of others in the form of idols, leaders or nationalities. Worship of what is other than Allah includes all of those. There are so many people whose hearts are completely empty of all care for Allah and are filled with seeking the pleasure of this one or flattering that one. The principle of false worship is included in this. It is the same with the principle of seeking fame.

When the believer prays, he is humble before Allah. When he gives *zakat*, he gives to Allah. When he strives, he is totally dedicated to Allah. His direction is unified and his conscience is at rest: *"Allah has made a likeness for them of a man owned by several partners in dispute with one another and another man wholly owned by a single man. Are they the same?"* (39:29)

The eighth comparison is contained in the words of the Almighty: *"Who could do greater wrong than someone who tells lies against Allah and denies the truth when it comes to him? Do not the rejecters have a dwelling place in Hell? He who brings the truth and he who confirms it – such are the godfearing."* (39:32-33) The earth seems filled with illusions and falsehoods. The people most entitled to respect and esteem are those who convey the truth and act by it. The worst people are those who invent lies against Allah. When someone does point them to the truth, they are recalcitrant and refuse to follow it. Allah has promised the party of the Truth that *"They will have anything they wish for with their Lord. That is the recompense of the good-doers, so that Allah may erase from them the worst of what they did and pay them their wages according to the best of what they did."* (39:34-35) What better news could one possibly receive?

This provocative question has come in *Surat az-Zumar*: *"Is not Allah enough for His slave, though they try to scare you with others apart from Him?"* (39:36) It is Allah alone Who abases and exalts, harms and benefits, and no one can criticise His judgement or avert His command or make it happen it, so how could a slave not rely on him? Who will protect people against Him? This idea is the basis of the ninth comparison. None but Allah can issue a command or carry out a judgement. He cannot even defend itself, so how could he protect others?

"*Say: 'So what do you think? If Allah desires harm for me, can those you call upon besides Allah remove His harm? Or if He desires mercy for me, can they withhold His mercy?' Say: 'Allah is enough for me. All who trust put their trust in Him.'*" (39:38) Allah very quickly orders His Messenger to inform the unbelievers of the results of their idolatry: "*Say: 'O my people! Do as you think best. That is what I am doing. You will soon know who receives a punishment to disgrace him and who unleashes on himself an everlasting punishment.'*" (39:39-40)

The tenth comparison expresses the yawning gulf between those who affirm the Divine Unity and the idolaters. Although some of the misguided know they are misguided and are devoting themselves to powerless substitutes, most of them really believe that they are in the right. They defend their falsehoods ferociously and believe that all other ways are wrong. Consider the *ayats* describing them: "*When Allah is mentioned on His own, the hearts of those who do not believe in the Next World shrink back shuddering, but when others apart from Him are mentioned, they jump for joy.*" (39:45) What can the Messenger do with such people? "*Say: 'O Allah, Bringer into being of the heavens and the earth, Knower of the Unseen and the Visible, it is You who will judge between Your slaves regarding the things about which they differed.'*" (39:46)

The eleventh comparison can be seen when the Almighty says: "*When harm touches a man He calls upon Us. But then when We bestow on him a blessing from Us, he says, 'I was only given it on account of knowledge.' Rather it is a trial, but most of them do not know. Those who came before them also said that, but what they earned did not avail them.*" (39:49-50) This is an internal comparison between a man and his own self when he is in ease and when he is in difficulty. When he is in difficulty, he resorts to supplication and asks Allah for deliverance and feels his powerlessness and is a penitent slave. But when times change and his blessings multiply, he forgets what he felt before and says: "This success is the product of my own cleverness." Did he not possess that cleverness before? Why did he not rely on it to remove the difficulty of what he was complaining before?

This heedlessness and disregard is the gateway to loss. It is vital for people to stay within the limits of slavehood. Hastening to repentance is one of the signs of sound faith. Deferring and delaying repentance, on the other hand, is proof of a person's inability to mend what has been broken, or may indicate lethargy in acting on one's capacity for good. The Messenger, may Allah bless him and grant him peace, said, "Follow an evil action with a good action which will efface it." A man might despair of himself and surrender to Shaytan and continue in that way for so long a time that he thinks it impossible for him ever to get away from him. The temptation to feel this way is dealt with once and for all in this *sura*: *"Say: 'O My slaves who have been profligate against yourselves, do not despair of the mercy of Allah. Allah forgives all wrong actions...'"* (39:53)

This leads us on to the twelfth comparison, which contrasts those spurred on by hope for Allah's pardon so that they continue in His path and hasten to please Him with those who are uninterested and lazy, so that they miss the good and feel regret when regret is of no longer of any benefit: *"Lest any self should say, 'Alas for me for neglecting what Allah was due, and for being one of the scoffers.'"* (39:56) Then he is told: *"No, the fact is that My signs came to you but you denied them and showed arrogance and were one of the rejecters."* (39:59)

Allah Almighty then says, comparing truthfulness and lying in in respect of faith, behaviour and character: *"On the Day of Rising you will see those who lied against Allah with their faces blackened. Is there not a home for the arrogant in Hell? Allah will save those who were godfearing in their victorious safe haven. No evil will touch them and they will feel no sorrow."* (39:60-61) This is the thirteenth comparison and the last of these comparisons for which this *sura* is so remarkable. The *sura* ends with the majestic and beautiful *ayats* for which it is justly celebrated. In them the word *zumar* (companies) which gives the *sura* its name and which was mentioned at the beginning is used twice once for the unbelievers and once for the believers. This is where the two sides of each of the comparisons we have been looking at are definitively separated. Each group is here sent to its final destination: *"Those who rejected will be driven to Hell in companies…"* (39:71) *"And those who were fearful of their Lord will be driven to the Garden in companies…"* (39:73) The people of Hell will realise, after the cessation of linear time, that their forgetfulness of Allah in this world has resulted in Him forgetting them. The people of Paradise will be in houses of bliss because of the remembrance and thankfulness which occupied them in this world. *"Their call there is: 'Glory be to You, O Allah!' Their greeting there is: 'Peace!' The end of their call is: 'Praise belongs to Allah, the Lord of all the worlds!"'* (10:10)

Sura 40
Ghafir or al-Mu'min:
Forgiver, or The Believer

Surat al-Mu'min is the first of the seven *suras* which begin with the letters *Ha-Mim*. They are together called the *Hawamim*. Ibn Mas'ud said, "The *Hawamim* are the brocade of the the Qur'an." Ibn 'Abbas said, "Everything has a nucleus, and the nucleus of the Qur'an is the *Hawamim*." This *sura* begins with the words: *"Ha Mim. The sending down of the Book is from Allah, the Almighty, the All-Knowing."* (40:1-2) Almighty and All-Knowing are among the Most Beautiful Names of Allah. Their effects extend to the Book sent down directly from Him so that His Might and Knowledge permeate the Qur'an and can actually be tasted in it.

"The Forgiver of wrong action, the Accepter of repentance, the Severe in retribution, the Possessor of abundance." (40:3) One of the practices of the Qur'an is to combine promise and threat so that its readers remain governed by a combination of fear and hope. *"Know that Allah is Severe in retribution and that Allah is All-Forgiving, Most Merciful"* (5:98) is another instance of this. Man is in constant need of the stimulants of hope and fear. If he despairs of success, that will lead him to fall; but if he is complacent, that will prevent him from striving.

According to Ibn Kathir, one of the men of Syria who was known for his great courage used to come regularly to visit 'Umar ibn al-Khattab. Then he failed to come for a considerable period and 'Umar missed him. He asked after him and was told, "Amir al-Mu'minin, he drinks all the time!" So 'Umar summoned his scribe and told him: "Write to so-and-so: 'Peace be upon you. I praise Allah to you. *"There is no god but Him, the Forgiver of wrong action, the Accepter of repentance, the Severe in retribution, the Possessor of abundance. There is no god but Him and to*

346

Him is the final destination."'" (the beginning of *Surat al-Mu'min*). Then he said to his companions, "Pray to Allah for your brother to accept him and turn towards him."

When 'Umar's letter reached the man, he began to read it and repeat it, saying, "'*The Forgiver of wrong action, the Accepter of repentance, the Severe in retribution.*' He warns me about His retribution and simultaneously promises me that He will forgive me!" He continued to repeat this to himself. Then he wept and turned over a completely new leaf.

When the news reached 'Umar, he said, "Do the same as this whenever you see that a brother of yours has gone wrong. Show him the right way and give him encouragement," meaning do not make him lose self-confidence, "and pray to Allah for him. Do not be Shaytan's helpers against him."

There are many today who could do with reading this story. There are far too many gloom and doom merchants who apparently have little regard for Allah's mercy and are very good at firing off blasts of rebuke and mortification. It is as if their goal in life were to destroy anyone whose foot slips. Rather than giving them a helping hand they push them into the ditch, and there are many enemies of the Muslims lying in wait to pick up those who have tripped up and bring them out of the *Deen*. Such people should remember that Allah has promised His forgiveness to all believers who turn to Him. They put themselves in a very dangerous position because by denying Allah's mercy to others they may very well be denying it, without realising, to themselves. Indeed, one of the names of this *sura* is *Ghafir* (Forgiver).

Allah says: *"No one disputes about Allah's signs except those who reject. Do not let their free movement about the land deceive you. The people of Nuh denied before them, and the Confederates after that. Every nation planned to seize its Messenger and used false arguments to rebut the truth. So I seized them, and how was My retribution!"* (40:4-5) The word 'dispute' is repeated five times in the course of the *sura*, which takes the lid off one of the ways that unbelievers often act when confronted by the Truth. They are obdurate and refuse to follow the clear evidence they are presented with. They are overcome by the force of their hostile prejudice and are determined to question and argue to the bitter end. The *sura* declares war against such disputation and the blindness to the Truth it indicates.

This is why Allah says of such people in another place: *"I will divert from My signs those who are unrightfully arrogant in the earth. Even if they see every sign, they will not believe in it. If they see the way of right guidance, they will not take it as a way. But if they see the way of error, they will take that as a way. That is because they denied Our signs and were heedless of them."* (7:146) Behind every hostile act and aggressive policy are people who dispute in this blind and obdurate way, who know the truth but refuse to follow it. The Prophets were exposed to this evil and their followers are also exposed to the same energy whenever and wherever they strive to implement the Prophetic teaching.

But life on earth is inevitably a period of testing whose difficulties the righteous are bound to encounter. The angels of the Merciful observe them from the heavens and pray for constancy and correctness for them. *"Those who bear the Throne and all those around it glorify the praise of their Lord and believe in Him and ask forgiveness for those who believe: 'Our Lord, You encompass everything in mercy and knowledge! Forgive those who turn to You and who follow Your way, and safeguard them from the punishment of the Blazing Fire.'"* (40:7)

In this *sura* the believer of the people of Pharaoh, from whom the *sura* takes its name and who provides an archetype for all time of a believer faced by hostile unbelievers, has to counter the arguments his people put forward in their determined opposition to faith. He shows that he knows that this is the nature of those who refuse to accept Divine Guidance. *"Yusuf came to you with the Clear Signs before, but you never ceased to be in doubt about what he brought to you..."* (40:34) Yusuf brought the true *deen* and attacked the prevailing paganism and ruled Egypt with a rule replete with justice and prosperity. Did the people enter the *deen* in droves? No, they continued to doubt and dispute what what he brought them until he died.

When Allah sent Musa after him, the pattern was repeated and the unbelievers once more produced their endless arguments:

"Thus does Allah lead astray those who are unbridled, full of doubt. Those who argue about the Signs of Allah without any authority coming to them do something very hateful thing in the sight of Allah and in the sight of the people who believe. Thus does Allah seal up the heart of every arrogant oppressor." (40:34-35) The believer of the people of Pharaoh was a most able advocate of the cause of belief. He was gentle at one time and harsh at another, travelled at one time and concealed himself at another, so as to spend the longest possible time in the service of the Truth in spite of the fact that Pharoah's power was widespread.

Even though this was in specific terms a defence of the message of Musa, it nonetheless provides an example for the effective defence of all Allah's messages. Abu Bakr later used some words from it to avert the aggression of the idolaters when he was Caliph of the Muslims.

Lack of sufficient knowledge, accompanied by inflated self-opinion, is an affliction without end. The only cure for it is to increase in true knowledge so that the horizon of the soul is expanded and the conscience strengthened until it no longer yields automatically to the gross appetites; and what applies to individuals also applies to societies.

In this context we find in *Surat al-Mu'min* that the Noble Qur'an twice bids us to travel through the earth and into the depths of the past so that we may benefit from the knowledge which past societies will enable us to grasp if we reflect deeply on their fate. The Almighty says: *"Have they not travelled in the earth and seen what was the end result of those before them? They were greater than them in strength and in the traces they left in the earth, yet Allah seized them for their wrong actions and they had no one to protect them against Allah."* (40:21)

Human history is full of lessons for us and shows us the unfolding of inexorable laws which, if we are intelligent, we will apply to our own situation. The study of the circumstances of past nations will reform the degenerate and guide the perplexed. To reinforce the importance of this Allah gives another almost identical *ayat* later in the *sura* when He says: *"Have they not travelled in the land and seen what was the end result of those before them?*

They were more numerous than them and greater in strength and traces left in the earth, but what they earned did not avail them." (40:82)

The Qur'an reveals the reasons for this defiant willfulness and describes it as originating from having only a little knowledge; a little learning truly is a dangerous thing. The delusion of having knowledge is responsible for the disputation and arrogance they evince. *"When their Messengers came to them with the Clear Signs, they exulted in the knowledge that they had and then were engulfed by the very things they mocked."* (40:83) Many of those who are misguided do not know that they are in error. They think that they are firmly rooted in what is correct. They only wake up when faced with a disaster which shatters their arrogance: *"Certainly those who argue about the signs of Allah without any authority having come to them have nothing in their breasts except for pride which they will never be able to vindicate. Therefore seek refuge with Allah. He is the All-Hearing, the All- Seeing."* (40:56)

This is the fourth place in this *sura* where that tendency to disputation is mentioned. Combating this interminable hostility on the part of the unbelievers demands great patience, turning to Allah and seeking His help, and Allah tells us in the *sura* how to go about this. *"So remain steadfast. Allah's promise is true. Ask forgiveness for your wrong action and glorify your Lord's praise in the evening and the early morning."* (40:55) However, this steadfastness should not be interpreted as waiting for punishment to befall the wrongdoers. Their punishment may be delayed and may not happen until after the death of the one striving in *jihad*. We must continue to perform our duty with zeal and never give up, however hopeless things might seem, entrusting the result to the knowledge and power of Allah. That is why the command to be steadfast is repeated later in the *sura*: *"So be steadfast. Allah's promise is true. Whether We show you part of what We promise them, or take you back to Us, they will in any case be returned to Us."* (40:77)

Another thing which is repeated in the *sura* is the command to call on Allah alone. The first time is near the beginning of the *sura*: *"So call upon Allah, making the* Deen *sincerely His, even*

350

though the unbelievers detest it. The Raiser of ranks, the Possessor of the Throne, He sends the Spirit by His command to whichever of His slaves He wills so that he may warn mankind of the Day of Meeting, the Day they will issue forth and when not one thing about them will be hidden from Allah..." (40:14-16) This idea is repeated in the *sura* a second time when the Almighty says: *"Your Lord says, 'Call upon Me and I will answer you. Those who who are too proud to worship Me will enter Hell abject.'"* (40:60) In both *ayats*, mention of calling on Allah is juxtaposed with that of the unbelievers who refuse to do so; and this can only make us look at our own civilisation, in which the worship of Allah has ceased to be even a secondary goal. It is not a goal at all! At best it has become a passing thought in the case of people who consider themselves religious. That is why this *sura* contains three *ayats* which all begin with the name of Allah, acknowledging Him and reminding us of His due.

> *"Allah is He who appointed for you the night, so that you might rest in it, and the day for seeing. Allah pours out His favour on mankind, but most people do not show thanks."* (40:61)

Each new morning is a blessing direct from Allah. The Messenger, may Allah bless him and grant him peace, reminded us of this when he said in the morning, "Praise be to the One has who returned my spirit to me and given me health in my body and granted me permission to remember Him." Do we breathe the air of a new day, aware that life is a gift for which we owe thanks to our Creator? Or do we merely occupy ourselves with the amusement and diversion that the world is full of and waste our lives on earth?

> *"Allah is He who made the earth a stable home for you and the sky a dome, and formed you, giving you the best of forms..."* (40:64)

It is miraculous that the earth remains firm when it is revolving so fast upon its axis every day and speeding on its orbit around the sun. But He who holds it and the heavens in His Hand prevents any turbulence or oscillation. I once experienced an earthquake which lasted scarcely any time but was terrifying. The Mercy of Allah which we take for granted is truly overwhelming.

> *"Allah is He who has supplied you with livestock, some to ride and some to eat. There are various uses for you in them..."* (40:79-80)

We human beings are full of self-admiration and pride in our intelligence and powers yet we do not even know who dwells in existence with us. This *sura* comes to tell us: *"The creation of the heavens and the earth is far greater than the creation of mankind; yet most people do not know."* (40:57) So we should develop humility and realise the extent and absurdity of the delusion under which we live. The Qur'an gives us a true perspective on existence. It answers every question an intelligent and open-hearted human being might wish to ask about the meaning and purpose of their life and their own place in existence. But many people are quite the reverse of open-hearted; on the contrary, they are determined to deny the truth at any price.

As we have seen, *Surat Ghafir* speaks several times about this arid and obdurate disputation on the part of bigoted unbelievers. The last time it does so it makes it clear that denying the Qur'an in fact means denying all Divine Revelation. *"Do you not see those who wrangle about the signs of Allah? How have they been turned about? Those who deny the Book and that with which We sent Our Messengers..."* (40:71)

How objectionable are Muslims who neglect their legacy and betray their Message in their headlong rush to follow the West! That does not prevent us from warning about the destruction to which we are being inexorably driven by a civilisation which abandons prayer and seeks only the satisfaction of appetites and ephemeral mastery of this world.

Sura 41
Fussilat: Made Plain

"Ha Mim. A Revelation from the All-Merciful, the Most Merciful." (41:1-2) The *ayats* of the Book descended from the fountains of Divine Mercy. It contains guidance which protects people from the evil of their own souls and their bad actions and guards them against idle thoughts, the confusion of untrammelled instinct, the oppression of materialism and the corruption of unbridled appetite. The blessed Revelation contains all good and all justice: *"A Book whose signs have been demarcated for people who know as an Arabic Qur'an, bringing good news and giving warning."* (41: 3-4) People of understanding perceive the excellence of these *ayats* which promise the godfearing pleasure and threaten fools with wretchedness. How few are the people who grasp this! That is why Allah says, *"But most of them have turned away and do not hear."* (41:4)

The fact that the Qur'an is in Arabic is part of its miraculous nature. If you translate its meanings into another language, that translation is not the Qur'an. Allah chose the language of the Arabs to be the medium of His Final Revelation and He chose the people of this language to guide the rest of mankind to good. But at first its people did not for the most part accept Islam. They turned away from it coarsely and harshly. Muhammad, peace and blessings be upon him, persisted with them until they recognised the truth and risked their lives and property for it, curtailing dynasties which had endured for many centuries, and ensured that Islam became firmly established in the world.

Now, however, two base qualities have returned to the Arabs of the modern *Jahiliyya*: the worst customs of their ancestors of the days before Islam, and the perversions of the materialistic West sunk in its pleasures and illusions. I do not know of anyone more

353

set in deviation than the Arabs and further from enlightenment and justice. The words addressed to Abu Jahl and those with him are equally applicable to them: *"They say, 'Our hearts are covered up against what you call us to and there is a heaviness in our ears and there is a screen between us and you. So act – we certainly are acting.'"* (41:5)

Allah wished the Arabs to carry the Message of Islam and to make its guidance clear in their own language. He says: *"If We had made it a Qur'an in a foreign tongue they would have said, 'Why have its signs not been made plain? What! A foreign language from an Arab?' Say: 'It is guidance and healing for people who believe.' Those who do not believe have heaviness in their ears and for them it is blindness. Such people are being summoned from a very distant place."*(41:44)

But Arabic does not belong to the Arabs. It is the possession of any person from any of the five continents who learns Arabic and masters the language of the Qur'an. Arabness is not a matter of ethnicity. Many Persians and Greeks who became Muslim in the past served the Qur'an and its language more than those born in the Arabian peninsula. The important thing is that there should be no covers on the heart or defects in the senses which preclude profitable listening and understanding.

So any upright human being can follow Muhammad, may Allah bless him and grant him peace, whose call was directed to the whole of mankind: *"Say: 'I am only a human being like yourselves. It is revealed to me that your god is One God. So be straight with Him and ask His forgiveness. Woe to those who associate others with Him: those who do not pay* zakat *and reject the Next World.'"* (41:6-7) Are going straight on the path and asking forgiveness for error such forbidding responsibilities? Are declaring the unity of Allah and showing mercy to the poor such arduous obligations? Yet those who are proud and egotistical refuse to take them on. Their end will be dismal.

That is why the Qur'an threatens the Arabs, the first and the last of them, with woe if their opposition to the truth and their harshness towards His Messenger continue. It reminds them of the fate of their forefathers 'Ad and Thamud: *"If they turn away, then*

354

say, 'I warn you of a lightning-bolt like the lightning-bolt of 'Ad and of Thamud.'" (41:13) Evil behaviour brings about the same consequences no matter how many centuries elapse.

Why were the people of 'Ad destroyed? *"'Ad were arrogant in the land without any right and said, 'Who is greater in strength than us?'"* (41:15) Why was Thamud destroyed? *"As for Thamud, We guided them, but they preferred blindness to guidance."* (41:17) It was arrogance without right and contempt for people in the case of 'Ad and preferring error to guidance and the false to the truth in the case of Thamud. Anyone else who manifests those qualities will inevitably suffer the same fate. I look at the Arabs today and their position in Islam and am overcome by pessimism.

Punishment in this world does not dispense with the punishment of the Next World: *"On the day We crowd the enemies of Allah into the Fire and they are driven in close-packed ranks, when they reach it their hearing, sight and skin will testify against them concerning what they did."* (41:19-20) Hearing and sight are blessings which Allah has bestowed on man so that he may recognise from the vastness of creation the sublimity of its Creator. But when man blocks his ears and blinkers his eyes and does not take the way to Allah, these thwarted senses will be the first to testify against him and ensure his punishment on the Day when he is cast into the Fire and meets a fate worse than that of the lowest animal!

It is noteworthy that between the presentation of the Message and the announcement of the repayment of those who deny it there is a passage discussing the formation of creation and the organisation of the universe: *"Say: 'Do you reject Him who created the earth in two days, and make others equal to Him? That is the Lord of all the worlds. He placed firmly-embedded mountains on it, towering over it, and blessed it and measured out its nourishment in it, laid out for those who seek it – all in four days.'"* (41:9-10) Man was formed from this earth and lives on its good things. When Allah established him in it, He made him master of it so that he might be a slave to his Lord who had fashioned him and breathed His spirit into him; but man forgets and transgresses.

The human race developed after Allah had prepared the earth for them to dwell in, blessing it and providing nourishment in it. In these *ayats* and in other places man's attention is drawn to the closest thing to him, the earth on which he lives. He can believe or disbelieve as he wishes. Mentioning these realities after presenting the Message is logical. Reflecting on them is the basis of belief and blindness to them is the way to perdition.

The middle part of *Surat Fussilat* mentions other worlds which intersect with that of man. It talks about the jinn and their whisperings and the angels and their inspirations. Materialists deny these things without producing any evidence except for saying they cannot be perceived by the five senses. Muslims acknowledge both matter and what lies beyond it, affirming the worlds of the jinn and the angels alongside that of the normal physical experience of human beings.

Some of the jinn are believers. But some of them are shaytans who cling to man and take advantage of his moments of heedlessness in order to delude him into disobeying Allah and neglecting what is due to Him. Iblis, the greatest of the shaytans, took advantage of Adam's heedlessness to tempt him to eat from the Forbidden Tree and swore false oaths to him that he was a trustworthy adviser. Adam ate and was expelled from the Garden. The first reason was his forgetfulness and weak resolve. The second reason was that Shaytan lay in wait for him and seized the opportunity to dupe him.

Shaytan did the same with the adversaries of Islam in the early days of Islam. The Almighty says: *"We have assigned close comrades to them, who have made what is before them and behind them appear good to them. And the statement about the nations both of jinn and men who passed away before them has proved true of them as well. Certainly they were losers. Those who reject say, 'Do not listen to this Qur'an. Drown it out so that perhaps you may gain the upper hand.'"* (41:25-27)

The unbelievers reject the Qur'an and hate to listen to it. Shaytan has deluded them into creating a hubbub when it is recited so that it does not reach people's hearts. That is an admission of failure by the unbelievers in the face of the Truth and of their inability to refute it. Everyone who denies the truth is deluded by Shaytan into actions of this kind. On the Day of Rising they will regret this deception: *"Those who reject say, 'Our Lord, show us those jinn and men who misguided us and we will place them beneath our feet so that they may be among the lowest of the low.'"* (41:29)

On the other hand, people of intelligence whose hearts have been opened to the truth and who have devoted themselves to helping it are surrounded by angels who ease their loneliness and help them to transcend difficulties: *"Those who say, 'Our Lord is Allah,' and then go straight, the angels descend on them, 'Do not fear and do not grieve: rejoice in the Garden which you have been promised.'"* (41:30) Most commentators think that this *ayat* was revealed about those who are dying, when they are in the final stage of this world and the first stage of the Next World, in order to put them at ease regarding things they love and are leaving behind and to prepare their hearts for the delight they are about to encounter.

There is nothing wrong in that view but the *ayat* certainly can bear a more general interpretation. There are many instances of the angels descending on the believers during *jihad* and inspiring them to right guidance and helping them in difficult situations, and the Messenger, peace and blessings be upon him, is known to have said to a man who praised Allah well: "A noble angel has helped you to it." The angels support the Truth as the shaytans support the falsehood.

Shaytan is clever in drawing man far from Allah and in obscuring the Straight Path. So calling people to Allah is an action which reminds people and stimulates the lazy to act. It protects the truth, repels shaytans, and expels illusions and erroneous ideas: *"Who could say anything better than someone who summons to Allah and acts rightly and says, 'I am one of the Muslims'?"* (41:33)

The Messengers are the models for all who call to Allah, and their deeds and words are a constant source of inspiration for people who desire to follow in their footsteps. The first thing that they do is to inform people about their Lord and inculcate love of Him in them. There are *ayats* in this *sura* which make it clear how this is done. *"Among His signs are the night and day and the sun and moon. Do not prostrate to the sun nor to the moon. Prostrate to*

Allah Who created them, if it is Him you worship." (41:37) *"Among His signs is that you see the earth laid bare and then when We sent down water on it, it quivers and swells..."* (41:39) *"The Knowledge of the Hour is referred to Him. No fruit emerges from its husk, no female gets pregnant or gives birth, without His knowledge."* (41:47)

It is sad that the Islamic call is very neglected and in some places non-existent. The way in which the Arabs neglect their duty is indefensible and will not be rectified as long as they are preoccupied with their desires and acts of disobedience which have made them a laughing-stock throughout the world. They have truly squandered their inheritance. *"Those who adulterate Our signs are not concealed from Us."* (41:40) *"Those who reject the Remembrance when it comes to them, truly it is a Mighty Book. Falsehood cannot come to it from before it or behind it..."* (41:41-42)

The Message of Muhammad, which the Arabs have all but lost sight of, is in fact the message of all the Prophets. *"Nothing has been said to you that was not said to the Messengers before you..."* (41:43) The People of the Book also squandered what they had and forgot its principles. *"And We gave Musa the Book and there were differences about it. Had it not been for a prior Word from your Lord, the judgement between them would already have been made."* (41:45) How strange it is, then, that these people are far more active than the Muslims in serving their distorted legacy and spend huge sums transporting missionaries to every part of the world!

The *sura* concludes with some *ayats* which concern both ancient and modern Arabs. *"Say: 'What do you really think? If it is from Allah and you reject it, who could be more misguided than someone who is in hostile opposition?'"* (41:52) Then the Almighty says: *"We shall show them Our signs on the horizon and within themselves until it is clear to them that it is the truth. Is it not enough for your Lord that He is witness of everything?"* (41:53) Every day the light of the Qur'an increases in radiance and its realities increase in substantiation. The truthfulness of the Prophethood of Muhammad is constantly verified. He called to sincere *tawhid.* No new way can be found. There is no way forward for humanity other than the Divine Guidance brought by the Last Prophet. He laid out a programme for the individual and for society and its governance. It lacks nothing but implementation. Is it marred by nothing but suspension and neglect. *"What! Are they in doubt about the meeting with their Lord? What! Does He not encompass all things?"* (41:54)

Sura 42
Ash-Shura: Counsel

After the five letters which begin *Surat ash-Shura*, Allah tells His Prophet: *"Thus He reveals to you and to those before you. Allah is the Almighty, the All-Wise."* (42:3) Prophets are sent with the language of their people and the words of Revelation are formed directly from letters. The Qur'an was sent down to Muhammad in clear Arabic and then he, may Allah bless him and grant him peace, conveyed it exactly as it was sent down to him and exemplified it in his character and behaviour. That is what his Companions and followers did after him: they fought to the utmost to efface evil from the earth and to correct the faults of humanity.

They did all they could, but since then the lower aspects of mankind have once more gained ascendancy on the earth and the Revelation has been all but forgotten. The earth has become a rebellious planet for want of the glorification and praise of its Creator. *"The heavens are all but rent apart above them when the angels glorify the praise of their Lord and ask forgiveness for those upon the earth. Allah is the Ever-Forgiving, the Most Merciful."* (42:5)

Revelation and its bearers are mentioned at the beginning and end of the *sura*, and in the middle we find the obligations imposed on the Arab nation, after Allah selected it for the Final Revelation, and the elucidation of its relationship to the people of the earlier Books. *"Thus We have revealed to you an Arabic Qur'an so that you may warn the Mother of the cities and all those round about it, and give warning of the Day of Gathering of which there is no doubt: one group in the Garden, the other in the Blaze."* (42:7)

It is clear that Islam is a universal and eternal *Deen* and that it is intended for the whole world until the end of time; but there must be a central point from which it spreads out. That point is *"the Mother of the cities and all those round about it"*. As for its area of dissemination, it is the entire world, North and South, East and West. Muhammad and his Companions performed their duty and hardly half a century passed before Islam had extended its rule over a good part of the world and the banners of the arrogant nations who had colonised Asia and Africa were pulled down.

What happened to the people of the previous Revelations to make this possible? The Jews relinquished all responsibility for calling other people to Allah and made the *Deen* their own exclusive property, allowing them to exploit others and exult in their own supposed superiority. The Christians imposed the doctrines of polytheism and redemption on the Revelation and indulged in endless discussion about the nature of 'the son of God'.

Islam came and proclaimed its firm connection with Musa and 'Isa, affirming that it confirmed and renewed the Revelations they brought: *"He has laid down the same* Deen *for you as He enjoined on Nuh: that which We have revealed to you and which We enjoined on Ibrahim, Musa and 'Isa: "Establish the* Deen *and do not make sects in it." What you call the idolaters to follow is very hard for them. Allah chooses for Himself anyone He wills and guides to Himself those who turn to Him."* (42:13)

The fact is that the *Deen* of Allah is one, from the beginning of creation until Allah inherits the earth and everyone on it. He is the Lord Whom the seven heavens and the earth and everything in them glorify. He has slaves whom He created by His power and raises in rank by His blessing. There are none among them who differ in respect of the attribute of slavehood. The closest of them to Him are those who prostrate the most to Him and have the strongest desire for Him and the most intense awe of Him. Affirmation of this is widespread throughout the entire Qur'an. It is the core of the *Deen* of Muhammad.

We recognise the truthfulness of Muhammad after we recognise Allah with our intellects and after we have seen that the Muhammadan revelation is never out of harmony with the intellect. The intellect is the best of mankind's gifts and what the utterances of Muhammad about Allah correspond to the most precise criteria of the human intellect. Yet people remain irrationally prejudiced against Muhammad and deny him, frequently justifying their antagonism on intellectual grounds. In reality, however, their hostility to him stems from their futile enmity towards his Master: *"They only divided after knowledge came to them, tyrannising one another. Were it not for a prior Decree from your Lord for a specified term, the judgement between them would already have been made. Those who inherited the Book after them are indeed in grave doubt about it."* (42:14)

So how should we deal with these tyrannical People of the Book in the light of this information about them? We should not pay attention to their hostility or have any truck with them. We must keep to our way our way calmly and fairly and as far as possible avoid conflict: *"So call and go straight as you have been ordered to. Do not follow their whims and desires, but say: 'I believe in a Book revealed by Allah and I am ordered to be just between you. Allah is our Lord and your Lord. We have our actions and you your actions. There is no argument between us and you. Allah will gather us all together. The final destination is to Him.'"* (42:15)

The early Muslims continued on their way of calling people to Allah and His Messenger, and large numbers of the People of the Book in the Middle East and North Africa responded to them, while at the same time countless pagans embraced the guidance of Islam in Iran, Azerbaijan, India and China. But the people of Europe for the most part rejected the Truth and their descendants in Europe and America, who have now, with the help of the Jews, now managed to dominate virtually the entire globe, still resist and fight *tawhid* and oppress Muhammad. And yet they do not harm Allah at all: *"The argument of those who argue about Allah, once He has been acknowledged, has no basis whatsoever with their Lord. There is wrath upon them and they will have a harsh punishment."* (42:16)

In spite of all their efforts the power of Islam has proved unstoppable and it has penetrated through to the point that there is now almost nowhere in the entire world where the *adhan* is not called. So Allah's Oneness and Muhammad's truthfulness are proclaimed daily in every land even though the unbelievers detest it!

Islam, when it is implemented properly, creates a community of people devoted to their Lord who make Allah their goal, His pleasure their hope, and preparation to meet Him their business! Does this mean that it produces a nation of monks? No, it produces a nation of people who work and worship, fight and pray, participating to the full in every aspect of life, serving both this world and the Next. The vital thing is that when you deal with the daily affairs of life you never lose sight of the fact that Allah is watching everything you do. We will be questioned about all our actions good and bad but if we keep Allah in mind we will have the good of this world and the Next: *"It is He who accepts repentance from His slaves, and pardons evil acts and He knows everything they do. He responds to those who believe and do right actions and gives them increase from His favour..."* (42:25-26) But a vast chasm separates a society worshipping this world from another whose focus is the Lord of all lords.

That is why the *sura* here reminds the believers about the incomparable greatness of the Originator of the heavens and the earth and *ayats* follow which use aspects of our earthly existence to connect our minds and hearts to Him: *"It is He who sends down abundant rain after they have become desperate and unfolds His mercy."* (42:28) *"Among His signs is the creation of the heavens and the earth and all the creatures He has scattered about in them."* (41:29) *"Among His signs are the ships sailing, like mountains on the sea."* (42:29) These *ayats* remind us that the natural laws which rule every aspect of existence are in themselves nothing other than the direct action of our Lord and so nothing that happens need or should distract us from Him.

For all its apparent superiority over previous civilisations, gained precisely by scientific manipulation of the natural world, the present civilisation has failed to understand this basic fact of existence which is in reality the secret of all its power. This blindness prevails because people's hearts are overwhelmed by their passion for this world and their refusal to acknowledge the existence of anything which cannot be measured by empirical means. This leads inevitably to the moral degeneration which inevitably incurs Divine anger and on account of which previous societies and peoples were destroyed, and which, in spite of all the rhetoric to the contrary, means that virtue and justice remain unattainable ideals.

In cautioning against that, the *sura* mentions nine qualities which are necessary for people to have if they wish to be safe from Divine anger: *"What you have been given is only the enjoyment of the life of this world. What is with Allah is better and longer lasting for those who (1) believe and (2) put their trust in their Lord, those who (3) avoid major wrong actions and indecencies and, (4) when they are angered, then forgive, those who (5) respond to their Lord and (6) establish the prayer, and (7) manage their affairs with mutual consultation, and (8) spend from what We have provided for them. Those who, (9) when they are wronged, defend themselves. The requital of a bad action is one equivalent to it. But if someone pardons and puts things right, his wage is with Allah. Certainly He does not love wrongdoers."* (42:36-40) As will be noticed, these few lines alone provide individual and communal guidelines for a complete social and political programme for any human community.

Mankind have the right to see among them a nation which implements this programme, which preserves the Revelation and observes its commands and prohibitions and establishes its rules in every place. The Arab nation which was honoured by the Final Revelation should certainly be among those who fulfil this role, and in the first years of Islam it can be said to have done so; but over the passage of time, it forgot and, indeed, returned to its original ignorance. In our time, we have seen something even worse. We have seen the Arabs disregard Islam and turn for their political identity to their ethnic and linguistic origins – Arab nationalism. This supposed nationalism has little or nothing to do with Islam and ironically it has gone hand in hand with the steady corruption of the very language on which its claims are based!

In the name of Arab nationalism, English, French and debased colloquial Arabic have flourished and the language of the Qur'an has become secondary and declined. A literature has been created lacking in moral values and imposed on the community at large, encouraging it to live outside the safety of the *Shari'a* laws.

Godlessness has succeeded in insinuating itself into the lands of Islam; up to now the Muslims have not succeeded in expelling it, and in some places they still welcome it in the name of enlightened progress! So in this *sura* we find a proclamation to the Arabs and a warning. *"Respond to your Lord before a day comes to you from Allah which cannot be turned back. On that Day you will have no hiding-place – there will be no way you can deny. But if they turn away, We have not sent you as a guardian over them. You are only responsible for delivering the Message."* (42:47-48)

Despite of copious rhetoric and some hot-headed action on the part of a few largely misguided extremists, the fact remains that the Arabs today have weakened their connection to Islam at a time when the Jews and others have strengthened their connection to their own religions.

As we have seen, *Surat ash-Shura* begins by speaking about the Divine Revelation and it also ends by speaking about it. It first explains how revelation occurs: *"It is not for any human being that Allah should speak to him except by inspiration, or from behind a veil, or He sends a messenger who then reveals that which He wills by His authority. He is indeed Most High, All-Wise."* (42:51) Allah sent Muhammad with a Book which contains healing for all humanity in every time and place.

The Book has conveyed knowledge and established a state, and bequeathed a legacy. It is a citadel to protect the entire world from deviation and decline: *"Accordingly We have revealed to you a Spirit by Our command. You had no idea what the Book was, nor faith. Nonetheless We have made it a light by which We guide those of Our slaves We will. You truly guide to a straight path: the Path of Allah, Him to whom everything in the heavens and everything in the earth belongs. Indeed all matters return eventually to Allah."* (42:52-53)

Sura 43
Az-Zukhruf: Gold Ornaments

As may well be gathered from its title, the main theme of *Surat az-Zukhruf* is the erroneous human tendency to ascribe all power to sensory phenomena and to fail to take account of what lies beyond the range of the five senses. It begins with the *ayats*: *"Ha Mim. By the Book which makes things clear. We have made it an Arabic Qur'an so that perhaps you may use your intellects."* (43:1-3) As we have noted several times elsewhere, the Arabic of the Qur'an only confers distinction on the people of its language, the Arabs, to the extent that they uphold and implement its Message. Allah chose Arabic as the language for His Final Revelation on account of its linguistic purity and its consequent ability to contain the depth and power of the meanings of His Uncreated Word.

The *sura* unveils the logical inconsistency into which idolaters fall since most of them in fact acknowledge that there is a supreme Deity. *"If you asked them, 'Who created the heavens and the earth?' they would say, 'The Almighty, the All-Knowing created them.'"* (43:9) *"If you asked them who created them, they would say, 'Allah!' 'How then are they perverted?'"* (43:87) If Allah, the Almighty and All-Knowing, is the One who created them and created the heavens and the earth, then what is the function of all the other things they worship? What is their business? Would it not be more sensible for them to recognise Allah alone and to direct themselves to Him alone? *"He who made the earth a cradle for you and made pathways in it for you so that perhaps you might be guided; He who sends down water in due measure from the sky by which We bring a dead land back to life. That is how you too will be brought forth."* (43:10-11)

The idolaters claim that Allah has sons who form part of Him. That is a lie. Allah has no composite parts and cannot be described as either son or father. He is Absolutely Singular and the Everlasting Sustainer of everything in existence. This *sura* cites this claim and refutes it. *"Say: 'If the All-Merciful had a son, I would be the first to worship him. Glory be to the Lord of the heavens and the earth, the Lord of the Throne, beyond what they describe.'"* (43:81-82)

The idolaters persisted in their lies and claimed that Allah led them to idolatry and authorised them to do it. So it is made clear that their rejection is stupidity and obduracy. *"Similarly We never sent before you any warner to any city without the affluent among them saying, 'We found our fathers following a religion and we are simply following in their footsteps.' Say: 'What if I have come with better guidance than what you found your fathers following?' They say: 'We reject what you have been sent with.' So We took revenge on them. See what was the end result of the deniers!"* (43:23-25)

Denial of the Truth in fact results from unbridled appetites overpowering the heart and intellect, not from weighed evidence. It is the passions and desires hidden in people's souls that impede them from affirming what is in fact self-evident. It precludes people from being able to acknowledge the reality of anything beyond the range of their ordinary experience and, as was mentioned above, that is the main theme of this *sura*.

The Noble Qur'an brings this to light in more than one place. *"Thamud denied the warnings, saying, 'Are we to follow a human being, one of us? Then we would truly be astray, completely mad! Has the Reminder been given to him out of all of us? No indeed! He is an impertinent liar.'"* (54:23-25) It is the envy and malice in people's hearts which provokes their denial. In *Sura Sad* we find in a similar vein: *"'Has the Reminder been sent down to him out of all of us?' No indeed! They are in doubt about My Reminder. No indeed! They have yet to taste My punishment."* (38:8) And here in this *sura*: *"Why was this Qur'an not sent down to one of the great men of the two cities?"* (43:31)

The two cities referred to here are Makka and Ta'if. The question is: "Why was the Qur'an not revealed to some powerful political figure, to one of the leaders of society?" Class prejudice dominated them as it dominates the people of our own time. People then as now were unable to distinguish between the appearance of power and its reality. Yet even a few moments' reflection would be sufficient to make one realise that worldly leaders are in fact the most unsuitable people of all to convey messages of moral reform and to deliver their nations from darkness to light!

In earlier times, the Tribe of Israel objected to Saul being appointed king over them. *"They said, 'How can he have sovereignty over us when we have more right to sovereignty than him? He has not even much wealth.'"* (2:247) The reply was: *"Allah has chosen him over you and favoured him greatly in knowledge and physical stature. Allah gives kingship to whomever He wills."* (2:257) The enlightenment of nations, true liberation and elevating whole peoples from the bottom to the top of the social scale requires special inner qualities and men of Divine inspiration. Men of great wealth or physical might are not suited to that task.

In ordinary life some people are in charge of others. The manager directs the worker and the general commands the soldier, and people gain and keep their positions through their aptitude for the job they do. How much more is this the case where the Prophetic function is concerned! Absolute purity of spirit, inner radiance by Divine choice and gift, and perfection of character in every situation are the necessary qualifications for Divine Messengers, none of which have anything to do with the normal human criteria of power and success.

That is why Allah Almighty says to reject the aim of the ignorant to select one of their chiefs as a Prophet: *"Is it they, then, who allocate the mercy of your Lord? We have allocated their livelihood among them in the life of this world and raised some of them over others in rank so that some of them are subservient to others. But the mercy of your Lord is better than anything they amass."* (43:32) People's differences of rank with regard to the tasks of this world is necessary and inevitable in every field of human endeavour but the Message of Allah is His business and He places it in those human containers He has chosen for the task of conveying it so that they may educate humanity in the deepest sense and raise them to the high possibilities Allah has made available to them.

This blindness regarding appearances does not stop here but is also very prevalent where wealth is concerned. Almost everyone is dazzled by it but the enjoyment of the goods of this world, which some people have in abundance, is not necessarily a token of good. Allah frequently expands the provision of people who are destined to end up in Hell while many individuals, of whom 'Ammar ibn Yasir and Bilal ibn Rabah are notable examples, are tested by extreme poverty and even slavery, although they are the kings of the Garden.

Allah makes it clear here that were it not for the fact that most people are deceived by wealth, He would have shown in what scant regard He holds it by bestowing it lavishly on the unbelievers! *"Were it not for the fact that people might become one nation, We would have given those who disbelieve in the All-Merciful silver roofs to their houses and silver stairways to ascend and silver doors to their houses and silver couches to recline upon, and gold ornaments. All of that is merely the trappings of the life of this world. But the Next World with your Lord is for the godfearing."* (43:33-35)

People who are deluded by this world into forgetting the omnipresence of Allah find themselves with unwelcome company. *"If someone shuts his eyes to the remembrance of the All-Merciful, We assign him a shaytan who becomes his bosom friend. They debar them from the path and yet they still think they are guided."* (43:36) These inseparable comrades make it very difficult indeed for their hosts to return to the path of right guidance and begin to make their lives unpleasant in many unexpected ways. The Prophet, peace and blessing be upon him, is informed how we can avoid this unfortunate fate. *"So hold fast to what has been revealed to you. You are on a straight path. It is most certainly a reminder to you and to your people, and you will be questioned."* (43:43-44)

The only way for people to be safe from the snare of this world is to cling resolutely to the core of the Prophetic teaching. *"Ask those We sent before you as Our Messengers: Have We ever appointed, apart from the All-Merciful, any other gods to be worshipped?"* (43:45) Otherwise there is always the danger of being deceived by the illusion of wealth and power in this world and, as an ultimate example of this, Allah once more cites the story of Pharaoh and Musa. Pharaoh was not just the leader of a small town like Ta'if but the King of Egypt, the cradle of civilisation, and the master of the Nile, the source of so much wealth.

Musa came to ask him to believe in Allah and refrain from his injustices towards those who were oppressed and persecuted. But Pharaoh suffered from the ultimate human delusion, one that is all too common in this time: that of making himself the measure of existence and arrogating to himself complete control over it. *"Pharaoh called to his people, saying, 'O my people! Does the kingdom of Egypt not belong to me, and all these rivers flowing under my control? Do you not then see? Am I not better than this man who is contemptible and can scarcely make things clear? Why then have gold bracelets not been put on his arms and why is there not a train of angels accompanying him?'"* (43:51-53) Again we note this propensity to judge by outward appearances alone.

Pharaoh denied Musa and pursued him and his people until they reached the Red Sea. The tribe of Israel crossed the sea, led by Musa, and Pharaoh would not let them go, but had to prove his power over them. He tried to catch up with them with the result that he and those with him were all drowned. When Pharaoh was aware he was drowning, he said, *"I believe that there is no god but Him in whom the tribe of Israel believe. I am one of those who submit."* (10:90) In the face of death all the illusions of this world evaporate; but at that point it is too late to do anything about it. What good were the much-vaunted gold bracelets then?

This human tendency to want to bring the Divine down to earth and to glorify this world finds another expression in the Christian heresy, and so Allah speaks of it here to show how the Christians misunderstood what 'Isa was calling them to and indeed how that misunderstanding could be used to justify outright idolatry. *"When an example is made of the son of Maryam, then your people laugh uproariously at it. They retort, 'Who is better, our gods or him?'*

They only say this to you for argument's sake. They are indeed a disputatious people." (43:57-58)

But in fact 'Isa's Message was no different from that of all the Prophets. *"And when 'Isa came with the Clear Signs, he said, 'I have come to you with Wisdom and to clarify for you some of the things about which you have differed. Therefore show fear of Allah and obey me. Allah is my Lord and your Lord, so worship Him. This is a straight path.'"* (43:63-64) The subsequent confusion was all of their own making, and the various positions they took were often more to do with power in this world than with concern for the Next. *"The various factions among them differed. Woe then to those who did wrong for the punishment of a painful Day!"* (43:64-65)

It is only in the Next World, however, that the reality of this world finds its true expression. It is there that those who held to the truth in this world and were not deluded by its appearance of permanence will find their reward. *"'Enter the Garden, you and your wives, delighting in your joy.' Platters and cups of gold will passed around among them and they will have there all that their souls desire and their eyes find delight in. You shall remain in it timelessly forever. That is the Garden you shall inherit for what you did."* (43:70) So it is there, in the true permanence of the Next World, that golden utensils have their real place.

Those who fell into the trap of this world will reap the reward of their short-sighted delusion. *"The evil-doers will be in the punishment of Hell timelessly forever. It will not be alleviated for them. They will be crushed there by despair."* (43:74-75) They thought that one thing was going on when the reality was very different. *"Or have they hatched a plot? It is We who are the Hatcher!"* (43:79) The implacable truth is that it is Allah who has absolute power at every moment in every sphere of existence. *"It is He who is God in heaven and God on earth. He is the All-Wise, the All-Knowing."* (43-84) And success in both worlds can only be obtained by those who truly understand this and therefore follow the guidance of the Qur'an and of Allah's final Messenger who conveyed it to us.

Sura 44
Ad-Dukhan: Smoke

Surat ad-Dukhan begins with an oath on the Noble Qur'an: *"By the Book which makes things clear, We sent it down on a blessed night;"* (44:2-3) this is generally understood to refer to the Night of Power in Ramadan. Commentators err when they suggest that it might refer to the middle night of Sha'ban. The night is blessed by the fact that the Final Revelation was sent down in it. It is a Revelation full of wisdom, light and abundant good, and the blessing it holds is mentioned elsewhere. *"A Book We have sent down to you, containing blessing, so let them ponder its signs..."* (38:29) *"And this Book - We have sent it down, blessed, so follow it ..."* (6:155) The blessing of this Book is that it produces transformed human beings. It produced from the uncouth Arabs a great and enlightened civilisation covering a large part of the world and has never ceased to transform those who recite it and implement its teaching.

"We are constantly giving warning." (44:3) This Divine warning concerns both the prevalent wrongdoing and its destruction in this world as well as its fate in the World to Come. The justice of Islam can only established after the elimination of the tyranny which precedes it and, by Allah, it will certainly succeed in doing so! The main theme of the *sura* is to point out the stupidity of people pitting themselves against Allah's power.

It is well known that at the beginning the Arabs resisted the call of Islam and that they persecuted those who took it on and drove them from their homes, until the Prophet called on his Lord: "O Allah! Help me against them with seven like the seven of Yusuf!" (referring to the seven years of drought which afflicted Egypt and the surrounding area at the time of Yusuf, which he foretold on the basis of Pharaoh's dream). There was a drought in the land and the rain stopped. The idolaters became hungry. The people went to the Messenger of Allah, may Allah bless him and grant him peace, to ask him to pardon his people. But after he pardoned them and well-being returned to them, they reneged. *"We remove the punishment just a little and you revert! On the day We launch the Great Assault, We will surely take Our revenge."* (44:15-16) Allah's revenge was taken on the Day of Badr when many of the leaders of Quraysh were killed and a humiliating defeat was inflicted on them.

That is the usual explanation of these *ayats* but, as is often the case, they are also open to a more general interpretation. The "distinctive smoke" which gives the *sura* its name and which is referred to as coming from the sky may well be a cosmic event which has yet to take place. We are now regularly warned about the holes in the ozone layer and the dangers they represent for mankind, which shows how the atmosphere can be affected by man's own unbridled use of the earth's natural resources. This has in fact come about through man's refusal to submit to Divine guidance and the limits which that imposes on human exploitation. It seems likely that if this is allowed to continue unchecked it will certainly lead to self-induced disasters on an unprecedented scale. In any case, the general Reckoning will come on the Last Day when every soul will be paid in full for what it did or failed to do.

Pharaoh had far more power than any of the leaders with whom the Prophet was confronted, and indeed more than those of our time, yet it was of no use whatsoever to him when Allah decided to help His Messenger. What was his end and the end of those with him? They were all destroyed. *"How many gardens and fountains they left behind, and ripe crops and noble residences! What comfort and ease they were delighting in! So it was! Yet we bequeathed these things to another people."* (44:25-27) Historical cycles endlessly repeat. The final result of injustice at all times is always the same.

The important thing is that those who follow Divine Guidance should implement it fully and that their actions tally with their words. But the sad thing is that the reign of righteousness is almost always short-lived. Passion and appetite quickly overpower people's hearts and they abandon the legacy of their Prophets. The Almighty says about the Jews: *"We chose them knowingly above all other people and We gave them Signs containing a clear trial."* (44:32-33) What did they do after they were liberated and given power? They soon became corrupt and implacable Destiny shredded them in turn. After them the Arabs inherited the Divine Message and flourished as long as they implemented it. Then they left it, except for a few of them, and were overtaken by inevitable punishment awaiting every degenerate. Now they are a passive flock preyed on by every tyrant!

The people of the modern civilisation possess a large measure of superficial cleverness although most of them do not pay any attention to the life of the Next World. It does not occur to their minds that they will meet Allah one day. They resemble the people of the *Jahiliyya* of the Arabs of the peninsula who mocked the idea of life after death and considered it to be a myth. *"These people say, 'There is nothing but our first death. We will not be raised up a second time. Produce our fathers if you speak the truth.'"* (44:34-36) In reality such people are not clever at all but deeply stupid. *"We did not create the heavens and the earth and everything between them as a game. We did not create them except with truth. But most of them do not know."* (44:38-40)

The truth by which the heavens and the earth were created is manifest in the precise laws which govern both atom and galaxy, ant and flea, plains and woods, land and sea. There are serious sciences which research all these areas and uncover wonders which proclaim the immensity of the Creator and Sustainer of all of them. The Truth will become manifest at the Reckoning when all resistance to Divine Power will be shown to have been completely futile. The difference between the Muslims and the wrongdoers, those who remember and the heedless, those with live consciences and dead consciences will become clearly apparent benefit! *"The Day of Decision is their rendezvous all together: the Day when friends will be of no use at all to one another."* (44:40-41) *"The Tree of az-Zaqqum is the food of the sinful, seething in the belly like molten brass as boiling water bubbles and seethes."* (44:43-

46) *"The godfearing will be in a safe place: amid gardens and fountains, wearing fine silk and rich brocade, face to face with one another."* (44:51-53)

Allah Almighty revealed the Qur'an to Muhammad to awaken the heedless and through him to produce a nation which would implement the Divine Guidance he brought. May we be among those who fulfil this task! *"We have made it easy in your tongue so that perhaps they may remember. So watch and wait. They too are waiting."* (44:58-59)

Sura 45
Al-Jathiya: Kneeling

Sura al-Jathiya is one of the *suras* devoted to Allah's signs as they appear both in His Revealed Book and also in the great Book of Existence. It begins by encouraging us to study the Book of Existence and examine its signs, because if we do reflect deeply on the domain of the heavens and the earth and the wonders they contain that will inevitably lead us to Allah – glory be to Him! *"Ha Mim. The Revelation of the Book is from Allah, the Mighty, the Wise. In the heavens and the earth there are certainly signs for the believers. And in your creation and all the animals He has scattered about there are signs for people with certainty. And in the alternation of night and day and the provision Allah sends down from the sky, bringing the earth to life by it after it has died, and the varying direction of the winds, there are signs for people who use their intellects."* (45:1-5)

There are similar *ayats* in *Surat al-Baqara*, *Ali 'Imran* and elsewhere. What is intended is the underpinning of the rational basis of faith. But reflection alone is not enough to ensure man's happiness. It is also necessary for us to utilise existence to provide for our needs. That is what it was created for. *"It is Allah who has made the sea subservient to you so that the ships sail on it at His command, enabling you to seek His bounty, so that perhaps you may show thanks. And He has made everything in the heavens and everything in the earth subservient to you. It is all from Him. There are certainly signs in that for people who reflect."* (45:12-13)

As mastery of the laws of existence benefits man materially in the life of this world, they also enable him to strengthen and protect his faith. The failure of the Muslims to grasp this has resulted in their abasement at the hands of their enemies. *"Those are the signs of Allah We recite to you with truth. In what discourse, after*

Allah and His signs, will they then believe?" (45:6) The Qur'an directs people by its *ayats* and existence indicates Allah by its signs, so why have people deviated after that and become misguided? *"Woe to every evil liar!"* (45:8)

In addition to this twofold guidance, as a mercy to His slaves, Allah defers the punishment of those who have strayed from His way. He increases the opportunity for them to be guided and orders the Muslims to be patient in presenting the call and to give every chance to the unbelievers. *"Tell those who believe to forgive those who feel no apprehension about the Days of Allah, when He will repay people according to what they earned. Whoever acts rightly, it is to his own benefit. Whoever does evil, it is to his detriment. Then you shall be returned to your Lord."* (45:14-15)

The two paths of guidance we have referred to are matched by two branches of knowledge: the intellectual and physical sciences and the transmitted knowledges of the *Shari'a*. These two kinds of knowledge can both lead man to the path of right guidance but what has happened is that the majority of those who study the material sciences are not guided by them. They have invaded space and yet continue to reject Allah. They see foetuses being created in the womb but instead of recognising the Creator they assert that the doer is blind chance.

This godlessness is the general hallmark of modern civilisation which now encompasses the whole globe. The worst thing is that this scientific obtuseness has even spread to those who study the branches of religious knowledge. Their studies have been transformed into a formal academic discipline which does not improve their souls or refine their moral character. They fit the Qur'anic description of donkeys carrying boxes of books with no connection to what they contain. Half of the corruption in the world derives from the indolence of the men of religion and their mental stupidity!

Unless religious knowledge results in the spread of truthfulness and justice, there is no good or worth in it. Now there are religious scholars and scientists with dead consciences, while it lies within the power of both to render much good to humanity. *"Have you seen him who takes his own desires to be his god – he whom Allah has misguided knowingly, sealing up his hearing and his heart and placing a blindfold over his eyes? Who then will guide him after Allah?"* (45:23)

Intelligence where this world is concerned and stupidity where the Next World is concerned make people the slaves of their own appetites and desires. That is the unfortunate fate of so many people in this time, and Allah makes it clear that even their claims to be atheists are false since the reality is that they have deified their own desires! But their sorry state means that they see this life alone and are prevented from preparing for what comes after it. *"They say: 'There is nothing but our life in this world. We die and we live and nothing destroys us except for time itself.' They have no knowledge of that. They are only conjecturing."* (45:24)

That is why the end of this *sura* is concerned with the reality of the Resurrection and Reckoning and describes the different positions people will have before their Lord when He questions them about what they did. *"The sovereignty of the heavens and earth belongs to Allah and on the Day that the Hour arrives – on that Day the liars will be lost. You will see every nation on its knees, every nation summoned to its Book: 'Today you shall be repaid for what you did. This is Our Book speaking against you with the truth. We have been recording everything you did.'"* (45:27-29)

Anyone who reflects on the civilisation of this time will see that scientific progress has made human life more comfortable and pleasures easy to obtain. It has attached people to the short span they spend here and distracted them from the endless eternity which awaits them beyond death. The People of the Book are incapable of bringing people back to Allah and they have joined with the enemies of all faith in striking at Islam and preventing its advance. The result is moral and social chaos throughout the entire world. It is no wonder that these words will confront them on the Day of Rising: *"They will be told, 'Today We have forgotten you as you forgot the meeting of this Day of yours. Your refuge is the Fire. You have no helpers.'"* (45:34) Those who worship this world have at best a small immediate profit; and their eventual loss is total.

"All praise belongs to Allah, Lord of the heavens and Lord of the earth, the Lord of all the worlds. All greatness belongs to Him in the heavens and earth. He is the Almighty, the All-Wise." (45:36-37) The end of the *sura* echoes its beginning by glorifying Allah and repeating two of His Names – the Almighty, the All-Wise.

Sura 46
Al-Ahqaf: The Sand Dunes

Surat al-Ahqaf is the last of the *suras* of the family of *HaMim*. Each one of these seven *suras* begins by confirming the revelation of the Noble Book from the Lord of the worlds. All mankind must attend to it as a student attends to his teacher, as a seeker of knowledge attends to him who imparts it to him, so that they may be guided and come into the light.

This *sura* also makes it clear at its beginning that Allah forms the cells in living bodies just as He manages the systems in distant galaxies and that one does not distract Him from the other in any way. This universe in which we live has a life-span at whose conclusion it will end, just as we end when our life-spans reach their conclusion. Then we will begin a second life in which we shall reap what we sowed here: *"We have not created the heavens and the earth and everything between them except with truth and with a designated term. Those who reject turn away from that about which they have been warned."* (46:3) They turn away from two things: from the true laws which regulate the universe and the from fate which awaits all when they are taken to account for what they did.

Then the *sura* discusses the debate which took place between the Messenger and the idolaters when the latter were trying to justify their beliefs and conduct. It points out the irrationality of the idolaters' position and their total lack of evidence to support it. *"Say: 'Have you really thought about the things you call upon apart from Allah? Show me what they have created in the earth. Or do they have a partnership in the heavens? Produce a Book for me before this one, or a shred of knowledge, if you are people who speak the truth.'"* (46:4) Nor is it effective in any real way that can be demonstrated – in fact quite the reverse. *"Who could be further astray than those who call upon things, apart from Allah, which will not respond to them until the Day of Rising and which are unaware of their prayers?"* (46:5)

The idolaters claim that the Qur'an was made up by Muhammad! *"Or do they say, 'He has invented it'? Say: 'If I have invented it, then you possess no power to help me against Allah in any way. He knows best what you hold forth about. He is witness enough between me and you..."* (46:8) Yet the Qur'an demonstrably did have a profound effect on those who heard it, either inspiring them with awe at the majesty and beauty of their Creator or repelling them like cockroaches fleeing from the light.

Hence the statement that the Qur'an was produced by Muhammad is itself irrational, since it is evident that he is simply a conduit for a powerful energy which far exceeded his normal style of self-expression. And this is known to have happened on previous occasions. *"Say: 'I am nothing new among the Messengers. I have no idea what will be done with me or you. I follow only what has been revealed to me. I am only a clear warner.'"* (46:9)

The people of Makka in fact had no excuse for denying the possibility of Prophethood. The Jews in Madina claimed to be following Musa and indeed those who were truly righteous among them became convinced of the truth of Muhammad's Message. So there was no reason to deny Revelation in general or to deny the Prophethood of Muhammad in particular. *"Say: 'What do you think? If it is from Allah and you reject it, when a witness from the tribe of Israel testifies to the like of it and believes while you are arrogant...! Allah does not guide wrongdoing people.'"* (46:10) Unfortunately the connection of the people of earlier Books to their own Books is often extremely tenuous; but it is impossible to find anyone with true knowledge of Allah who dislikes a man who tells people: *"Those who say, 'Our Lord is Allah' and then go straight, they will feel no fear, they will know no sorrow. Those are the Companions of the Garden, in it timelessly forever, as recompense for what they did."* (46:13-14)

When the Message was presented it began to divide families into believers and unbelievers. Sometimes parents would be guided and children misguided, or the other way round. Sometimes Islam permeated the whole family and it was possible to say: *"O my Lord, keep me thankful for Your blessing You bestowed on me and my parents, and keep me acting rightly, pleasing You. Make my descendants righteous. I have turned in repentance to You and I am truly one of the Muslims."* (46:15) But in the former case the unity of the family was disrupted. *"But what of him who says to his parents, 'Fie on you! Do you promise me that I will brought forth when generations before me have passed away?' They both call on Allah for help: 'Woe to you! Believe! Allah's promise is true.' But he says, 'This is nothing but the myths of earlier peoples.' Those are people about whom the statement regarding the nations of jinn and men who passed away before them is also proved true. Truly they were the losers."* (46:17-18)

Frequently the lives of unbelievers are devoted to pleasure, to the gratification of their appetites, concerned mostly with amusement and entertainment. That is why Allah says about them: *"The Day when those who rejected are exposed before the Fire: 'You dissipated your good things in your worldly life and enjoyed yourself in it. Therefore today you are being repaid with the punishment of humiliation...'"* (46:20) For this reason 'Umar ibn al-Khattab used to forgo many of the pleasures of this life. Ibn 'Atiyya mentioned that when 'Umar went to Syria, Khalid ibn al-Walid brought him some fine food and 'Umar said, "Is this for us? What about the poor Muslims who died without ever having had their fill of barley bread?"

"They have Paradise," Khalid replied.

'Umar wept. "If this is our portion and they have Paradise: we are very far apart!"

'Umar was frugal in his life and never had more food than the poor Muslims. We know that Allah has not forbidden His slaves good things but it is to be feared that people of plenty will become people of luxury and forget their duties and obligations.

The pagans' unreasoning hostility towards Islam was fierce and they opposed it at every opportunity. The Muslims were steadfast in the face of this aggression and the Qur'an strengthened them, offering them lessons from history to reassure them of the eventual success of the Mission, however fierce and oppressive the enemy might seem at the time. *"Remember the brother of 'Ad when he warned his people by the sand-dunes, and warners passed away before him and after him: 'Worship none but Allah. I fear for you the punishment of a terrible day.'"* (46:21) Is it the punishment of the Day of Rising which is being referred to here, or is it the punishment of destruction in this world?

The people of 'Ad lived in the south of Yemen in the sands which extended near Hadramawt. We have already mentioned how they were distinguished by sturdiness, might and strength. They reviled their Prophet Hud and dismissed him. Allah admonished them by years of drought in which He denied them rain but the crisis did not make them relent and did not restrain their evil. They said to Hud: *"Have you come to us to divert us from our gods? Bring us what you promised us if you are one who speaks the truth."* (46:22)

It was not long before what they sought to hasten came to them! They looked at the horizon and saw a cloud coming and rejoiced in the rain that they had been long awaiting to relieve the drought. *"When they saw it as a storm cloud approaching their valleys, they said, 'This is a storm cloud which will give us rain.' No, rather it is that you wanted to hasten on: a wind containing painful punishment, destroying everything at its Lord's command. When morning came you could see nothing but their dwellings."* (46:24-25) The living were destroyed and the houses remained desolate and empty.

'Ad were far stronger than Quraysh but that fact did not enable them to overcome Allah's Messenger. People are prevented from believing because they put their intellects to sleep, blindfold their eyes and block up their ears against the truth. *"We established them firmly in a way that We have not established you, and gave them hearing, sight and hearts. But their hearing, sight and hearts did not avail them in any way when they repudiated Allah's signs. The things they mocked at encompassed them."* (46:26)

Quraysh lived in the middle of the Arabian peninsula. They used to pass by the destroyed cities of Salih and the towns of the people of Lut which had been overturned, and they knew what had happened to Sheba and to the people of Tubba'. Their idols did not help any of them. *"No, in fact they have forsaken them. That was their fantasy, something they fabricated."* (46:28) To combat the renowned obduracy of the people of Makka, the Qur'an was forced to cite enough examples to suffice all who call to the Truth until the end of time to enable them to defend the Truth and make its guidance available.

Then *Surat al-Ahqaf* mentions that in spite of the fact that so many people did not respond to the Noble Qur'an, a group of jinn listened to it and were guided by it. This leads us to a slight digression. Superstitious people tend to put too much emphasis on unseen things and to loosen the reins of their imagination too far. The Qur'an says about Shaytan, *"He and his tribe see you from where you do not see them."* (7:27) Such people write books about the life of the jinn and about their intermarriage with human beings and how they can be angered, and other things which make people spend far too much time worrying about things that do not concern them in any way, to the point that it can really distract them from the worship of Allah.

Notice what the Noble Qur'an relates about the jinn in this instance: *"And We diverted a band of the jinn towards you to listen to the Qur'an. When they were in earshot of it, they said, 'Be quiet and listen.' When it was over they went back to their people, warning them."* (46:29) This shows that the power of the Qur'an is such that it penetrates the Unseen. *"O people, respond to Allah's caller and believe in Him. He will forgive you some of your wrong actions and guard you from a painful punishment."* (46:31)

Nevertheless most of Quraysh resisted every attempt to bring them out of their darkness and warn them of the Resurrection and Reckoning. *"Do they not see that Allah – He who created the heavens and the earth, and was in no way wearied by creating them – has the power to bring the dead to life? On the contrary, He has power over all things."* (46:33) 'Ad were stronger than Quraysh and the jinn are stronger than both of them but that still does not restrain the arrogance of human prejudice.

Surat al-Ahqaf ends with an *ayat* which instructs Muhammad to adopt the firm resolve of the Messengers who preceded him –

Nuh, Ibrahim, Musa and 'Isa – who also suffered at the hands of their peoples in the same way as him but who nevertheless remained steadfast until their Missions were fulfilled. *"Therefore be steadfast as the Messengers with firm resolve were also steadfast. And do not seek to hasten it on for them...."* (46:35) Remember that time is entirely relative and that even if the struggle takes years, once it is over it will seem as if no time has passed at all. *"On the Day they see what they were promised, it will be as if they had tarried for just one hour of a single day."* (46:35) This is all they remember: *"It has been delivered! Will any be destroyed except degenerate people?"* (46:35)

Sura 47
Muhammad

This is also called the *Sura* of Fighting (*Surat al-Qital*). It explains that the Messenger of Allah, may Allah bless him and grant him peace, is both the Prophet of Mercy and the Prophet of Battles, and that he will take revenge on the unjust for those who have been wronged and allow people who have been injured to retaliate. He will not leave injustice and outrage strutting arrogantly on the earth. He will curb them and pull their teeth.

In order to recognise the tone of this *sura*, first ask yourself: what do the people of Bosnia harbour in their hearts towards the Serbs who slaughtered their men and raped their women? They harbour nothing but anger and hatred. What do the people of Palestine feel about the Jews who drove them out of their homes and killed so many of them and usurped their rights? They feel nothing but anger and hostility.

What do you expect the Noble Qur'an to say to someone who has been oppressed and persecuted when he meets his tormentor? It says to him: *"Fight them! Allah will punish them at your hands, and disgrace them and help you against them, and heal the hearts of a people who believe. He will remove the rage from their hearts."* (9:14-15) And what we find in this *sura*: *"So when you meet those who reject strike their necks. Then when you have decimated them, tie their bonds tightly and set them free or ransom them – until the war is finally over. That is how it is to be. If Allah willed, He would avenge Himself on them. But it is so that He may test some of you by means of others."* (47:4) War is a bitter medicine, but the illness incurred by not fighting is more bitter still, as Shawqi says:

> War is a law for you
> and a cure for latent poisons.

The *sura* begins with *ayats* which express a timeless universal law: *"Those who reject and bar from the way of Allah, Allah will make their actions go astray. But those who believe and do right actions and believe in what has been sent down to Muhammad – and it is the truth from their Lord – He will erase their bad actions from them and put their affairs right. That is because those who reject follow falsehood, whereas those who believe follow the truth from their Lord. In that way Allah coins likenesses for mankind."* (47:1-3) The *sura* is unified by having the same idea repeated at its end where Allah says: *"Those who reject and bar from the way of Allah, and split off from the Messenger after the guidance has become clear to them, do not harm Allah in any way and He will make their actions come to nothing."* (47:32)

Muslims often recite this *sura* out loud in groups on the battlefield because it has a particular rhythm, unique in the whole Qur'an, which unsettles the hearts of the enemy. The whole tone of the *sura* is very martial and urges on the believers, assuring them of success in battle so long as the fight is for the Cause of Allah. *"O you who believe, if you help Allah, He will help you and make your feet firm. And those who reject will have utter ruin and He will make their actions go astray."* (47:7-8)

In the course of these military instructions, the Qur'an mentions the fate of the martyrs and the reward which awaits them. *"Those who fight in the Way of Allah, He will not let their actions go astray. He will guide them and better their condition. He will admit them into the Garden which He has made known to them."* (47:4-6) And later the Garden is described in graphic, alluring detail. *"The likeness of the Garden promised to the godfearing: in it there are rivers of water which will never spoil and rivers of milk whose taste will never change and rivers of wine, a pure delight to those who drink, and rivers of honey of undiluted purity..."* (47:15)

In the midst of this examination of the necessary physical struggle between the believers and the unbelievers, the discussion extends to the hypocrites so that their sick secrets may be disclosed and society protected from its hidden enemies. These were the people who joined with the Muslims in their assembly around

the noble Messenger and listened to the directives which came –
but whose hearts were sick. They participated in the acts of worship which required little effort and informed the opponents of
Islam about what took place between the Prophet and his
Companions. But they could not help giving themselves away by
making comments which revealed their concealed disbelief.
*"Among them are those who listen to you and then, when they
leave your presence, say to those who have been given knowledge,
'What was that he just said?' They are those whose hearts Allah
has sealed up and who follow their own desires."* (47:16)

This is a question tainted with either the affectation of ignorance or mockery. It is clear that they are terrified at the prospect
of having to fight and tremble lest the command to fight be
revealed. They have no faith to defend and are only concerned
with protecting their own best interests, which makes them cowards. *"But when a clear-cut* sura *is sent down and fighting is mentioned in it, you see those with sickness in their hearts looking at
you with the look of someone about to faint from fear of death."*
(47:20)

The hypocrite's sin is twice as grave as that of the unbeliever.
There are unbelievers who do not know anything about Islam and
fight it out of stupidity. These hypocrites were in the midst of the
Muslims, listened to the Revelation as it was being revealed, and
were able to observe the behaviour of the Messenger, so they have
no excuse. *"Those who have turned back in their tracks after the
guidance became clear to them, it was Shaytan who urged them on
and filled them with false hopes."* (47:25)

In our own time the hypocrites have revived the behaviour of
those earlier impostors. They receive instructions from worldwide
missionary groups or from the centres of cultural invasion and
infiltrate the masses seeking to provoke sedition. They spread mis-
information, preferring hostile points of view, and dishearten people engaged in the struggle to re-establish the *Deen*. *"That is
because they said to those who hate what Allah had revealed, 'We
will obey you in respect of some of the matter.' But Allah knows
their secrets. How will it be when the angels take them in death,
beating their faces and their backs? That is because they followed*

what angers Allah and found hateful what is pleasing to Him. Therefore He made their actions come to nothing." (47:26-28) Allah has branded these hypocrites, but their behaviour would disclose them in any case, and their actions give them away. Their words betray their secret. *"If We willed, We would show them to you and you would know them by their mark and know them by their ambivalent speech. Allah knows your actions."* (47:30)

The *sura* ends firstly by telling the believers not to surrender, however fierce and long the battle – *"Do not become fainthearted and call for peace when you are the uppermost and Allah is with you. He would never cheat you of your deeds"* (47:35) – and then by condemning those who shrink from spending what they have in the cause of the Truth. *"Here you are then: people who are called upon to spend in the Way of Allah and then some of you are stingy! But anyone stingy is stingy only to himself. Allah is the Rich. You are the poor. If you turn away, He will replace you with a people other than yourselves and they will not be the same as you."* (47:38) Generosity and courage go hand in hand, and stinginess can be just as destructive to society as cowardice.

Sura 48
Al-Fath: Victory

The Muslims returned dispirited from the failed *'umra* expedition of al-Hudaybiyya. They had been hoping to visit the Sacred House, perform *tawaf* around the Ka'ba, and run between Safa and Marwa, but had not achieved their purpose. They were returning from Makka after difficult negotiations with the idolaters in which they appeared to have been worsted and war would have broken out between the two groups had it not been for the wisdom of the Messenger, may Allah bless him and grant him peace. While they were returning by stages to Madina, a *sura* was revealed which was full of good news: *"Truly We have granted you a manifest victory, so that Allah may forgive you your earlier errors and any later ones, and complete His blessing upon you, and guide you on a Straight Path and so that Allah may help you with a mighty help."* (48:1-3) Help – the best thing you can have is help from Allah! That was the beginning of the Great Victory.

What occurred was the beginning of the spread of Allah's *Deen* and the removal of the obstacles which had been impeding it. After the treaty which the idolaters dictated to the Prophet and which the Muslims reluctantly accepted, the diffusion of the Message increased, many more people entered Islam, and the Islamic polity established itself. Not two years passed before Makka surrendered to the Message-Bearer who came at the head of an army of 10,000 fighters. The idols which had been worshipped instead of Allah for centuries were smashed, the banner of Divine Unity was raised once and for all, and Bilal called the *adhan* from the top of the Ka'ba!

The wisdom of the Messenger at Hudaybiyya brought all these later fruits and that is why Allah gave him the good news of forgiveness and victory and then extended the good news to the masses of the believers. *"It is He who sent down Serenity into the believers' hearts, thus increasing their belief with more belief. To Allah belong the legions of the heavens and the earth. Allah is All-Knowing, All-Wise. So that He may admit the believing men and believing women into gardens with rivers flowing under them..."* (48:4-5)

Their enemies would experience woe in this world and the Next. They would be defeated and the standard of idolatry fall, and neither their strength nor their zeal would be of any use to them. No one can overcome Allah. *"To Allah belong the legions of the heavens and the earth. Allah is Almighty, All-Wise."* (48:7)

Allah sent Muhammad with the Truth to eradicate ignorance and he built a nation which establishes glorification and praise of Allah. The first Companions were the vanguard of this community of worship and *jihad.* They pledged their allegiance to the Prophet at a time of dire constriction. None of them held back. That is not surprising, since they lived for Allah and died in His Path. Allah says about them: *"Those who pledge you their allegiance pledge allegiance to Allah. Allah's Hand is over their hands. He who breaks his pledge only breaks it against himself. But as for him who fulfils the contract he has made with Allah, We will pay him a huge reward."* (47:10)

They were true to Allah and He announced His pleasure with them and their eligibility for immediate and later good: *"Allah was pleased with the believers when they pledged allegiance to you under the tree. He knew what was in their hearts, and sent down Serenity upon them and rewarded them with an imminent victory and with much booty which they will take."* (48:18-19)

Surat al-Fath was sent down while the Muslims were returning to Madina, and it soothed and reassured them. The truth about the people who had failed to come out with them was also revealed to them: they were informed of what the hypocrites said about them and their resentment towards them. The hypocrites in Madina were saying, "They will not return. Quraysh will punish them and inflict a horrible defeat on them."

The strange thing is that those hypocrites had not learnt anything at all from the defeat of the Confederates who had failed in their attack on Madina in the Battle of the Ditch the previous year. It is clear that hypocrisy becomes so deeply embedded in people's hearts that their whole view of existence is permanently coloured by it. They are continually on the wait for a disaster to befall the Muslims and they see events through the screen of their hidden rancour.

When what they hoped for did not happen they took refuge in lies. *"Those Arabs who remained behind will say to you, 'Our wealth and families kept us occupied, so ask forgiveness for us.' They say with their tongues something that is not in their hearts. Say: 'Who can control Allah for you in any way whether He wants harm for you or wants benefit for you?" Allah is aware of everything you do. No, you thought that the Messenger and the believers were never going to come back to their families and that seemed pleasing to your hearts. You thought evil thoughts and were a blighted people. Whoever does not believe in Allah and His Messenger, We have prepared a Blazing Fire for the rejecters."* (48:11-12)

The hypocrites had full knowledge of the nature of the idolaters because they were related to them. They knew that Quraysh would not allow the Muslims to enter Makka, and they thought that if a battle took place the Muslims would suffer a defeat because they were few in number. There is no doubt that they were surprised to see the Muslims return safe, and to discover that the desired *'umra* had been postponed until the following year and that Allah had devised a way out for the Muslims and ordered their affairs in a way that guaranteed good and success for them. *"To Allah belongs the sovereignty of the heavens and the earth. He forgives whoever He wills and punishes whoever He wills. Allah is Ever-Forgiving, Most Merciful."* (48:14)

One aspect of the mercy of Allah is that He left the door of repentance open for any of the hypocrites who wished to return to His Path. But there was a precondition on them: that they should cease to worship this world and stop sitting on the fence. Their repentance would only be valid if they fought the strong unbelievers and were firm in fighting them. *"Say to the desert Arabs who remained behind, 'You will be called up against a people possess-*

ing great force whom you must fight unless they submit. If you obey, Allah will give you an excellent wage. But if you turn your backs as you turned your backs before, He will punish you with a painful punishment.'" (48:16)

There is some controversy as to who the people with 'great force' were. It is said that they were the tribes of Hawazin and Thaqif on the Day of Hunayn. It is said that they were the apostate tribe of Musaylima the Liar, the Banu Hanifa. It is said that it was the Persians and Byzantium. But whoever was intended, fighting requires a sacrifice and a steadfastness that will obliterate every trace of hypocrisy.

Those who had stayed behind tried to join the Muslims on the Khaybar expedition in order to get some of its booty, but Allah refused to allow that. The Jews were clearly not the people with 'great force'. *"Those who remained behind will say, when you go out to take the spoils, 'Allow us to follow you,' desiring to alter Allah's words. Say: 'You may not follow us. That is what Allah said before.' They will say, 'It is only because you envy us.' No, they have not understood except for very little."* (48:15)

The conquest of Khaybar and the appropriation of its wealth was appointed by Allah as a recompense for those who had been present at al-Hudaybiyya. It took place forty days after their return, about twenty years after the beginning of Islam. Khaybar was the strongest and wealthiest of the Jewish settlements in the north of the Hijaz. With its elimination, the banner of the Jews fell and the petty states in which they sought shelter in that area ended and this world was relieved of the contentiousness of the Jews until power was re-established for them.

They had not served the Revelation which had been revealed to them, nor honoured it with noble conduct. They never tried to save the Arabs from the worship of idols which was widespread among them. Indeed, the reverse was true. They lent their support to idolatry against the Prophet of Divine Unity and they wanted the Muslims to revert to idol-worship. The bane of the Jews is that they have confused religion and nationality and made it into a token to distinguish them from other people. When they claimed for themselves a special position in the sight of Allah, they did not offer Him anything that would bring them near to Him. They spread obscenity and usury and worshipped the life of this world, as if the *deen* were a legacy given to them so that they could lord it over other peoples.

When he first arrived in Madina the Prophet treated them well and did everything possible to accommodate them. But they never ceased wishing him ill even though they originally concealed their treachery. Allah, however, expressed what their true feelings were. *"Many of the People of the Book would love it if they could change you back to being rejectors after you have believed, showing their innate envy now the truth is clear to them. But pardon and overlook until Allah gives His command. Truly Allah has power over all things."* (2:109)

Allah brought about His command and the Jews were punished time after time so that perhaps they might take heed. When they persisted in their aggression, the last of their fortresses in Madina fell at the beginning of 7 A.H. They were stripped of the strength on which they had relied in their misdoings and they and their property became booty for the Muslims whom they used to disdain. *"Allah has promised you much booty which you will take, and has hastened this for you and held back people's hands from you, so that it would be a sign to the believers, and that He might guide you to a Straight Path."* (48:20) Allah allocated this good to those who had gone with the Prophet to al-Hudaybiyya and pledged allegiance under the Tree.

Surat al-Fath makes clear the wisdom shown in the Messenger's refusal to fight the idolaters in Makka on that occasion. If he had fought them, he would have inflicted a heavy defeat on them as the Almighty says: *"If those who reject had fought you, they would have turned their backs and then not found any protector or any helper."* (48:22) So why did he leave them? For one thing it was important that the sacred status of the *Haram* should not be compromised, and there was something else as well. Islam had spread in every place and many people had embraced it in Makka itself, but the fear of persecution had made them conceal their belief. If there had been a battle and the Muslims had used the sword against the people of Makka, those unknown believers might have been slain unjustly.

Allah Almighty says: *"Had it not been for some believing men and believing women whom you did not know and whom you might trample underfoot, and so unknowingly incur blame on their account – so that Allah might admit into His mercy whoever He wills – and had those among them who reject been clearly distinguishable, We would have punished them with a painful punishment."* (48:25) In any case, the Muslims who were prevented from performing the practices in 6 A.H. would be able to perform them in 7 A.H. and would then enter Makka victorious in 8 A.H.

One thing which is not widely known is the extraordinarily small number of people who fell in battle in these years. It was a number small enough to count on your fingers. Islam resulted in surprisingly little loss of life on both sides. If the dead were to be counted from the beginning of Islam until it was fully established, their number would be found to be very much less than that of those who were slaughtered in one night on St Bartholomew's Day in the struggle between the Catholics and the Protestants. But the world is beset with liars and those who spread shameful rumours.

This is particularly apparent in what is symbolically probably the greatest of all the military victories of Islam which Allah announced in this *sura*, the conquest of Makka. It was achieved without a single life being lost. *"Allah has confirmed the vision of His Messenger with truth: 'You will enter the Sacred Mosque, Allah willing, in safety, heads shaved, hair cut short, without fear.' He knew what you did not know and ordained, apart from that, an imminent victory."* (48:27)

Then came this great *ayat* which appears in slightly different forms three time in the Qur'an: *"It is He who sent His Messenger with the Guidance and the* Deen *of Truth to raise it over every other* deen *Allah is enough as a witness."* (48:28) What this *ayat* makes explicit is that victory is a necessary adjunct of Islam in the past and in the future. The victorious banner of Islam will remain flying until the Last Hour arrives, as we are informed in *hadith*: "My Community is like the abundant rain. It is not known whether its beginning is better or its end." (Related by at-Tirmidhi) But the victory depends on certain qualifications that are needed by each generation. If these qualifications are not present, achieving victory will elude us. We shall have no one to blame except ourselves and will not harm Allah in any way.

The *ayat* which concludes *Surat al-Fath* explains the special qualities of the victorious Community. Allah Almighty says: *"Muhammad is the Messenger of Allah, and those who are with him are fierce to the rejectors, merciful to one another..."* (48:29)

Perhaps we should stop there and look at two recent reports which show just how far we are away from even this basic Muslim position. In one of these reports we read that an Arab government killed thirteen Muslim 'fundamentalists' in a single punitive raid. In the other we find that an American mediator between Syria and Israel had offered the Jews a guarantee that Syria would make every effort to find five Jewish soldiers who were either killed, wounded or captured in Lebanon some years ago. Israel wanted their bodies if they were dead and their persons if they were alive. The Jewish people are terribly eager for their sons.

I compared the two reports and realised the disparity in this time between the two communities. Of old we were, as Allah describes, *"fierce to the rejectors, merciful to one another."* Today we are merciless with one another and aid our enemies to show mercy to one another! If this is our situation how can victory be near? By what token do the Muslims deserve to inherit the earth?

Sura 49
Al-Hujurat: The Private Quarters

One of the rights of the aged is to be honoured and shown the proper tokens of respect, as it is the right of the young to be shown compassion and to be treated kindly. The Prophet, may Allah bless him and grant him peace, made these things fundamental aspects of Muslim society: "Anyone who does not respect our old, show mercy to our young and acknowledge the due of our scholars is not one of us." *Surat al-Hujurat* contains a number of instructions about correct behaviour which enhance the community and protect it. The first relate to how Muslims should behave with their Messenger, the next to how Muslims should behave with one another, and the last deal with how the entire community should relate to other nations.

Regarding how the Muslims should behave with their Prophet, the Almighty says: *"O you who believe, do not put yourselves forward in front of Allah and His Messenger. Show fear of Allah. Allah is All-Hearing, All-Knowing. O you who believe, do not raise your voices above the voice of the Prophet and do not be as loud when speaking to him as you are when speaking to one another..."* (49:1-2) This corroborates what we have already seen in *Surat an-Nur*: *"Do not make the Messenger's summons of you the same as your summons of one another."* (24:63)

Particular courtesy is needed when addressing the Messenger, may Allah bless him and grant him peace, and conversing with him, characterised by humility, lowering the voice and being respectful. He conveyed the Message from Allah and transmitted His guidance. Respect for him is part of the *Deen*. He has enough to bear with the trouble he meets from the unbelievers and hypocrites. Those who observe proper behaviour with the Messenger of Allah have their position and reward. As for those who are ill-behaved and lacking in good character, they too will get what they deserve.

Part of true belief is to be careful when listening to reports. Many a baseless rumour has provoked widespread dissent and unrest: *"If a degenerate person comes to you with a report then scrutinise it carefully in case you should attack a people in ignorance and then become regretful for what you did."* (49:6)

What is certain is that Shaytan watches the children of Adam expectantly and listens to their conversation, attempting to provoke dissent between them. When a small error occurs, he tries to expand it so that it turns into a huge mistake. He tries to fan insignificant sparks into a blazing fire, sparing no efforts to increase conflict and hostility wherever possible. The body of the Muslims must hasten to control the situation and rectify the division. To combat this, whenever someone becomes unjustly aggressive all the Muslims should help one another against him and make him stop at the limits. How much unnecessary violence and destruction could be prevented if the Muslims would only apply the guidance we have been given!

"If two parties of the believers fight, make peace between them. But if one of them unjustly attacks the other, fight the attackers until they revert to Allah's command. If they revert, make peace between them with justice, and be even-handed. Allah loves those who are even-handed." (49:9) The present lack of cohesion among the Muslims bodes ill. It is a pretext which allows non-Muslims to exploit the decadence of the Muslims for their own ends and Islam is the loser, first and last.

Surat al-Hujurat draws our attention to several ignoble characteristics which we must avoid. It is thoughtlessness and groundless insolence to mock others, supposing yourself to be better than them. Only Allah Almighty knows the true state of people. The true rectitude of any man can only be determined by a thorough knowledge of his heredity and environment, by comparing his own nature and the currents which surround him and affect him. You may mock a man who will be successful when you fail, and then he goes forward and you go backwards. *"O you who believe! People should not ridicule others who may very well be better than themselves. Nor should women ridicule other women who may very well be better than themselves..."* (49:11)

Islam rejects fault-finding, insults, spying, bad opinion, slander and backbiting. The unfortunate fact is that most gatherings of people are not free of these banes. If people refrained from them, they would spend half of their lives in silence! The *sura* mentions all these things and indeed, as the Prophet himself made clear to us on several occasions, nothing is more destructive to human society than our own tongues. They sometimes work more havoc in the community than all that our enemies can muster against us.

We Muslims must make our Message known to other people. We were not created to look up to them. We are the people with the Message which we are obliged to explain with courtesy, wisdom, mercy and love. I fear that our failure to immerse the world in it derives largely from our poor presentation of it, our lack of enthusiasm for it, and, worryingly, our tendency to be disinclined to share it with other people. *"O mankind! We created you from male and female, and made you into peoples and tribes so that you might come to know each other. The noblest among you in Allah's sight is the one with most fear of Him."* (49:13)

The *sura* ends by explaining the situation of the desert Arabs who entered Islam without being bound by its behaviour or abiding by its judgements. They are very similar to the people who have inherited Islam in name only and whose hearts are empty of real faith. Their actions are far from righteous. *"The desert Arabs say, 'We believe.' Say: 'You do not believe. Say rather, "We submit," for belief has not yet come into your hearts.'"* (49:14) Allah points out to these people that it is their actions, not their words, which are judged for them or against them. *"If you obey Allah and His Messenger, He will not deplete your actions for you in any way."* (49:14)

People who fail Islam when they are asked for help, or abandon its practices when crises arise, are not true Muslims. *"The believers are only those who have believed in Allah and His Messenger and then had no doubt, and performed* jihad *with their wealth and themselves in the Way of Allah. It is those who are the truthful."* (49:15) In this time we find among the common and the elite Muslims people who resemble these desert Arabs of the distant past. They affiliate themselves with Islam and yet do not respond to its call or support it in times of difficulty.

Sura 50
Qaf

Surat Qaf is one of the many *suras* basically devoted to the Resurrection and the Reckoning which provide evidence from the natural world and from historical sources as well as direct information about the Unseen realities themselves. *"Yet they are amazed that a warner has come to them from among themselves, and those who reject say, 'This is an extraordinary thing! What when we are dead and turned to dust...? That would be a most improbable return!' We know exactly how the earth reduces them. We possess an all-preserving Book."* (50:2-4)

The fact is that death and resurrection are repeated every hour of the day and night in every body as cells die off and become regenerated, so the restoration of creation is not really such an extraordinary idea at all. Look at the constant interaction between our bodies and the earth on which we live. We witness resurrection on a daily basis but the unbelievers are heedless and thoughtless.

Our food is one of the things mentioned in the *sura*. *"And We sent down blessed water from the sky and by it made gardens grow, and grain for harvesting, and soaring date-palms with layered spathes, as provision for Our slaves."* (50:9-11) Let us just reflect a moment about the food we eat. Some of it is transformed into energy which maintains body temperature. Some of it is transformed into cells in which life flows and by which bones and flesh are formed with their own qualities. Yet no one really knows exactly how these processes occur.

Biologists describe a cell as something resembling a city with fields and lanes and electrical lines and watercourses – all this in something which cannot even be seen by the naked eye! The part of the food the body does not use reverts to the earth by the process of the elimination, from where it will once again emerge as barley, wheat or corn which people eat, and the whole process starts again.

The Qur'an bases faith on the receptivity of the active questing intellect and then causes it to grow in a receptacle of miraculous luminosity, the human heart. Transmitters report that one of the women Companions memorised *Surat Qaf* directly from the Messenger when he uttered it one Friday. The words were engraved in her mind and she was constantly repeating it. Then she was transformed in her conduct, character, worship and way of life.

We do not hold the Resurrection to be a theoretical notion. It is one of a number of unseen realities of which it is possible for us to become vibrantly aware. *"We created man and We know what his own self whispers to him, and We are nearer to him than his jugular vein, while the two recording angels are recording, sitting one on the right and one on the left. He does not utter a single word without a watcher by him, pen in hand."* (50:16-18) All these things are going on around us all the time. The Qur'an describes existence as it really is.

There is a great difference between the life of faith and the life that contemporary civilisation posits as reality. It is a civilisation which rarely remembers Allah or prepares to meet Him or even thinks of Him. The dominant religions have failed to revive religious awareness and restore people's innate consciousness of Allah, their Creator. Death, as far as most Europeans and Americans are concerned, is the end of existence. So what follows it will come as a most unexpected and unpleasant surprise. *"You were unmindful of this, so We have removed from you your covering and today your eyesight is sharp."* (50:22)

Unfortunately many Muslims have also been carried away by this trend and consider this world more real than the Final Reckoning, saying with az-Zahawi "I will not exchange something physical for something imaginary." For such people, the Next World is imaginary as it is to their unbelieving mentors. But the Last Day is a certainty and people will reap what they sowed.

Two scenes are described for us in this *sura*: firstly the fate of the unbeliever, and secondly the fate of the believer, on the Last

Day. As we have learned elsewhere, Allah allots the unbelievers bosom friends from the jinn who never leave them, and we learn here that they even accompany them to the Next World. *"His inseparable comrade will say, 'This is what I have ready for you.' 'Hurl every obdurate unbeliever into Hell, impeder of good, doubt-causing aggressor, who set up, together with Allah, another god. Hurl him into the terrible punishment.'"* (50:23-25)

And this shaytan who undertook the task of misguiding and deluding his human host will further say, *"Our Lord, I did not make him inordinate. He was, in any case, very far astray,"* (50:27) meaning that that man was already corrupt before he corrupted him. But none of this affects the outcome. *"He will say, 'Do not argue in My presence when I gave you advance warning of the Threat. My Word once given does not change and I do not wrong My slaves.'"* (50:28-29)

The second scene is the fate of those who are good and god-fearing. *"And the Garden will be brought up close to the godfearing, not far away: 'This is what you were promised. It is for every careful penitent.' Anyone who fears the All-Merciful in the Unseen and comes with a contrite heart: 'Enter it in peace. This is the Day of Endless Timelessness.'"* (50:31-34)

Surat Qaf then returns to discussing the universe and its creation, mentioning that Allah brought it into existence by His power and did not experience fatigue of any kind when doing so. If He had felt any fatigue after this creation, how could He sustain the heavens and the earth and nourish the awesome numbers of human beings and animals and every other created thing throughout the passage of time? How could He control the stars in their galaxies? The ordering of the universe would slip from His grasp! That is why He says: *"We created the heavens and the earth, and everything between them, in six days and We were not affected by fatigue."* (50:38)

The Qur'an bases faith on human intellect and the free acceptance of the overwhelming evidence we have been given for Allah's existence. That is why the *sura* ends with the statement that the Prophet is not a dictator who tries to change people's beliefs by force as dictators force political and social changes onto people. He is simply a truthful and sincere adviser and guide. *"We know best what they say. You are not a dictator over them, so remind with the Qur'an all those who fear My Threat."* (50:45)

Sura 51
Adh-Dhariyat: The Scatterers

Surat adh-Dhariyat begins with a number of oaths. *"By the scatterers scattering, and those bearing weighty loads, and those speeding along with ease, and those apportioning the command: what you are promised is certainly true – the Reckoning will certainly take place!"* (51:1-6) Although there is more than one opinion about what Allah is referring to here it is generally accepted that the winds are intended. Wind is of course the movement of air through the atmosphere. If when we are deprived of air, we suffocate and die. Air currents rise and fall above the surface of the earth and then the winds blow, veering to east, west, north and south. These winds move the clouds for whose rain thirsty men and animals and the parched earth are eagerly waiting. So this daily event which we take so much for granted is absolutely vital for the continuance of life on the earth.

I used to be amazed at the air in automobile tyres supporting enormous weights until I looked at the rivers of the earth which are also borne by the air as clouds before the rain which fills them descends to us. So there is immense power involved. Anyway, perhaps for these and other reasons Allah chose in this *sura* to swear by the winds that the Reckoning is true and that human beings will soon be questioned about what they did and left undone.

Then after that there is another oath: *"By heaven with its oscillating tracks, you are certainly of differing opinions."* (7-8) The order of the heavens is very finely balanced and there is no neglect or chaos in them whatever. All that moves in them is completely in accordance with undeviating laws. Nothing is out of place and yet within this determined order there is still room for variation.

We leave heaven for the earth and its inhabitants. *"There are certainly signs in the earth for people with certainty, and in your-*

selves as well. Do you not then see? Your provision is in heaven – and what you are promised. By the Lord of heaven and earth, it is most certainly the truth, just as you have speech." (51:21-23) The human body is a very intricate organism. Glory be to the One who created it and fashioned it and gave it hearing and sight! In spite of that, a deluded man sits on his sofa and says, "There is no god. Life is matter and nothing more." If it is matter, then who constructed it and ordered it and set up the laws it follows so rigorously?

We leave aside the middle of the *sura* for a minute in order to look at the end of it which contains the reply to this question. *"As for heaven: We built it with great power and gave it its vast expanse. And the earth: We spread it like a carpet and how well We smoothed it out! And We created all things in pairs so that perhaps you might remember."* (51:47-49)

The godless unbeliever with all his stupidity and heedlessness is about to be overcome by a catastrophe which he cannot evade. That is why Allah says to him and those like him: *"So flee to Allah. Truly I am a clear warner from Him to you. Do not set up another god together with Allah, Truly I am a clear warner from Him to you."* (51:50-51) But unbelievers have always possessed a complacency and impudence by which they justify to themselves and each other their total belief in the permanence of material existence. *"Likewise, no Messenger came to those before them without them saying, 'A magician or a madman!' Did they bequeath this to one another? Indeed they are unbridled people."* (51:52-53)

In the middle, *Surat adh-Dhariyat* describes the fates of a number of those unbelieving peoples of the past. It begins by mentioning the honoured guests of Ibrahim: angels who had come to bring him the good news that Allah would give him a knowledgeable son but also to inform him that Allah would destroy the impure towns which Lut was powerless to reform.

Then the *sura* speaks about Pharaoh and his army and how they persecuted the tribe of Israel. *"So We seized him and his armies and hurled them into the sea, and he was to blame."* (51:40) Then Ad who used to ask, "Who could be stronger than us?" *"And also in 'Ad when We sent against them the barren wind. It left nothing it touched without bringing it to ruin."* (51:41-42) Then Thamud and the people of Nuh. All were destroyed for their refusal to accept their Messenger.

Allah does not need His creation. He is rich beyond need of anything in existence. If He obliges us to worship Him, it is only so we may show ourselves thankful for His blessings and aware of His immensity and our need of Him – *"I did not create jinn or man except to worship Me. I do not desire any provision from them. I do not desire for them to nourish Me. Certainly Allah, He is the Provider, the Possessor of Strength, the Sure."* (51:56-58) – and so that we may avoid the fate of those who came before us. "Those *who do wrong will get their due the same as the due their predecessors got. So they should not try to hurry Me."* (51:59) If we fail to heed the warning and follow the Messenger in his worship of Allah we will have only ourselves to blame. *"Woe then to those who reject, on account of their Day which they are promised."* (51:60)

Sura 52
At-Tur: The Mount

Surat at-Tur provides a dazzling example of how the Noble Qur'an acts on the soul when it brings it to guidance, just as morning breaks in upon the night, obliterating its darkness and illuminating it. Jubayr ibn Mut'im was an idolater who came to Madina to negotiate for the ransom of the captives after the defeat sustained by his people at Badr. The Muslims entered the mosque to pray the *Maghrib* prayer behind the Prophet and he remained outside the mosque. He listened to *Surat at-Tur,* which the Prophet was reciting in the prayer, and was transformed by it on the spot. This was by no means an isolated example of that phenomenon. Many similar incidents have been recorded of the astonishing power that the Qur'an can have on those who hear it for the first time. In this case Jubayr's idolatry was swept away and his heart flooded with indelible faith.

Jubayr said about the incident, "I heard the Prophet reciting *at-Tur* in *Maghrib* and when he reached these *ayats*, *'Or were they created out of nothing, or are they the creators? Or did they create the heavens and the earth? No, the truth is that they have no certainty. Or do they possess of the treasuries of your Lord or do they have control of them?'* (52:35-37) my heart almost took flight." In another transmission, he said, "I came to the Messenger of Allah in Madina to speak about the captives from Badr. I was brought to him while he was leading his Companions in the *Maghrib* prayer and I heard him recite, *'By the Mount and an inscribed Book on an open page, by the Visited House, by the Raised Canopy and by the Overflowing Ocean: your Lord's punishment will certainly take place. No one can ward it off.'* (52:1-7) It was as if my heart would burst and I became Muslim on the spot out of fear of the descent

408

of the punishment. I thought that the punishment might alight on me before I rose from my seat."

There is a correspondence between ancient Revelation and later Revelation. It was from the side of Mount Sinai that Musa was called to bear the double burden of confronting Pharaoh and guiding the Tribe of Israel; and it was from the side of the Visited House that Muhammad was called to re-establish the foundations of *tawhid* and restore truth to the world. It is said that 'the Unfurled Scroll' refers to the scriptures of Musa and 'the Overflowing Ocean' is the Red Sea when it drowned Pharaoh and did away with false divinity.

Whatever the case may be, the Qur'an contains the final form of faith and *Shari'a* and is the Final Revelation which will endure until the end of time. It is the only reliable document about the Revelations which earlier Messengers received. *Surat at-Tur* stresses the threat to the enemies of Revelation and that they are endangering their future prospects. On the other hand, the godfearing will have a pleasant future and everlasting bliss: *"They will say, 'Beforehand we used to go in fear among our families, but Allah was gracious to us and safeguarded us from the punishment of the searing wind. Beforehand we certainly used to call on Him, that He was the Good, the Most Merciful.'"* (52:26-28)

After the promise and the threat, the middle of the *sura* contains the command to the Messenger of Allah to persevere in delivering the Message despite anything the unbelievers might do or say to stop him. *"Remind them then! For, by the blessing of your Lord, you are neither a fortune-teller nor a madman."* (52:29)

Islam is based on the fact that humanity in its natural state will not go crooked, err, fabricate, and deviate. This is why this *sura* poses fifteen successive questions appealing to healthy intellects, to induce us to reflect on our present state and ultimate end.

• *"Or do they say, 'A poet – for whom we await the uncertainties of fate'? Say: 'Wait then! I am waiting with you.'"* (52:30-31) Muhammad was not a poet: *"We did not teach him poetry, nor would it be fitting for him."* (36:69) His

Book contains truths, not fantasies: *"We have sent it down with Truth and with Truth it has come down."* (17:105)

• *"Is it their intellects that direct them to say this?"* (52:32) People with intelligence would rise above concocting these accusations.

• *"Or is it that they are an unbridled people?"* (52:32) Excessive love of this world is the first incentive to denial.

• *"Or do they say, 'He has made it up'? No, the truth is they do not believe. Let them produce a discourse like it, if they speak the truth."* (52:33-34) If the Qur'an had been the words of a human being, what would prevent human beings from producing something equivalent?

• *"Or were they created out of nothing?"* (52:35) There is nothing that can come from nothing.

• *"Or are they the creators?"* (52:35) Man is created and a vassal and cannot create anything.

• *"Did they create the heavens and the earth? No, the truth is they have no certainty."* (52:36) We found the universe prepared for us and we did not create either its atoms or its galaxies.

• *"Or do they possess the treasuries of your Lord?"* (52:37) Most of the unbelievers ask, "Why were the Prophets not chosen from among us? Why were we not chosen?"

• *"Or do they have control of them?"* (52:37) If they had control they would never be able to distribute them justly.

• *"Or have they a ladder on which they listen? Then let their listeners bring clear evidence."* (52:38) If they are able to intercept the Revelation then why do they not do so?

• *"Or does He have daughters whereas they have sons?"* (52:39) The idolaters of Makka did not want daughters. In spite of that they ascribed daughters to Allah!

• *"Or do you ask them for a wage so they are weighed down with debt?"* (52:40) The Prophets do not ask people for anything, or seek any worldly goods from them.

• *"Or is the Unseen in their possession so they can write out what is to happen?"* (52:41) The unbelievers have no knowledge of the Unseen and only a little of the Visible.

• *"Or do they desire to dupe you? But it is those who reject who are the duped."* (52:42) The struggle is long between truth and falsehood but the end belongs to the godfearing.

• *"Or do they have some god other than Allah? Glory be to Allah above any idol they propose!"* (52:43) All that is other than Allah is false.

After all these questions, Allah Almighty says: *"If they saw a lump of heaven falling down, they would just say, 'Banked-up clouds!'"* (52:44) This means that they are people of prejudice and pride and are not at all concerned with the Truth and its evidence. That is why the Messenger was told to wait with them for some time during which they would be humbled to the Truth and their power would be stripped away from them. It is Allah alone who controls existence, so we should occupy ourselves with worship and striving and what is pleasing to Him. *"So wait steadfastly for the judgement of your Lord – you are certainly before Our eyes."* (52:48)

Sura 53
An-Najm: The Star

Ordinary human knowledge is acquired by means of certain known faculties, primarily the intellect and the five senses. But there is another kind of knowledge particular to some people, which is Divine Inspiration. Ya'qub indicated it when he said to his sons, *"I know things from Allah which you do not know."* (12:86) Anyone who learns something directly from the Knower of all things has obtained irrefutable knowledge. Allah does not give this kind of direct knowledge from Himself to every man. People are lodes. Revelation is only conveyed to chosen beings, beings of an elevated nature who disdain pettiness and falsity. The stars set, but these guides do not set. Muhammad was one such person, or rather he was their Imam!

Surat an-Najm describes how Revelation is received. *"By the star when it descends, your companion is not misguided or misled. Nor does he speak from whim. It is nothing but Revelation revealed, taught him by one immensely strong, possessing power and splendour."* (53:1-6) As we know, Musa was called by Allah from *"the right hand side of the valley in the part which was full of blessing, from out of the bush..."* (28:30) so that he could become a shepherd of men after having been a shepherd of sheep for some years. These *ayats* tell us what happened to the last of the Prophets, who withdrew from people into the Cave of Hira' where the angel appeared to him in his awesome form with the beginning of the final Revelation. "His *heart did not lie about what he saw. Will you then contradict him concerning what he sees?"* (53:11-12)

The Muhammadan Revelation came from Reality Itself to a people who were immersed in ignorance and delusion without even knowing it. *"They are following nothing but conjecture and what their own selves desire – and that when guidance has come to them from their Lord!"* (53:23) There are religions which have no basis in reality whatsoever and others which were Divine in origin but whose horizons have become clouded by illusion and falsehood. Wrong things are said about Allah. How many misguided religious people lead others terribly astray by their erroneous ideas! *"They have no knowledge of this. They are following nothing but conjecture. Conjecture is of no avail whatsoever against the truth."* (53:28)

The truth is that the Revelation came with the path of Islam containing all good for all mankind. Allah is free of any need of His creation but requires certain actions from us for the sake of our own right guidance and salvation. The Qur'an is the Way of Rectitude, the Stairway of Ascent. Whoever wishes to, does good. Whoever wishes to, does evil. *"Everything in the heavens and everything in the earth belongs to Allah, so that He can repay those who do evil for what they did and repay those who do good with the Best. Those who avoid the major wrong actions and indecies except for minor lapses, truly your Lord is Vast in forgiveness. He had most knowledge of you when He first produced you from the earth, and when you were embryos in your mothers' wombs. So do not claim purity for yourselves: He knows best those who have fear of Him."* (53:31-32)

Yet so many people prove unable to see where their best interests lie. Their obduracy and stupidity in the face of Divine Guidance blind them to the truth. *"Have you seen him who turns away and gives little, and that grudgingly? Does he have knowledge of the Unseen enabling him to see?"* (53:32-34) This is not so much the description of one particular individual as that of an archetypal unbeliever in all times and places. The godless of today have the same aversion to the truth, suffer from the same delusions and are equally anxious concerning their provision.

Both faith and the rejection of it are constant factors of the human story and this *sura* summarises concisely and beautifully the tenets of all Divine Revelation. *"Or has he not been informed what is in the texts of Musa and of Ibrahim, who paid his dues in full? That no bearer of a burden can bear the burden of another. That man will have nothing but that for which he strives. That his*

413

striving will certainly be seen. That he will then receive repayment of the fullest kind." (53:36-41)

The core of faith is belief in the Creator and to see that everything in creation points to His existence. Both the living and the inanimate indicate Allah. Anyone who imagines that life itself originated within this existence itself is foolish. The source of life is the Living who never dies. *"And that the ultimate end is to your Lord. That it is He who brings about both laughter and tears. That it is He who brings about both life and death. That He created the two kinds – male and female – out of a sperm-drop when it spurted forth."* (53:42-46) The life in ourselves and around us and in our sons and daughters is bestowed on us by the One who controls all existence. He is Allah - glory be to Him!

Earlier peoples were destroyed for their refusal to acknowledge and submit to their Divine provenance; and the later ones will not have a better end. *Surat an-Najm* ends with some short *ayats* which state this truth with great power and eloquence. *"That He is responsible for the second embodiment. That it is He who enriches and who makes content. That it is He who is the Lord of Sirius. That He destroyed 'Ad, the earlier people, and Thamud, sparing none of them, and the people of Nuh before – they were unjust and intemperate in the extreme – and the Overturned City which He inverted it so that what enveloped it enveloped it. Which one of your Lord's blessings do you then dispute?"* (53:47-55)

Since that is how Allah dealt with those sinful societies there is nothing to prevent Him from dealing similarly with the godless of today. But do godless people of today grasp that? Muhammad is just repeating the same Message that the previous Messengers brought to their societies. *"Nothing has been said to you that was not said to the Messengers before you."* (41:43) It is no laughing matter and it is as relevant and urgent now as it was fourteen hundred years ago. *"Are you then astonished at this discourse and laugh and do not cry, treating life as a game? Prostrate before Allah and worship Him!"* (53:59-60)

Sura 54
Al-Qamar: The Moon

"The Hour has drawn near and the moon has split." (54:1) The apparent meaning is that this splitting will occur at the end of the time with the break up of the heavens. However, there is a *hadith* related from Ibn Mas'ud which states that the splitting of the moon took place in the time of the Messenger, may Allah bless him and grant him peace, but the idolaters still refused to believe him and continued their arrogant assertion that the Messenger was a magician. *"They have denied and followed their whims and desires, but every matter is fixed."* (54:3)

They thought that the efforts of the Messenger to destroy paganism would prove futile and that they would be able to continue in their beliefs. They thought that their system would endure and that the Muslims would not tangibly affect their way of life. But in a very short time the Revelation swept away falsehood and eliminated the darkness. *"News has come to them with a threat in it. Consummate wisdom – but warnings are profitless."* (54:4-5) When someone's heart is dead and not moved to submission or faith, there is no point in your calling him, however eloquent your words may be.

Allah threatens the idolaters with the Day of Resurrection and Reckoning and then reminds them of the misguided nations who met a painful fate in the past, recounting briefly and succinctly the results of misguidance and obduracy from the time of Nuh onwards. *"Before them the people of Nuh denied. They denied Our slave, saying, 'A madman,' and he was driven away with jeers. He called upon his Lord, 'I am overwhelmed, so help me!' We opened the gates of heaven with torrential water and made the earth burst forth with gushing springs. And the waters met together in a preordained way."* (54:9-12)

415

After Nuh came 'Ad, an arrogant and deluded tribe who had been given great wealth and bodily strength but did not hesitate to call their Messenger a fool when he called them to acknowledge the Oneness of Allah. They soon had cause to regret their arrogance: *"We sent against them a howling wind on a day of unremitting horror. It plucked up men like uprooted palm-stumps."* (54:19-20)

Thamud came after 'Ad and the noble *sura* begins with what they said to their Prophet Salih because it was basically the same as the people of Makka said to the Seal of the Messengers. They said: *"'Has the Reminder been sent down to him out of all of us?'"* (38:8) Before that they said: *"They are astonished that a warner should have come to them from among them, and the rejectors say 'This is a lying magician.'"* (38:4) How similar that is to what Thamud said about their Prophet, Salih! *"Are we to follow a human being, one of us? Then we would truly be astray, completely mad! Has the Reminder been given to him out of all of us? No indeed! He is an impertinent liar."* (54:24-25)

Thamud killed the She-Camel which Allah had miraculously created for them and which they were instructed to care for. A punishment befell them, said to have been a great earthquake, which left them like straw strewn over the ground. *"We sent against them a single Blast and they were just like a thatcher's reeds."* (54:31)

Now we move to the depraved city whose appetites overstepped all bounds. They took their pleasure in the abnormal, and societies devoted to perversion were opened. Their righteous Prophet, Lut, proclaimed his detestation of this outrage and tried to reform them but they refused and even attempted to seduce his angelic guests. Their punishment was the destruction of their city. Some people think that it was an atomic explosion which overturned their city and afflicted those who saw it with blindness, but in any case there was certainly fire involved. *"They even wanted to seduce his guests. Therefore We blotted out their eyes: 'Taste then My punishment and warnings!' Early morning brought them enduring punishment."* (54:37-38)

Thus the people of Nuh were destroyed by water, the people of Hud by air, the people of Salih by the earth, and the people of Lut by fire. These are the four familiar elements so essential to our lives on earth, but we see from this that if we abuse the gifts He gives us and refuse to live within the limits he has prescribed for us for our own well-being, Allah can, if He wishes, use them to destroy us.

"We have made the Qur'an easy to remember. But is there any rememberer there?" (54:17, 22 ,32, 40) This phrase is repeated several times during the course of the *sura* as a kind of refrain. It states a plain truth for, as millions have shown throughout the centuries since its revelation, the memorisation of the entire Qur'an is, despite its considerable length, well within the capacity of almost all who seriously set out to accomplish it. But also in this instance it powerfully reinforces the message of this particular *sura*, striking the hearts of those who hear it, bringing home to all of us the urgency of our own situation. This is eloquently backed up by a second repeated phrase – *"How terrible are..."* or *"Taste then... My punishment and warnings!"* – which well and truly drives the message home!

This account of the behaviour of the earlier peoples concludes by mentioning the Pharaohs who ruled people by force and began to deify themselves: *"Warnings came to the people of Pharaoh. They denied every one of Our signs. Therefore We seized them with the seizing of One who is Almighty, All-Powerful."* (54:37-38)

Then the message is brought right into the present. The enemies of Islam should know that they too will not escape the fate of their predecessors. *"'Are your rejectors better than those peoples'? Or do you have exemption in the Sciptures? Or do they say, 'We are an assembly who will win.' The assembly will be routed and turn their backs in flight."* (54:43-45) This threat was realised in the case of the people to whom the Revelation was originally addressed and they suffered a humiliating and conclusive defeat at the Battle of Badr in which many of their leaders were killed.

The *sura* concludes with words about the Day of Reckoning when justice will finally be done.

"The evil-doers are indeed misguided and insane. The Day when they are dragged face-first into the Fire: 'Savour the scorching touch of Saqar!'" (54:47-48)

"The godfearing shall be amid Gardens and fountains, on seats of honour, in the presence of an All-Powerful King." (54:54-55)

Sura 55
Ar-Rahman: The All-Merciful

The All-Merciful (*ar-Rahman*) is one of the Most Beautiful Names of Allah. It is often used to refer to the Divine Essence Itself: *"Say: 'Call on Allah or call on the All-Merciful.'"* (17:110) It is also, of course, used together with its corollary the Most Merciful (*ar-Rahim*) to introduce all the *suras* of the Qur'an – except for *Surat at-Tawba*.

Among the great mercies of Allah is that He did not leave mankind without the guidance they needed to direct their steps and define their goal. The Noble Qur'an contains the essence of what was in all the previous Revelations and guarantees the means of right guidance for the whole of mankind up until the time the Last Hour arrives. *"The All-Merciful taught the Qur'an."* (55:1-2)

One of the characteristics of the human species is the blessing of clear expression and transmission of the meaning to others in various languages. *"He created man and taught him clear expression."* (55:2)

Then Allah explains that existence is governed by precise laws and that the planets do not roam about freely in space in a haphazard fashion. They have a defined course and exact speed and are managed precisely. The same applies to the plants which grow on the earth – and indeed to everything else in creation. *"The sun and moon both run with precision. The stars and trees all bow down in prostration. He erected heaven and established the balance, so that you would not overstep in the balance."* (55:5-8)

Corruption and pollution only appear in existence because of people's tendency to go to excess in their pursuit of power and pleasure. Holes appear in the ozone layer and all the rest of the rampant pollution of land sea and air now so prevalent is on account of people's excessive exploitation of natural resources.

This does not mean that management of existence has gone out of the hands of its Creator, for in His wisdom He has allowed us leeway to do our worst. Nevertheless He has continually warned us against excess and instructs us to establish justice, whether in the exchange of goods or in giving everyone with a right his right in governmental and social contexts: *"Give just weight; do not skimp in the balance."* (55:9)

Among the blessings of Allah to His creation are the fruits of agriculture. The sweet fruits are accompanied by seeds in their containers, like wheat and rice which blow with the wind. Most of humanity rely on them for their nourishment, just as their plants are eaten by animals, and then there is water and sweet herbage as enjoyment for whoever wishes.

The refrain, *"Which of your Lord's blessings do the two of you then deny?"* which comes first in *ayat* 11 is repeated thirty-one times in the course of the *sura*. The "two" referred to in it are men and jinn, the two clasees of being who are under obligation to worship Allah in this world and accountable for their actions in the next.

The entire *sura* is divided into four distinct parts. The first speaks about creation and origination. The second discusses annihilation, resurrection and reckoning. The third speaks about the highest reward for those who excel in this existence. The fourth is about the reward of the ordinary believers.

It is known that Adam was created from earth, then from mud, then from 'dried clay made from fetid black mud,' (15: 26, 27, 33) and then 'dry earth like baked clay' (55:12) and his offspring were created from a sperm drop, then a clot and then a lump of flesh, and so forth. (see 20:13-14) That was the first genesis. People will fill up the earth and then death will overtake all of them: *"Everyone on it will pass away. And the Face of your Lord will remain, Possessor of Majesty and Generosity."* (55:26-27) Then they will be awakened to meet their Reckoning. No one will escape. The righteous will go to abiding bliss and the corrupters will be led to the end they have prepared for themselves.

"The evildoers will be recognised by their mark and seized hold of by their forelocks and their feet." (55:41) Those evildoers

will pass through various stages. They might dispute the Reckoning for a time and they will be questioned about what they did, as happened in this world. But after affairs are settled it only remains to carry out the sentence, and they will dragged to Hell. For these people the refrain acts as a kind of rebuke: *"Which of your Lord's blessings do the two of you then deny?"* (55:41) It emphasises the disobedience of those who neglect what is due to Allah before mentioning what will be done to them. Then comes the concluding description of the punishment for faithlessness: *"This is Hell which the evil-doers deny. They will go between fire and scalding water, back and forth"* (55:42-3)

Surat ar-Rahman ends with a fine and beautiful description of the Gardens which are in store for the godfearing. There are two gardens for the people of high degrees: *"For him who fears the station of his Lord are two Gardens."* (55:46) The objects of description and the description itself are often interspersed with the refrain, for instance when Allah describes the dark-eyed houris: *"In them are maidens with eyes for them alone, untouched before them by either man or jinn – which of your Lord's blessings do the two of you then deny? – like precious stones of ruby and coral."* (55:56-58) In this case the refrain acts to emphasise the immensity of the value of the blessing which is being portrayed.

Another example of this occurs when Allah describes the lesser Gardens. *"As well as them there will be two other Gardens – which of your Lord's blessings do the two of you then deny? – of deep viridian green."* (55:62-64) Nowhere in any literature is the otherworldly reality and beauty portrayed as vividly and immediately as in this supremely beautiful *sura*. Its sounds and images combine to paint a picture which becomes indelibly engraved on the hearts of those who hear it and which will only be matched by the reality it describes when we are face to face with it. May Allah place us among those whose destiny is this!

Sura 56
Al-Waqi'a: The Occurrence

'*Al-Waqi'a* (the Occurrence)' is one of the various names for
the Day of Rising, like *al-Haqqa* (the Undeniable), *al-Qari'a* (The
Crashing Blow) and *as-Sa'a* (the Last Hour). The hallmarks of this
sura are clear. It begins with a brief account of the end of the
world and the beginning of the Reckoning. Then it mentions the
categories of people after the Resurrection. They are the Front-runners, the Companions of the Right, and the Companions of the
Left. After that, it produces five proofs that the Resurrection is true
and that it is insanity to deny it. It ends with a description of the
journey of mankind from this world in death and summarises the
fates of the three categories – the Front-runners, the Companions
of the Right, and the Companions of the Left – which were mentioned at the beginning.

Many people are captivated by the distractions of life, the pressure of appetites and the intoxication of the present, and are only
aware of their material existence. One of them who is heedless
says, "I do not think there will be a Last Hour." Another says,
"There is only biological life and then we disintegrate into dust.
Only time destroys us!" They take oaths to this insanity and affirm
that there is no life after death: *"They swear by Allah with their
most earnest oaths that Allah will not raise up those who die."*
(16:38)

You see people who will be dead tomorrow accompanying the
dead of today. They talk to their companions about their hopes and
desires for this world and fail to benefit in any way from the funeral procession which is such a potent reminder for them of their
own mortality. Generations continue and peoples are swallowed
up, and those who deny are increasing rather than decreasing. The
voice of disbelief holds sway in the East and the West. The Last

Hour will arrive suddenly without warning and the voice of god-lessness will be silenced for ever. *"When the Great Event occurs, none will deny its occurrence."* (56:1-2)

"Bringing low, raising high." (56:3) There are leaders and kings who will be raised as vile paupers because they have not prepared anything for that Day. There are obscure people who will be at the summit of existence on the Day of Rising. "Many a person who is dressed in this world will be naked on the Day of Rising." (al-Bukhari) It is a day in which all injustices will be rectified, all falsehood annihilated and truth disclosed in all its brilliance.

There will be a physical shaking whose beginning is described in the words of the Almighty: *"When the earth is convulsed and the mountains are crushed and become scattered dust in the air."* (56:4-6) When the Last Hour comes, an earthquake will shake everything and by it solid stone will be transformed into atoms like those specks which we see dancing in the rays of sunlight. *"On the day the earth is changed to other than the earth, and the heavens likewise, and they parade before Allah, the One, the Conquering."* (14:48) We do not know how long we will continue before the earth is transformed. Tens or hundreds of generations? The lack of temporal definition is not important. The important thing is that it will most certainly occur.

Allah Almighty declares that the sons of Adam will be divided into three groups: *"And you will be classed into three. The Companions of the Right: what of the Companions of the Right? The Companions of the Left: what of the Companions of the Left? And the Front-runners, the Front-runners: those are the Ones Brought Near in Gardens of Delight."* (56:7-12)

After describing the states in the Next Life of these three categories *Surat al-Waqi'a* gives five proofs, drawn from people's experience of this world, for the Resurrection being true.

The first is *"We created you so why do you not confirm the truth?"* (56:57) How can the Master of the first creation be suspected of incapacity to create it a second time? Allah says about this in another *ayat*: *"It is He who originated creation and then brings it back again. That is easy for Him."* (30:27) There is no easy or hard, easier or harder, with Allah. That is why He follows this with His words, *"His is the Highest Designation in the heavens and the earth. He is the Almighty, the All-Wise."* (30:27) This is repeated in many *suras* and is a self-evident truth which it is arrogant to reject. *"They say, 'What! When we are bones and crumbled dust, will we then be raised up as a new creation!' Say: 'It would not matter if you were rock or iron or indeed any creation that you think is harder still!' They will say, 'Who will bring us back again?' Say: 'He who brought you into being in the first place.'"* (17:49-51)

The second proof is that the One who created the universe the first time did not expend any effort in it and His command is carried out. Every day, indeed every hour, every second, He renews His creation. That is clearly evident in the formation of human beings and the process of procreation. *"Have you thought about the sperm that you ejaculate? Is it you who create it or are We the Creator? We have decreed death for you and We will not be forestalled from replacing you with others the same as you and reforming you in a way you do not know."* (56:58-61)

Sperm is a wondrous liquid. As determined by the All-Powerful, one drop of this base liquid contains millions of live sperm. This life, which is invisible owing to its minuteness, carries in it all the qualities of a fully grown human being, both physical and mental. See how physical and mental characteristics move from father to child by way of the living sperm. Are there factories in the testicles which are managed by geniuses who produce that? There is no such thing. The One who oversees these changes, first and last, is Allah, *"He who has created all things in the best possible way. He originated the creation of man from clay, then produced his progeny from an extraction of mean water, then formed him and breathed into him something of His spirit. And He assigned for you hearing and sight and hearts. What little thanks you show!"* (32:7-9)

The third proof is the very earth on which we live. There we find gardens with and without trellises, fields, woods and countless varieties of agricultural produce – grains, fruits, nuts, oils and fabrics, and flowers with a multitude of scents and shapes. Who produces all that? The farmer ploughs the earth and casts seed into it and that is all he knows. *"Have you thought about what you cultivate? Is it you who make it germinate, or are We the Germinator? If We willed We could have made it broken stubble."* (56:63-65) Bringing the dead land to life is a symbol repeated many times in the Qur'an. Our emergence from our graves on the Last Day to meet Allah and encounter our Reckoning is like those plants which emerge from the dead earth containing sugar, oil and starch and all the colours of the spectrum. Why deny the Resurrection, when there is a resurrection taking place every moment?

The farmer imagines that the harvest is a foregone conclusion, so Allah explains to him that it is only by His Power and Generosity that the whole process of growth and ripening takes place, and that if He wished He could destroy what emerges from the earth so it would be of no use to anyone. *"If We willed We could have made it broken stubble. You would then be left devoid of fruit, distraught: 'We are ruined. No! In fact we are destitute!'"* (56:65-67)

We find the fourth proof in *Surat al-Waqi'a* that the Resurrection is a reality in His words: *"Have you thought about the water that you drink? Is it you who brought it down out of the clouds or are We the Sender?"* (56:68-69) Water is the source of physical life and the basis of its continuance. The Almighty says: *"And We made from water every living thing. Will they not then believe?"* (21:30) Water covers four-fifths of the surface area of the earth. It has a role which merits profound thought. The wind drives the clouds, for instance, so that water from the Indian Ocean falls on the land and animals of Egypt. Then the used water goes down the drains and sewers and follows courses we do not know to return to the seas and oceans and come full cycle. Then it begins another cycle with increase or decrease. The Almighty says, *"We sent down a measured amount of water from heaven and lodged it firmly in the earth; and We are well able to remove it."* (23:18)

Yes, the One who brought it into existence is able to remove it! *"If We willed We could have made it bitter. So why do you not give thanks?"* (56:70) Divine will alone is the source of bringing into existence and annihilation. Water, which is the natural means of life here and life after death, is an element subject to this absolute Will. We find in the *Sunna*: "Allah will send down a rain like dew and the bodies of people will grow from it," after having been dead in their graves.

The fifth proof is in the element of fire. *"Have you thought about the fire that you light? Is it you who make the trees that fuel it grow or are We the Grower? We have made it to be a reminder, and a comfort for travellers in desert wastes."* (56:71-73) I believe that this evidence is displayed by modern science. When we breathe we inhale oxygen and exhale carbon dioxide, and the reverse of that is done by the plants: they take in carbon dioxide and give off oxygen. Charcoal is carbon. The wonder is that those plants are the source of fuel and although they glisten with life, they conceal the means for combustion. The tree with its trunk, branches, and green leaves soon becomes dry and is transformed into fuel for fires. That is how we see death in the midst of life.

The characteristics of matter, simple or compound, are a matter worthy of study and benefit. A chemical compound may display attributes which are diametrically opposed to those of the elements from which it is compounded. For example, we drink water to quench our thirst and our thirst disappears. At the same time we see that the two elements – oxygen and hydrogen – from which it is formed are closer to burning than they are to quenching. We see in gardens and fields signs of vigour and growth and then after a short time we see disappearance and burning. Thus opposites follow one another. How easy that is for Divine power! *"You merge the night into the day. You merge the day into the night. You extract the living from the dead. You extract the dead from the living. You provide for those You will without any reckoning."* (3:27)

✳✳✳✳✳✳

The main subject of *Surat al-Waqi'a* – the fate of mankind in the Next World – gives rise here to an important digression. There are theologians today, both Muslims and non-Muslims, who deny that Paradise has any physical reality and denigrate that idea. They think that theirs is an elevated concept, whereas in reality it is great ignorance. Anas ibn an-Nadr saw the promised reward when he objected to the action of those who retreated at Uhud and he advanced alone to fight the idolaters and bore the slash of the swords on his flesh, shouting, "I smell the fragrance of the Garden beyond Uhud!" Was this great believer a man subject to delusion? No, he is the man of whom the Lord of the Worlds said: *"Among the believers are men who were true to the contract which they made with Allah. Some of them have fulfilled their pact by death and some of them are still waiting to do so."* (33:23)

There was Ja'far at-Tayyar (Ja'far ibn Abi Talib) who held the banner of Islam in his hand, and did not let it fall until his arms were severed. Then another was swift to bear the precious banner. He was looking forward to martyrdom, saying, "How excellent the Garden is! so near! So good and cool its drink!" Is such a man's expectation of resting in the shade of the Garden an illusion or feebleness of mind? That is what the people of flawed nature and thought say. Our sources of knowledge are the Book of Allah and the *Sunna* of His Messenger. May we hold fast to them! They give us a clear and unequivocal view of both this world and the Next.

They make it absolutely evident to us that it is in the Next World that things take on their true appearance whereas here in this world they appear only in a shadowy way. *"Give good news to those who believe and do right actions that they will have Gardens with rivers flowing under them. Whenever they are given fruit there as provision, they will say, "This is what we were given before." But they were only given a simulation of it. They will have there spouses of perfect purity and they will remain there timelessly, forever."* (2:24) So the truth is that, if anything, we will not really experience reality until the Next World!

I read that a famous Christian missionary mocked the 'Golden Garden' and 'Fiery Hell', disparaging the physical rewards Islam explicitly describes. Such people are in fact trapped in this world and espouse philosophies which have no connection to Revelation whatsoever. What good has humanity obtained from these concepts? Their false understanding of the true nature of existence has succeeded only in driving people away from religion. They suppose themselves to be enlightened but bring nothing but darkness to people's lives.

The human being, who comprises both matter and spirit, is only put right by teachings which acknowledge his combined physical and spiritual nature. The banner of this teaching was borne by all the Prophets. Among them was Musa, who said to intercede for his people: *"You are our Protector so forgive us and have mercy on us. You are the best of Forgivers. Prescribe good for us in this world and the Next World. We have truly turned to You."*(7:155-156) Before him Ibrahim had called on his Lord, saying: *"My Lord, give me right judgement and unite me with the righteous; and make me highly esteemed among the later peoples; and make me one of the inheritors of the Garden of Delight; and forgive my father – he was one of the misguided. Do not disgrace me on the Day they are raised up, the Day when neither wealth nor sons will be of any avail, except to those who bring to Allah sound, flawless hearts. The Garden will be brought near to the godfearing. The Blazing Fire will be displayed to the misguided."* (26:83-91)

The people of bliss are divided into two groups in this *sura*. The first are those who race ahead to good deeds. The second are those whose good deeds outnumber their bad. The rest are the Companions of the Left. The greatest pleasure of the first group, the Front-runners, is nearness to Allah Almighty: *"And the Front-runners, the Front-runners: those are the Ones Brought Near in Gardens of Delight."* (56:10-12) The belief in the Unseen which they professed in this world becomes direct witnessing in the Next. The Greatness of Allah which they affirmed hypothetically before will be directly witnessed then. They will constantly praise Allah and praise and glorify Him without effort, fatigue or boredom. The *ayat* says: *"Their call there is: 'Glory be to You, O Allah!' Their greeting there is: 'Peace!' The end of their cry is: 'Praise belongs to Allah, Lord of all the Worlds!'"* (10:10)

In their tasting, the people of the Garden enjoy the reality of the *'right actions which are lasting'* which they did in this world. The exact nature of the delights of the Garden cannot be appreciated by people in this world because, as the Prophet told us, they are 'what eye has not seen nor ear heard nor occurred to the heart of man.'

But what we do know is that the delights and torments of the Next World will correspond exactly to the descriptions we have been given of them by Allah and His Messenger. There is no doubt that the people of the Garden are more than content with the gifts they receive there but it is known that their greatest pleasure is in the contemplation of the Face of Allah which they will enjoy.

Some unusual words are used in this *sura* to describe the Next World and it is worth investigating their exact meanings. *"On sumptuous woven couches,"* which are woven with precious gems *"reclining on them face to face,"* (56:15:19) meaning they will have congenial assemblies in which they will speak to one another. *"There will circulate among them ageless youths."* (56:27) They will be served by youths who will remain forever young. There will also be an abundance of things to drink in Paradise: milk, honey, water, and wine. The wine is a wine which Allah has allowed which will not cause headache or disorientation. *"It does not give them any headache nor does it leave them stupefied."* (56:19) Stupefaction is the confusion and mental derangement commonly found in those who are drunk.

Among the well-known blessings of Paradise are the dark-eyed houris. The dark-eyed houris are maidens with enchanting eyes whom the people of Paradise will enjoy. It is clear that all the inhabitants of Paradise have houris and also that the great changes will occur in the bodies of both men and women – changes of honour and perfection. Part of the perfection of Paradise will be the beauty of everyone in it.

No *sura* in the Qur'an contains an exhaustive description of all the good prepared for the godfearing. We are given various views and certain pictures of aspects of bliss appropriate to each *sura* and that gladdens the hearts of the readers and arouses hope and yearning. In this *sura* we see some of the delights prepared for the Front-runners and for the Companions of the Right, who are greater in number. *"A large group of the earlier people and a large group of the later ones."* (56:39-40) Some of the words reported about their reward need to be clarified. Lote-trees give fruit and they grow where there is abundant water. Perhaps that is the secret of why they are so precious in the desert. They always have thorns which scratch, but in Paradise they will be green and thornless.

As for 'the fruit-laden acacias,' this could mean a banana-like plant which bears fruit in bunches, or it may simply refer to the blossoms of the acacia tree. The 'wide-spreading shade' is one which does not decrease in the burning sun. *"Its foodstuffs and cool shade never fail. That is the final destiny of the godfearing."* (13:35) The 'outpouring water' is what flows under the palaces of the Garden or what plays in the fountains. The fruits of the earth are seasonal, appearing some in months but lacking for the rest of the year. The fruits of the Garden, however, are *"never failing, unrestricted."* (56:33) *"Urub'* are women who are loving and welcoming to their husbands. They may be women of this world after their otherworldly transformation or houris produced for the people of the Garden. They are close in age. That is the meaning of His words, *"Devoted, passionate, like of age, for the Companions of the Right."* (56:37-38)

Then the *sura* moves to the Companions of the Left. They are the group of the godless and depraved and the deniers who made trouble for the Messengers and attacked the *Deen*. They were pleased with the life of this world and were content with it and mocked what is beyond it, not caring for anything but their own desires in their life here. Special words are also used to describe their punishment: *"Amid searing blasts and scalding water"* (56:43) are those winds which scorch with their heat. The word for them, *'samum'*, is derived from *'samm'* (poison) because of the intensity of their venom.

"The murk of thick black smoke" is a dense black smoke whose shade gives no relief. It is also referred to elsewhere: *"Proceed to a shadow which forks into three but gives no shade or help against the flames."* (77:30-31) By why do the People of the Left deserve this punishment? Because they did not protect themselves against it in this world by righteous actions. They did not believe in it at all. Their life on the face of the earth was filled with pleasures or spent in quest of them, whether they found them or not. Allah describes the life of the unbeliever in this world and his confining himself to it alone, saying, *"He used to be joyful in his family. He thought that*

he was never to return." (84:13-14) He returns to His Lord. *"But on the contrary his Lord was always watching him."* (84:15)

The unbelievers based their lives on the notion that they would not be resurrected. This idea now almost envelops the entire world. It is the basis for lapsing into acts of disobedience and pre-occupation with them without any sense of repugnance or regret. That is the 'immense wrongdoing' of this *sura. "Before that they were living in luxury, persisting in immense wrongdoing and saying, 'When we are dead and turned to dust and bones, shall we then be raised again, or our forefathers, the earlier people?' Say: 'The earlier and the later people will certainly all be gathered to the appointment of a specified Day."* (56:45-50)

Then the *sura* returns again to describing the punishment which the godless will receive: *"Then you, O misguided, O deniers, will eat from the tree of Zaqqum."* (56:51-52) Zaqqum is a repulsive bitter fruit. We seek refuge with Allah from it. When anyone eats it, he becomes crazed in quest of water, but he will not find anything but boiling water: *"They are given boiling water to drink which tears apart their bowels."* (47:15) In addition to its hideous taste, eating Zaqqum causes the person to seek water frantically because of the thirst he experiences. It is like the thirst-crazed camel whose intestines are disordered with a fever which makes it seek water unendingly. *"Gulping like thirst-crazed camels. This will be their hospitality on the Day of Repayment."* (56:56)

These vivid pictures of reward and punishment all encourage hope and fear and are especially needed now in a time in which science, technology and communications are making people heedless of the Next World and are diverting them from acting for it. Mankind has never been in greater need of being reminded of the Day of Rising. This reminder may discipline their appetites and restrain their desires. When the ordinary mind knows that the Last Day is a reality, it will not prefer a little to a lot or the ephemeral to the lasting; it will not forgo the reward of the Next World for the sake of this world as modern civilisation does.

Surat al-Waqi'a ends with a type of challenge before which creatures are powerless. Is anyone able to escape their end? Can human beings, however much they support one another, defend themselves against death or even help a friend or relative escape it? *"Why then, when death reaches the throat and you are at that moment looking on – and We are nearer him than you but you cannot see – why then, if you are not subject to Our command do you not send it back if you speak the truth?"* (56:83-87) But you will never bring back a soul to its body in this world after it has fulfilled its prescribed term. Rather human beings will be divided into groups and parties according to what they prepared for the Next World and they will be divided according to what they earned.

"But the truth is, if he is one of Those Brought Near, there is solace and sweetness and a Garden of Delight." (56:88-89) This, of course, refers to the elite group of the Front-runners.

"And if he is one of the Companions of the Right, 'Peace be upon you!' from the Companions of the Right." (56:90-91) That is the greeting of the angels to those who are saved and were victorious in the Battle of Life. They receive them with the joyful good news on the day that they return to Allah.

"And if he is one of the misguided deniers, then there is hospitality of scalding water and roasting in the Blazing Fire." (56:92-94) Those are the Companions of the Left and their fate is bleak.

Then the end of the *sura* reinforces its beginning, and summarises its contents. Will people realise the fates that await them? Whether they heed or are heedless, that will not change the facts: *"This is indeed the Truth of Certainty. Glorify then the Name of your Lord the Magnificent!"* (56:95-96)

Sura 57
Al-Hadid: Iron

Surat al-Hadid is an entirely Madinan *sura* as we shall see. In consequence it is directed to social rather than individual considerations. One of the distinguishing characteristics of Muslim society is that all its activities are directed to Allah. From before the rising of dawn until after the sun has set, the Muslims, both ruler and ruled, hasten to the mosques and the call of the *adhan* is heard in every quarter to call Muslims to the prayer and the fulfilment of their daily obligations to Allah. The whole society is dedicated to playing its destined part in the universal order. *"Everything in the heavens and the earth glorifies Allah. He is the Mighty, the Wise. The sovereignty of the heavens and the earth belongs to Him. He gives life and causes to die. He has power over all things."* (57:1-2)

The age in which we live heralds itself as the age of science. This is not surprising, for man has been able to venture into space and walk on the moon. Now other stars outside our solar system are being studied with the aim of reaching them. It is certain that the sun and the planets of our solar system are merely grains of sand in the vast expanse of space with its myriad stars and suns. Yet the universe, in spite of its huge size and mass, is controlled by precise laws which also control the metabolism of our bodies, the ebb and flow of the seas and oceans, the solar and lunar eclipses, and the distances which defy both eyes and instruments. This dominion of awesome vastness is preserved by the Lord and Master of everything. "Glory be to Allah and may He be praised in number as great as His creation and His pleasure and the weight of His Throne and the extent of His words!"

All of these phenomena are means of revealing the Divine Power and Wisdom which sustain the whole of existence: *"It is He who created the heavens and the earth in six days, then settled*

Himself firmly on the Throne. He knows what goes into the earth and what comes out of it, what comes down from heaven and what goes up into it. He is with you wherever you are. Allah sees everything you do." (57:4) The task of the Muslim community is to recognise Allah and to make Him recognised, and to worship Him and to make it easy for others to worship Him. It must strive to protect the right of worship and to prevent trouble-makers from imposing their misguidance on others.

The *sura* begins by defining for the Muslim community the path by which they can convey the global message. We read the words of the Almighty: *"Believe in Allah and His Messenger and spend from that to which He has made you successors. And those of you who do believe and spend will have an enormous wage."* (57:7) Faith and spending are two principal elements for the success of the Community in achieving its end. Then this general statement is followed by detailed instruction so that it will not be difficult for the Muslims to hold to their *Deen* and live by it to the end of time. A Prophet came to them who brought them out of the darkness to the light and complemented the Divine Revelation for them, making them the best community ever to appear among mankind.

Yet modern civilisation is continually urging Muslims to abandon Islam and embrace other ideologies – it does not particularly matter which – just so long as they abandon the Book of their Lord and the *Sunna* of their Prophet! Many have responded to these modern proposals and preferred them to Islam, which in turn has led to the persecution of hundreds of thousands who are pleased with Allah as their Lord and Islam as their *Deen*. They have provoked terrible civil wars which have done untold harm to Turks, Kurds, Persians, Berbers, Indians and Africans and so many others.

These ideologies are new paganisms forbidden by the words of the Almighty: *"And what is the matter with you that you do not believe in Allah when the Messenger calls you to believe in your Lord, and He has made a covenant with you if you are believers? It is He who sends down clear signs to His slave to bring you out of the darkness to the light. Allah is All-Gentle with you, Most*

Merciful." (57:8-9) The Arabs who supposedly understand the language of the Qur'an are now one of the wealthiest peoples on earth. There is an abundance of assets in their possession and their fertile land overflows with oil and honey. Their barren deserts are full of riches and minerals. But is their wealth devoted to serving the promotion of the Message, or have their unbridled appetites overcome them in this ephemeral world?

In fact the wealth of the Muslims helps others more than it helps the Muslims themselves. Indeed it is used to shore up the economies of the enemies of Islam. The Arabs should certainly be asked: *"And what is the matter with you that you do not give in the Way of Allah when the inheritance of the heavens and the earth belongs to Allah? Those of you who gave and fought before the Victory are not the same as those who gave and fought afterwards. They are higher in rank. But to each of them Allah has promised the Best. Allah is aware of everything you do. Who will make a good loan to Allah so that He may multiply it for him? He will have a generous wage."* (57:10-11)

Good use of money in the service of belief is the practice of the people of sincere belief. As for the slaves of this life and the people of hypocrisy, their spending only supports the enemies of Islam. That is why they will be told on the Day of Rising: *"Today no ransom will be accepted from you, nor from those who rejected. Your refuge is the Fire. It is your master. What an evil destination!"* (57:15)

The basis of accepted faith is acknowledgement of Allah, self-denial, mercy to creatures and kind-heartedness. There are some people affiliated with belief whose hearts contain arrogance and selfishness which makes their hearts hard and their manner harsh. The Jews, after they broke their covenant with Allah, are examples of this kind of degeneration. Allah says about them: *"But because of their breaking of their covenant, We have cursed them and made their hearts hard."* (5:13) Although Allah forbids us to follow such people, a pernicious superficiality has spread among the Muslims and you will see people clinging to unsubstantiated opinions without budging and imagining that they alone possess the keys to Paradise. Such people look down on others and treat them with stern harshness.

Surat al-Hadid warns such people: *"Has the time not arrived for those who believe that their hearts should be submissive to the remembrance of Allah and to the Truth He has sent down, and not to be like those who were given the Book before? The time seemed too long for them and their hearts became hard..."* (57:14) This sickness causes people's actions to come to nothing. It prevents the Muslim nation from carrying out its task of transmitting Allah's Message. Humility and mercy cultivate acceptance and love. Pride and severity only result in contention and fighting.

The *sura* returns to outlining the characteristics of the community which bears the Message of Goodness and Truth. It stresses what was said earlier about faith and spending: *"The men and women who give* sadaqa *and make a good loan to Allah will have it multiplied for them and they will have a generous wage. Those who believe in Allah and His Messengers – such people are truly sincere – and the martyrs who are with their Lord will have both their wages and their light..."* (57:18-19) The 'martyrs' may be those martyred fighting in *jihad* or they may be 'witnesses', those who call people to Allah, following in the footsteps of the Prophets and explaining the Revelation.

True religion lies in maintaining the correct balance between this world and the Next World. People in our time are forgetful of the Next World. The dominant civilisation makes people ignorant of it and bars them from it. Religions have failed to conduct the battle, claiming that success in Heaven is dependant on failure on the earth. This is of course nonsense and plays right into the hands of the enemies of faith.

Recently a conference on water which was held in the Gulf states was attended by Israel! Why? Because the Jewish state has the experts. Our expertise is limited, it appears, to love of wealth and rank alone. *Surat al-Hadid* points out that we are participants in a race in this world which can only be won by someone who has trained for it properly. *"Race each other to forgiveness from your Lord and to a Garden whose breadth is that of heaven and earth together, made ready for those who believe in Allah and His Messengers."* (57:21)

The people of faith present what they have and support it and the people of disbelief present what they have and support it. That is how Allah wished for the mill of activity to turn in the earth. *"That is how it is. If Allah willed, He would avenge Himself on them, but it is so that He may test some of you by means of others."* (47:4) Anyone who looks at the opposing sides now will see something extraordinary. Nowhere on the surface of any ocean from the North Sea to the South Sea will you see any warship flying the banner of Islam, yet you can see warships, fighter jets, and submarines serving every single enemy of Islam.

Allah Almighty says: *"We sent Our Messengers with the clear signs and sent down with them the Book and the Balance so that people might establish justice. And We sent down iron in which there lies great force and many uses for mankind, so that Allah might know those who help Him and His Messengers in the Unseen. Allah is All-Strong, All-Mighty."* (57:25) Allah created iron with many properties for use as instruments of both war and peace. Have we studied these properties and made full use of them in our civilian and military activities? Have we undertaken for Allah activity which is pleasing to Him? Our Islamic nation continually looks to others. We can scarcely produce nuts and bolts, let alone weapons with which to defend our rights and beliefs.

We are strongly attached to the goods of this world and weakly attached to the Next World, but we do not even do that properly. Our knowledge of earthly sciences is practically nil! How can the world be led by people who do not understand any of its laws? Today the Muslims find themselves in a tight corner. The Jews, whose number worldwide is less than that of the inhabitants of Syria, control the resources of the Muslim world, which makes up more than a fifth of the world's population! The followers of other religions and the pagans have subdued us on many fronts. Will those for whom *Surat al-Hadid* was revealed finally wake up to what it is telling them?

The *sura* ends with two *ayats* which advise the Muslims to return to Allah and to follow His Prophet. The truth is that the first

Muslims moved from ignominy to glory when they gathered around this Qur'an and reflected on its *ayats*. They were a group whom you could count on your fingers and then became a small party which pursued its course with unwavering effort. Within the space of a few years they had become an immense nation which swallowed up nations who had ruled the world for centuries. There is absolutely no doubt that history can repeat itself if the Muslims resume their connection to their Book and follow their Prophet. *"O you who believe! Show fear of Allah and believe in His Messenger. He will give you a double portion of His mercy and grant you a light by which to walk, and will forgive you. Allah is Ever-Forgiving, Most Merciful. So that the People of the Book may know that they have no power at all over any of Allah's favour..."* (57:28-29)

Sura 58
Al-Mujadila: The Disputer

Surat al-Mujadila is the first of a group of shorter *suras* which were all revealed in Madina. Madinan society was comprised of various types of people. There were the believers whom the Revelation had transformed into leaders of mankind. There were pagans still attached to a vanishing past. There were Jews who worshipped their race and wanted to impose their errors on everyone else. There were hypocrites who sought their own interests and manifested in a thousand guises.

Despite of its brevity, this *sura* deals with all of them. It settles the problem of *dhihar*[1] which was still troubling Muslim marriages. It is made clear that it does not constitute divorce and the means of its expiation is mentioned. Islam is concerned with all family matters and lays down the parameters for Muslim family life. Allah says here: *"These are Allah's limits. The rejectors will have a painful punishment."* (58:4)

The Qur'an declares in several places that these domestic matters have great importance in the sight of Allah. After all, the family is the basic building block of society and if it is weak the whole of the community will be weak as well. Allah says in *Surat al-Baqara*: *"These are Allah's limits; so do not go beyond them,"* (2:229) after the judgements of divorce. He says in *Surat an-Nisa'*: *"These are Allah's limits. Whoever obeys Allah and His Messenger, We shall admit him into Gardens with rivers flowing under them"* (4:13) after the judgements concerning inheritance.

As we have noted before, a characteristic of the Qur'an is that it interweaves legal rulings with reminders of Divine existence to show that adhering to them is an integral part of faith and a mani-

---

1. *Dhihar*: when a man says to his wife, "Be as my mother's back." This was a divorce before Islam, but was not considered one after Islam came.

festation of reverence for Allah. *"Do you not see that Allah knows everything in the heavens and everything in the earth? No three men confer together secretly without Him being the fourth of them, nor five without Him being the sixth of them..."* (58:7)

After that the *sura* goes on to mention the behaviour of the Jews in Madina. When they greeted the Muslims, they would say, "Poison be upon you," turning 'peace' (*salam*) into 'poison' (*sam*) with the aim of cursing the Muslims and wishing for their destruction. 'A'isha heard them and rebuked them, but the Prophet, may Allah bless him and grant him peace, preferred a different and more suitable approach. The *ayat* was revealed: *"Then when they come to you they greet you with words Allah has never used in greeting you and say to themselves, 'Why does Allah not punish us for what we say?' Hell will be enough for them. They shall roast in it. What an evil destination!"* (58:8)

Then Allah commanded the Muslims that their conversations in their own assemblies or with their adversaries should avoid rancour and needless provocation and they should avoid imitating the Jews. They should not be troubled when the Jews and hypocrites went off together to confide in one another with the aim of causing injury to the believers and making them conscious of their isolation: *"Conferring in private is from Shaytan, to cause grief to those who believe. But it does not harm them at all unless by Allah's permission. So let the believers trust in Allah."* (58:10)

Islam ranks people according to their faith and knowledge. Regarding the rows of the prayer, the Messenger said, "Let those of you with discernment and intelligence be directly behind me." Allah Almighty says about general gatherings: *"Allah will raise in rank those of you who believe and those who have been given knowledge."* (58:11)

The Muslims love their Prophet deeply. How could they not love him when He has brought them out of the darkness to the light and acquainted them with their Creator and Provider? His noble person should be loved and honoured. However, the inclination to gather around the Messenger and sit with him must be regulated somewhat so that the affairs of this world and the *Deen* can be in order and so that he may have some time to devote to himself and his family. That is why this *ayat* was sent down: *"O you who believe, when you consult the Messenger privately precede your private consultation by giving* sadaqa: *that is better for you, and purer. But if you cannot find the means, Allah is Ever-Forgiving, Most Merciful."* (58:12)

If that is difficult for the believer, then the good actions available to him which he can do to please his Lord are numerous. That is better for him than simply preferring to converse with the Messenger. Speaking with great men may be a pleasure but it is more important to uphold their message: *"Are you afraid to give gifts of* sadaqa *before your private consultation? If you do not and Allah turns to you, at least establish the prayer and pay the* zakat..." (58:13)

In a society in which believers, idolaters and People of the Book are mixed together and their moral and financial interests are intertwined, principles are strongly tested. A man may prefer his relatives or commerce to his religion. Hypocrisy is a foul and very serious disease. It is one of the easiest of things for a hypocrite to take a false oath. That is why the Almighty says about this category of person: *"Do you not see those who have turned to a people with whom Allah is angry? They belong neither to you nor them. They swear to falsehood, and do so knowingly. Allah has prepared for them a terrible punishment. How evil is what they have been doing."* (58:14-15)

It is clear that a person who becomes habituated to a way of life will die following it and be raised following it. That is what makes the ordinary people in our land say, "The flautist dies but his fingers keep playing." If he dies like that, he will be raised up like that. Probably a person who was an impostor in this world will be one in the Next World and swear to lies as he swore to save himself: *"The Day that Allah raises all of them up together they will swear to Him just as they have sworn to you and reckon they have something to stand upon. But certainly it is they who are the liars."* (58:18) He will fail! *"Those who oppose Allah and His Messenger, such people are among the most abased."* (58:20)

Regarding salvation from these seditions and distinguishing between true belief and counterfeit belief, Allah commands the believers to make their beliefs known and define their principles, and to hold to their principles and be harsh to their adversaries. *"You will not find people who believe in Allah and the Last Day having love for anyone who opposes Allah and His Messenger, though they be their fathers or their sons or their brothers or their clan. Those people, Allah has inscribed belief within their hearts and will reinforce them with a Spirit from Him..."* (58:22)

Sura 59
Al-Hashr: The Gathering

"Everything in the heavens and everything in the earth glorifies Allah. He is the Mighty, the Wise." (59:1) The glorification of Allah here before the announcement of the expulsion of the Jews from their homes resembles His praise in *Surat al-An'am* after the eradication of the wrongdoers and the purification of the earth of them: *"So the last remnant of the people who did wrong was rooted out. Praise belongs to Allah, the Lord of all the worlds!"* (6:45) Freeing the world of evildoers is a tremendous blessing and enabling every man to fully enjoy his rights is a great benefit. How excellent it is when a man has peace of mind and has a healthy body over which no wrongdoer has power!

The Jews remained in and around Yathrib and claimed to pay allegiance to the Torah but did not in fact respect their Revelation or uphold justice or tell people about the Divine Unity or warn them about the Last Day. When Islam came and began to guide those who worshipped idols to Allah, they were angered by it and defamed its Prophet. They were proficient in the craft of war and transformed their homes into fortresses, thinking that no one would have any power against them. *"You did not think they would leave and they thought that their fortresses would protect them from Allah. Then Allah came upon them from where they least expected it and cast terror into their hearts. Their houses were pulled down by their own hands and by the hands of the believers..."* (59:2)

They had been quite at liberty to remain where they were but suddenly they had the idea of murdering the Messenger while he was secure and relaxed among them. When he became aware of their treachery, he immediately left the place and returned to Madina. Then their expulsion was confirmed: *"That is because*

443

they opposed Allah and His Messenger with hostility. If anyone opposes Allah, Allah is severe in retribution." (59:4) That is how they came to be sent back whence they had come.

The *sura* says that this was the first gathering, just as there is another gathering which awaits the people in the near or distant future. We are waiting for it with them. The Jews now, thanks to the heedlessness of the Muslims, have set up a state for themselves. How did they manage it? Did they remember Allah well? Did they forge a modern civilisation which believes in the Last Day? They merely took advantage of the powerlessness and negligence of the Muslims and, to make things worse, they agreed with Europe and America to reject the legacy of their Revelation and to worship the Golden Calf.

When the Muslims return again to right guidance and put things right with their Lord, they will once more regain their land and the Tribe of Israel will be dispersed again. The Prophet, peace and blessings be upon him, gave the land of the Banu'n-Nadir as a gift to the poor Muhajirun. By that balance was restored to the Muslim society in Madina. The Muhajirun had had their property and houses in Makka confiscated and they had endured that affliction for the sake of Allah. The Ansar had been wonderfully magnanimous and opened their hearts and houses to them but still the best solution lay in the Muhajirun inheriting what the Jews had left. The reason mentioned in the *sura* is: *"...so that it does not become something which merely goes by turn to the rich among you."* (59:7) This refers to wealth.

Then it describes the state of those Muhajirun. It says, *"It is for the poor of the Muhajirun who were driven from their homes and wealth desiring the favour and the pleasure of Allah and in support of Allah and of His Messenger. Those are the truly sincere."* (59:8)

In our time, as in the time of the Prophet, there are hypocritical Muslims who do not see any harm in cohabiting with the Jews and allying themselves with them. The fact is that the two groups have no *deen*. The *deen* with the Jews is not cleansing of the heart, purification of behaviour and generosity. It is overweening selfishness and extraordinary arrogance. The hypocritical Muslims do not believe that Allah chose them to elevate the spiritual and intellectual level of people. They only seek this life. It is no wonder that they reinforce each other: *"Did you not see the hypocrites saying to their brothers, those among the People of the Book who reject, 'If you are driven out we will leave with you and we will never obey anyone in respect of you, and if you are fought against we will help you'? Allah bears witness that they are truly liars."* (59:11)

The connection of the Jews to the Next World is weak. The first books of the Torah do not speak much about the reward and punishment and the Garden and the Fire. It is a dry history of a stiff-necked people. That materialistic thinking has permeated modern society and misled people into worshipping the present moment and forgetting what lies beyond it. After the Christians abandoned the few remnants of the teachings of 'Isa that remained with them they too were unable resist this crookedness and so the entire world was infected with this pernicious disease.

That is why this *sura* urges people to the recognition of Allah and preference for what He holds in store and brings the Next World near so that it makes it an actualised future. *"O you who believe, show fear of Allah. Let each self look to what it has sent ahead for Tomorrow. Show fear of Allah. Allah is aware of everything you do. Do not be like those who forgot Allah, and so He made them forget themselves. Such people are the degenerate."* (59:18-19)

A violent conflict will occur between the Arabs and the Jews and the Jews will not cease to have helpers among the European peoples who bear malice towards Islam and do not recognise either 'Isa or Muhammad. The question which must be answered is: When will the Muslims truly enter Islam? When will they be immersed in the spirit of Islam and live according to its rulings? When will they march under the banner of the Qur'an? Their Prophet led his community from the mosque and raised the levels of knowledge and character in the tightly-knit ranks behind him. When they reached the East and West, they moved whole peoples from the earth to Heaven: *"Had We sent down this Qur'an onto a mountain, you would have seen it humble, smashed in pieces out of fear of Allah. We coin such likenesses for people so that perhaps they may reflect."* (59:21)

The *sura* about the Banu an-Nadir ends with about twenty of the Most Beautiful Names of Allah. It explains the nature of the connection to Allah, the One, and exalts this connection which encompasses all human activity. The world is under the sway of deficient religions and is only ruled by evil instincts and as humanity strives only for the sake of a higher standard of living! There is no thought or predisposition for the recompense is held in store by Allah and the meeting with Him.

Sura 60
Al-Mumtahina: The Woman Tested

The believer does not accept subjection nor is he content with humiliation. He exerts every effort to repel his oppressors. If he is overcome, he conceals his opposition and waits for the day when he will achieve his goal. In him the words of Allah Almighty are realised: *"Those who, when injustice is done to them, defend themselves."* (42:39)

The Muslims were worsted at the beginning of their history in Makka and expelled from their homes in the harshest possible manner. They refused to surrender to aggression, or to compromise with their enemy. Some people find the path of conflict difficult and take any opportunity to accept the existing situation. Such people do not see any harm in submitting to an enemy out of the desire to save themselves and their family. Allah Almighty says to those: *"O you who believe, do not take My enemy and your enemy as friends, showing love for them when they have rejected the truth that has come to you..."* (60:1)

It is a failure on your part to be gentle towards those who want to oppress you and belittle your *deen* and try to seduce you. *"If they come upon you, they will be your enemies and stretch out their hands and tongues against you with evil intent, and they would dearly love you to reject."* (60:2)

Holding fast to creeds and principles requires complete constancy on the part of those who support them, abandonment of all who oppose them, and active resistance to all who obstruct them. That has been the path taken by the true followers of the Prophets in all ages. That is why Allah says to the Muslims: *"You have an excellent example in Ibrahim and those with him when they said to their people, 'We wash our hands of you and what you worship apart from Allah, and we reject you. Between us and you there will*

447

be enmity and hatred forever unless and until you believe in Allah alone.'" (60:4) This does not mean that the Muslims become aggressors. They repel aggression and proclaim that they will hold to their *Deen* to the last breath.

In defining the relations between the Muslims and their enemies, Allah Almighty says: *"Allah does not forbid you, in respect of those who have not fought you in the* Deen *nor driven you from your homes, from being good to them and being just towards them. Allah loves those who are just. Allah merely forbids you, in respect of those who did fight you in the* Deen *and drive you from your homes and supported your expulsion, from taking them as friends. Whoever does take them as friends, they are the wrongdoers."* (60:8-9) We have seen complete disregard for international treaties and human rights and hundreds of thousands of Muslims have been invaded and forced to abandon their homes to others and then been forced to live in the open for decades. Is it honourable to be content with that? Is anger on that account religious fanaticism?

Allah loves justice. Where is the justice in victimising the Muslims in this sinful manner? The answer is that aspirations should be awakened to the desire to change this situation worldwide so that worship of Allah, justice to human beings and respect for humanity may be re-established. As a general rule, the major nations are only concerned with their own best interests. They do not care what happens to others. That is not permissible. Love for the sake of Allah and hatred for the sake of Allah are vital elements of faith. If you like a tyrant just because of some benefit you have had from him, or dislike someone else just because he has not given you what you wanted, question your faith! Unsound feelings show defective faith.

At the end of the *sura* we are instructed to show fervour for the truth alone and to turn away from the people of doubt and deviance. *"O you who believe! Do not make friends of people with whom Allah is angry, who have despaired of the Next World in the same way that the unbelievers have despaired of the inhabitants of the graves."* (60:13) When the idolaters dictated their conditions to the Muslims in the treaty of al-Hudaybiyya, they imposed this strange condition: "If anyone leaves Makka as a Muslim, the people of Madina are not to receive him as an emigrant. If anyone leaves Madina as an apostate, the people of Makka may offer him security and safety." The Messenger, may Allah bless him and grant him peace, accepted this clause despite its apparent unfairness. But there were some women in Makka whose hearts had been opened to Islam. Where could they go?

A Revelation was sent down announcing that they were to be accepted in Madina and it was not permitted to leave them in the hands of the unbelievers. *"O you who believe, when believing women come to you in emigration, submit them to a test. Allah has best knowledge of their belief. If you know them for believers, do not return them to the rejectors..."* (60:10) At the same time the Muslims were commanded to compensate those idolaters whose womenfolk believed in Islam, and not to remain married to unbelieving women. *"Do not hold to any marriage ties with women who disbelieve. Ask for what you paid and let them ask for what they paid. That is the judgement of Allah: Allah will judge between them..."* (60:10) These just directives indicate the spirit of the *Deen* and this treaty did not last long. Makka was soon conquered and the strongholds of paganism were demolished.

Surat al-Mumtahina then lays down the terms under which the Prophet was to accept the allegiance of women: *"O Prophet, when believing women come to you pledging allegiance to you that they will not associate anything with Allah or steal or fornicate or kill their children or give a false ascription of paternity – making up lies about their bodies – or disobey you in respect of anything right – then accept their allegiance and ask forgiveness for them."* (60:12) This prescription is really extraordinary in that it gave social equality to women in a society in which they had previously been treated as chattels.

Sura 61
As-Saff: The Ranks

To achieve victory and protection, the great Message requires complete commitment and sincerity. People who voice empty words and claims are not competent to support it; nor are the cowards who, when they are obliged to undertake *jihad*, roll their eyes as if they were about to swoon from fear of death. Atheists and adherents of sects are bold in serving what they embrace. They can only be resisted by strong believers who are prepared to die in defence of the truth and ready to spend their lives and wealth for it. Such people close ranks against the enemy. Whenever one hero is martyred another takes his place. Words alone will not achieve anything. That is why the believers, who did not rise to this level, were rebuked: *"O you who believe, why do you say what you do not do? It is deeply abhorrent to Allah that you should say what you do not do."* (61:2-3)

When the believer dedicates himself wholeheartedly to the pleasure of his Lord, he will be answered by everything in existence praising its Lord. As for the one who rebels against Allah, he is out of touch with existence and puts himself outside of the norm of obedience. That is why *Surat as-Saff* begins with this *ayat*: *"Everything in the heavens and everything in the earth glorifies Allah. He is the Almighty, the All-Wise."* (61:1) A rebuke comes after that, followed by affirmation of the true believers, and then the nations are mentioned which did not affirm Allah but opposed Allah and His Messengers.

The first of those are the Jews who injured Musa. They followed him but lacked the courage to confront his enemies. They quickly squandered the blessing of the Scripture which had been sent down to them. *"When Musa said to his people, 'O my people! Why do you injure me when you know that I am the Messenger of*

Allah to you?' So when they deviated, Allah made their hearts deviate." (61:5) Any Prophet would be disappointed if scant heed is paid to his teachings and people are afraid to face his enemy.

Then the *sura* mentions 'Isa and his people. It is clear that 'Isa, peace be upon him, had a message for a specific time and place. He was sent to the foolish ones of the misguided tribe of Israel to reconnect them to the Torah whose true teaching they had rebelled against and to treat their spiritual and social ills. He also paved the way for the universal Prophethood which would guide all mankind to Allah, the One God. *"When 'Isa son of Maryam, said, 'O Tribe of Israel, I am the Messenger of Allah to you, confirming the Torah which came before me and giving good news of a Messenger coming after me whose name is Ahmad.'"* (61:6)

When we look at the books which are attributed to the disciples of 'Isa and which are metaphorically called 'Gospels', we find apt words which give us pause for thought. In the Gospel of Matthew (24:11-14) 'Isa, peace be upon him, says, "And many false prophets shall rise, and shall deceive many. And because iniquity shall abound, the love of many shall wax cold. But he that shall endure until the end, the same shall be saved. And this Gospel of the Kingdom shall be preached in all the world for a witness until all nations, and then shall the end come."

We ask ourselves: "Who is this who claims the kingdom and offers himself to all the world and will remain until the end of the world?" Do these qualities apply to any other person but Muhammad? The Gospel of John (14:15-16) says: "If ye love me, keep my commandments. And I will pray the Father, and he shall give you another Comforter, that he may abide with you for ever." This Greek word means the 'merciful who drives away sorrows'. Who is this who will come whose Message will endure forever? It is, of course, none other than the last of Allah's Messen-gers, Muhammad, may Allah bless him and grant him peace.

"Who does greater wrong than he who fabricates a lie against Allah when he is called to Islam? Allah does not guide wrongdoing people. They desire to extinguish Allah's light with their mouths but Allah will perfect His light even if the rejectors are averse." (61:7-8) The intellect is the most precious gift which

Allah has given people. Faith which is based on suppressing or denying the intellect, as Christians do, has no substance and no good.

The *sura* concludes with two noble ideas which affirm its beginning. The first is that life consists of both faith and active struggle: *"That you believe in Allah and His Messenger and fight to the utmost in the Way of Allah with your property and your-selves."* (61:11) The second is the readiness of the believer in every place to support Allah and raise His Banner. He walks in the highways and by-ways of life with his ears alert. When he hears a call to Allah, he rushes to answer the caller. There is an echo of this when we respond to the *mu'adhdhin* when his voice pierces the air, calling to the prayer.

'Isa relied on this support when he saw that the Jews doubted him and turned from him. He called out: *"'Who will be my helpers to Allah?' The Disciples said, 'We will be the helpers of Allah.'"* (61:14) The disciples of 'Isa were like the Companions of Muhammad – like everyone who is devoted to the Truth and raises its banner. They are the only hope for the Message to be established and upheld. Now is the time for us to grasp the meaning of this *ayat* and put it into practise: *"O you who believe, be helpers of Allah..."* (61:14)

Sura 62
Al-Jumu'a: Congregation

"Everything in the heavens and everything in the earth glorifies Allah, the King, the Most Holy, the Mighty, the Wise." (62:1) *Surat al-Jumu'a* begins with this *ayat* which encourages the believers to perform their obligation and listen to the *khutba*. Since everything glorifies the praise of Allah, the Muslims must not delay in participating in the obligatory public gathering of the Friday Prayer. They are urged to go to the mosques to join the body of the Muslims and strengthen their ranks. Friday is our weekly celebration. It contains a blessed moment. If that moment coincides with any of us directing supplication to Allah, Allah will accept it from him and forgive him. It is recommended to have a bath and for men to put on perfume for this day.

That the *sura* begins with glorification is a sort of rebuke to those who left the mosque when they heard the caravans arriving with goods: *"But when they see a chance of trade or some entertainment they scatter off to it and leave you standing there. Say: 'What is with Allah is better than entertainment or trade, and Allah is the best of providers.'"* (62:11)

The beginning and middle of the *sura* discuss the sending of the Final Messenger to the unlettered Arabs. The fact is that Allah re-directed the Universal Message from the People of the Book because the disorders of false religiosity were numerous, combining pride, harshness and stupidity. When people do not help themselves, how can they help others? When the nature of ordinary people is sound and their desires are few, they are quicker to answer Allah and able to help Him. That is why Allah did not send His Prophet among the Jews but preferred the Arabs to them: *"It is He who raised up among the unlettered people a Messenger from them to recite His signs to them and purify them and teach them the Scripture and Wisdom, even though before that they were clearly misguided."* (62:2)

The Arabs conveyed the Message to all the world and made efforts with other peoples. They eventually acted as excellent conduits for the Revelation, whereas the Jews worshipped their ethnicity, forgot their Lord, and remembered their appetites: *"The likeness of those who were charged with the Torah, but then have not upheld it, is that of a donkey loaded with weighty tomes. How evil is the likeness of the people who deny Allah's signs! Allah does not guide wrongdoing people."* (62:5) Past and present, the Jews continue to turn people away from seeking the Next World and are ruthless participants in the free-for-all to gain the goods of this world. They are good at everything except leading people to Allah: *"Say: 'O you who are Jews, if you claim to be the friends of Allah, to the exclusion of all other people, then wish for death if you are telling the truth.' But they will never ever wish for it because of what they have done."* (62:6-7) The unfortunate truth is that many Muslims have taken the same path.

Sura 63
Al-Munafiqun: Hypocrites

Hypocrisy is one of the basest qualities that a human being can have. It begins by people being two-faced and continues to grow until they become like a chameleon, which takes on different colours according to the environment in which it finds itself. Lying and perjury are the foremost qualities of the hypocrite. They come near or distance themselves according to the way the wind blows. They have no firm pivot upon which to revolve or definite direction in which to aim. They only consider their private interests: *"When the hypocrites come to you they say, 'We bear witness that you are indeed the Messenger of Allah.' Allah knows that you are indeed His Messenger – and Allah bears witness that the hypocrites are indeed liars."* (63:1)

However, daily events and the various situations in which they place people do not allow hypocrisy to remain hidden. It will inevitably be exposed, either by slips of the tongue or through reactions to unexpected events. *Surat al-Munafiqun* unmasked the leaders of hypocrisy and revealed their hidden motives and plans. They were eager for their outward appearance to be impeccable and their slogans admirable so their inward secrets would remain concealed, but their spite overcame them and they things that pained the Muhajirun and made the Ansar[1] angry.

If any trivial disagreement occurred between people the hypocrites would try to fan it into a major conflict and provoke hatred and fighting. *"They are the people who say, 'Do not spend on those who are with the Messenger of Allah, so that they all may go away.' But the treasuries of the heavens and earth belong to Allah.*

---

1. The Muhajirun, or the Companions of the Messenger of Allah who accepted Islam in Makka, emigrated to Madina where they were welcomed and given hospitality by the Ansar or "Helpers" in Madina.

But the hypocrites do not understand. " (63:7) Allah tested the Muhajirun by making them leave their houses and property in Makka and He tested the Ansar with the duty of receiving them and making them welcome in Madina. Was it permitted for Ibn Ubayy to say: "We should watch out for them. Remember the saying 'Fatten your dog and it will eat you!'"? Thus he encouraged the Ansar to injure the Muhajirun. Then he said, *" 'If we return to Madina, the mightier will drive out the inferior.' But all might belongs to Allah and to His Messenger and the believers, yet the hypocrites do not know."* (63:8)

'Abdullah ibn Ubayy hated Islam and its Prophet because he had been a candidate for the leadership of Madina before the *hijra*. When the Messenger of Allah came, he lost his opportunity to become king, which had been his dream. If the fool had only believed sincerely in Allah and the Last Day, he would have had glory far greater than this world and everything it contains. Disbelief is unbounded stupidity. If he had gone to the Messenger of Allah to apologise when he erred, he would have asked forgiveness for him and Allah would have turned to him, but he refused.

The *sura* ends with what makes the intelligent prefer Allah and what is with Him. They do not direct their aspirations to ephemeral concerns: *"O you who believe! Do not allow your wealth or your children to divert you from the remembrance of Allah. Whoever does that, it is they who are the losers."* (63:9)

Sura 64
At-Taghabun: Profit and Loss

"Everything in the heavens and everything in the earth glorifies Allah. Sovereignty and praise belong to Him. He has power over all things." (64:1) Existence acknowledges its Lord: it acknowledges that its existence derives from Him and continues by Him. That is why it glorifies His praise and carries out His command. As for human beings, they act differently. How often they are insolent to Him and deny His rights and fight His Messengers! *"He created man from a drop of sperm and yet there he is, an open challenger"* (16:4) meaning: "What is this disobedience?"

What a marvel! How can man rebel against God?
How can the denier deny Him?
Everything is a sign showing that He is One!

Surat at-Taghabun begins with this glorification to call attention to the fact that man's disobedience is out of harmony with everything else in existence. *"It is He who created you, but among you are those who reject and those who believe. Allah sees all that you do."* (64:2) It is illogical that Allah should have given you such an excellent form and, that in return you show such poor esteem for Him. He bestows countless blessings on you and yet you remain heedless and denying.

People denied Revelation because those who brought it were humans like them. It is difficult for us to recognise the superiority of another person. We want to go our own way and lord it over others. This is especially true of the rich, who often take pleasure in humiliating others. *"Has the news not reached you of those who rejected before and then tasted the evil consequences of what they did? They shall have a painful punishment. That is because their*

457

Messengers came to them with the Clear Signs but they said, 'Are human beings going to guide us?' So they rejected and turned away. Allah is completely independent of them: But Allah is Rich beyond need, Praiseworthy." (64:5-6)

"Those who disbelieve claim that they will never be resurrected. Say: 'Oh yes, by my Lord, you certainly will be resurrected, and then you will informed about everything you did. That is easy for Allah.'" (64:7) Denying the Resurrection is an ancient error but the sway that it enjoys in modern times is totally unprecedented. The civilisation which overshadows us glorifies the life of this world and heaps ridicule on what lies beyond it. They express their disbelief that someone intelligent can accept the the Last Day as a reality! The People of the Book have allowed themselves to indulge in this denial which encourages people to forget Allah and to deny the encounter with Him. They are vexed by the Qur'an when it depicts the events of the Next World. The true *Deen* needs to be represented in all its freshness and vigour to counter this widespread godlessness.

"So believe in Allah and His Messenger and the Light We have sent down." (64:8) The light is the Qur'an. It is called that in many *ayats. "But We have appointed it to be a light by which We guide those of Our slaves We will."* (42:52) Nothing can reliably be said to have truly come from Allah except this Book. It contains articles of faith which rescue people from error accompanied by evidences and proofs which produce certainty in people whose hearts are open to the truth. If only the Muslims would rise to the level of their Book and implement and transmit their Message!

"The Day He gathers you for the Day of Gathering. That is the Day of Profit and Loss." (64:9) The feelings of people on the Day of Rising require explanation. Some of them will say, *"Oh, if only I had prepared for my life to come!"* (89:24) Many will regret that they wasted their ample time to no avail and did not use the good health they were given to good effect, as is mentioned in the *hadith,* "There are two blessings about which many people are duped: health and free time." There were many opportunities for salvation which they missed through great foolishness! *"It may be that those who reject will wish they had been Muslims."* (15:2)

Too late! The days of action are gone and the Days of Reckoning have arrived!

Since this *sura* is Madinan, and the Muhajirun and Ansar had the task of establishing the governance of Islam in the face of terrible difficulties and fierce opposition, Allah Almighty said, to make the people steadfast and to strengthen their faith: *"No misfortune occurs except by Allah's permission. Whoever believes in Allah, He will guide his heart. Allah has knowledge of all things."* (64:11) Compelling a man to leave his homeland is something arduous which not every man can endure. Some people responded to the summons to make *hijra;* others did not, preferring to remain where they were with their wives and children, and so missed this honour. *"O you who believe! In your wives and your children there is an enemy for you so beware of them. And if you pardon and exonerate and forgive, Allah is Ever-Forgiving, All-Merciful."* (64:14) Preoccupation with this life is a path of deception and loss: *"Your wealth and your children are only a trial. But with Allah there is an huge reward."* (64:15)

Resisting misguidance and holding to the truth inevitably mean loss and sacrifice on the part of people of faith, which they should accept with resolve and contentment. We have seen atheists in our time who do not care about anything and it is impossible for any to overcome them except "men who are true to their contract with Allah."

Our greatest enemy lies within ourselves and if we can truly master ourselves our other enemies too will soon also be overcome. *"So show fear Allah as much as you are able, and listen and obey, and spend for your own benefit. It is the people who are safe-guarded from the avarice of selves who are successful."* (64:16)

Sura 65
At-Talaq: Divorce

Surat at-Talaq is called the lesser *Sura an-Nisa'* (*Sura* of Women) because of the rules concerning marriage which Allah has put in it. It deals with some of the problems and troubles to which marriage is subject. The entire *sura* revolves around this single theme and is an excellent example of how the *ayats* of the Qur'an interconnect and are woven together to produce a coherent meaning in a specific context. The rulings of *fiqh* taken from the *sura* which are mentioned here are selected from the opinions of classical scholars and commentators of the Qur'an and are not intended to be definitive legal judgements.

The beginning of the *sura* directly addresses the Prophet, peace and blessings and be upon him, because he is the leader of the community. Directly addressing the Messenger concerning a matter relevant to all the individuals of the community indicates that it is something important and that it extends beyond the bounds of the private arena into the public social arena.

The fact is that divorce can cause a man to disregard his wife, children and family and so there have to be rules regulating it in order that it will not be completely arbitrary and a gateway to corruption and injustice. For this reason the Divine Legislater specified a specific time for divorce, declaring that it is not permitted during menstruation and lochia. There must be two witnesses, and afterwards the divorced woman should remain in the marital home. The pronouncement of divorce is not necessarily the end of married life: it may end, or it may continue. The marriage may be given a new lease of life if the circumstances which led to divorce change. The provocations may vanish and the desire for harmony and reconciliation may predominate during the three months before the expiry of the *'idda* period.

460

All these points are contained in the first *ayat*: *"O Prophet, when any of you divorce women, divorce them during their period of purity and calculate the waiting-period carefully. And show fear of Allah, your Lord. Do not evict them from their houses, nor should they leave unless they commit an outright indecency. Those are Allah's limits, and anyone who oversteps Allah's limits has wronged himself. You do not know: it may be that after that Allah will cause a new situation to develop."* (65:1) Here once again we see the order to fear Allah occurring in an *ayat* concerned with legal rulings, showing that the law is based not so much on punishment – although that may in certain situations be appropriate – as on the desire of the individuals in society to be pleasing to their Lord.

In this *sura* the benefits of fearing of Allah are specified. *"Whoever shows fear of Allah, He will give him a way out and provide for him from where he does not expect... Whoever shows fear of Allah, He will make his affair easy for him."* (65:2-4) Thus it can be seen that fear of Allah is an active principle which produces practical results in everyday life such as the resolution of family crises and other worldly problems.

The Noble Revelation goes on to mention the details of maintenance under all circumstances and clarifies the particulars of suckling and other connected matters. It is clear that part of the Divine Guidance is to prevent divorce from being a depressing social evil and to limit its deleterious effects as far as possible. When Allah's instructions are adhered to correctly it is remarkable how divorce, one of the most potentially painful human experiences, becomes far less fraught with emotional turmoil and embitterment. It is also remarkable that in spite of the comparative ease of divorce in Islam marriage is on the whole a very stable institution. Look at the contrast with Western society, where half of all marriages now end in divorce, causing untold suffering to individuals and damage to the social fabric.

However, safety in these social matters as in all other aspects of human life depends upon following Allah's guidance, and the *sura* continues by reminding us of how the two things are interconnected. This begins with the Almighty saying: *"How many a city spurned its Lord's command and His Messengers, and so We called it harshly to account and punished it with a dreadful punishment. It tasted the evil consequences of what it did..."* (65:8-9) So the Revelation is a blessing but it is also a great responsibility and the penalties for ignoring it are dire. No people whom Allah honours with Revelation and Guidance can afford to be prodigal with any of its stipulations – and that includes all questions from macro-economics to details of domestic life. Nor should they place obstacles in the path of the spread of Allah's Message by setting a poor example of Islam and improperly implementing its judgements.

The *sura* ends with an *ayat* reminding us that these injunctions do indeed come to us directly from Him and are, as it were, part of the very fabric of existence of which He is totally and continually aware and over which He has absolute power. *"It is Allah who created the seven heavens and of the earth the same again, the Command descending down through all of them, so that you might know that Allah has power over everything and that Allah encompasses everything in His knowledge."* (65:12) Are we then going to show fear of Allah and gain the innumerable benefits He has promised us for doing so, or to continue to follow the path of slavish adherence to man-made legal systems which can only result in chaos and degradation?

Sura 66
At-Tahrim: Making Unlawful

The wives of the Prophet, the Mothers of the Believers, were the best and highest of the women of the community as regards purity and fear of Allah. They accompanied the Noble Prophet and helped him to convey his Message and responded to and passed on all the *ayats* of Allah and the wisdom of His Messenger which were revealed in their houses. Despite all this, or perhaps because of this, Allah rebuked them for their lapses and warned them that their supremely privileged position was no guarantee of salvation.

The Qur'an refers to two instances of less than perfect behaviour on the part of the Prophet's wives. One was when they sided together against the Prophet to ask him for more maintenance, out of resentment at the frugal lives they were forced to lead in spite of the growing prosperity of the Muslims. But they entirely abandoned their complaint when it became clear to them that that was necessary for those who desired Allah and His Messenger and the Next Abode.

The second incident referred to in this *sura* was when two of the Prophet's wives tried to take advantage of his gentle nature for their own ends. He was a perfect companion, kind and mild-tempered, and on this occasion that led two of his wives to be bold towards him. The whole affair was sparked off by jealousy. They concocted a plot to discredit the wife of whom they were jealous and, knowing that he had just come from her, one of them claimed that she smelt an unpleasant odour coming from him. He said, "I drank honey with Zaynab." She said, "Perhaps the bees visited noxious plants." He said, "I will never do not it again. Do not tell anyone." The idea was to make him less keen on her company.

When the Messenger discovered the ruse he was angered by what had occurred, andhe kept away from all his wives until it was rumoured that he had divorced all of them. This was the reason for the revelation of *Surat at-Tahrim* which put an end to the situation and reprimanded those who had injured the Messenger and behaved badly. It begins with the *ayat*: *"O Prophet, why do you make forbidden what Allah has made lawful for you, seeking the good pleasure of your wives? Allah is Ever Forgiving, Most Merciful. Allah has made the expiation of your oaths obligatory for you."* (66:1-2) It is not permitted for anyone to make an oath which makes unlawful something that is lawful. Such an oath must not be held to and should be expiated by the expiation of an oath. No one can make unlawful what Allah has made permitted.

Then the Revelation alludes to the actual incident. Commentators say that Hafsa bint 'Umar and 'A'isha bint Abi Bakr were the two wives concerned and that it is those two who are referred to in the *sura*. *"If the two of you would turn to Allah, for your hearts clearly deviated... But if you support one another against him, Allah is his Protector and so are Jibril and every right-acting man of the believers, and furthermore the angels too will come to his support."* (66:4) The meaning is: "Your hearts deviated and you should put them right. Unless you do so, your actions will come to nothing and you will no longer be part of the body of those who are righteous."

Then the discourse is extended to include all the wives of the Prophet, to advise them to take note and to point out to them the high standard of behaviour which they should follow. *"It may be that if he does divorce you his Lord will give him in exchange better wives than you: submitted women, believing women, obedient women, penitent women, women who worship, women who fast much, both previously married women and virgins."* (66:5)

The house of Prophethood has no room for jealousy and mutual envy. It must be an example for the community and a means of advancing to the Next World and gaining Allah's pleasure. The end of the *sura* is a severe warning to those of the Prophet's wives who took part in angering him and causing him sorrow – and, by extension – to anyone who thinks that a privileged position in this world is a guarantee of security in the Next. The wives of Nuh and Lut did not help their husbands to convey the Message. Indeed, they helped the enemies of Allah and the opponents of the Revelation: *"Allah has coined a likeness for those who reject: the wife of Nuh and the wife of Lut. They were married to two of Our righteous slaves but they betrayed them and were not helped at all against Allah and it was said, 'Enter the Fire along with all who enter it.'"* (66:10) The betrayal mentioned is not sexual; it was betraying the Message and the privilege of their high position.

There is no position whatsoever in this world – for what position could be higher than the intimate companionship of a Messenger of Allah? – which of itself guarantees salvation from Allah's punishment. Individual responsibility is the basis of accountability in Islam. No father will be able to help his son and no husband his wife. And the reverse is also true: a bad position in this world does not preclude the attainment of Allah's mercy in the Next.

Another theme of the *sura* is the need for the masters of every household to supervise their homes and make them a place of the *deen* so that each family will be a healthy cell in a sound society. *"O you who believe, safeguard yourselves and your families from a Fire whose fuel is people and stones..."* (66:6) At the same time Allah makes it clear that He does not expect us to be impeccable and never go wrong. But when we do make mistakes we should return to right guidance and learn from our experience. *"O you who believe, turn to Allah in sincere repentance..."* (66:8)

Certain orientalists have taken the fact of this *sura* being concerned with a domestic dispute in the Prophetic household as a reason for doubting the Divine origin of the Revelation, but if anything quite the reverse is true. It is absolutely essential for us to realise that Allah is present in every part of our lives, and it is incidents such as these which make the Divine involvement in even the most mundane aspects of life so vividly apparent. Were it not for *ayats* such as these we might be in danger of relegating Allah to the mosque, as our predecessors have to the synagogue, church and temple, and removing Him, as they have done, from day-to-day existence. Furthermore, the shedding of the light of Divine guidance on such incidents enables us to apply it to our ourselves more easily in our own daily lives.

Sura 67
Al-Mulk: The Kingdom

This world is a realm beyond which lies a different reality. False religiosity faces this fact with lamentation and pessimism instead of serious action and preparation for endless timelessness. The position of the Next World must be defined to counter the ignorance of contemporary civilisation and this definition obliges us to study this life and to learn about eternity from temporal existence. Only a foolish mind could study this existence and not prepare for what comes after it – that is not the mentality of the believer. *Surat al-Mulk* calls attention to this in a vivid way. *"He who created death and life to test which of you is best in action."* (67:2) *"He who created the seven heavens in layers. You will not find any flaw in the creation of the All-Merciful."* (67:3) *"We have adorned the lowest heaven with lamps…"* (67:5)

The sad thing is that nowadays the Muslim mind is ignorant of the phenomenal world, confused about its laws, weak in experience of it and lacking the power to utilise it. But there is another factor besides this powerlessness: greed for pleasure and devoting one's life to it: "This world is laughter and amusement. Enjoy your days! Enjoy your nights! The passing day will never return. Why waste it?" That is the main reason for all the material and spiritual defeats which the Muslims have suffered. It is not surprising that they are threatened with the same fate as the unbelievers when they are cast into Hell. *"Its custodians will question them: 'Did no warner come to you?' They will say, 'Yes indeed, a warner did come to us but we denied and said, "Allah has not revealed anything…"'"* (67:8-9) *"They will say, 'If only we been listening and using our minds, we would not have been the Companions of the Blaze.'"* (67:10)

466

It is assumed that the believing intellect will be better informed about life and more intelligent about existence than the godless intellect, because belief in Allah is based upon reflection on existence and perceiving the signs of Allah in the universe. It is a matter for sorrow and unease to find the Muslims at the tail-end of the human caravan. Belief in the Unseen is the cause of good in both worlds. *"Those who fear their Lord in the Unseen will have forgiveness and an enormous wage."* (67:12) The reality is that belief in the Unseen gives its possessor mastery of the visible world and skill in managing all aspects of the earth in a balanced way without the excessive exploitation which has now caused such irretrievable damage to our terrestrial environment. *"It is He who made the earth subservient to you, so walk its trails and eat of its provision..."* But our true future is not here. It is with Allah: *"...The Resurrection is to Him."*(67:15)

The first *ayat* of this *sura* indicates that all sovereignty is in Allah's Hands just as other *ayats* explain that all bounty is in His Hands (3:73; 57:29) and all good is in His Hands. (3:26) The whole earth is a mere handful to Him and the heavens will be rolled up in His Right Hand. (39:67). His control over His kingdom is total and it is impossible for any to oppose Him in it. (23:88) *"Do you feel secure against Him who is in heaven causing the earth to swallow you up when suddenly it rocks from side to side? Or do you feel secure against Him who is in heaven unleashing against you a sudden squall of stones..."* (67:16-17)

Although Allah is seated on His Throne, He knows, hears, sees and supervises everything and manages every affair and sustains every atom in the heavens and the earth. Nothing is hidden from Him and He is not absent from anything. The Book of Allah is full of *ayats* to this effect. *"Both East and the West belong to Allah, so wherever you turn, there is the Face of Allah: Allah is Boundless, All-Knowing."* (2:115) *"No three men confer together secretly without Him being the fourth of them, nor five without Him being the sixth of them, nor less than that nor more than that without Him being with them wherever they are."* (58:7) *"He is with you wherever you are."* (57:4) These are a few such *ayats,* and there are many more.

There is no doubt that Allah witnesses us but it is presumptuous to investigate the nature of this witnessing. We do not even know how Allah transforms the morsels which we eat into our eyes and ears, so who could we possibly know the true nature of His essence and nearness? Allah is nearer to us than ourselves but we do not have the capacity to see! It is enough that we know that and seek help from Him and provision from Him and realise that nothing other than Him has any real existence or power – as this *sura* explains to us. *"Who is there who could be a force for you, to come to your support, apart from the All-Merciful? The rejectors are only living in delusion. Who is there to provide for you if He withholds His provision? Yet still they obstinately persist in insolence and flight."* (67:20-21)

At the end of the *sura* it speaks about the unbelievers who try to take the battle to the Messenger and the believers who follow him. Allah asks them: "What use is it for you if you are rich but blind to the true state of things until you collide with Reality? Will the alleged shortcoming of others justify your misguidance?" *"Say: 'Do you not see? If Allah destroys me and those with me, or if He has mercy on us, who can shelter the rejectors from a painful punishment?' Say: 'He is the All-Merciful. We believe in Him and put our trust in Him. You will soon know who is clearly misguided.'"* (67:27-28)

The *sura* ends with a question directed at the devotees of the material world who deny their Lord and think that they themselves are lords of existence. *"Say: 'Do you not see? If your water disappears one morning into the earth, who will bring you running water?'"* (67:30) It is reported that one of the godless heard this *ayat* and said, "So bring us axes and shovels!" meaning that he would dig the well deeper and it would bring out water for certain. To make him understand the true meaning of the *ayat* Allah dried up his tear ducts and so he went blind. We see refuge with Allah from being forsaken by Him!

Sura 68
Al-Qalam: The Pen

"Nun. By the Pen and what they write down!" (68:1) Does the pen sworn by here mean the common writing implement? Perhaps. Writing is one of the most important means to knowledge. Or does it mean the angels writing on the Preserved Tablet? Or does it refer to the writing down of the Qur'an itself and the vast wisdom it contains? This last seems the most likely interpretation. The Noble Qur'an is the most important Book ever to appear in the world. From first to last it is pure Revelation – *"Falsehood does not come to it from before it or behind it."* (41:42)

Allah chose to convey it to the foremost man in existence in respect of intellect, honour and behaviour. The words of those enemies of Allah who seek to detract from his incomparable stature are worthless. *"By the blessing of your Lord, you are not mad. For you there is a never-failing wage. Indeed you are truly vast in character."* (68:2-4)

The enemies of the Revelation are a band of people ungraced by anything good and time will expose their claims and states just as those of the past were also exposed. They have disappeared but the Qur'an and Islam have remained. The Almighty says, *"We have tried them as We tried the owners of the garden."* (68:17) It is known that the idolaters of Makka first rejected Islam and then acknowledged the Truth and entered Islam and supported it. That is what happened. The owners of the garden mentioned here were niggardly about the rights of the poor to one-tenth of it and so Allah destroyed its fruits, causing them to regret their wickedness. *"They said, 'Woe to us! We were indeed excessively greedy. Maybe our Lord will give us something better than it in exchange. We make entreaty to our Lord.'"* (68:31-32)

If anyone sincerely makes entreaty to Allah, Allah will turn to him and receive him well. Allah elevated Quraysh through Islam after they had debased themselves with disbelief. But as for those who persist in their deviation, they have no future. *"Would We make the Muslims the same as the evildoers? What is the matter with you? On what basis do you judge?"* (68:35-36) The logic of the unbelievers in various states has no basis in reason or Revelation. That is why Allah Almighty says to deride them: *"Or have you have a Scripture which you study so that you may have anything in it you choose?"* (68:37-38) They have nothing to rely on but self-deception and delusion. Before them lies a harsh reckoning in which they will experience bitter regret. *"The Day that legs are bared and they are called on to prostrate, but they will not be able to do so."* (68:42)

The 'baring of the leg' means when the business reaches its end and the unbelievers have no excuse to offer. They were informed but they were obdurate. They were given various opportunities and wasted them. *"So leave to Me anyone who denies this discourse! We will lead them, step by step, into destruction from where they do not know."* (68:44) The Prophet, may Allah bless him and grant him peace, was commanded to convey the Message, to be steadfast under its burdens, and to endure the persecution of the idolaters however severe it might be. *"So wait steadfastly on the judgement of your Lord. Do not be like the Companion of the Fish..."* (68:48)

The Message-bearer endured difficult nights full of such distress and pain that even mountains would have been shaken by it; but he remained firm until he had completely conveyed the trust imposed upon him and left the Message protected by a generation of Muslims into whom he had breathed his spirit and force, and so it was spread throughout the world.

The universality of Islam is mentioned in many *ayats* and the fact that it was intended to be universal from its inception is shown by the fact that they first appear in the earliest Makkan *suras* such as this one. *"Those who disbelieve all but strike you down with their evil looks when they hear the Reminder and say, 'He is quite mad.' But what is it except a Reminder to all the worlds?"* (68:51-

52) Muhammad, upon him be blessings and peace, knew from very early on in his Mission that he was the Messenger to the entire world. The Makkan *Surat al-Qalam* was one of the first *suras* to be revealed.

Sura 69
Al-Haqqa: The Undeniable

"The Undeniable! What is the Undeniable? What will teach you what the Undeniable is?" (69:1-3) We suppose this world to be the reality which is indisputable. Will that supposition remain after death takes us and we advance to another world which is in fact the lasting reality? Most people are overtaken by death without preparing for what comes after it. But all of us will meet a Day on which the first and last will meet and when everyone will know the truth about what they did and did not do.

Various nations denied their Messengers. Some of them were punished and some of them are awaiting their punishment. But the Day will come when all will be faced with the final Reckoning. *"So when the Trumpet is blown with a single blast, and the earth and the mountains are lifted and crushed with a single blow, that Day the Occurrence will occur."* (69:13-15) It will be the time when good-doers and evil-doers will be clearly distinguished one from the other. *"As for him who is given his Book in his right hand, he will say, 'Here, come and read my Book! I counted on meeting my Reckoning.'"* (69:20) *"But as for him who is given his Book in his left hand, he will say, 'If only I had not been given my book and had not known about my Reckoning!'"* (69:26)

Belief in the material alone dominates the world at this time. There is an insane race to gain wealth and satisfy animal passions. There is general apathy towards prayer, selflessness, and speaking about Allah. What remains of earlier Revelations has not been translated by their people into clear faith and righteous action. The bearers of the truth are an almost vanished species to which people are entirely indifferent.

It is to be regretted that the guidance of the Messengers is in the possession of people with weak resolve and little insight. You find them in possession of great heaps of gold and silver but niggardly about giving anything to help the poor. It is about such people that it will be said: *"Seize him and truss him up. Then roast him in the Blazing Fire. Then bind him in a chain which is seventy cubits long. He used not to believe in Allah the Most Great, nor did he urge the feeding of the poor."* (69:30-34)

Then there are many peoples and nations with power in the world who have inherited from their ancestors the idea that Muhammad was an impostor and his Message was a lie. Yet what was his Message? Insistence that Allah is One and all mankind will definitely meet Him; insistence that fear of Allah is the sole route to salvation; and insistence that the servant of Allah cannot harm or help himself except as Allah wills. The order to bow and prostrate to Allah and bear weapons to defeat tyranny. Nowhere in this is there any possibility of private gain or personal aggrandisement. Muhammad was the worthiest of all people to speak about Allah. There has never been anyone so utterly devoted to Him as he was.

This is the secret of the oaths used in the *ayats* here: *"I swear both by what you see and by what you do not see, that this is the word of a noble Messenger. It is not the word of a poet – how little you believe! Nor the word of a fortune-teller – how little you remember! A Revelation from the Lord of all the Worlds."* (69:38-43)

If it had happened that the Prophet had concocted this Revelation, his punishment would have been severe: *"If he had made up any sayings and ascribed them to Us, We would have seized him by force, and then We would have cut off his life-blood and not one of you could have protected him."* (69:44-47) This Qur'an will remain as long as the world endures, as the support of true faith and a foundation for pure souls and a proof of the truthfulness of its Bearer.

Sura 70
Al-Ma'arij: The Ascending Steps

At the beginning of this *sura* Allah describes Himself as 'Lord of the Ascending Steps'. That is similar to His words in another *sura*, *"The Raiser of ranks, the Possessor of the Throne."* (40:15) The Divine Dominion extending from the Carpet to the Throne or from the lowest earth to the Lote-tree of the Limit is a fifty thousand year journey for man. As for the Trusty Spirit (Jibril) and the company of angels, they travel the distance in a far shorter time. We have seen how the Throne of Bilqis, the Queen of Sheba, was transported from Yemen to Palestine in a flash.

What is meant here is that anyone who invites the punishment which will come from Allah, the Lord of the Ascending Steps, is not asking for something difficult. His destruction is no more difficult than that of a gnat but this questioner does not believe in any punishment, near or far. He is either stupid or an unbeliever. He will certainly see this punishment: *"The Day that the sky will be like molten brass and the mountains like tufts of coloured wool, no good friend will ask about his friend."* (70:8-10)

Allah created human beings with animal instincts which drag them down and then asks them to resist these instincts so that they can rise higher. Whoever sinks to the earth is destroyed and whoever follows the Revelation is saved. Faith in it provides one with the strength to climb higher and higher on the path of Allah's pleasure: *"Truly man was created headstrong, when bad happens, desperate; when good happens, begrudging, except for those who pray and are constant in their prayer, those in whose wealth there is a known share for beggars and the destitute, those who affirm the Day of Repayment..."* (70:19-26)

We read this question in this *sura*: *"What is the matter with those who reject, that they rush headlong in your direction with*

474

necks outstretched and eyes transfixed, on the right and on the left in scattered groups? Does each one of them aspire to be admitted into a Garden of Delight? Certainly not! We created them from what they know full well." (70:36-39) The idolaters formed into groups around the Messenger, desiring to trip him up. They drew near him and did not believe him or follow him. Will someone like this achieve his hope? No, there must be following, sincerity and struggle. Allah created life and death to test which of us will be the best in action.

Any generation that falls short of the truth and wearies of the race will be overwhelmed by destruction and buried in ignominy and will be replaced by one purer and more active than it. *"No! I swear by the Lord of all the Easts and all the Wests that We have the power to substitute better than them. We will not be out-stripped."* (70:40-41) That happens in this world when indolent communities fail to implement the guidance they have received. In the Next World, the disparity between individuals and peoples will put some nations in the depths of Hellfire and others in the highest reaches of Paradise.

Sura 71
Nuh (Noah)

One of the most extraordinary things about the life of Nuh is that he spent 950 years calling his people to Allah without receiving a positive response from them. That is a tremendously long era during which nations could flower and decline and ideologies begin and end. But the people of Nuh remained in their misguidance without repenting or even considering repenting. That man of firm resolve and forbearance returned to his Lord to complain about how he was received and the obduracy of his people's disbelief: *"He said, 'My Lord, I have called my people night and day, but my calling has only increased them in evasion. Indeed every time I called them to Your forgiveness, they stuck their fingers in their ears and wrapped their garments around themselves and were overweeningly arrogant.'"* (71:5-7) Is the disbelief which makes a man worship stones and abandon the worship of the Lord of the worlds supported by any logical premise?

It is obvious when you study unbelievers that the driving force of their denial and unbelief is emotional rather than intellectual. It is psychological defects which distract people from their Lord. How can you explain the conduct of those who reject the transparent wisdom of Divine Revelation and devote themselves to patently fallible and flawed human beings? The evidence for the existence of Allah is not difficult of access. It provides a constant stimulus for the sleeping intellect to wake up and to see: *"Do you not see how He created seven heavens in layers, and placed the moon as a light in them, and made the sun a lamp? Allah caused you to grow out of the earth. Then He will return you into it and bring you out again."* (71:15-18)

We continually feed upon the fruits of the earth and they are transformed in our bodies into muscle and blood. Are we the ones

476

who bring about this transformation, or is it the All-Penetrating, the All-Aware, the One who manages all existence, who does it? Is it Allah or is it Wadd and Suwa', the pagan gods of Nuh's people? The stupidity of disbelief is incredible and nothing is more extraordinary than the pride and arrogance people have in it. This is why Nuh called to his Lord after the long centuries he had spent in conveying the Message and reminding the people: *"My Lord, do not leave a single one of the rejectors on the earth! If You leave any they will lead Your slaves astray and spawn nothing but dissolute rejectors."* (71:26-27)

Sura 72
Al-Jinn: The Jinn

Surat al-Jinn contains indications of the true nature of Christian belief and how the Christians turned the Messiah into a 'Son of God' and a god alongside Allah Almighty. This allegation has spread throughout the earth. Generations were born adhering to it until the Qur'an came and refuted it, stressing that Allah is One and has no offspring. The Christian creed had reached the jinn and they embraced it. Then in their wandering around the earth they happened upon the Qur'an. *"Say: 'It has been revealed to me that a band of the jinn listened and said, "We have heard a most extraordinary Recitation. It directs people to right guidance. Therefore we believe in it and will not make anyone a partner with our Lord."'"* (72:1-2)

The jinn then explained in detail what they had repented of and acknowledged their mistake. *"He – exalted be the Majesty of our Lord! – has taken neither wife nor son."* (72:3) They mentioned that those who had conveyed that notion to them were totally delinquent. *"The fools among us have uttered a vile slander about Allah."* (72:4) Then they apologised for their heedlessness in accepting this slander which only happened because they did not think it was possible for anyone to lie deliberately about Allah: *"We never thought it possible for either men or jinn to speak a lie against Allah."* (72:5)

But some human beings listened to that nonsense, spread it in the world, and misled many people with it: *"Certain men among mankind used to seek refuge with certain men among the jinn and they increased them in wickedness."* (72:6) They maintained that the Gates of Heaven were closed and no angel would descend with Revelation and no human being would bear any other message to restore belief to its correct basis and support the previous Messen-

478

gers in their affirmation of the Oneness of Allah and of His absolute power over all existence.

But Allah sent His Final Prophet among the Arabs and His Message spread to the East and West, proclaiming that Allah has no son and no parents. This message came as a shock to those in error: *"They thought, as you also think, that Allah was never going to send anyone."* (72:7) But the truth is that the state now uses its power to reinforce erroneous beliefs about existence, establishing fortresses for them where they are studied and preserved, and so false beliefs are now ingrained in people's consciousness and mistaken theories form the basis of their lives.

Roman imperialism spread the doctrine of the Trinity and was able by inducements and terror to compel people to embrace it. Since the Renaissance, outright unbelief has been disseminated in a similar way. If Muhammad had not defended the Truth with which he was sent and fought for it with everything he had, the Romans would have made it a thing of the past.

The jinn were aware that a change had occurred in existence and that the new Revelation was protected by fierce guards so that it could not be got at or interfered with. *"We tried as usual to travel to heaven in search of news but found it filled with fierce guards and meteors. We used to sit there on special seats to listen in. But anyone listening now finds a fiery meteor in wait for him."* (72:8-9) The extraordinary thing is that the protection which accompanied the descent of the Qur'an from Heaven did not leave it when it reached earth. Here it was assumed by those who have preserved every single letter and sound of the Revelation by memorising it and reciting it throughout the centuries.

Some of the jinn accepted Islam with vigour and conviction: *"And when we heard the guidance, we believed in it. Anyone who believes in his Lord need fear neither diminishment nor wickedness."* (72:13) But it is evident that a number of the jinn refused to follow the Truth and made known their rejection of it. There is nothing astonishing in that. Is that not what the children of Adam also do? *"Some of us are Muslims and some are degenerates. Those who have become Muslim are those who sought right guidance. The degenerates will be firewood for Hell."* (72:14-15)

Inevitably in the context of this *sura* the thorny question of the existence and nature of the jinn raises its head. This has already been dealt with above. It is sufficient to say here that there are many things in phenomenal existence that we cannot see and yet whose presence we wholeheartedly believe in. There are many subtle forces whose power is known but which are little understood. The truth is – and the greatest scientists admit this – that we have barely scraped the surface of what can be known. We live in a many-storeyed universe and do not even know everything about the ground floor, let alone the upper storeys! There is in fact plenty of evidence throughout the ages for the existence of those unseen co-dwellers of ours on the earth; but it is not a subject which it is wise to delve into since it can prove a time-wasting and dangerous distraction. We simply believe in Allah who created men, jinn and angels. *"No one knows the legions of your Lord but He."* (74:31)

Some people are attached to Allah and enjoy His blessings but they are distracted by the blessings from their Giver and live for themselves alone. I have seen masses of people of this sort. Indeed, the spread of disbelief in the earth can be traced to the conduct of people who had the Revelation but did not devote themselves to it and establish it properly. Allah says about those people: *"If only they were to go straight on the Path, We would give them overflowing water to drink to test them by it. Whoever turns aside from the Remembrance of his Lord, He will introduce him to an arduous punishment."* (72:16-17) One of the trials we face is that what Allah has given us distracts us from that which He imposes on us.

The final *ayats* of this *sura* testify that the Message-bearer, may Allah bless him and grant him peace, conveyed it and devoted himself to it: *"Say: 'I call only upon my Lord and I do not make anyone else a partner with Him.' Say: 'I possess no power to do you harm or to guide you right.' Say: 'No one can protect me from Allah and I will never find any refuge apart from Him.'"* (72:20-22)

Now in this world there are a group of men who claim that they possess the power to absolve wrongdoers of their sins and that the keys of the eternal kingdom are in their possession! These claims are only the result of ignorance of Allah and a weak connection to Him. Muhammad, the Seal of the Prophets, had a true understanding of Allah's power. *"Say: 'I do not know whether what you are promised is imminent or whether my Lord will appoint a longer time for it. Knower of the Unseen, He does not divulge His Unseen to anyone."* (72:25-26) He is the slave of Allah, the One, who struggled against idolatry and superstition and propagated belief in the Divine Unity so that it would spread throughout the entire world. There is no instant when someone somewhere on earth is not calling, "Allah is greater! Allah is greater! There is no god but Allah."

Sura 73
Al-Muzzammil: The Enwrapped

An *ayat* in *Surat al-An'am* depicts the framework which defines the life of the Prophet: *"My prayer and my rites, my living and my dying, are for Allah, the Lord of all the worlds. He has no partner. To that I have been commanded and I am the first of the Muslims."* (6:162-163) The life of some people is a mixture of truth and falsehood, gravity and levity, relaxation and exertion. This majestic man spent his life in continuous struggle and worship. The level of his effort was not just in order to fulfil the task of Prophethood in a defined place but to form a generation of men who would map out the path of mankind up until the Last Day and to create a lighthouse of Truth which no tempest or hurricane would ever be able to blow out. The sixty-three years which Muhammad lived in this world did not just put things right in a particular age. His life was spent protecting unitary belief for all time and preparing the men who would protect it after him until the end of time.

This *sura,* revealed right at the beginning, paves the way to that end. The Messenger is told: *"O you enwrapped in your clothing, stay up the night, except a little, half of it, or a little less, or a little more, and recite the Qur'an distinctly."* (73:1-4) The time for replete sleep and complete relaxation had come to an end. *"We shall impose a weighty word upon you."* (73:5) It is a word filled with difficult obligations and exhausting struggle. When he has finished standing in prayer in the night he faces the struggle of the day in conveying the Message and striving against his enemies with no helper but Allah. So he should devote himself to Him and seek His help and take Him as a guardian and be steadfast in the face of their persecution. Their future reckoning will be harsh:

"With Us there are shackles and a Blazing Fire and food that chokes and a painful punishment." (73:12-13)

When will this happen? *"The Day the earth and mountains shake and the mountains become like shifting dunes."* (73:14) The earth is depicted as shaking with its highlands and lowlands, land and sea, as impotent people quake before its unexpected terror. It is a description which provokes anxiety and terror, but the people *'play at plunging'*. (52:12) Muhammad, peace and blessings be upon him, was of all people the most fearful of Allah and the strongest in awareness of the nearness of the encounter with Him. The generation that surrounded him took him as their model and followed his example of how to live, so it is natural that they should have stood in the night in prayer like him and girded themselves for the struggle against oppressive misguidance.

As a mercy to the people of the community, Allah Almighty made the night prayers an obligation only for His Prophet. The obligatory acts they perform during the day are enough for the believers: *"Allah determines the night and day. He knows you will not keep count of time, so He has turned towards you. Recite as much of the Qur'an as is easy for you. "* (73:20) This dispensation is not an open permit or *carte blanche*. No rather it is to give importance to other actions: *"He knows that some of you are ill and that others are travelling in the land seeking Allah's bounty, and that others are fighting in the Way of Allah."* (73:20) The fact is that the economic and social struggle are both necessary for the protection of the community and the implementation of the Message. The enemies of the truth regard us with rancour. When they find a gap they penetrate it to our heart. This is the disaster which endangers the truth and its supporters.

Sura 74
Al-Muddaththir: The Enveloped

It is evident that *Surat al-Muddaththir* was revealed before *Surat al-Muzzammil*. It has been said that it was the first *sura* to be revealed, but that is not correct. It is the first *sura* to be revealed after the hiatus in the Revelation and the yearning of the Messenger for its recommencement. The first *ayats* contain the contours of the behaviour which Allah recommended for His Prophet: *"O you enveloped in your cloak! Arise and warn."* (74:1-2) This means that he should make the idolaters fearful of the consequences if they remained pagans.

"And magnify your Lord" (74:3): ascribe to the Essence of Allah every glory, majesty and splendour. The *takbir, or* magnifying, of Allah begins the *adhan,* the prayers, and the battles of *jihad*. It is the motto of Islam. *"And purify your clothes"* (74:4): what is meant is both body and clothes. Cleanliness is part of the nature of Islam. *"And shun all filth"* (74:5): you should avoid all ugly things. *"And do not give desiring gain"* (74:6): give without seeking to indebt others to you in any way, aiming only to please your Lord. *"And be steadfast for your Lord"* (74:7): bear whatever befalls you for the sake of Allah.

After making the idolaters fear the Day of Reckoning, the *sura* then mentions one of their great men who rejected the Message, describing the Revelation as magic. He was a man of great rank and wealth called 'the unique' because of his social and material position. *"Leave him to Me whom I created alone [unique] and whom I have given great wealth and sons who stay in his presence."* (74:11-13) It scorns this leader who will incur what all who follow him incur. *"I will roast him in Saqar. What will convey to you what Saqar is? It does not spare and does not let up, ceaselessly scorching the flesh. Over it there are nineteen."* (74:26-30)

That is the number of the angels of torment who are charged with punishing the tyrants, degenerates and corrupters.

Next, the *sura* returns to the most evident manifestation of Revelation in physical existence: the end of the night and the appearance of the day. *"No Indeed! By the moon and the night when it withdraws and the dawn when it grows bright, it is truly one of the greatest things, a warning to human beings, for any of you who want to go forward or hang back."* (74:32-37) Going forward and hanging back are connected to activity and passivity; it is not a question of blind fate. That is why Allah then says: *"Every soul is held in pledge against whatever it has earned except for the Com-panions of the Right. In Gardens they will ask the evildoers: 'What caused you to enter Saqar?' They will say, 'We were not of those who prayed and we did not feed the poor.'"* (74:38-44) What this means is that you will harvest what you sowed and crooked steps do not lead to a straight outcome: *"The intercession of the interceders will not avail them."* (74:48)

But why did the idolaters resort to this stubborn resistance and complete aversion to Islam? Pride! Each of them wanted an angel to descend to him and tell him, "I am the messenger of Allah to so-and-so so" in order for him to believe and acknowledge his Creator. Why did He single out Muhammad for the revelation for the Message? This is unacceptable! *"What is wrong with them that they turn away from the Reminder like panicked donkeys fleeing from a lion? In fact each man of them desires to be given an unfurled scroll."* (74:49-52)

People's sense of their own importance still remains a barrier to the truth and is the cause of their dislike of its upholders! What do the Prophets do when that happens? It is enough for them to remember Allah and His signs, blessings and rights. Whoever is guided is saved and whoever rejects guidance is destroyed: *"No indeed! It is truly a reminder to which anyone who wills may pay heed."* (74:54-55)

Sura 75
Al-Qiyama: The Resurrection

When the believer falls into error, he is overcome by anxiety and the earth becomes constricted for him where before it had been wide. That is because faith is a swift incentive to rise and is a painful impediment against decline. Someone who is a self-critical about what he does is not content with defects in himself – in fact they impel him to move forward to a purer realm. Allah swears by the self-reproaching soul because of the belief it holds in Allah and the Last Day. As for souls and societies which do not acknowledge Allah or look ahead to the meeting with Him, they do not care about any vice they have or fear the Day of Reckoning because they think it is a fantasy!

The beginning of *Surat al-Qiyama* indicates these states: *"No! I swear by the Day of Rising. No! I swear by the self-reproaching soul. Does man reckon We will not re-assemble his bones? On the contrary, We are well able to re-shape his fingers."* (75:1-4) Allah, Who causes bodies to decay, is capable of bringing them back again with exactly the same traits. People will be brought to life again in order to receive the recompense for what they did. *"On that Day man will be told what he did and failed to do."* (75:13) It has been a fault of human beings throughout the history of the human race that their awareness of the Day of Reckoning has been non-existent or very weak. If they had understood, they would have acted very differently.

Surat al-Qiyama contains a true description of this Day and what precedes and follows it. But incorporated into this description is the instruction to the Noble Messenger not to seek to hasten the reception of the Revelation. How is it possible for any man to retain this celestial Revelation without changing a single letter and then go and recite it to the people exactly as it was revealed? What earthly intellect is capable of that? But Allah calms him: *"Its collection and recitation are Our affair. So when We recite it, follow its recitation. Then its explanation is also Our affair."* (75:17-19) That Divine promise has ensured that we have received the entire Qur'an just as it was revealed.

There is an end that comes before the Day of the Final Reckoning and which a man cannot avoid: his own death! Why are men heedless of this? *"No indeed! When it reaches the gullet and it is said, 'Who can heal him now?' and he realises it is indeed the final parting and one leg is entwined with the other – that Day the driving will be to your Lord."* (75:26-30) Intoxication with life in this world blinds the eyes to this inescapable end.

"Does man reckon he will be left to go on unchecked?" (75:36) The One who created this life and filled it with activity throughout the world did not do so without reason. Mankind must stand before their Creator who will ask them about what they did in this first existence and whether they prepared in it for their final existence. The strange thing is that human science has progressed as much in recent years as it progressed in all of earlier history. But in spite of that, its knowledge of Allah is shallow, and no preparation is made to meet Him!

Sura 76
Al-Insan: Man

A swift caravan passed some graves and one of the people in it said to his companion, "Do you know what these graves say about us?" He asked, "What do they say?" He replied, "They say, 'As you are so we were and you will be as you we.'" *"Has man ever known a point of time when he was not something remembered?"* (76:1) We were nothing and Allah created us hearing and seeing, and then He will return us to Him and the earth will be rid of us! But to what will we return? Allah says in *Surat al-Insan*: *"We have made ready for the rejectors shackles and chains and a Searing Blaze."* (76:4) *"The truly good will drink from a cup mixed with the coolness of Camphor, a spring from which Allah's slaves will drink."* (76:5-6)

It is interesting that this *sura* contains only a brief description of the punishment which the unbelievers will meet but goes into great detail about the description of bliss and the delights which await the believers: *"Seeing them, you see there delight and a great kingdom."* (76:20) Then they will be reminded of what has passed: *"This is your recompense, and your striving is acknowledged."* (76:22)

The last half of the *sura* speaks about the final Message and its role in life in general. The effect of the environment on our character is important and undeniable. When the Messenger was able to change the direction of a society and to fill hearts which were empty with the Divine Revelation, he produced a nation which was firm and guided people to a straight path. Hence he is told, *"We have sent down the Qur'an to you piece by piece. Therefore wait with patience for the judgement of your Lord. Do not obey any evil-doer or thankless man among them."* (76:23-24)

Allah should be remembered at the beginning and end of the day: *"Remember the Name of your Lord morning and evening,"* (76:25) and He should be glorified in the night: *"And in the night, and prostrate to Him, and glorify Him through the long hours of the night."* (76:26)

The Noble Qur'an describes the nature of people at the time of the Message and before and after it: *"Those people love this fleeting world and have put the thought of a Momentous Day behind their backs."* (76:27) The truth is that people have practically no guidance when they are intoxicated with life and its pursuits and pleasures. In modern times, it is almost taboo to mention the Next World and the mention of death leaves people indifferent. This does not mean that people should be gloomy or obsessed with death; but the present heedlessness of the human race and their refusal to reflect on their own inevitable mortality is short-sighted to the point of stupidity.

It is vital for human beings to recognise where they have come from and where they are going. *"This is truly a Reminder. So whoever wills should take a way towards his Lord."* (76:29) Allah increases in guidance those who are guided and removes the obstacles before them. As for those who forget Allah and are blind to His signs, He will leave them in their benighted state. *"He admits whomever He wills into His mercy. But for the wrongdoers He has prepared a painful punishment."* (76:31)

Sura 77
Al-Mursalat: Those Sent Forth

"By those sent forth in succession, by the violently gusting blasts, by the scatterers scattering, by the winnowers winnowing, by those hurling a reminder, excusing or warning" (77:1-6) All these phrases describe the winds whose directions are delineated for us in the weather reports. The beginning of the *sura* resembles the beginning of *Surat adh-Dhariyat*. Air is the basis for human life, whether it is still or blows lightly or becomes a gale. When the air is calm we have little sensation of it. When it rages in some areas, we see trees uprooted and cars thrown about from place to place. It moves the clouds here and there and parts them so that the rain can fall wherever Allah wills.

Let us reflect on the words of the Almighty: *"By those hurling a reminder, excusing or warning."* (77:5-6) Here the 'reminder' is the Noble Qur'an and the air is the means of transmission for the sound waves. The revelation is heard both by those who benefit from it and those who impede it. It is an 'excusing' for those who are guided and a 'warning' for the misguided. Most commentators suppose that the last two *ayats* describe the angels. They resort to that meaning because they do not know that the air is the means for the transmission of sound although that has become one of the facts ascertained by the science of physics.

Allah swears by the winds and their attributes that the Resurrection is real and that the Repayment for disbelief and belief will undoubtedly occur. Then He describes the Day on which all this will take place. *"When the stars are extinguished, when heaven is split open, when the mountains are pulverised, when the Messengers' time is appointed – until what Day is that deferred? Until the Day of Decision. And what will teach you what the Day of Decision is?"* (77:8-14) The structure of this seemingly solid existence will disintegrate and dissolve. Then its regeneration will take place in another dimension. In the days of this world, the base people were elevated and the Prophets were humiliated and persecuted. In the Next World the truthful will not be denied and liars will not be honoured.

We notice in this *sura* that Allah repeats the words, *"Woe upon that Day to the deniers!"* (77:15) This refrain is repeated ten times in all. It comes sometimes after a divine warning or an existential sign or an historical stage or after instructive advice. The first time it is followed by the threat of destruction in this world for rejecting faith, which befell earlier peoples. Then we learn of the origin of the human creature. Man is not engendered on a golden path surrounded by precious gems! He originates with a base liquid which goes down the same drains as human excreta. *"Did We not create you from a base liquid and then place it in a secure repository until a recognised predetermined time?"* (77:20-22) Human beings, clever and stupid, are all formed in this repository. Who oversees this process? *"We do the determining. What an excellent determiner!"* (77:23)

Then Allah Almighty says: *"Did We not make the earth a receptacle for both the living and the dead?"* (77:25-26) It is a place which draws together and contains. These *ayats* allude to the gravitational force of the earth which holds the living and dead on it. Everything adheres to it and is prevented from flying off into space. Who holds the water, which covers four-fifths of the globe, onto its surface? Why does not it rise up into the air? Because Allah made the earth a place which attracts every drop to it. What subtle force flows in the layers of the earth and sea to make this happen? *"Did We not place firm-seated mountains in it, soaring high, and give you sweet fresh water to drink?"* (77:27)

Then the *sura* moves to the Reckoning in the Next World and describes the fates of the believers and unbelievers and the masses of the creatures who have lived on the earth throughout time: *"'This is the Day of Decision. We have gathered together you and the earlier peoples. So if you have a plot, plot against Me now!' Woe upon that Day to the deniers!"* (77:38-40) There is nothing

491

they can do. Allah has stupefied them and the Hour has come suddenly upon them; and nothing can be heard but whisperings.

The noble *sura* ends with this *ayat*: *"In what discourse after this will they then believe?"* (77:51) Is there any speech with more guidance than the words of this Book? Is there anything that acquaints people with Allah and His rights better than this Qur'an? Has any human ever conveyed anything more truthful than this Message? This Book, which Muhammad recited to us, is Truth itself and eliminates all doubts. *"In what discourse after this will they then believe?"* (77:51)

Sura 78
An-Naba': The News

It is the duty of anryone who finds out about a Prophet to study his words and his personality and then to make their own decision for or against him. What message did Muhammad bring? He told us that Allah is Real and detailed the proofs of His existence and His perfection in an unprecedented manner. He stated that He is One and that all in the heavens and the earth was created by Him and is in need of Him, whether angel, human being or jinn, and that we will certainly meet Him for a Reckoning in which everyone with responsibility will be called to account. In his life, recorded in every detail, the Prophet substantiated this and demonstrated the meaning of it for us. So why should we reject Muhammad?

Surat an-Naba' tells the idolaters: "If the call of Muhammad does not satisfy you, will you not reflect on the creation of the heavens and the earth?" *"Have We not made the earth a flat bed and the mountains its pegs? We have created you in pairs."* (78:6-7) We are now in the fifteenth *Hijri* century, at the end of the twentieth century of the Christian calendar, and are the inheritors of various Messages. It is our right to compare and state our preference. It is not possible to find anything better than the legacy of Muhammad in the Book and *Sunna* – indeed, his Message contains what is best of all the previous Revelations. *"Nothing has been said to you that was not said to Messengers before you."* (41:43) This means when we follow Muhammad, we also follow Musa and 'Isa as well, and Nuh and Ibrahim and all the earlier Prophets.

This *sura* consists of four distinct sections. The first is a description of the world and its inhabitants, up to His words: *"We sent down from the clouds cascading water to bring forth by it grains and plants and densely growing gardens."* (78:14-16) The second is a brief description of the Day of Reckoning: *"The Day of Decision is a fixed appointment: the Day the Trumpet is blown and you come in droves."* (78:17-18) The Qur'an frequently mentions the Resurrection to counter the love of the immediate which tends to dominate us. The third is a description of the punishment which awaits the wrongdoers: *"Hell lies in wait: a homecoming for the profligate, remaining in it for countless aeons."* (78:21-23) And the fourth is the description of the bliss which awaits the righteous believers: *"For the godfearing there is triumph, Gardens and grape vines, and nubile maidens, of similar age."* (78:31-33)

The spiritual repayment is a reality, and the faces of the believers will be radiant when they are with the throngs of angels glorifying the praise of Allah and proclaiming His majesty. Part of their perfect enjoyment is that they will be in radiant gardens with intimate companions of like age, and after that alluring description it people of intelligence are told: *"That is the True Day. So whoever who wills should make his way back to his Lord."* (78:39)

Whoever feared his Lord will be successful. Whoever lived in heedlessness here and comes to Allah empty-handed will be full of remorse after having missed his one and only chance: *"We have warned you of an imminent punishment, the Day a man will see what his hands have sent ahead, and the rejector will say, 'Oh, would that I were dust!'"* (78:40)

Sura 79
An-Nazi'at: The Pluckers

"By those who pluck out harshly, and those who draw out gently, and those who glide serenely, and those who outrun easily, and those who direct affairs." (79:1-5) Most commentators assert that these *ayats* refer to the angels and that Allah swears by them about the coming of the Last Day. *"The Day the first blast shudders, and the second blast follows it."* (79:6-7) In the great convulsion everything will lose its equilibrium and commotions will follow one after another. Hearts will be in turmoil and eyes cast down.

The idolaters will say when they hear this warning: *"Are we to be restored to how we were?"* (79:10) "Are we to be returned to life again? That is what the Messenger was telling us." When? *"When we have become rotted, worm-eaten bones?"* (19:11) "After we were dead and decayed?" *"That then will be a losing restoration!"* (79:12) "It will be a return with no good in it because we did not affirm it nor prepare for it."

"There will be but one Great Blast, and suddenly they are on the surface, wide-awake!" (79:12) That is the Hour of gathering and repayment. The followers of scientific materialism will be in exactly the same position as the idolaters of the desert when they say, *"There is nothing but our existence in this world. We die and we live and nothing destroys us except for time."* (45:24) How will they feel when they find themselves alive without having gained anything whatsoever from their lives in this world?

The *ayats* proceed to tell of Pharaoh who was an archetypal evildoer. The fact is that pharaohism is a common disease whose symptoms are disregard of truth and rights and contempt for other people. It is found in rulers, administrators, artists and road sweepers. When a man is obsessed with himself, he lives arrogantly and tyrannically without supporting the truth or abolishing falsehood.

Hell will be fuelled by all such people. The Qur'an points out the absurdity of this arrogance on the part of man. *"Are you stronger in structure or is heaven? He built it: He raised its vault and levelled it out..."* (79:27-28) In relation to much else man is a weak being. He must not be blind and oppressive but must fear his Lord and purify himself. When he has power over other beings, he should make use of this favour by thanking Allah and fulfilling his responsibilities.

The *sura* returns to its first theme, speaking about the Resurrection and the Reckoning to encourage us to make our lives here a preparation for the Next Life: *"When the Great Calamity comes, the Day man remembers what he has striven for and the Blazing Fire is displayed for all to see."* (79:34-36) On that Day there will be two sorts of people: those who were slaves of their appetites and who lived to satisfy them, and those who were slaves of Allah, aware of His sustaining and watching them and not forgetting what is due to Him: *"Then as for him who went to excess and preferred the life of this world, the Blazing Fire shall be his refuge. But as for him who feared the Station of his Lord and forbade the self its appetites, the Garden will be his refuge."* (79:37-41)

Curiosity and mockery dominate most people and they ask about the Hour: *"When will it come? What are you doing mentioning it? Its coming is your Lord's affair."* (79:42-43) Knowledge of it rests with Allah alone. What benefit is there in your knowing about it if you do not prepare for it? Existence is continuous and death is a brief hiatus between one existence and the next. We will know the true measure of this world on the Day of the Encounter: *"The Day they see it, it will be as if they had only tarried for the evening or the morning of one day."* (79:46)

Sura 80
'Abasa: He Frowned

The Prophet, may Allah bless him and grant him peace, was concerned to call some of the great men of Quraysh to Islam because if they were guided the masses would follow them in embracing the *Deen*. 'Abdullah ibn Umm Maktum, a blind man, came seeking guidance and to speak with the Prophet while he was talking to these people. The Prophet was annoyed with him and turned away and continued to speak with the important idolaters. So the *sura* was revealed: *"He frowned and turned away because the blind man came to him. But how do you know? Perhaps he would be purified or reminded and the reminder benefit him."* (80:104) The noble Prophet heeded this rebuke and after that received 'Abdullah warmly and used to say to him, "Welcome to him on whose account my Lord rebuked me!" When the Prophet was absent from Madina, after the *hijra*, he appointed 'Abdullah amir over it until his return.

Then the *sura* proceeds to explain how the Divine Message is transmitted. It consists of *ayats* which are heard or pages which are prepared by *"the hands of scribes, noble, virtuous"*, meaning those who write down the Revelation and those who memorise the Qur'an. So the one to whom the Message is conveyed must reflect and remember and take refuge in Allah and prepare to meet Him.

But are most people like that? How many people we see with closed minds, rooted to the earth, unaware of how they came into this world! They began as drops of impure liquid and then developed and became properly formed human beings. Who put us into this existence and gave us that form? How can man forget his Lord who has complete control over him and has given him so many blessings? *"From what thing did He create him? From a sperm-drop He created him and determined his form, then He eases the way for him, then He makes him die and buries him, then, when He wills, He resurrects him."* (80:18-22)

Man is heedless of all that and thinks only of achieving his goals and fulfilling his desires. Has he fulfilled the rights he owes to Allah? *"No indeed! Man has not done what He ordered him."* (80:23) The argument with the idolaters and the unbelievers in every age is based on the Resurrection and Reckoning. They only believe in the life of this world, so the Qur'an brings one of the proofs of the Resurrection in order that they may recognise their Lord and make their preparations to meet Him. *"Let man but look at his food. We pour down plentiful water, then split the earth into furrows. Then We make grain grow in it and grapes and herbs and olives and dates and luxuriant gardens."* (80:24-30)

How are these full ears of wheat and splendid clusters of grapes created? How are sweetness and scent and flavour imparted to them? He Who brings these things forth from earth and dung is the same One who will bring our bodies from the earth, and then every man will be faced with what he did. *"When the Deafening Blast arrives – the Day a man will flee from his brother and his mother and his father, and his wife and his children – every man among them will be that Day fully occupied with his own concerns."* (80:33-37)

Man is veiled by his immediate concerns and what directly conforts him from the Garden and the Fire, the Reward and the Punishment. *"Some faces that Day will be shining, laughing, rejoicing. Some faces that Day will be dust-covered, overwhelmed with gloom."* (80:38-41) The sorry thing about our time is that scientific research investigates only phenomenal existence and does not desire to learn what is beyond it. That is why it is impossible to discuss the Next World or to deal with it in a serious gathering.

Sura 81
At-Takwir: The Compacting

Surat at-Takwir begins with twelve events closely linked with to the arrival of the Last Day and the return of people to their Lord for the Great Reckoning.

"When the sun is compacted in blackness." (81:1) It will implode and darkness will prevail.

"When the stars fall in rapid succession." (81:2) They will fall and their order will be disrupted.

"When the mountains are set into motion." (81:3) They will be atomised and vanish.

"When the camels in foal are neglected." (81:4) People will no longer be concerned with this world.

"When the wild beasts are herded together." (81:5) They will come together from their distant habitats.

"When the oceans boil over into each other." (81:6) They will overflow and flood the land.

"When the souls are grouped into classes." (81:7) People will be categorised according to how they lived.

"When the baby girl buried alive is asked for what crime she was killed." (81:8-9) Everything will give testimony about what happened to it.

"When the pages are opened up." (81:10) Everyone will be presented with the book of their actions.

"When the heaven is peeled away" (81:11) Time-space as we know it will cease to exist.

"When the Blazing Fire is set alight" (81:12) The reality of Hell will appear.

"When the Garden is brought up close." (81:13) The reality of Paradise will appear.

"Then will each soul know what it has done." (81:14) What we were really doing in this world will be made known to us.

These *ayats* provide a summary of what will occur before the Final Hour and the division of people to face their final fates.

We know that the earth is one of the smallest planets revolving around the sun and that the sun and its solar system are minuscule in relation to the universe as a whole. In spite of that, the earth contains the species for whose sake the whole universe was created. So in this *sura* Allah swears by the planets subject to His command that the Qur'an is true and that Muhammad was sent by Him as guidance for mankind and a mercy from Allah: *"No! I swear by the planets with their retrograde motion, swiftly moving, self-concealing, and by the night when it draws in, and by the dawn when it exhales, truly it is the speech of a noble Messenger."* (81:15-19)

This is an oath swearing by the unimaginable vastness of Existence to the truth of the Revelation. Both of them are proofs of Allah: one implicit, the other explicit. The Qur'an is the only book which truly gives a sense of the profound connection between the earth and the rest of the universe and between the whole universe and its Incomparable Creator.

The *ayats* mention Jibril, the Spirit of Purity, and declare him to be an angel near to Allah with the status of a trusty servant: *"Possessing strength, securely placed with the Lord of the Throne, obeyed there, trustworthy."* (81:20-21) He carried the Revelation to Muhammad who received it and transmitted it. He was coloured by its meaning and imbued with its character. He fought to the utmost to implement it in the face of deviants and deniers and through him governance by it was established in the East and the West.

Surat at-Takwir was one of the first *suras* to be revealed but it nevertheless confirms the universality of the Message to all mankind. *"It is simply a Reminder to all the worlds, to any of you who wishes to go straight."* (81:26-28)

Sura 82
Al-Infitar: The Splitting

In the life of this world, man is told, "Look up!" *"He who created the seven heavens in layers. You will not find any flaw in the creation of the All-Merciful. Look again - do you see any gaps?"* (67:3) There are no rips and no holes. The heavens are completely interwoven and the planets are guided without pause or hesitation. But when the Last Hour comes all that will change: *"When the heaven is split apart, when the stars are strewn about, when the seas flood and overflow, when the graves are emptied out, each soul will know what it sent ahead and left behind."* (82:1-5) The fabric of existence will come apart. The planets will leave their orbits and no order will control them. The seas will flood the shores and the people of the graves will prepare to emerge feeling constricted and bewildered.

In the context of that overwhelming power Allah addresses us, asking us how we can possibly be so foolhardy as to ignore our Creator to Whom we will have to answer for our lives. *"O man! What has deluded you respecting your Noble Lord, He who created you and formed you and proportioned you and put you together in whatever form He wished?"* (82:6-8) What did you do yesterday which has vanished without a trace? What have you advanced for your eternal future? Allah's instructions are the easiest of things to follow yet man shoots to his passions like an arrow and when he is called to *jihad* or the prayer he shows the utmost reluctance!

The abode of the Next World will come suddenly as a disaster for most people: *"Yes indeed! But still you deny the* Deen; *standing over you are guardians, noble, recording, who know everything you do."* (82:9-12) The recording angels are firm in their recording of everything and so a man will be confronted by everything he did or failed to do without increase or decrease. Then all creatures will go to their eternal homes. *"The truly good will be in perfect Bliss. The dissolute will be in a Blazing Fire."* (82:13-14)

Sura 83
Al-Mutaffifin: The Stinters

Surat al-Mutaffifin comes after *al-Infitar* as if it were intended to complete it. It details the relationship between actions and their repayment – that is a connection that is impossible to break. There are egoists who are only aware of their own needs, even if they are unreal, and are annoyed by the needs of others, even if they are real. They range the cities and towns like wild beasts knowing nothing more than gratification of their appetites. The attitude of such people is that of stinters: *"Those who, when they take a measure from people, exact full measure, but when they give them a measure or weight, give less than is due."* (83:2-3)

They are only interested in what they can get. They have no respect for the property of others. It is impossible for society to be just when personal gain is the mainspring of people's actions and the result is bound to be social disorder and injustice. *"As for those who do not believe in the Next World, We have made their actions seem good to them and they wander about blindly. Such people will receive an evil punishment and will be the greatest losers in the Next World."* (27:4-5)

Belief in Allah and the Last Day protects people against these base motives and restricts people's greed so that self-gratification is not their only concern and they do not sink into injustice and iniquity. If people are aware of their coming Reckoning they will not behave like animals. *"Do those people not realise that they will be raised up on a Mighty Day, the Day all people stand before the Lord of all the Worlds?"* (83:4-6)

People's fates are not decided by slips of the tongue or stumbles on the path. They are decided by planned courses of action and engrained behaviour. The believer is able to purify himself from passing error but a well-laid plan for a debased life is a certain path to destruction. A *hadith* says, "When someone commits a sin, a black spot is marked on his heart. If he stops it and asks forgiveness and repents, his heart is polished. But if he returns to it, the spot increases in size until it covers his whole heart." That is the rust about which Allah says: *"No indeed! Rather what they have earned has rusted up their hearts. No indeed! Rather that Day they will be veiled from their Lord. Then they will roast in the Blazing Fire."* (83:14-16) Al-Hasan al-Basri said, "The rust is wrong action on top of wrong action until the heart becomes blind and dies."

Such people are at home with infamy and live like vermin in cellars and pits, afraid of the light and not even wanting the gates of Heaven to be opened. *"No indeed! The book of the dissolute is in Sijjin. And what will teach you what Sijjin is? A clearly written Book. Woe that Day to the deniers!"* (83:7-10)

As for those who take on the responsibilities of *taqwa* and hardships of purification, those who support the Truth and are steadfast in bearing its burdens, they will have a very different fate: *"No indeed! The book of the truly good is in 'Illiyun. And what will teach you what 'Illiyun is? A clearly written book. Those brought near will witness it. The truly good will be in perfect bliss."* (83:18-24) The first strivers were adorned with radiant truthfulness and unassailable faith but their small number and lack of arms exposed them to harm, so Allah will recompense them with this glorious end and will repay them for enduring mockery and injury with an exalted place and sealed wine. (83:29)

"Those who did evil used to laugh at those who believed, and, when they went by them, would wink at one another and, when they returned to their families, would make a joke of them." (83:29-31) This scene is often repeated now, and we find those who deny the existence of God who are snide in their criticisms of believing people and make fun of them in gatherings.

The early believers were an exemplary generation with liberated minds and great hearts. When Allah gave them victory after their trials, they filled the world with civilisation and prosperity. The later ones are like the children of a great man who have inherited his fame but not his greatness. How can they advance Islam when they have not purified themselves or paid any attention to it?

Sura 84
Al-Inshiqaq: The Bursting

"When the heaven is split apart, hearkening to its Lord as it is bound to." (84:1-2) We think that heaven is just this blue dome above us and we do not know anything about its layers and inhabitants or the nature of life in it. Allah informs us that heaven will be split apart: it is a true announcement and this will certainly happen at the Last Hour. Similarly the earth will be stretched out and disgorge what is inside it, both precious and base.

At the beginning of creation, the heaven and earth were told: *"'Come willingly or unwillingly.' They both said, 'We come willingly.'"* (41:11) At the end of the world, earth and heaven will respond to what is desired of them. Allah says of each of them *"hearkening to its Lord as it is bound to"* (84:2), meaning that they obey Him. Can they do otherwise than hear and obey?

"O Man! You are toiling laboriously towards your Lord but meet Him you will." (84:4) This world was the abode of responsibility and of serious and difficult trial, and it is up to each man to choose which path he will take, straight or crooked. *"As for him who is given his book in his right hand, he will be given an easy reckoning and return to his family joyfully. But as for him who is given his book behind his back, he will cry out for destruction but will be roasted in a Searing Blaze."* (84:7-12) The meaning of 'behind his back' is that he will take it with his left hand behind his back, as if Allah hates to see his face! He denied Allah's existence in this world and spurned His Revelation, acknowledging only matter and its disappearance: *"But the fact is his Lord was always watching him"* (84:15), with full knowledge of all he did.

Then the *sura* contains an oath by the twilight: *"No, I swear by the evening glow, and the night and all it shrouds, and the moon when it is full, you will certainly mount up stage by stage!"*

506

(84:17-19) This means "state after state". The evening glow is the redness which extends on the horizon just after sunset. It is possible that these *ayats* refer to the history of the Muslims and the hardship and ease, and defeats and victories which have accrued to them. That would harmonize with the *hadith* which at-Tirmidhi related from Abu Sa'id al-Khudri who said, "The Messenger of Allah, may Allah bless him and grant him peace, led us in the *'Asr* prayer. Then he stood to address us and did not omit anything which would occur until the Final Hour without telling us about it. Whoever remembered it remembered it, and whoever forgot it forgot it."

Part of what he said about it is, "This world is sweet and verdant. Allah has appointed you in it and He will see how you act." Then he, peace and blessings be upon him, said, "Awe of people should not prevent a man from speaking the truth when he knows it." He continued in his sublime words. Abu Sa'id said, "We began to look at the sun to see if any of the day was left. The Messenger of Allah, may Allah bless him and grant him peace, said, 'All what remains for this world, in relation to its past, is like what remains of this day and what has passed of it.'"

That short period remaining before the Final Hour is the time of our Muslim community and comprises the present time and what remains. We have come in the late afternoon of the world or its twilight hour. The important question is: Have we conveyed our Message and fulfilled our responsibility to the rest of mankind? Have we progressed stage by stage or have we regressed? Have we reflected? *"What is wrong with them that they do not believe and, when the Qur'an is recited to them, do not prostrate?"* (84:20-21) The Muslims will be asked about their Scipture and whether they established it and gave people a correct example of it.

Sura 85
Al-Buruj: The Houses of the Zodiac

"By Heaven with its Houses of the Zodiac" (85:1) refers to the astronomical cycles through which the planets pass. *"And the Promised Day"* (85:2) is the Day of Reckoning, *"And the witness and the witnessed,"* (85:3) are Allah and His angels and Messengers who will be witnesses against people. *"Death to the Companions of the Trench."* (85:4) They were cursed and destroyed. The Trench was a pit in the earth filled with firewood into which the believers were thrown to be burned. Martyrs for the truth are numerous in the history of mankind and the cruelty of wrongdoers knows no bounds.

Martyrs despise falsehood and its adherents and see no hindrance to sacrificing their lives for the Truth. I heard one of them speaking before his death. He said, "Annihilation in Allah is the same as living on." Some young men came to me to say farewell as they going to fight in Palestine. They went and did not return.

Historians say that the trench referred to in this *sura* was dug specifically to burn the believers: *"The fire well stocked with fuel – when they were seated right beside it, witnessing what they did to the believers. The only reason that they punished them was because they believed in Allah, the Almighty, the All-Praiseworthy."* (85:5-8) How many individuals and groups have died for the Cause of Allah and have gained the Next World!

Allah threatened the people of Makka unless they abandoned their crimes: *"Those who persecute believing men and believing women, and then do not repent, for them there is the punishment of Hell, for them there is the punishment of the Burning."* (85:10) The repayment received corresponds exactly to the action performed.

The *sura* then mentions some of the Attributes of majesty and beauty in order to provoke fear of Allah and repentance. *"Your Lord's Assault is fierce indeed. He originates and regenerates. He is the Ever-Forgiving, the All-Loving, the Possessor of the Throne, the All-Glorious."* (85:12-15) In addition to this reminder of the Attributes of Allah, there is a brief allusion to what He did to the ancient tyrants. He allowed them a little space and then seized them with the seizing of One who is powerful and mighty. The normative pattern of Allah does not change, so let the tyrants of today take note!

Sura 86
At-Tariq: The Night-Comer

"By Heaven and the Night-Comer! And what will convey to you what the Night-Comer is? The Piercing Star!" (86:1-3) In the sky there are planets which resemble the earth in that they are dark without any heat or light. In it are radiant stars like the sun or stronger or weaker than it. The Night-comer may be one of these stars. The Arabs called it 'the Witness' and it appears at sunset. What is sworn to by it is what immediately follows it: *"There is no soul which does not have a guardian over it."* (86:4) The great Creator has appointed a guardian for every person, to record what he does and fails to do.

The sequence of the evidence continues: *"Man has only to look at what he was created from. He was created from a spurting fluid, issuing from between the back-bone and breast-bone."* (86:5-7) The details of human creation have been elaborated in biology. Both ordinary people and specialists know that the beginning of human conception is a fluid which passes down the same tracts as urine, controlled by glands connected to the nervous system. This is the beginning, but what is man formed from once conception has taken place? From foods made up of every element. It could be said that the entire surface of the earth has participated in forming the cells of our flesh, bone, hair and so on.

But man is ungrateful. In any case he will be returned to an exacting reckoning: *"The Day that the innermost selves are scrutinised and he has no strength nor any helper."* (86:9-10) The sequence continues to discuss Divine power. The earth splits open and the rain comes; the grains and fruits are harvested and appear here and there. The son of Adam whose weight when he is born is a few pounds becomes a mass of muscles and limbs. Who transforms radishes and millet into brain tissue which is able to process

510

thought? Who transforms plants and animals into a body with skin, sinews and sensation and intelligence? Who if not Allah?

Various media sources accuse Islam of backwardness and claim to be the arbiters of progress. What do they say? They say that existence is based on chance. This is disgraceful. How can the complex layers of existence be formed by chance? They will find out how mistaken they were. *"It is truly a Discriminating Word. It is no joke. They are hatching a plot and I too am hatching a plot. So bear with the rejectors. Bear with them for a while."* (86:13-17)

Sura 87
Al-A ʿla: The Most High

"Glorify the Name of your Lord, the Most High, He who creat-ed and moulded, He who determined and guided." (87:1-3) Height in a metaphorical sense is nobler than height in a physical sense. When we describe our Lord – may He be glorified – as having height, we mean height of power and height of glory. We do not mean the stupidity of Pharaoh when he said, *"Haman, kindle a fire for me over the clay and build me a lofty tower so that perchance I may be able to climb up to Musa's god!"* (28:38) It is not the stu-pidity of a Russian astronaut who said that he went into space and did not find God! A Muslim prostrates before Allah frequently, and in his prostration he says, "Glory be to my Lord the Most High," affirming His words, *"Glory be to Him! He is exalted above what they say in greatness and sublimity."* (17:43)

There is no doubt that the All-Merciful has settled on the Throne and that the Throne encompasses all the worlds, but the dimensions of time and space and the special qualities of matter cannot contain Allah, the All-High, the All Great. We recognise that Allah has sublime power. If a single ray of His light were to shine forth, unveiling a tiny portion of His sublimity, the rest of existence would be wiped out. We are bewildered by the secrets of atom, so what would we do in the realm whose distances and dimensions are invisible to us? The splendour of Him who origi-nated everything from non-existence is radiant beyond our capaci-ty to perceive. "Glory be to You, O Allah, and praise. Blessed is Your Name and exalted are You."

"He created and moulded," and gave everything the best cre-ation and defined for everything a function which it precisely ful-fils. The quantity of water on the earth does not increase or decrease. Many human beings, animals, plants and various forms

of life continually consume it but it does not increase or decrease. *"He who determined and guided, He who brings forth green pasturage and then makes it blackened stubble."* (87:3-5) Its freshness withers and then the cycle recurs again and will do so as long as this world lasts, crops being followed by stubble until the final annihilation is decreed for it.

"We will cause you to recite so that you do not forget." (87:6) "O Muhammad, be at peace. The One who chose you will help you to convey your Message. He sent down to you an eternal Book and sent you with the true religion." *"And We will ease you to the Easy Way. Remind, then, if the reminder benefits."* (87:8-9) "You must convey it. Whoever is guided will follow you and whoever is stupid will abandon you." *"He who has fear will be reminded, but the most miserable will shun it, those who will roast in the Greatest Fire."* (87:10-13)

Man is able to descend or to rise. His salvation does not lie in property or rank. What is the value of our obtaining this world if we deny our Lord and reject His Revelation? *"He who has purified himself will have success, he who invokes the Name of his Lord and prays."* (87:14-15) The sad thing is that people want instant gratification and are blind to their true best interests. *"But still you prefer the life of this world when the Next World is better and longer lasting."* (87:16-17)

Sura 88
Al-Ghashiya: The Overwhelmer

"Has news of the Overwhelmer reached you?" (88:1) This is one of the names of the Resurrection because it will overwhelm people's senses and stun them. The *sura* begins with a threat and a promise, to provoke both fear and hope. Then it stimulates the mind to reflect on the elements of the environment, turning to camels, the mountains and the wide horizons in order to move from that to affirm Allah as the sole the object of worship. The *sura* ends with the definition of the Mission of the Muslim community among people, which is to warn and to remind. When people failed to perceive the wisdom behind their existence, the Muslims shouldered this burden and fought godlessness, denial and heedlessness of Allah. Their support on this path was the Eternal Book with which they were honoured, but then they ignored it in these barren years.

The threat which comes at the beginning of the *sura* is a description of the fate which awaits those who reject the Message. *"Some faces on that Day will be downcast,"* (88:2) in despair, *"labouring, toiling endlessly,"* (88:3) overwhelmed by heat. Their drink will be hot water and their food will be of no benefit to them. The godfearing will have a very different end. *"Some faces on that Day will be radiant, well-pleased with their efforts in an elevated Garden,"* (88:8-10) and one of the attributes of Paradise is that prattle has no place in it, since foolishness and intelligence do not mix.

Intelligence involves applying the intellect to what is unknown until it is made clear. *"Have they not looked at the camel - how it was created? And at heaven - how it was raised?"* (88:17-18) The word 'how' is used here to encourage the human intellect to investigate existence and what is in it, not for its own sake but to see how it points to its own Creator.

We will pause a little at the words of the Almighty: *"Remind them then! You are only a reminder. You are not in control of them."* (88:21-22) Islam does not establish a colonial empire to abase people and steal their wealth and raw materials. It liberates people and ennobles them, and encourages them to perfect themselves. The establishment of Islamic governance is not a privilege belonging to a particular race or elite group. Truly it is the struggle for self-determination which so many of us claim to want. Will we undertake it?

People have become discouraged by the apparent strength of the unbelieving powers in defending of their economic hegemony and unjust systems. Islam alone stands as a real counterweight to them, promising purity and justice for everyone. In any case, however long or short life is, the end is to Allah, the Just. *"Certainly their return shall be to Us and then their reckoning is Our responsibility."* (88:25-26)

Sura 89
Al-Fajr: The Dawn

"By the dawn" (89:1) is an oath by the retreat of darkness and birth of light. Other oaths are added to it: *"And ten nights,"* (89:2) and according to most of the commentators which are the ten days of Dhu'l-Hijja appointed for the Standing at 'Arafa and the Day of Sacrifice. *"And the even and the odd, and the night when it departs."* (89:3-4) The oath by time is added to what precedes it. Time is one of the secrets of existence whose effects are known but whose reality is not known.

What is this oath about? It is clear that what is sworn to is elided, and it is indicated afterwards. What is meant is that Allah will help your *Deen* and raise your banner and will confound disbelief and its adherents, whatever their power and however great their force. Today's unbelievers are in no way superior to their predecessors.

"Do you not see what your Lord did with 'Ad – Iram with its columns, whose like was not created in any land – and Thamud who carved out rocks in the valley-side, and Pharaoh of the Stakes?" (89:6-10) Earlier peoples did not invade space and delve into the sciences of matter but they were skilful engineers and their monuments continue to astonish us. Allah said to the Arabs who denied Muhammad: *"Have they not travelled in the earth and seen the end of those before them? They had greater strength than they have and they cultivated the land and they inhabited it in greater numbers than they do..."* (30:9) Their oppression and arrogance brought disaster on themselves. When they rejected their Messengers and were arrogant towards Allah *"Your Lord unleashed on them a scourging punishment. Your Lord is always lying in wait."* (89:13-14)

The middle of *Surat al-Fajr* speaks about the evil side of man. He is deceived by the present day and forgets what preceded it and what will follow it. He does not recognise that Allah alternates good and ill fortune between people. Many people are deceived by their immediate present and they do not know that they are being tested by good and bad. *"As for man, when his Lord puts him to the test, by honouring him and blessing him, he says, 'My Lord has honoured me.' But then when He puts him to the test by restricting his provision, he says, 'My Lord has humiliated me.' No indeed!"* (89:15-17)

All of this is the parcelling out of provision whose secret is known to Allah alone. There is no evidence in it of preference or disdain. Allah tests by both wealth and poverty, defeat and victory. Ease does not necessarily indicate His pleasure nor hardship His wrath. It is simply the division of livelihood by which all people are tested and in the light of which their positions will be defined on the Day of Resurrection. The only safety lies in fear of Allah.

Allah does not give a wealthy man wealth so that he may tell someone else, *"I have more wealth than you, more people under me."* (18:34) He gives it to him so that he may let others share in it. He should strive to help those in need and to alleviate their distress. And poor people should not weep over their lack of the things of this world or envy those who possess them. They should be patient and struggle and grow in virtue.

From the beginning of creation Allah made a distinction between people by a decree and a deliberate test. That is why He says, after drawing this contrast willed by Him: *"You do not honour orphans nor do you urge the feeding of the poor; you devour inheritance with voracious appetites and have insatiable love of wealth and property."* (89:17-20) The battle for bread has raged since ancient times. Everyone's energy has been directed to it, and wars have occurred because of it. It is only the *Deen* of Allah that can keep it in check and it is disastrous that the injunctions of the *Deen* have been neutralised and animal instincts have prevailed. Communism tried to rectify this by appropriating to itself Allah's role in the allocation of provision but the result was, of course, the same pattern of injustice and oppression.

But what have the Muslims offered the wayward masses on the surface of the earth? Nothing! They have covered up the face of Islam and distorted its teachings. Indeed, in the lands of Islam I have seen free men begging for generosity from another country and seeking the justice which is all too rare in their own land! It only remains to await the Last Resurrection: *"No indeed! When the earth is crushed and ground to dust and your Lord comes, and the angels rank upon rank and that Day Hell is brought up, that Day man will remember. But how will the reminder be for him? He will say, 'Oh! If only I had prepared for my life to come!'"* (89:21-24) This cry of regret on the Day when regret is of no use!

For the righteous slaves of Allah this will be a Day of good news and faces will glow with triumph. At-Tabari related from Sa'id ibn Jubayr that a man recited in the presence of Allah, *"O self at rest and at peace! Return to your Lord, well-pleasing and well-pleased."* (89:27-28) Abu Bakr said, "How excellent is this!" The Prophet, may Allah bless him and grant him peace, said to him, "The angel will say it to you when you die." Abu Bakr was the first of the just and rightly guided Caliphs and one of the people most entitled to it. But the context is general in the Noble Qur'an. Every Muslim who surrenders himself to Allah and makes his actions righteous can obtain it. The beautiful words are awaiting for him to enter Paradise and participate in the glorification and praise which fill it. May Allah place us among them by His grace and favour!

Sura 90
Al-Balad: The City

"No, I swear by this city," (90:1) meaning "I swear by Makka," *"and you are resident in this city,"* (90:2) meaning you are an inhabitant of it. Furthermore, it is a sacred place in which plants and animals are protected. Nonetheless it was deemed lawful to harm Muhammad and commit aggression against him. Why this oath by a land in which that violation occurs? Because the call to Islam originated there and it was the home of the core of a new generation of human beings who responded to Allah and established His *Deen* for future generations.

The Prophets Ibrahim and Isma'il said about it, *"Our Lord, raise up among them a Messenger from them to recite Your signs to them and to teach them the Book and Wisdom and to purify them."* (2:120) That is the explanation of the next part of the oath: *"By a father and what he has fathered."* (90:3) The father is Ibrahim and Muhammad, one of the descendants of Isma'il, is his descendant who will seal Divine Revelation and establish its rule on earth. *"We created man in a state of trouble."* (90:4) The human species bears the burdens of responsibilities and the restraint of the *Shari'a* prevents him from giving free rein to the gratification of his appetites.

A man may disbelieve and deny that he will be brought to life again. Is Allah unable to bring him back after making him die? *"Does he reckon that no one has power over him?"* (90:5) That is like His words in another *sura*: *"Does man imagine that We will not re-assemble his bones?"* (75:3) He may be deluded by what he has been given and the wealth he can spend: *"He says, 'I have consumed vast quantities of wealth.'"* (90:6) That is the nature of the Arabs when they boast of rank, wealth and giving. What is the value of all that if a man meets his Lord naked and unadorned by belief or righteousness? *"Does he suppose that no one was watching him?"* (90:7) Allah will question every man about his wealth and how he earned and spent it.

Allah reminds His slaves of the blessings He has entrusted to them which call for thankfulness: *"Have We not allotted him two eyes, and a tongue and two lips and shown him the two clear ways?"* (90:8-10) Will he not break the bonds of disbelief and blind following of tradition and embark on his path to Allah believing in Him and obeying His command? What must he do to achieve this? *"But he has not braved the steep ascent – and what will teach you what the steep ascent is? Freeing a slave or feeding on a day of hunger an orphaned relative or a poor man in the dust."* (90:8-10)

Here the *sura* talks of true faith. Faith is not just a question of words. It is giving, sacrifice, intelligence and light. It produces true humanity and nobility in each individual and in society as a whole. *"Then to be one of those who believe and bid each other to steadfastness and bid each other to compassion. Those are the Companions of the Right,"* (90:17-18) meaning the people of Paradise. Bidding to steadfastness and mercy is the hallmark of the people of perfection and striving. Believers are not lazy or base. They are active in the path of good until death overtakes them and elevates them to their high place in the Garden of Delight. But the people who are addicted to wrongdoing and enamoured of darkness will have a different end: *"Those who reject Our signs, they are the Companions of the Left. Above them is a sealed vault of Fire."* (90:19-20)

Sura 91
Ash-Shams: The Sun

"By the sun and its morning brightness, and the moon when it succeeds it." (91:1-2) When you look at the sun high in the sky, it appears to be a little smaller than the size of a hand. But remember what the scientists say about how much greater it is than the size of our earth; that the distance between us and the sun is 120 million kilometres; and that there are nine planets orbiting it of which our earth, which contains billions of people, is only one of the smaller ones. Then bear in mind that the sun and its planets are travelling among countless other stars in an unimaginably vast expanse and that these innumerable galaxies take up only a small corner of space.

One cannot help but be overcome with wonder and awe at the utterly unknowable power of the Creator of all this. And yet we know that the whole physical universe is merely a minute part of what Allah has made! On this small planet live the sons of Adam who have been given the gift of freedom of will, but our only real choice is to believe or not to believe in Him who brought us into being.

Surat ash-Shams and the short *suras* like it contain terse pronouncements and short instructions but they are completely self-sufficient. That is why they are repeated in the five prayers to provide a beneficial spiritual provision. Allah has made seven oaths at the beginning of the *sura* that success belongs to those who purify themselves and that failure is the lot of those who follow their lower appetites. People are only ever destroyed by their own arrogance and heedlessness. Thamud was corrupt and despotic. What was their end? They became stubble trodden underfoot.

Sura 92
Al-Layl: The Night

"By the night when it conceals and the day when it reveals..." (92:1-2) The darkness of night covers the world and the light of day illuminates it. With the unceasing alternation of night and day people pass their lives and prepare for their future, either in the Garden or in the Fire. Virtuous striving purifies people for a prosperous future and base action paves the way to a vile end. *"As for him who gives out and is godfearing and confirms the Good, We will pave his way to Ease. But as for him who is tight-fisted and self-satisfied, and disavows the Good, We will pave his way to Difficulty."* (92:5-10)

The problem is that there have been generations of Muslims who have abnegated their responsibility and become lazy, thereby losing both their present and their future because they have failed to understand the nature of the Divine Decree and embraced the superstition of blind fate. Much empty rhetoric has been expended to lament and even justify their failure and lack of power. But the true causes of this situation have rarely been addressed. It is necessary to actively seek the Pleasure of Allah and purify one's intention of all insincerity.

This is a difficult goal. Most people revere wealth and rank. They base their ambitions and hopes on them. Sometimes it seems that self-seeking is the pivot of human activity and that sincerity is rarer than the legendary Philosopher's Stone! *"Those who give their wealth to purify themselves – not to repay someone for a favour done – desiring only the Face of their Lord Most High; they will certainly be well-pleased."* (92:18-21) If people's actions were free of love of this world and accompanied by sincere desire for the Next World, then the earth would be spared much bloodshed and many destructive wars. We ask Allah to take us by our forelocks to what pleases Him!

Sura 93
Ad-Duha: The Forenoon

In many *ayats* the Qur'an is described as light: *"So believe in Allah and His Messenger and the Light We have sent down."* (64:8) *"But We have appointed it to be a light by which We guide those of Our slaves We will."* (42:52) There is no doubt that the Divine Revelation was a constant illumination to the heart of Muhammad and remained with him throughout his life. However, the Revelation was broken off once or twice for natural reasons and one time when that occurred was very near the beginning. It did not mean that the Lord of Muhammad hated him, as was claimed by some of the enemies of the Message. So this *sura* was revealed: *"By the brightness of the morning and the night when it is still, your Lord has not abandoned you nor does He hate you."* (93:1-3)

The scholars state that these two oaths indicate the time of the descent of the Revelation and the time of its stopping. There must be a time for recuperation and rest because the descent of Revelation is accompanied by intense physical distress. That has nothing to do with abandonment or dislike: *"The Last will be better for you than the First."* (93:4)

At the beginning of the Prophetic Mission the followers of the Prophet, may Allah bless him and grant him peace, could be counted on the fingers. Then the Message began to spread and became the basis of the formation of a great community. That community constituted the firm foundation of the Islamic edifice which will endure until the Last Hour. In the course of that process the Prophet received much Revelation and expended great effort until he had altered the course of human history and founded a new civilisation. The Book which produced that still is in our hands as a truthful testimony to the greatness of Islam and its

Messenger: *"Your Lord will soon give to you and you will be satisfied."* (93:5)

Allah had said to Musa before *"So that you would be brought up under My eye."* (20:39) He said to Muhammad after he had taken on the awesome Message: *"Therefore wait steadfastly for the judgement of your Lord - you are certainly before Our eyes. And glorify the praise of your Lord when you arise."* (52:48) Allah Himself oversees the upbringing of the Prophets whom He chooses from precious lodes and then polishes throughout their lives with harsh events. He *"has closer ties to the believers than their own selves."* (33:6)

"Did He not find you an orphan and shelter you? Did He not find you wandering and guide you? Did He not find you impoverished and enrich you?" (93:6-8) 'Wandering' here refers to bewilderment in knowing the Way and how to guide the world. Muhammad and all the other Prophets were protected from all misguidance or wrong action of any kind. That cannot be ascribed to them at all.

Then Allah made him independent of people; but although his basic needs were guaranteed he did not possess any stored wealth or even any surplus. After Allah reminded him of his previous and future blessings, He told him, *"So as for orphans, do not oppress them. And as for beggars, do not berate them. And as for the blessing of your Lord, speak out."* (93:9-11) Speaking out about blessings is a basic function of Prophethood. Allah says in another *sura*: *"So remind them, for, by the blessing of your Lord, you are neither a fortune-teller nor a madman."* (52:29) "You are chosen to convey the Message and bring people to salvation, so speak out. You are not a soothsayer or pretender." *"You are but a warner; and Allah is Guardian over all things."* (11:12)

Sura 94
Al-Inshirah: The Expanding

Surat al-Inshirah is a continuation of *Surat ad-Duha*. The question with which it begins is a continuation of the successive questions which ended the previous *sura*. Allah expanded the breast of the Prophet, peace and blessings be upon him, to perfect the knowledge and good behaviour He had given him. He says elsewhere: *"Allah has revealed the Book and Wisdom to you and taught you what you did not know before. Allah's favour to you is immense."* (4:113) The Messenger of Allah grew up in an environment full of darkness. Indeed the entire world was lacking in guidance and overwhelmed with paganism. So on what could someone who called to the Truth rely? From whom should he seek help? His back would have been exhausted by the weight of the burden had it <u>not</u> been that Allah chose him and blessed him: *"Did We not expand for you your breast and remove your load from you which weighed down your back?"* (94:1-3)

The unitary belief which Muhammad brought is a pure kind in which there is no contradiction or illusion or anthropomorphism or polytheism. The testimony that Muhammad is the Messenger is joined to the testimony that Allah is One. This connection between the Prophet's name and that of his Lord is one meaning of *"Did We not exalt your name for you?"* (94:4)

Allah instructs His Prophet to be steadfast and persevere in countering those who deny Him, however severe their persecution. The future belongs to Allah and His helpers. *"For truly with difficulty comes ease. Truly with difficulty comes ease."* (94:5-6) The rules of Arabic rhetoric in this construction make the ease great and hardship little. That is why they say, "For the one who overcomes hardship there are two eases."

Finally Allah instructs His Messenger never to give up the struggle and to turn to Him. When he completes one task, he must get on with the next. There is no place in his life for slackening off: *"So when you have finished, work on and make your Lord your goal."* (104:7-8) Muhammad spoke the truth when he spoke and was just when he judged. The world, especially now, is in desperate need of truthfulness and justice.

Sura 95
At-Tin: The Fig

"By the fig and the olive and Mount Sinai and this Safe Land!" (95:1-3) Allah swears by these four things that He created man in the finest mould. The fig and olive are well-known fruits and a group of scholars think that Allah means to swear by fruit in general, so that if He had sworn by other fruits that would have come to the same thing. All the plants which grow on the earth are evidence of His power. Other scholars believe that the oath is connected to earlier Divine Revelations and this understanding draws all four things together. Ibn 'Abbas related that at-Tin (the fig) was the mosque of Nuh which he built on al-Judi after the Flood; az-Zaytun (the olive) is the Aqsa Mosque which Ibrahim built after he built the Ka'ba; Mount Sinai is the place where Allah revealed Himself to Musa and honoured him with the Commandments; and the Safe Land is Makka, the place where the Qur'an was first revealed.

What is sworn to is the creation of man in the finest mould. Does "finest mould" refer to his beautiful form and tall stature? No, that is not what is meant. In the *hadith* we find, "Allah does not look at your bodies or your forms: He looks at your hearts." Only some of the Children of Adam have been distinguished by tall stature. Their first and perhaps their ultimate distinguishing feature is the intelligence of the intellect and the uprightness of their natural patterning.

The breath from the Spirit of Allah Most High flowed throughout the parts of man and made him a being of paramount importance in existence. The circumstances of his original creation show that man is born with innate belief in Allah and natural rectitude. Then his environment overcomes him and he deviates and forgets his noble origin. Allah says: *"So set your face firmly towards the*

527

Deen *as a pure natural believer, Allah's natural patterning on which He made mankind. There is no changing Allah's creation. That is the right* Deen - *but most people do not know."* (30:30)

When people forget their Lord and their natural patterning is corrupted, they commit sins which make the flesh creep. Why do they bury baby girls alive? Why do they burn healthy women with their dead husbands? Why do they torture prisoners to death? Why do some people conceal the Truth? Why do misers begrudge giving when they have no need of what they have? Why do we deny Allah who is our Creator? All of these are base actions to which mankind has degenerated and which puts them far from the natural form given by Allah.

The naturally beautiful form of man is lost when belief dries up. This is the meaning of the *ayat: "Then We reduced him to the lowest of the low, except for those who believe and do right actions: for them there is a never failing wage. What could make you deny the* Deen *after this? Is not Allah the justest of all judges?"* (95:7-10) Why do some deny the *deen* and fight it and bar people from it? What idea led them to do that? People have left the wisdom of the Wise and replaced Islam with contemptible laws which produce no good at all. How extraordinary!

The Prophet said that whoever recites this entire *sura* should say, "I am one of those who testify to that."

Sura 96
Al-'Alaq: The Blood Clot

The Prophet, may Allah bless him and grant him peace, used to go to the Cave of Hira' at times and withdraw from the tumult of the *Jahiliyya* and contemplate, full of certainty and humility, the existence of the Creator of this vast universe. He disdained idols and detested their worship and the festivals and customs held under their auspices, but he did not know more than that until a voice came to him: *"Recite: In the Name of your Lord who created, created mankind from a clot of blood. Recite: And your Lord is the Most Generous, He who taught by the pen, taught man what he did not know."* (96:1-5) These five *ayats* were the first *ayats* of the Qur'an to be revealed to the heart of the Messenger. The rest of the *sura* was revealed later.

The One who is able to create man from a blood clot is able to make an illiterate man knowledgeable. Muhammad did not aspire to Revelation or the Prophetic Mission; it came to him unexpectedly and suddenly. When he was certain he had been chosen by Allah, he began to build the new community, as Ibrahim and Musa had done before. Any impartial observer of his behaviour, the Book he brought, and his struggle will be convinced that the world has never known any leader even close to his qualities and virtues.

After a gap the *ayats* were revealed: *"No indeed! Truly man is inordinate in seeing himself as totally self-sufficient. Truly to your Lord is the return."* (96:6-8) Need might abase man but why does he become arrogant when he has no need. It is so often the case that when people become wealthy they disdain the Next World and rebel against the Truth! Their reckoning is in the Next World.

The *sura* mentions some characteristics of the unbeliever who denies the signs of his Lord and forbids prayer and purification: *"Have you seen him who prohibits a slave when he goes to pray?*

Do you think he is rightly guided or commands to godliness?" (96:9-12) In *Surat al-Muddaththir*, Allah mentions these qualities and more: *"'What caused you to enter Saqar?' They will say, 'We were not of those who prayed, we did not feed the poor, we plunged with those who plunged, and we denied the Day of Repayment.'"* (74:42-46)

This was the battleground for Muhammad and His opponents in Makka for about ten years, and the same battle will continue until the Day of Rising because the vast majority of unbelievers reject the prayer and *zakat*. They wrangle about the existence of Allah and the encounter with Him and hearkening to His commands and prohibitions. Islam is a particular source of exasperation to them because it will not compromise about the obligation to hear and to obey. *"Or do you see how he has denied and turned away? Does he not know that Allah sees?"* (96:13-14)

The battle will certainly continue between the two factions: one of them observing the lawful and unlawful, duty and obligation, and the other thinking that man is his own master and that no one has any authority over him. *"No indeed! If he does not desist, We will grab him by the forelock"* (96:15): he will be grabbed and dragged by his forelock so that he will not be able to escape. *"A lying, sinful forelock."* (96:16) The leaders of Makka heard this threat but did nothing.

Sura 97
Al-Qadr: Power

The Revelation of the Qur'an began on a night which the Muslims call the 'Night of Power'. Scholars disagree about exactly when this night was but most believe that it was in the last ten nights of the month of Ramadan. Since the waxing and waning of the moon varies throughout the lunar year, it is difficult to say the exact moment when it happened and so those who want to pray on that night should offer night prayers throughout the last third or last half of the blessed month of Ramadan. The Qur'an is the Word of Allah by which He sealed and completed His Revelation and by which He perfected His blessing upon the human race. The extent of the blessing which descends on this night is clear in the words of the Almighty: *"And what will convey to you what the Night of Power is? The Night of Power is better than a thousand months."* (97:2-3)

"During it the angels and the Spirit descend at their Lord's command with every ordinance." (97:4) This expression is like His words in *Surat ad-Dukhan*: *"In it every wise decree is specified by a command from Our presence – We are constantly sending out as a mercy from your Lord."* (44:4-6) The Qur'an contains all the right guidance needed for human beings to fulfil themselves and establish a just society, and there is no other source of true knowledge about existence. Since things are made distinct by their opposites, any reader can compare the Qur'an with all the Scriptures which are ascribed to God and then see what conclusion he reaches. Which has the greatest evidence of Allah and is more effective in making people fear Him?

The night on which the Qur'an was revealed is a night of peace. Peace is our objective as Muslims. But what is the situation when the idolaters say to those who believe in one God, "There is no place for you here!"? Those who disbelieve said to their Messengers, *"We will drive you from our land unless you return to our religion."* (14:13) There must be pure worship and justice before there can be peace.

Sura 98
Al-Bayyina: The Clear Sign

This *sura* is illustrated by a general overview of history. Anyone who examines at a map of the world as it was in the sixth century CE will see that North Africa and western Asia were Christian, ruled by the Romans, and the lands beyond that were peopled by idolaters as far as India and China. When the seventh century came, the world changed. Before the end of that century all North Africa, the Nile Valley, Anatolia, Syria, and Yemen were governed by Islam and the *adhan* could be heard right across the two ancient continents.

Sincere Christians welcomed Islam and embraced it eagerly, realising that the prophethood of Muhammad was the fulfilment of what they saw in their own scriptures. We find in *Surat al-Isra'*: *"Certainly, when it is recited to them, those who were given knowledge before it fall on their faces in prostration, saying, 'Glory be to our Lord! The promise of our Lord is truly fulfilled!' Weeping, they fall to the ground in prostration, and it increases them in humility."* (17:107-108) And in *Surat ar-Ra'd*: *"Those to whom We gave the Book rejoice at what has been sent down to you but some of the parties refuse to acknowledge part of it. Say: 'I have been ordered only to worship Allah and not to attribute any partners to Him. To Him I call people and to Him I will return.'"* (13:36).

Historical evidence confirms that the spread of Islam in the face of Christian superiority was truly remarkable and that it later halted temporarily owing to internal circumstances which we will not go into here. Just as the Christians entered Islam, so did many Zoroastrians, Buddhists and pagans. How did this come about? It was the effect of the Noble Qur'an! *"The People of the Book who reject and the idolaters would not be cut off,"* i.e. abandon their prior doctrines, *"until the Clear Sign came to them: a Messenger from Allah reciting purified texts containing upright precepts."* (98:1-3)

There is no reason whatsoever why the Qur'an should not cause history to repeat itself. It just needs people to exemplify it and convey it as our ancestors did. There are thousands of people ready to recognise the truth if only it is presented to them with energy, wisdom and sincerity. But among the People of Scripture, both today and in the past, there are also those who are willing to sell their religion for worldly gain. Some of them murdered the Prophets and tortured the righteous. The study of history unfortunately reveals too many men of religion of every faith who indulged in all kinds of cruelty.

"Those who were given the Book did not split up until after the Clear Sign came to them. They were ordered only to worship Allah, making their Deen *sincerely His as people of natural pure belief and to establish the prayer and pay the* zakat: *that is the* Deen *of uprightness."* (98:4-5) It appears that the illumination of the intellect does necessarily bring illumination of the heart. Allah will excuse people of limited intelligence, but not people overpowered by passion and fraudulent intention. Among the custodians of religious practices are those who are enslaved by avarice and uncurbed egotism. *"The People of the Book who reject and the idolaters will be in the Fire of Hell, remaining in it timelessly forever. Those are the worst of creatures."* (98:6)

The *sura* ends with a generous promise to the believers provided that they show awareness of Allah and act with due fear of Him: *"Those who believe and do right actions, they are the best of creatures. Their repayment is with their Lord, Gardens of Eden with rivers flowing under them, to remain in them timelessly forever without end. Allah is pleased with them and they are pleased with Him. That is for him who fears his Lord."* (98:7-8)

Sura 99
Az-Zalzala: The Earthquake

Before the Last Hour there will be an enormous earthquake which will overpower all the inhabitants of the earth. Earthquakes vary in duration and intensity. An earthquake can last only few seconds and yet leave cities in ruins; I have seen an earthquake of half a second which destroyed houses and threw people on their faces. The earthquake at the end of time will be accompanied by the eruption of volcanoes and the release of hot water from inside the earth. *"When the earth is convulsed with its quaking and the earth disgorges its charges and man says, 'What is the matter with it?'"* (99:1-3)

What has happened to it? What does it want from us? *"That Day it will tell all its news because your Lord has inspired it to do that."* (99:4-5) On that Day people will be aware that the promised Day has arrived and that people's Reckoning of people for what they did has come. *"That Day people will emerge segregated to see the results of their actions."* (99:6)

Their awareness of what they did will be extremely vivid. *"On the Day that each self finds the good it did and the evil it did present there in front of it, it will wish there were a great distance between it and that time."* (3:30) The reckoning will be accurate to within an atom's weight on that terrible Day. According to a *hadith*, the Prophet was asked about the *zakat* payable on a donkey and said, "Allah has not revealed anything about it except this single general verse: *"Whoever did an atom's weight of good will see it. Whoever did an atom's weight of evil will see it."* (99:7-8)

535

Sura 100
Al-'Adiyat: The Chargers

Fighting protects belief, defends the Truth, guards the land and protects things that should be inviolable. Falsehood reaches out for any gaps in its defences. When it encounters only weak resistance, it attacks and achieves its goal. I have seen corruption impose itself on people because it is supported by strong forces, and I have seen nobility melt away before it and disappear. Recall the words of the young men of the Cave to one another: *"If they find out about you, they will stone you or make you revert to their religion and then you will never prosper."* (18:20)

For this reason Allah swears by the vivid image of a dawn raid: *"By the charging horses panting hard, striking sparks from their flashing hooves, raiding at full gallop in the early dawn, leaving a trailing dust-cloud in their wake, cleaving through the middle of the foe, truly man is ungrateful to his Lord."* (100:1-6) When the cavalry charges with their horses and their breath is heaving in their chests, their hooves striking sparks from the intensity of the pace of their galloping, and the men riding them are facing death in attack or defence, then the thwarters will know the gravity of their error and pay its price in their blood.

The truth is that in our time we need the energy evoked by these *ayats*. We need to go out and fight the people of ingratitude and recalcitrance who are stealing our faith and virtue. They desire to impose lies and injustice on people: *"Truly man is ungrateful to his Lord and certainly he is a witness to that."* (100:6-7)

There has never been a time when the Next World was denied as it is denied in our time, nor has this world ever been worshipped as it is worshipped in our time: *"Does he not know that when the graves are emptied out, and the contents of the hearts are brought into the open, that Day their Lord will certainly be aware of them."* (100:9-11)

Sura 101
Al-Qari'a: The Crashing Blow

Immediately before the Last Hour there will be an ear-splitting blast which will terrify all who will awaken and wake up any who are asleep. Is it the clash of bells or the beating of drums or a shriek which pierces the ears? It is the Crashing Blow: *"The Crashing Blow! What is the Crashing Blow? What will make you realise what the Crashing Blow is? The Day that mankind will be like moths strewn through the air, and the mountains like tufts of coloured wool."* (101:1-5) The mountains will lose their cohesion and fall apart like bits of carded wool.

People will be like swarms of moths or scattered locusts, everyone searching out his future, anxious to know where his fate lies. You have already determined your future in the days which have past. *"As for him whose balance is heavy, he will have a very pleasant life."* (101:6-7) What is meant is the scale of good people filled with good actions. As for the one who has little good and whose evil overflows, *"His motherland is Hawiya."* (101:9) This expression conforms to Arab usage in which the state of a mother is held to indicate the state of her son in either sorrow or happiness. 'Hawiya' is the name of a low place. What is meant here is Hell. Allah says after it: *"And what will teach you what that is? A raging Fire!"* (101:10-11)

538

Sura 102
At-Takathur: Competition

"Fierce competition for this world has distracted you until you go down to the graves." (102:1-2) This is addressed to the idolaters who worship idols but it includes all who are devoted to seeking this world. When we examine people's aspirations, we find that the Next World does not come to their minds at all. They may hear some passing reference to the Next World but they do not retain anything at all about it or express any concern for what will happen there. It is not a matter of being concerned with the basic needs of life. It is about competition with others to amass the greatest amount of goods possible. This rivalry will only end with the cutting off of breath and the sudden event of death.

"Going down to the graves" in Arabic is literally 'visiting' them. It is called 'visiting' because the grave is not our final destination. We will emerge from them after a time to face the Reckoning: *"The Trumpet will be blown and suddenly they will be emerging from their graves towards their Lord. They will say, 'Alas for us! Who has raised us from our resting-place? This is what the All-Merciful promised, and the Messengers were telling the truth.'"* (36:51-52) The grave is a passageway or interspace to what lies beyond it.

"No indeed! You will soon know. Again no indeed! You will soon know." (102:3-4) There is sudden recognition at the direct witnessing of the Abode of Eternity. Then those who were slaves of the life of this world will be told: *"No indeed! If you only knew with the Knowledge of Certainty – you will certainly see the Blazing Fire."* (102:5-6) "If you had believed the Messenger, you would have followed another course of action to protect yourselves from the punishment of Hellfire." A man can protect his

539

face from the Fire by away giving half a date; but they failed to act, and so the Fire of the Day of Repayment has come upon them. *"Then you will certainly see it with the Eye of Certainty. Then you will be asked that day about the pleasures you enjoyed."* (102:7-8) In the Next World man will be asked about every blessing he enjoyed for which he was not grateful.

Sura 103
Al-'Asr: The Late Afternoon

"By the Late Afternoon, truly man is in a state of loss." (103:1-2) In spite of its brevity, this *sura* is a summary of the results of all human action throughout the entirety of space-time. Those who are cut off from Allah will be the fuel of Hell and those who hold fast to belief, righteousness, truth and steadfastness are the ones who will win the battle of life. These four qualities are rare and precious. Mankind has passed through many times when these qualities have not been valued, but Allah has good news for the people who have them: *"Except for those who believe and do right actions and exhort each other to the truth and exhort each other to steadfastness."* (103:3)

The Companions took *Surat al-'Asr* as their byword in their meetings. It is related in *hadith* that "When two of the Companions of the Messenger of Allah, may Allah bless him and grant him peace, met, they would not part until one of them had recited all of *Surat al-'Asr* to the other. Then they would greet one another." Imam ash-Shafi'i said, "If no *sura* other than this one had been revealed for mankind, it would have been enough for them."

Sura 104
Al-Humaza: The Backbiter

One of the ways in which evildoers fight against the people of belief is by mockery and derision: *"Those who did evil used to laugh at those who believed, and, when they passed by them, would wink at one another."* (83:29-30) When this Revelation was sent down, there were rich people and others in Makka who sat in assemblies devoted to amusement and made fun of the Muslims. So this *sura* was revealed: *"Woe to every fault-finding backbiter, who has amassed wealth and hoarded it! He thinks his wealth will make him live forever."* (104:1-3)

Fault-finding and backbiting involve attacking others by gesture or expression, sometimes verbally and sometimes by movements of the eyes and lips. Books may also contain mocking satire. The satirizers are idle people who live for their wealth or for things which make them act in dubious dways. Alas for those people in this world and the Next! Allah says about this mocker: *"No indeed! He will be flung into the Shatterer. And what will teach you what the Shatterer is? The kindled Fire of Allah reaching right into the hearts. It is sealed in above them,"* like a lid shutting in what it covers, *"in towering columns."* (104:4-89) The supports of this prison are high columns through all of which the punishment spreads.

Sura 105
Al-Fil: The Elephant

The Abyssinians mobilised a huge army to attack the Ka'ba and destroy it and put an end to worship in its precincts. They left their homes according to Allah's description: *"…who left their homes in arrogance, showing off to people and barring them from the Way of Allah."* (8:48) Elephants formed part of the attacking force. The people of Makka were aware that they lacked the power to repel this attack and they fled to the tops of the surrounding mountains, leaving the fate of the House of Allah and their own houses to the decisionof the Divine Decree.

The Abyssinian Christians erred in sending this attack against the Sacred House and their expedition met with a disastrous end. They were attacked by flocks of birds which cast stones on the men. It is understood from the Noble Qur'an that the stones were the same kind as were cast down on the people of Lut, which demolished their city and turned it upside-down.

Historians recount that these flocks spread smallpox and annihilated the attackers, and that the general of the army, Abraha, died while returning to San'a' after his crushing defeat. Allah says about this incident: *"Do you not see what your Lord did with the Companions of the Elephant? Did He not bring all their schemes to nothing, unleashing upon them flock after flock of birds, bombarding them with stones of hard-baked clay?"* (105:1-4)

It is noteworthy that it is transmitted that the Seal of the Messengers, may Allah bless him and grant him peace, was born in the Year of the Elephant. It appears that Allah protected Makka by His blessing and Quraysh remained provided for in Makka and in full security as a divine preparation for the manifestation of Islam from the Mother of Cities to the rest of the world. That is indicated by the next *sura*.

Sura 106
Quraysh

"In acknowledgement of the established tradition of Quraysh, their tradition of the winter and summer caravans." (106:1-2) The Arabian peninsula is located between Europe and Asia. Its inhabitants carried out trade between the two continents as they dwelt in an isthmus connecting the Byzantines in Syria with the Indian trade to Yemen in the south. Their caravans were the regular means of transport for the goods between those two groups of people. The Arabs in Makka and around it benefited greatly from the geographical location Allah had given them, travelling south in winter and north in summer.

"They should worship the Lord of this House who has kept them from hunger and secured them from fear." (106:3-4) These words indicate the stability of security and the negation of fear. They are the basic conditions for political freedom, abundant food and ease of exchange, and they form the basis of economic freedom. This gave the Arabs of the peninsula strong character and fierce independence from others and made them ideal candidates for bearing the message of Islam and taking it to the east and west. Some scholars think that *Surat al-Ilaf* is an extension of *Surat al-Fil*, and consider them to be a single *sura*.

Sura 107
Al-Ma'un: Helping Others

True people of religion seek to discover the needs of others and hasten to fulfil them. The *Deen* is there to help the weak so that they may become strong, the poor so that their needs may be met, orphans until they have grown up, and travellers to return home. But some of those who claim affiliation with the *Deen* have been negligent in these duties and consequently social theories based on unbelief have been devised to compensate for this. One of them was Communism, which succeeded in controlling half the world and influencing the other half! If only the people of religion, especially the Muslims, had clung to their *Deen* and implemented it properly, this godlessness which denies the *Deen* would not have appeared.

Belief is the brother of generosity and justice, and idolatry is the brother of egotism and harshness. Consider the words of Allah Almighty: *"Have you seen him who denies the* Deen*? That means him who harshly rebuffs the orphan and does not urge the feeding of the poor."* (107:1-3) *Surat al-Ma'un*, in spite of its brevity, refutes worship that is a mere formality and shows that helping the needy is a precondition for belief, as well as the establishment of the prayer and performing it with humility. It threatens with woe those who refuse to help people who need it!

Sura 108
Al-Kawthar: Great Abundance

Surat al-Kawthar, which is scarcely one line long, contains an immense abundance of good news. As is well known, all the sons of the Prophet, may Allah bless him and grant him peace, died and only his daughters survived. In the *Jahiliyya* this was considered a calamity because sons were needed to carry on their father's name; because of this people taunted the Prophet as being 'cut off without an heir'.

This *sura* was revealed to confirm that Allah has the vastest possible gift for His Prophet. The Qur'an came down upon on his heart and Allah chose him as a Messenger to all the worlds. He inspired the people of the earth and heaven to mention him and praise him. Not a moment of passes without a prayer being said by an angel or mortal which increases his reward and elevates his renown. Muhammad is the most fortunate of the creatures of Allah, thanks to the favour and honour shown to him by Allah. He is the Master of the Children of Adam and the Imam of the first and the last. *"Truly We have given you the Great Abundance. So pray to your Lord, and sacrifice."* (108:1-2)

What is meant here is the *'Id* Prayer, after which animals are sacrificed and their meat is distributed to the poor. The sacrifice can be of either sheep or camels.

Then Allah tells His Prophet: *"It is the one who hates you who is cut off without an heir."* (108:3) "He who hates you is the one whose repute will be terminated and whose traces will be obliterated. As for you, the angels which encircle the Throne glorifying the praise of their Lord join with you when you are calling out the glories of Allah and praising His blessings."

546

Sura 109
Al-Kafirun: The Rejectors

"Say: 'O rejectors! I do not worship what you worship and you do not worship what I worship." (109:1-3) To unify divergent belief systems and religions is impossible. The sound policy is to acknowledge the multiplicity of persuasions and positions and to confront that situation with wisdom and understanding. *"If your Lord had willed, He would have made one nation of mankind; but they persist in their differences except for those on whom your Lord has mercy. That is the reason why He created them."* (11:118-119)

We Muslims do not strive to obliterate other religions. The scholars agree that Islam only fights to establish justice and repel aggression. Any battle to compel someone to adopt a particular belief stems from the instigation of Shaytan: it only results in greater rancour. That is why it is repeated in this *sura* after that: *"Nor am I going to worship what you worship and you are not worshippers of what I worship. You have your* deen *and I have my* deen.*"* (109:4-6) This *sura* is the clear demarcation line between belief and disbelief.

Oppressing Islam and denying it the right to life cannot be tolerated. It must be explicitly stated that blood will continue to flow until this evil desire is removed and the power of Islam is restored and its *Shari'a* protected and its complete implementation guaranteed. Do the oppressors understand?

Sura 110
An-Nasr: Help

"When Allah's help and victory have arrived and you have seen people entering Allah's Deen *in droves."* (110:1-2) This *sura* was sent down at the end of the life of the Prophet, may Allah bless him and grant him peace, and it is clear, as the intelligent Companions understood, that it announces his death to him and makes him aware of the nearness of the journey from this world and of the need to be ready for death.

The victory consisted in the overthrowing of the idols and the system they represented and the spread of Islam throughout the Arabian peninsula. Muhammad had fulfilled his Mission by making the word of Allah uppermost (9:40) and effacing the prevailing superstitions. It only remained for him to return to his Lord so that might reward him well for his long striving. He prayed at night until his feet became swollen, and he was deeply preoccupied with intimate conversation with His Lord.

Victory in this world had no effect on him at all. Towards the end of his life, the Prophet asked a Jewish merchant for food for his family and the Jew refused to give it to him without a pledge. The Prophet was at the peak of his power. He had wiped out all resistance to him in the peninsula and confronted the Byzantine menace beyond its borders. The Messenger could have requested one of his wealthy followers to pay for the food he wanted and the man would have done so without hesitation.

But the Messenger did not do that. He said to the Jew, "I am trustworthy in the earth and heaven. Take the pledge for which you ask," and he gave him his armour. The Prophet died while his armour was still in pawn to a Jew for his family's food! So Muhammad did not want any of the things of this world. He was offered the choice of remaining here or meeting Allah. He said, "Rather the Higher Friend!" Muhammad met his Lord and enjoys His presence. He is now with the first Messengers and the angels brought near in *"on seats of honour in the presence of an All-Powerful King."* (54:55)

Sura 111
Al-Masad: Palm Fibre

"Death to the hands of Abu Lahab and death to him! His wealth has not helped him, nor anything he has earned." (111:1-2) This prayer for the destruction of Abu Lahab was answered. His great wealth and high rank did not help him. Abu Lahab was the uncle of the Messenger of Allah, but he was the boldest of people against him and the quickest to deny him. The transmitters tell us that the Prophet climbed the hill of Safa and called, "Banu Fihr! Banu 'Adi!" mentioning all the clans of Quraysh, until they gathered. Anyone who could not come sent someone in his place to bring him the news. Abu Lahab came.

The Prophet asked them whether they would believe him if he told them that there were horsemen in the valley intending to attack; they replied that they would because they had always found him to be truthful. But when he announced that he was warning them of a terrible punishment ahead of them and mentioned that Allah had sent him, Abu Lahab said, "Death to you! Is this the reason you called us to meet?" And the *ayat* was revealed.

Abu Lahab was implacably hostile and remained so until his death. This enmity extended to his sons, who divorced those of their wives who were the daughters of Muhammad. It extended to his wife, who was a vicious, sharp-tongued woman of inveterate enmity. She used her venomous tongue against Muhammad, going from house to house lampooning him. Abu Lahab's wife was the sister of Abu Sufyan, the chief of Makka and its standard-bearer.

This *sura* was revealed in the earliest period of Islam and Abu Lahab could have refuted it by entering Islam, but he remained an enemy of the *Deen* and its followers until the day he died and the threats proved true of both him and his wife. *"He will burn in a Fire of blazing flame as will his wife, the firewood-carrier, with a rope of twisted palm-fibre round her neck."* (111:3-5)

Sura 112
Al-Ikhlas: Sincerity

The Lord of the Universe is One. There is no second or third. He has no consort or child. The attributes which are ascribed to His sublime Essence alone make other than Him non-entities: *"Allah says, 'Do not take two gods: He is only One God, so have dread of Me alone.'"* (16:51) *"...Do not say, 'Three': it is better that you stop. Allah is only One God. Glory be to Him – that He should have a child!"* (4:171) Unitary belief is the mainspring of Islam and the core of the Qur'an. The attributes which Allah ascribes to Himself mean that He alone possesses effective power and that all else is powerless and has no power over itself, let alone the ability to harm or benefit anyone else.

Elsewhere in the Qur'an we find: *"Allah has no son and there is no other god accompanying Him, for then each god would have gone off with what he created and one of them would have been exalted above the other. Glory be to Allah above what they describe, Knower of the Unseen and the Visible! Exalted is He above the partners they attribute to Him!"* (23:91-92) And in another place: *"If there had been any gods except Allah in heaven or earth, they would both be ruined. Glory be to Allah, Lord of the Throne, above what they describe! He will not be questioned about what He does, but they will be questioned."* (21:22-23)

Those who believe in the Trinity believe that God is three although in reality the three comprise one God, who is 'Father, Son and Holy Ghost'. No difference is imagined between them. So what do they say about the crucifixion? If three are one, then all are crucified. In that case the universe would lose its Lord for a certain time. But if the crucified was the 'Son' alone, then he is certainly not a god.

"Say: 'He is Allah, Absolute Singularity, Allah the Everlasting Sustainer of all, He has not given birth and was not born, and no one is comparable to Him.'" (112:1-4) This text is equal to a third of the Qur'an because it encapsulates the basis of our belief. There is nothing like Allah. No one is his equal and it is impossible that there be a Lord and a son. He is the Everlasting Sustainer, the Master to whom all in the heavens and the earth direct themselves. What does anything other than Him control?

The structure of the universe cannot support a plurality of gods. It is ludicrous to suppose that the sun is a god and the earth is a god, or that animals or plants are gods, or that Africa has one god and Europe has another. The cosmic system is one, and is defined by one will and controlled by one power. He who oversees the secretions in the digestive system of living things is the One who oversees the movements of the spheres in the furthest reaches of space. After profound reflection and deep thought, we can but say: "There is no god but Allah alone with no partner. His is the Kingdom and His is the praise, and He has power over everything."

Sura 113
Al-Falaq: Dawn

"I seek refuge with Allah" means "I seek His protection and safeguarding." Allah Almighty answers anyone who asks of Him and gives shelter to anyone who seeks shelter with Him. The last two *suras* of the Noble Qur'an were revealed to teach us how to seek protection with Allah from all kinds of evil. Life contains things which can be evil. The Almighty says: *"We test you with both good and evil as a trial."* (21:35) *"We tried them with good and evil so that perhaps they might return."* (7:168) The two *suras*, *"Say: I seek refuge with the Lord of Daybreak"* (113:1) and *"Say: I seek refuge with the Lord of mankind"* (114:1) are strong protections for anyone who desires to seek the protection of Allah and attain His safekeeping.

Daybreak is the morning, or the light which splits the darkness. The sources of evil are very numerous: microbes, reptiles, wild beasts and men. *"The darkness when it gathers"* is the night when it begins and its darkness becomes intense. The night is the playground of thieves, prostitutes, and usurpers of rights and liberties. *"Women who blow on knots"* are said to be sorceresses. Sorcery is a reality and the *shaytans* among men and jinn use it, but seeking refuge annuls its power. *"The evil of an envier when he envies."* Envy is a vice based on the wish to see blessings removed, dislike of other people having them, and contriving against them. Envy is one of the most widespread human vices.

This *sura* protects us from evil that comes from outside ourselves.

Sura 114
An-Nas: Mankind

"Say: I seek refuge with the Lord of mankind, the King of mankind, the God of mankind." (114:1-3) Refuge is sought in this *sura* from *shaytans* among men and jinn and the whisperings they cast into our hearts. We do not know exactly how the jinn act but we are aware of what they seek of us and we try to avert it. That is why we seek refuge with the Lord, the King, the God, to protect us. This repetition acknowledges the extremity of our need and reinforces our request.

"From the evil of the insidious whisperer." (114:4) The 'insidious' one is one who hides in order to injure and to seize the opportunity to attack. What is whispered is foul and deceitful and one must be on guard against it. The only power Shaytan and his followers among the jinn possess over us is that of suggestion and instigation to evil. Our safety lies in not responding to them.

This *sura* speaks about the danger of inward impulses and the need to be saved from them. The believer who remembers his Lord and seeks refuge with Him will live within Allah's limits and be protected from evil coming from within himself.

Glossary

Abu Jahl: the most embittered opponent of the Prophet among the idolaters in Makka, killed in the Battle of Badr.

adhan: the call to prayer.

Ansar: the "Helpers", the people of Madina who welcomed and aided the Prophet.

'Arafa: a plain 15 miles to the east of Makka where the *Hajjis* stand on the 9th of Dhu'l-Hijja during the *Hajj*.

'Asr: afternoon, and in particular the afternoon prayer.

ayat: a verse of the Qur'an.

Badr: a place near the coast, about 95 miles to the south of Madina, where, in 2 AH in the first battle fought by the newly established Muslim community, three hundred outnumbered Muslims led by the Messenger of Allah overwhelmingly defeated one thousand Makkan idolaters.

Dar al-Islam: Muslim-ruled regions of the world.

Dajjal: the false Messiah whose appearance marks the imminent end of the world.

Dhu'l-Hijja: the last month of the Muslim calendar, during which the *Hajj* takes place.

deen: the life-transaction, literally the debt between two parties – in this usage, between the Creator and created.

dhihar: A form of divorce in pre-Islamic Arabia in which a man said to his wife, "You are like my mother's back"

Fajr: dawn, and in particular the obligatory prayer at dawn.

Fatiha: The first chapter of the Qur'an,

fiqh: science of construction and application of the *Shari'a*.

hadd: Allah's boundaries between the lawful and unlawful. The *hadd* punishments are specific fixed penalties laid down by Allah for specified crimes.

hadith: reported speech of the Prophet

hadith qudsi: those words of Allah on the tongue of His Prophet which are not part of the Revelation of the Qur'an.

Hajj: the annual pilgrimage to Makka.

Hajji: someone who is performing or has performed *Hajj*.

Hijaz: the region along the western seaboard of Arabia in which Makka, Madina, Jidda and Ta'if are situated.

hijra: emigration for the sake of Allah, in particular, the *Hijra* of the Prophet from Makka to Madina.

hudud: plural of *hadd* (see above).

'Id: a festival.

'idda: a legally fixed period after divorce or the death of her husband during which a woman must wait before re-marrying.

ihram: the condition adopted by people on *Hajj* or *'Umra*, especially robed and under special renstrictions of behaviour.

ijtihad: to struggle, exercise of personal judgement in legal matters by those qualified to do so.

Injil: the Evangel or Gospel, the actual Revelation given to the Prophet 'Isa.

'Isha': evening, and in particular the *'Isha'* prayer, the evening obligatory prayer.

Jahannam: one of the names of the Fire, Hell.

Jahiliyya: the Time of Ignorance, before the coming of Islam.

jihad: struggle, particularly fighting for the Cause of Allah to establish or defend Islam.

jinn: unseen beings created from smokeless fire who inhabit the earth together with mankind.

jizya: a protection tax imposed on non-Muslims under the protection of Muslim rule.

Ka'ba: the cube-shaped building at the centre of the Masjid al-Haram in Makka. Also known as the House of Allah.

Khaybar: Jewish colony to the north of Madina which was besieged and captured by the Muslims in the seventh year after the *Hijra* because of those Jews' repeated treachery.

khul': a form of divorce initiated by the wife.

Malakut: the Angelic Realm.

Muhajirun: Companions of the Messenger of Allah who accepted Islam in Makka and emigrated (made *hijra*) to Madina.

qadi: a judge, qualified to judge all matters in accordance with the S*hari'a* and to dispense and enforce legal punishments.

qibla: the direction faced in the prayer, which is towards the Ka'ba in Makka.

sadaqa: giving charity for the sake of Allah.

Sha'ban: the eighth month of the Muslim calendar.

Shari'a: literally a road, the legal and social modality of a people based on the revelation of their Prophet, in particular, the *Shari'a* of Islam.

shaytan: a devil, particularly Iblis.

shirk: to associate anything as a partner with Allah.

Sunna: the customary practice of a person or group of people. It has come to refer almost exclusively to the practice of the Messenger of Allah.

sura: a chapter of the Qur'an.

Tabuk: a town in Northern Arabia close to Syria. In 9 AH the Messenger of Allah, hearing that the Byzantines were gathering a large army to march against the Muslims, led a large expedition to Tabuk.

tafsir: commentary on the Qur'an.

Ta'if: an important town fifty miles to the east of Makka which was the basis of the tribe of Thaqif and which resisted Islam until well after the Conquest of Makka.

taqwa: awe or fear of Allah, which inspires a person to be on guard against wrong action and eager for actions which please Him.

tawaf: circling the Ka'ba (q.v.), *tawaf* is performed in sets of seven circuits.

tawhid: affirmation of Divine Unity.

Uhud: a mountain near Madina where, five years after the *Hijra*, the Muslims lost a battle against the Makkan idolaters. Many great Companions, and in particular Hamza, the uncle of the Prophet, were killed in this battle.

Umm al-Mu'minun: literally Mother of the Believers, an honorary title given to the wives of the Prophet.

'umra: the lesser pilgrimage to Makka which can be done at any time of the year.

wudu': the minor ritual ablution required in order to be pure for the prayer.

Yathrib: the name of Madina before the Prophet's *Hijra* (emigration) to it.

Zabur: the Psalms, in the sense of the original Revelation given to the Prophet Da'ud.

zakat: The wealth tax obligatory on Muslims each year, usually payable in the form of one-fortieth of surplus weath in excess of more than a certain fixed minimum amount. It is one of the indispensable pillars of Islam.